Making the Connections

BEVERLY WILDUNG HARRISON

Making the Connections

ESSAYS IN FEMINIST SOCIAL ETHICS

Edited by Carol S. Robb

Beacon Press   Boston

Grateful acknowledgement is made to the following for permission to reprint copyrighted material:

"The Effect of Industrialization on the Role of Women in Society" first appeared in *Concilium, Sociologie de la Religion 1976*, Vol. III, pp. 91–103.

"Theology and Morality of Procreative Choice" from *The Witness magazine*, The Episcopal Church Publishing Company.

"The Politics of Energy Policy" from *Energy Ethics*, edited by Dieter Hessel. Copyright © Friendship Press, 1979, reprinted by permission of Friendship Press.

"The Early Feminists and the Clergy" from *The Review and Expositor*, Volume LXXII #1, Winter 1975.

Beacon Press books are published under the auspices of the Unitarian Universalist Association of Congregations in North America, 25 Beacon Street, Boston, Massachusetts 02108

Library of Congress Cataloging in Publication Data

Harrison, Beverly Wildung, 1932–
    Making the connections.

    Includes bibliographies and index.
    1. Feminism — Moral and ethical aspects — Addresses, essays, lectures.   2. Social ethics — Addresses, essays, lectures.   3. Christian ethics — Addresses, essays, lectures.   I. Robb, Carol S.   II. Title.
HQ1221.H27 1985   305.4'2   84–45718
ISBN 0–8070–1524–5

Preface

It is not possible to do feminist ethics without a commitment to a collaborative style of work. Even so, neither of us was fully aware of just how much collaboration had gone into this book until it was concluded.

The collaboration between us began in 1975, when the Consultation on Social Ethics in Feminist Perspective first became an annual event for women studying, teaching, and practicing feminist ethics in the northeastern area of the United States. It was there that we became aware of the direction of each other's work.

In 1980–1981 Carol was a Research Associate in Women's Studies in Ethics at Harvard Divinity School, and decided to focus a course on Beverly's work. To assist in that process, Beverly channeled a melange of published essays, mimeographed presentations, articles in progress, sermons, even one course outline to Carol who in turn constituted what became known as the "Blue Monster," otherwise known as the "Blue Book." That Xeroxed document bound in blue not only became a reading resource for the course, "The Contribution of Beverly Harrison to the Construction of Christian Social Ethics," but it also became a coveted possession amongst a wider circle because then, as now, there were few resources that connected feminism with the moral and political praxis of overcoming racism and class-based society. Those of us who connected gender justice with socialist theory found in Beverly's work the theoretical and theological perspective that was largely missing in most available material in both feminist ethics and Christian social ethics.

When we began revising the Blue Book for publication, we (probably naively) expected it to be a one- or two-year project. However, *Making the Connections* is a far different work than the Blue Book. Three essays previously published elsewhere and contained in the Blue Book have been included here in all but identical form. However, everything else is different. Five essays have been substantively edited, and another one has been recast so totally as to be unrecognizable. Some things have been dropped and two essays have been written especially for this volume. Two others not yet written in 1980 have been added here as well.

None of this would have reached fruition without the collaboration far broader than our own team effort. Students in

Carol's class at Harvard Divinity School were enthusiastic and critical in their response to Beverly's material. Brinton Lykes made the initial (offhand) suggestion to revise the Blue Book for publication. The women in the Consultation on Social Ethics in Feminist Perspective have sharpened our comprehension of several matters discussed here. So have students in Beverly's seminars in ethical method, who responded in particular to the last essay in its various versions.

In addition, support has come in many material and emotional forms from Shirley Cloyes, who did editorial work on several essays, including the one that carries her name as co-author, Carter Heyward, Nancy Richardson, Kate Cannon, Anne Gilson, Taeko Tsujimoto, Pat Rathbone, Chrissy Atkinson, Amelie Ratliff, Elaine Huber, Tim Wright, Bill Krumske, Richard Horsley, Bonita DiRafaele, Vendela Carlson, Maria Gonzales, Celeste Deroche, Chris Blackburn, Sydney Howell, and Gail Geisenheiner. Marie Cantlon, our editor at Beacon, has been a source of great encouragement, as has Nancy Lattanzio, editorial assistant there. Barbara Flanagan has provided superb copy editing, and Jeff Smith has extended his meticulous work and cordial spirit throughout the production stages of the book. We also express appreciation to the Union Theological Seminary for funds from a Faculty Research Grant that enabled us to meet more often than we could otherwise have done.

Our ongoing collaboration has only strengthened our initial conviction about how feminists work together and how feminist theory develops. Beverly Harrison can attest that, quite literally, she understands her own thought better because of Carol's engaged, even dogged, determination to get this book in feminist ethics into print. Carol Robb, for her part, attests that it is exciting to work with someone who consistently casts new light on familiar terrain, thus revealing it to be quite different territory. It is also rewarding to encourage a woman with such visionary and analytic power and discipline to commit herself to paper.

Finally, Beverly Harrison wants a personal word: my indebtedness to Carol Robb is greater than anything contained within the covers of this book can explicitly convey. Like so many gifted contemporary feminist voices, I have a diffidence about publication that is excessive, not to say absurd, given prevailing academic standards. Many of the pieces published here would most certainly never have reached an audience without Carol's perception as to their value in one or another connection. Even more basically, though, Carol's persistent role, along with those of other sisters in the Consultation on Social Ethics in Feminist Perspective, has been to press me to take my own voice seriously, and, above all, to recognize that seeing work all the way to publication is important, not only personally, but in relation to our urgent shared agenda. Nothing would please me more, or stand as a better tribute to Carol's work, than the knowledge that the method of our joint venture has done something to strengthen the resolve of other feminists to find sisters with whom to collaborate in emptying out those files of promising, unpublished manuscripts.

Contents

Introduction

Carol S. Robb

No adequate understanding of debates about contemporary social issues can neglect the contribution of feminists. One of the major feminist theorists in religious social ethics is Beverly Wildung Harrison. Her writing, speaking, and teaching have helped ethicists do ethics, address specific social issues, and reflect on the Christian churches as a locus for moral thought. It is an occasion for rejoicing that her book on the ethics of procreative choice[1] and now this collection of essays are available for the religious and nonreligious reading public.

Harrison's essays mark the development of a genre of feminist ethics that is motivated by social consciousness, based on a thorough-going critique of existing forms of political economy, and related to Christian tradition. For these reasons, we can identify Harrison's ethics as feminist socialist Christian ethics.

The work of no other feminist ethicist covers the range of Harrison's in this volume. Her work encompasses the social sciences, philosophy, and theology, all the while making explicit commitments to women's full dignity, a new society with class, racial, and gender justice, and a community of faith rooted in the Jesus story. The essays in this collection reflect her work in feminist ethical theory since 1972. During this time she has taught Christian ethics at Union Theological Seminary in New York. (Her address at her inauguration as full professor opens the collection.) The publication of this portion of her work demonstrates the significance of her contribution to social ethics and furthers the dialogue about what feminist ethics entail.

The diversity of thought about how Christian social ethics should be done is compounded by the diversity of thought about the foundation of feminist ethics. Although little has been published before this collection to sharpen these lines of distinction among feminists, we can allude to the nature of the differences by characterizing the approaches to feminist ethics. I focus here on differences in analyzing the roots of women's oppression and the appropriate social change strategies such analyses require; the manner of assessing the significance of biological differences between men and women; and the view of the possibility of relating to historical religious traditions. These three issues are not analytically distinct; they are related to each other in any feminist analysis and vision. Yet they are specific matters every feminist ethicist must face, and discussion of them may introduce Beverly Wildung Harrison and prepare the way for a genre of feminist ethics to which she contributes.

These essays by Harrison are exemplary in the field of feminist ethics that analyzes women's oppression in historical perspective, relating the role and religious valuation of women in society to concrete social developments and specific forms of political and economic organization. This genre of ethics assumes that appropriate social change strategies must challenge the hierarchies in which women and racial, ethnic, minority men have been forcibly kept in secondary positions. This challenge must include adopting a socialist program and vision for society because participation in decision-making and fair access to the wealth created in a society are fundamental to gender justice and social justice. Alternative modes of feminist ethics follow different directions from Harrison's on this question of the nature of women's oppression and strategies to resist it. One perspective collapses women's oppression into a transhistorical fear or hatred of women; its corresponding social change strategy prescribes that women separate from male-organized society.[2] Another mode accepts the necessity that structural change include women in all of society's institutions but does not interlink sexism with class and racial oppression and sees no contradiction between the liberation of women and a capitalist political economy. Its social change strategy tends to ignore the oppression of workers and the poor and racial, ethnic minorities, thereby avoiding concrete reference to these deep divisions among women.

A growing literature is attempting to clarify the biologically based differences between men's and women's ways of thinking, perceiving, and relating to the world. The assessment of the import of such material is another way of characterizing the diversity in feminist ethical theory. Several of Harrison's essays contain an assertion that whatever the evidence as to biologically based gender differences, the ethical issue is the degree of moral relevance given to such evidence. She takes the stance that women and men are more alike than different and that biologically based gender differences are not sufficient moral reason for unequal participation in society and access to wealth. Some feminist views ascribe greater moral significance to biologically based gender differences, implying that there is no serious possibility of achieving gender justice in a society where men and women live and work together.[3]

Finally, feminist ethicists diverge over the question of whether women can be religiously affiliated with historic religious traditions and still maintain their full dignity. For some, Christianity and all the other historic religious traditions are worldviews created by men to rationalize the inferior status of women, and women can find no integrity at all within them. In this view, any effort by feminists to relate to selective aspects of those traditions only sustains ideologies that are antifemale. Consequently, women must create new spiritual communions using resources from our contemporary lives in our struggle toward liberation.[4] Harrison takes a rather more complicated view of this question. In reference specifically to Christianity, she agrees that church institutions are pervaded with sexism and acknowledges that the religious tradition has reflected and sustained the socially created notion of spiritual and social inferiority of women. Christianity is also simultaneously the carrier of convictions about the profound value of human life and the ultimate possibility of a just society. Harrison contends that women who have been encouraged by this justice tradition to claim the value of their own lives are de facto related, albeit ambiguously, to Christian tradition. Not every woman can or should remain self-consciously affiliated with the religious tradition in which she was raised, but taking the feminist option also does not necessarily require leaving one's tradition. In response to the separatist perspective, Harrison confesses that the Christian story is still her own but acknowledges that pre-Christian and post-Christian resources are indeed necessary to affirm the full value of women's lives.

The reasons Harrison offers for her position among other feminist ethicists unfolds in the course of these essays, as does the wider tenor of the genre to which she contributes. While feminist ethicists are not all doing ethics in the same way, Beverly Harrison serves the wider project of feminist ethical reflection by illustrating specifically how feminist socialist ethics illuminates concrete tensions and possibilities encountered in the struggle for gender justice. Hers is the most significant articulation of this genre of feminist ethics to date.

In my analysis of how Harrison's work relates to the discipline of Christian social ethics, the term "feminist ethics" presumes not the whole range of feminist ethical theory but the specific stream of socialist feminist Christian theory. This stream of feminist ethics is in many ways analogous to mainstream religious ethics, sharing substantive assumptions and questions with the wider discipline. We must observe these similarities if we are to appreciate the depth of the challenge such feminist ethics pose to it.

There are at least five ways in which this genre of feminist ethics shares methodological continuity with mainstream ethics. The first is that feminist ethics, like much religious social ethics, is justice-centered. It is a justice ethic in accordance with the familiar and traditional view that like cases should be treated alike. Some of the arguments feminists make emphasize justice as equality (as in support for the Equal Rights Amendment); others appeal to justice according to merit (as in support for affirmative action programs). Some of our arguments emphasize justice by virtue of work (as in comparable pay for comparable work), by virtue of need (as in income maintenance programs), or by virtue of legal entitlement (as in court cases in general). Overall, however, we challenge whether the status or rank into which we are born is itself just, particularly when status is defined in terms of race, sex, or class.[5] What is new and distinctive in these arguments is the assumption that *women* deserve justice, not the appeal to justice *per se*.[6]

Beyond the view that like cases should be treated alike, however, this feminist agenda is to press the norm of justice beyond a procedural norm to a substantive norm. Harrison argues that justice is a substantive norm in that it requires social-institutional change as a precondition for meeting its demands. She feels that justice is also the central animating theological image for religious ethics and that it is Christian and biblical but also shared with other justice movements. She does not claim that it is in any way distinctive to feminist ethics.

The claims made in feminist ethics about the centrality of the norm of justice and, in addition, the theme of objectivity stand in tension with some other perspectives on feminism and ethics, such as the approach developed by Carol Gilligan. Gilligan asserts that it is uncharacteristic of women's moral voice to appeal to justice or objectivity, thereby indicating a radical discontinuity between women's and men's ways of knowing morally and of embracing particular norms.[7] The tension between Gilligan's and Harrison's perspectives is grounded in at least two theoretical issues: whether gender yields basic differences not only in men's and women's moral experience but also in the norms to which we appeal and whether it is possible to develop any basic moral theoretical perspective without reference to both procedural and substantive conceptions of justice. Gilligan appears to answer both questions yes. Obviously the feminist ethicists I am characterizing answer no. Harrison argues that what Gilligan rejects, rightfully, is a liberal notion of justice central to a capitalist worldview.

A second continuity of feminist ethics with other ethics is

the concern for objectivity when making claims. That is, we want our arguments to carry weight because of their merit, and we assume that the basis of such merit is not coercion, but persuasion; not obfuscation, but clarification; not personal preference, but interpersonal accountability and public scrutiny.

Objectivity in the feminist perspective involves aspects of traditional expectations such as fairness and consistency, or moral universalism (treating like cases alike), and feminists agree that these are all related terms essential to our understanding of what constitutes rationality. These are characteristics of judgment that feminists such as Harrison want to enhance. To be sure, this view of objectivity is very different from one that precludes advocacy and fails to allow for challenges to ideas and practices that subjugate women. Feminists decry the kind of objectivity that explains evil by blaming it on women, for instance,[8] or that fails to notice or challenge the coercion that has been used to protect male privilege. Such coercion is not consistent with the moral point of view.[9] Thus we need to recognize that feminist ethicists, including Harrison, dissent from the view that objectivity involves emotional disinterestedness or that appeals to objectivity require us to assume a homogeneous reality such that all rational human beings will perceive the world similarly.

Perhaps most important, feminist ethicists — and Harrison has been key in this area — have emphasized that objectivity itself is a social product that results when we put forward our perspectives, are self-assertive, hear the perspectives of self-assertive others, particularly those who will bear the brunt of any decision, and allow ourselves to be challenged and changed.[10] The case is being made that to be objective and to be self-assertive are not irresolvably in tension; they can be held together with a commitment to the common good. Further, objectivity is a result of engaged reflection with people who are also immersed, but in different circumstances.[11] Feminists contend that this is the way everyone gropes toward objectivity, though those who argue that they can be rationally unimpaired by self-interest, emotions, and commitment do not admit it. Even so, feminist ethicists make no claim to a unique view of objectivity. Any ethicist who asserts that the truth of ethical claims is tested in a community's practice shares this view. As Harrison observes, this involves feminist ethicists in an implicit theory of the common good which, although it must be scrutinized, is recognizably continuous with the heritage of Roman Catholic moral theologians, many of whom are not feminists.

Feminist ethicists also presume that the aim of ethics and the moral point of view is the enhancement of personhood, defined as the capacity for responsible self-direction. Insofar as this is what is meant by the principle of autonomy in ethics, which most ethicists agree is foundational for moral action, feminists embrace that principle. Moral autonomy is at once a goal that persons ought to achieve, the basis for moral reflection and action, and an aspect of emerging personhood. There is no basis for accountability without the freedom to be responsible, to make decisions about what responsibility requires. Decisions and policies that open up arenas for responsible choice and encourage persons to take responsibility are essential aspects of moral agency. At the same time — and this is a point Harrison makes frequently — we have inherited a notion of moral autonomy associated with a conception of individuals as basically unrelated monads, selves who may avoid interpersonal and intercommunal accountability or who believe in some degree that moral agency is enhanced when we are "unencumbered" by relationships. A feminist understanding of personal autonomy in no way involves a solitary or disengaged self; rather, it stresses the social foundation of optimal self-directing action.[12]

Feminist challenges to sex roles are an extension of this conception that moral autonomy is the responsible direction of the social self. While sex roles are characteristic of every society and expectations vary from society to society, they have become a central moral issue because they have been used to legitimate the absence of moral autonomy for women. Unfortunately for women, social expectations of how men should behave correlate very closely with how adulthood is defined; expectations about how women should behave correlate more closely with immaturity.[13] In other words, it is contradictory in our society to be both mature and female. The work of feminists like Harrison challenges this assumption at every point.

This challenge is so important to the feminist ethic because religious justifications for sex roles remain powerful. One of the most pernicious justifications is teleological natural law, wherein nature (or selective perceptions of nature) is viewed as the mirror of God's intention for human behavior. Two key phrases that indicate the presence of such a natural law theory in relation to sex roles are "complementarity" and "according to the design of the Creator," which usually mean that males and females have their respective natures and that from their natures, which are divinely or naturally established, flow certain social roles appropriate to each. In spite of a continuity between feminist and Roman Catholic moral theory in terms of how we evaluate the social order by the norm of the common good, there is also fundamental discontinuity between feminist ethics and any theological or ethical tradition that dictates natural or divinely willed constraints on male and female destiny. This discontinuity between traditional moral theology and feminism is repeatedly illustrated in Harrison's work.

The sort of natural law theory Harrison rejects is exemplified in interpretations of male and female nature that are invoked to justify women's secondary status in the churches, including our unsuitability for ordination.[14] Other arguments for such restricted status, such as biblical literalist appeals, are equally sham. However, justifications for traditional sex roles or against the ordination of women are often buttressed by appeals to just such natural law. For the unconvinced, of course, appeals to such traditions are not morally compelling, since these traditions themselves are explicitly being questioned by feminist norms. A segment of the community of scholars in theology and ethics now rejects church authorities and their justifications for limiting the participation and leadership of women. The work of such scholars is certainly welcomed by those whose vision of the church requires participation of women in all roles. Those who control the institutions can no longer assume they enjoy the aura of legitimate authority. With respect to views of sex roles and autonomy of women in the churches, feminists in no way stand alone; we have the comradeship of many who are firmly situated in the mainstream of Christian social ethics who have found no good reasons to define women's participation in the churches differently than men's.

Another social issue related to the question of the moral autonomy of women, one frequently encountered in natural law theories that reinforce sex roles, is that of abortion and the social policy regulating it. As Harrison indicates,[15] there are few issues that reveal so many indicators of distrust of women's moral agency as the abortion issue. Assumptions of women's selfishness, irresponsibility, turpitude, and immaturity are as salient in arguments against reproductive choice as are any other concerns, including concern for the rights of the fetus.[16] Clearly the intent of measures restricting access to reproductive choice is to remove this issue from the sphere of the moral autonomy of women, in particular women who are pregnant. Women have been and want to continue to be responsible, but feminists challenge self-sacrifice as a norm uncritically accepted by women. In most ethical theory, when people are asked to be self-sacrificing, a wide range of turf called "prudence" is assumed to exist on which they may stand to demur or to weigh conflicting claims. However, since a central part of what is understood to be "feminine" is to be nurturant and other-regarding to the extent of self-sacrifice, women are exempted from the option of prudence. In the abortion decision, many women struggle to be self-assertive as the necessary step to making an autonomous decision.[17] Christian feminists like Harrison call into question the relevance of these expectations of women's self-sacrifice from people who do not assume women to be fully valuable moral persons.[18]

It may be a unique contribution of feminist ethics to insist that it is morally good for a woman, reflecting on what responsibility to herself and others requires, to decide to terminate a pregnancy and therefore to eschew self-sacrifice in favor of the selfhood that expresses appropriate autonomy. Harrison has made an important contribution, arguing that a right to bodily integrity foundational to moral well-being must operate in the abortion decision. If the Christian tradition does not evidence concern for this right, Harrison challenges us to reconsider the abortion dilemma. Legal precedents exist for not sacrificing one's body for the purpose of supporting the dependent life of another; as with other issues, the feminist position on the abortion question is not distinctive.[19] The challenge that feminist ethical theory offers on this issue is to bring the notion of autonomy to bear on the evaluation of both sex role constraints and procreative choice.

The fourth area of continuity with the wider ethical discipline relates to the sources of the norms we invoke. As Harrison's work demonstrates, the sources of norms in this genre of feminist ethics are the same as in religious social ethics generally. They include appeal to scripture, tradition, other disciplines, and contemporary experience, all sifted through critical reflection.[20] Because the boundaries of what may be appropriately invoked as scripture or tradition are so large, there are always criteria for selection of what is most compellingly authoritative. Even biblicists use criteria for selection; criteria are impossible to avoid, and it is undesirable to try to do so. The criterion feminist ethicists use is to select that which promotes the full personhood and agency of women. This criterion is unique to feminists, but even this must be qualified: We understand the full personhood and agency of women to be fundamental to the creation of a genuinely common good. Feminists may use a criterion unique to our perspective, but we are not distinctive in using criteria for selecting that which is appealed to as authoritative for morality or theological norms.

I stress scripture and tradition as two sources of norms in feminist ethics, and in Harrison's in particular, because it is clear that Harrison and others refer to other disciplines and acknowledge contemporary experience as sources for justifying feminist norms. The prophets and the Jesus tradition figure prominently in Harrison's work, but she relates to the scriptural tradition particularly through a version of natural law morality: With other feminists, Harrison holds that claims made in feminist ethics should also appeal to assent by any person who experiences, or could effectively imagine, solidarity with women struggling to achieve justice. This is common ground with ethicists who reject biblicism or fundamentalism and so consider moral norms to be discernible through critically perceptive human reasoning.[21] Feminists, however, stress what Harrison and others call "embodied reason," rationality that is grounded in sensuousness, integrating feeling/thought.

Embodied reason, as the way norms are critically tested, constitutes the fifth point indicating continuity with segments of the wider discipline. This feminist norm of embodiment is indicative of several agendas critical to feminist ethics. The effort to overcome the body/mind split in both intellectual and social life is central to our work. We emphasize the connection between body/mind dualism and negative attitudes toward women, as Harrison's work demonstrates. Another agenda is learning to attend to our bodies and emotions both as sources of moral data and the foundation of our moral power. A third agenda — the one that yields the most distinctive and specific guidelines for action — is challenging traditional sexual ethics with such a conception of body-mediated reasoning.[22] All these agendas suggest why the question of gender justice leads directly to the question of sexuality and sexual expression, a direction illustrated thoroughly in Harrison's essays. In developing these agendas, however, feminists are closely supported by and supportive of progressive segments of Protestantism and Roman Catholicism, including male colleagues who have developed related themes; even in this dimension our work is not unique.

The term "embodiment" with respect to feminist theory and specifically feminist ethics means, minimally, five things: (1) Our sexuality and body-selves are to be celebrated rather than deprecated, and are to be respected as the ground of our personhood. (2) Mutuality, rather than control, ownership, or paternalism, is a major moral norm for social, including sexual, communication. (3) Sex role rigidity is destructive of possibilities for mature interpersonal relations; hence sex role fluidity is to be practiced. (4) We are to recognize and honor all expressions of sexual communication between people who care for each other in mutuality and equal regard, whether they are homosexual or heterosexual relations. (5) At the level of social policy, a woman's moral agency should be trusted above anyone else's to decide what responsibility requires, especially with respect to the predicaments of procreation.

The argument I have been making is that the genre of feminist ethics to which Harrison contributes is founded on justice, objectivity, moral autonomy, appeals to traditional moral norms critically appropriated through contemporary experience, and an embodied rationality and rational embodiment, all of which are shared with other segments of the religious social ethics community. If we define the discipline of ethics in terms of people who evaluate and construct moral arguments, there are certainly feminists who dissent from some of these assumptions. But many feminists, and certainly Beverly Harrison, share this large area of common theoretical ground with other ethicists. Clearly there is a significant area of overlap between what feminists mean in their ethical theory and what other ethicists mean in theirs. In fact, few ethicists would say that, theoretically, they do not support the full human dignity and agency of women.

Granted all of this, why is there so much conflict over gender justice and feminist ethical norms? Within religious ethics a very high level of conflict exists about the guidelines for action attendant to this theoretical common ground.

Harrison is one of the most explicit about the sources of this conflict. She identifies how the implications of the Equal Rights Amendment are too deep-seated for business interests, particularly the insurance industry, to bear and observes that comparable pay for comparable work would significantly upset the current sex segregation of the labor force and undermine the economy.[23] Women's control over our bodies with respect to sexual expression and reproduction flies in the face of men's expectations about how they will be taken care of emotionally and how the labor force will be reproduced. Justice for women and our moral autonomy are very threatening to current social-economic organization. Current societal structures are suffering severe strain because of the increased pressure for justice of people all around the globe.

The requirements for change to accommodate women's claims to justice challenge an order in which ethicists are participants. Underneath the ethical theory held in common with feminists, there remains a worldview that includes rationales for unequal access to the common good. These rationales have enormous emotional valence because they "explain" the world. Racism and misogyny are rationales for unequal access to the common good. They "explain" why people of color and women do not have control over resources, not even our own bodies. They "explain" why some people deserve what they have and other people deserve not having it. It is these ideological justifications to privilege that Harrison and other feminists target in their work.

In the face of this hidden world of meaning, feminist ethicists, making claims based on justice, objectivity, moral autonomy, involving religious tradition and reason to achieve mutuality and equal regard, acting as though we belong to the relevant moral community, discover that these claims are freighted with controversy. We have appropriated the moral tradition, taken it seriously, as though it were our tradition too.[24] But the power and depth of the resistance to our work indicate to us that those moral concepts and traditions were never intended to refer to women's reality! We discover this only when we use them in communicating that reality and find that the claims based on these concepts convince so few. We were told that *he* was the generic term inclusive of both he and she; we found out that *he* really did mean "he" only when we tried to substitute *she* as the generic. We were told that God is not bound by human limitations of gender; we found out that god really is god the father when we tried to substitute god the mother. Feminist ethicists have had to learn also that when we appeal to justice, women's situations turn out to be "different" and not relevant to the justice arena. It is in applying the theory that we learn what the limits of the theory are. Even so, all of us, including Beverly Harrison, have proceeded, convinced that our moral theory will become more responsive and accountable to other women who join us in challenging and extending moral imagination. The essays in this volume were collected, revised, and published to this end — to exemplify this feminist challenge to ethical theory and moral imagination and to extend the dialogue regarding what feminist ethics entails.

Beverly Wildung Harrison is a woman among women doing feminist ethics, and she is distinctive in this field because of her simultaneous commitments to historical research, social analysis, philosophical integrity, the Christian community and ministry, and a socialist vision of human community. These commitments are significant because they indicate the range of ways she is willing to be held accountable for adequacy in her moral vision. Not many have been willing to be held accountable in so many ways, and these commitments together affect all the work she does. Thus, each of the three sections of this book contains an essay that illustrates Harrison's work in historical and social analysis, and in each section is some emphasis on the vision that undergirds her theology of ministry; the latter are more personal and concrete than the former. It will be obvious that these essays were prepared for very divergent audiences, some religious and some not. We have included pieces that began as lectures, others prepared for publication, and still others presented within their respective disciplines. Given the assumptions of feminist ethics, the original audiences clearly shape the content of Harrison's message.

This book has been organized into three sections to show how, in each, Harrison, with her combination of approaches, addresses a focal question. What are the fundamental challenges a feminist ethicist brings to those doing Christian and religious social ethics? This is the organizing question for the first section. Here one will find all the major methodological principles, or basepoints, in Harrison's terms, which are crucial for understanding how she both affirms and criticizes the traditions of moral reflection to which she is related.

What does a feminist ethical approach to concrete social issues look like, and what sort of perspective on social policy does it yield? The essays in the second section illustrate Harrison's response to this question. They address both social policy and the practice of the churches with respect to sexuality, procreative choice, homosexuality, age, the Equal Rights Amendment, and energy policy. The essays are for the most part independent of each other.

Is it possible to be a feminist and remain with integrity affiliated with one of the most obstinate perpetrators of patriarchy, the Christian church? As I have said, Harrison answers this question with a qualified yes. Yet she challenges the history of the Christian tradition to its roots, in ways that may be relevant to feminists from other religious traditions as well. The third section contains essays germane to her distinctive way of answering this question, illustrating how she integrates theology and ethics and how she reads the religious roots of feminism.

The reader should be forewarned that these sections are not analytically discrete. While the first contains essays that illustrate Harrison's methodological approach, that is, how she does ethics, the methodological issues reappear throughout the book. The second section emphasizes specific social policies, but there is ample evidence of her concern for method here as well as her vision of what it means for the churches to be accountable for the public welfare. The third section will be of particular interest to those who want to understand how theological and moral assumptions interrelate and how Harrison's own critical-constructive relation to Christianity works. Yet essays in the other two sections speak to these matters as well.

I

FEMINISM AND ETHICS

Challenges to the Discipline

The four essays in this section illustrate the significance to
ethics of starting with reflection on real women's real experiences,
however different those experiences are, before moving induc-
tively to a definition of the moral situation and claims about what
we ought to do. The alternative, which Harrison criticizes, involves starting moral reflection with statements about the nature
of God, the nature or essence of the universe or human nature, or
the nature of femininity and masculinity. These "nature of" statements are very abstract, usually defined by someone with a status
verging on the sacred, and therefore not open to challenge, and
they serve as first principles from which we are to deduce what
to do in our particular situations. An important discussion in
ethics, particularly in religious ethics, revolves around which of
these approaches is most appropriate. Harrison argues for the inductive approach, starting with the observation of our lived-world
experience; when the other approach is used, the first principles
obscure the morally relevant circumstances of our diverse realities. Moral principles, whether formulated in an ancient or a more
contemporary manner, are important in such an inductive approach. However, if we are not attuned to the contingencies of
the situation, we will be unable to discern what principles may
mean or which principles should take priority in the case of a
conflict between them, or what specific values or ideals shape the
way we interpret our principles. This issue of how best to go about
doing ethics is addressed in each essay. The moral principles to
which Harrison appeals are familiar ones: Love as mutuality and
equal regard and human dignity in the context of social justice
are moral norms rooted in the traditions of religious ethics.

The challenge to begin ethical reflection with our actual experience is one of the characteristic methodological basepoints
Harrison stresses for doing theology and ethics. While a list of
other basepoints necessarily risks oversimplification, such a list
would include minimally these:

1

Our bodies and sexuality are the source of our moral power. This means we are to affirm our bodies ourselves as a way of appropriating the moral universe.

Relationships are the source of our experience of the divine. Since power conditions all our relationships, it also conditions our experience of God. Reciprocal and mutual relations enable genuinely creative power to emerge. For this reason, we should be oriented toward relationships marked by mutuality and equal regard.

Justice is the meaning of religious promise. It is not an inferior norm to which we must tailor our minimal moral expectations in the social and political arena, but the heart of moral faithfulness and of our experience of God.

There are no female and male natures. We are accountable to social justice regardless of our gender.

The analysis of structural dynamics of race, class, and gender in our society is an irreducible aspect of ethical method. Such analysis informs the description of the moral situation and affects the way we assess what responsibility requires given our historical contingencies.

The reader might add to this list of methodological basepoints while encountering Beverly Harrison in these moments of moral reflection.

In "Anger in the Work of Love," Harrison identifies herself as Christian because of the norm of love in Christianity that is set within the biblical framework of justice. In "Sexism and the Language of Christian Ethics," she identifies herself as an ethicist in the context of the discipline of religious ethics. In "The Effect of Industrialization on the Role of Women in Society," Harrison situates herself in the feminist movement, from a stance critical of liberal bourgeois feminism. Finally, in "Reconsidering the Case for Marxian Political Economy," she makes clear why she believes that a socialist feminist stance and critical social theory are necessary to religious ethics and to feminist ethics.

THE POWER OF ANGER IN THE WORK OF LOVE*

Christian Ethics for Women and Other Strangers*

Undoing Patriarchal Processions

Readers who are knowledgeable in feminist theology and who have had sufficient intellectual energy to read and appropriate Mary Daly's powerful, angry book *Gyn/Ecology: The Metaethics of Radical Feminism*, may already understand why it was important then, as now, to begin a discussion of feminist ethics by focusing on the issue of academic processions. Processions, Daly argues, exemplify all that is wrong with the patriarchal world; they are the essence of "the deception of the fathers." [1] Daly believes that this "deception of the fathers" — the way we were all taught to view the world through rigidly compartmentalized, static categories and academic disciplines — is killing us all. This fixation with processions, she contends, has its origins in Christianity, beginning with the procession of the trinitarian god. The god of Christian orthodoxy — with its threefold, exclusively male manifestation — is, she suggests, expressive of the male homosexual fixation that underlies the dominant spirituality of our culture, whether in an ecclesiastical or an academic expression. In either

---

* This essay is an expansion of my inaugural lecture as Professor of Christian Ethics at Union Theological Seminary in New York. Those who heard it in its original form in 1980 also witnessed an academic procession. On that occasion, however, the academic procession was planned to ritualize — that is, to express in embodied form — what I believe the work of radical love involves. It would be possible, in retrospect, to describe that procession in a way that would emphasize its similarity to other such academic processions. It could be reported merely that participating were faculty colleagues as well as representatives of the Board of Directors, distinguished clergy and lay leaders from a number of denominations and scholars from other seminaries and academic departments of religious studies. Yet those present, seeing and hearing my lecture, also saw a procession radically unlike most others of its genre because seventy percent of the marchers were women and most were arrayed in garb of breathtaking color. This essay is a slightly amended version of one that appeared in the *Union Seminary Quarterly Review*, vol. 36 Supplementary, 1981.

academic or ecclesiastical contexts, processions mark out clearly, and protect, male privilege and control. Daly stresses that this sacralizing and deification of male functions in our world will be ended only if women who understand the idolatry involved give up participation in processions altogether. In fact, she is so serious in this claim that the power of procession sustains the patriarchal oppression of women that she designates "procession" as the *first* (the very first) of the eight deadly sins of Phallocracy.[2] These eight deadly sins represent Daly's alternative way of viewing human evil; they replace the traditional seven deadly sins of Christian teaching. It should not be lost on any of us that on the traditional list of deadly sins the "sin" of anger was usually given conspicuous emphasis. Happily, no feminist analysis could perpetuate the notion that anger, per se, is evil, and Daly's analysis surely does not do so.

I acknowledge that Mary Daly would not exempt even an academic procession numerically dominated by females from her unequivocal indictment of processions as instruments of patriarchy. She is adamant that processions can be only a "frozen mirror image" of "Spinning," which is her metaphor for the wholistic, spontaneous, intellectually imaginative modes of knowing, being, and doing of which women — when not dependent on patriarchy for self-definition — are capable. There can be no doubt that the mere presence of a *few* women in traditional processions serves, first and foremost, to disguise the devastation that dominant institutions wreak upon women and others who do not "fit in" — for example, males of color or males whose ideological viewpoint or sexual orientation does not reinforce the dominant cultural mode. Even so, my theory of social change obviously diverges from hers or I would not have organized a procession at all.

I agree with Daly that a chief evidence of patriarchal control in our world is women's subtle conditioning that reinforces our reluctance to develop a sense of our own power to identify, name, and characterize our world. For all of the methodological differences that separate my position from Daly's,[3] it is no part of my argument with her to deny the depth of the problem of misogyny in human history or in the dominant forms of historical Christianity. Among the many debts we owe Mary Daly is this: She has described the problem in an uncompromising way and has made it impossible for any intellectually honest person to deny the necessity of a feminist critique of Christianity. I have long argued this point in light of Daly's analysis — that it should never be the business of any feminist who remains within the Christian community to mitigate the painful encounter that the Christian church must have, and has yet to have, with the full force of a feminist critique. We have very far to go before Christianity acknowledges adequately its complicity in breeding and perpetuating the hatred and fear of the real, full, lived-world power of female persons! Misogyny, as Daly claims, is hydra-headed, having as many forms as there are cultures, languages, and social systems. She is right to insist that what is feared is not "femininity," that clever nineteenth-century invention, but the spooking, sparking power of *real* women who do not need to stand around waiting for male approval. Misogyny's real force arises only when women assert ourselves and own our power. Mark this point well: It is never the mere presence of a woman, nor the image of women, nor fear of "femininity," that is the heart of misogyny. The core of misogyny, which has yet to be broken or even touched, is the reaction that occurs when women's concrete power is manifest, when we women live and act as full and adequate persons in our own right. Even when Daly's specific historical portrayal of misogyny is carelessly done,[4] she still has a firm sense of the *depth* of what must be undone in human life if the culturally diverse patterns of woman-hating are to end. It would be a form of deep intellectual dishonesty not to acknowledge that only Mary Daly's profound rage has produced a feminist critique strong enough to assure that some minimal attention must be given it within ecclesiastical and academic circles.

At times I wish I believed, with Daly, that the power of patriarchy could be overthrown if only we women would absent ourselves from patriarchal processions altogether. If only the *withholding* of power were adequate to bring about social change in our world, undoing oppression would not be difficult. However, we women should be the last to allow ourselves to be trapped in a "spiritualizing" notion that real change in our flesh and blood world ever comes from absenting ourselves from what is going on in that world. Only a few women are in a position even to fantasize such options of withdrawal. Hardly any of our foresisters had such an option.

Even if many contemporary women were to choose the option of nonparticipation, we may be sure that processions would continue precisely because they are such powerful human actions, which is to say that they express energy, movement, and festivity. If men have enjoyed them, why should women not enjoy them too? Like all powerful public rituals, all dramatic human activity, processions shape our sense of who we are as actors, or what in the language of ethics we call "moral agents." They shape not only what we call our "personal moral sense" or sense of identity and self-worth but also our sense of destiny and community — what we call our "moral ethos." They always have and they always will. Processions cannot be abandoned because we *all* live by a sense of plausibility and legitimacy that we gain from them. Be assured that whatever passes in our common life as sacred truth or profound wisdom has been and will always be shaped and celebrated through such occasions. So those excluded from processions in our flesh and blood world suffer very palpable loss, real injuries to dignity, real assaults on self-respect and sense of worth.

This is why I cannot concur with Daly's call to women to abandon processions and join the "Journey to the Otherworld" of segregated feminism. The joyful world of Womanspace, which she commends to us as a permanent habitat, can be at best only an occasional sanctuary for the feminist *for whom life itself, and the embodied world of flesh and blood,* are the true gifts of God. For this reason the turn in Mary Daly's writing, marked by a new emphasis on the language of otherworldliness, disturbs me. In contrast to Daly, my basic ethical thesis is that women, and other marginated people, are *less* cut off from the real, material conditions of life than are those who enjoy the privileges of patriarchy and that, as a result, an otherworldly spirituality is far removed from the life experience of women. Even if Daly were clear, as I hope she is, that her use of the language of otherworldiness is metaphorical, her imagery still seems misguided. Our need is for a moral theology shaped and informed by women's actual historical struggle. Women's experience, I submit, could not possibly yield an "otherworldly" ethic. Nor can feminists ignore the growing but morally dubious fascination with forms of world-denying spirituality in our culture. In light of a massive trend toward escapist religiosity, Daly's imagery, even if it stems from poetic license, is dangerous. It gives aid and comfort to those who have very strong political and economic reasons to encourage a spirituality that does not focus on injustice and the personal suffering it generates. Feminists, whose commitments must be to deep and profound change, should have no part in supporting a world-denying spirituality or in encouraging ways of speaking about the world that may invite withdrawal from struggle.

"Otherworldliness" in religion has two very different sources in our social world of knowledge. One sort of otherworldly religion appears among the poor and downtrodden, reflecting a double dynamic in their experience: It reflects a hopelessness about this world that is engendered by living daily with the evil of oppression, but it also fuels and encourages an ongoing struggle against the present order by conjuring a better time and a better place, beyond the oppressive here and now. However, an entirely different form of otherworldliness appears amongst those of us who have never been marginated, who have lived well above the daily struggle to survive, when our privileges are threatened. This form of otherworldliness is merely escapist, and its political consequences are entirely reactionary. Its result is to encourage denial of responsibility for the limited power that we do have, and it always results in reinforcing the status quo.

Daly's metaphorical leap into Otherworldly Womanspace may well come from the real agony and pain she has experienced in the face of misogyny.[5] The inexhaustibility of her rage suggests that this is so. However, a feminist metaethics must not fail to affirm and generate our power to affect the existing world. We must wrest this power of action from our very rightful anger at what has been done to us and to our sisters and to brothers who do not meet patriarchy's expectations. The deepest danger to our cause is that our anger will turn inward and lead us to portray ourselves and other women chiefly as victims rather than those who have struggled for the gift of life against incredible odds. The creative power of anger is shaped by owning this great strength of women and of others who have struggled for the full gift of life against structures of oppression.

We need not minimize the radicality of women's oppression in varied cultures and communities nor minimize Christianity's continuing involvement in that oppression, but we must not let that recognition confirm us in a posture of victimization. Let us note and celebrate the fact that "woman-spirit rising" is a *global* phenomenon in our time. Everywhere women are on the move. Coming into view now, for the first time, on a worldwide scale, is the incredible *collective* power of women so that anyone who has eyes to see can glimpse the power and strength of women's full humanity. We dare not forget, in spite of the varied forms of women's historical bondage, that we have also been, *always*, bearers of many of the most precious and special arts of human survival. The Chinese revolutionary slogan "Women hold up half the sky" is not mere hyperbole. In spite of a literary historical tradition that has ignored the fact, women always have held up half, or more than half, of the sky. This astonishing cross-cultural phenomenon of women's rising consciousness going on all around us could not have happened if this deep human power of women were not already grounded reality. I submit that even the present widespread cultural and political backlash against feminism is strong testimony to this fact. To be sure, the full world historical project that feminism envisages remains a distant dream — that is, that every female child in *each* and *every* community and culture will be born to share a full horizon of human possibility, that she will have the same range of life options as every male child. This is, and remains, "the longest revolution." But this revolution, for which we have every right to yearn, will come sooner if we celebrate the strength that shines forth in women's lives. This strength and power must stand at the center of the moral theology that feminism generates.

What I propose to do in the space remaining is to identify several positive dimensions of women's historical experience that I believe are most urgent to the reshaping of traditional Christian theological ethics to bring that ethics closer to a moral norm inclusive of all humanity. I also invite you to consider what difference it would make to our understanding of "the great commandment" — our love of God and our love of neighbor — if these basepoints drawn from women's experience received their due. It is out of such a process that we can begin to develop an adequate feminist moral theology.[6]

My basic thesis that a Christian moral theology must be answerable to what women have learned by struggling to lay hold of the gift of life, to receive it, to live deeply into it, to pass it on, cannot be fully defended here. My theological method is consonant with those other liberation theologies that contend that what is authentic in the history of faith arises only out of the crucible of human struggle.[7] This I take to be *the* central, albeit controversial, methodological claim of all emergent liberation theologies. That the locus of divine revelation is in the concrete struggles of groups and communities to lay hold of the gift of life and to unloose what denies life has astonishing implications for ethics. It means, among other things, that we must learn what we are to know of love from immersion in the struggle for justice. I believe that women have always been immersed in the struggle to create a flesh and blood community of love and justice and that we know much more of the radical work of love than does the dominant, otherworldly spirituality of Christianity. A feminist ethic, I submit, is deeply and profoundly worldly, a spirituality of sensuality.[8]

Basepoints for a Feminist Moral Theology

Activity as the Mode of Love

The first point at which women's experience challenges the dominant moral theology is difficult to see historically because of the smoke screen created by a successful nineteenth-century male counterattack on the first women's liberation movement. Because of this counterattack, most educated, middle-strata women have internalized an ideology about ourselves that contradicts our ac-

tual history. Historically, I believe, women have always exemplified the power of activity over passivity, of experimentation over
routinization, of creativity and risk-taking over conventionality.
Yet since the nineteenth century we have been taught to believe
that women are, by nature, more passive and reactive than men.
If women throughout human history have behaved as cautiously
and as conventionally as the "good women" invented by late
bourgeois spirituality, *if* women had acquiesced to "the cult of
true womanhood," and *if* the social powerlessness of women that
is the "ideal" among the European and American "leisure classes"
had prevailed, the gift of human life would long since have faced
extinction.

This very modern invitation to us women to perceive ourselves under the images of effete gentility, passivity, and weakness blocks our capacity to develop a realistic sense of women's
historical past. The fact is that while there are few constants in
women's experience cross-culturally, the biological reality of
childbearing and nursing (never to be confused with the cultural
power of nurturance) usually gave women priority in, and responsibility for, those day-to-day activities that make for human
survival in most societies. For example, women — not men — are
the breadwinners and traders in many precapitalist societies. If
we modern women acquiesce in the seductive invitation to think
of ourselves primarily as onlookers, as contemplators, as those
who stand aside while men get on with the serious business of
running the (public) world, we should at least recognize what a
modern "number" we are doing on ourselves! The important
point here, however, is that a theology that overvalues static and
passive qualities as "holy," that equates spirituality with nonin-
volvement and contemplation, that views the activity of sustaining daily life as mundane and unimportant religiously, such a theology *could not have been formulated by women.* In contrast,
Sojourner Truth spoke authentically, out of the real lived-world
experience of women, when she defined her womanhood in this
way:

> Nobody ever helped me into carriages, or over mud
> puddles, or gave me the best place. And ain't I a
> woman? Look at me! Look at my arm! I have ploughed
> and planted and gathered into barns, and no men could
> head me! And ain't I a woman? I can work as much and
> eat as much as any man when I can get it and bear the
> lash as well. And ain't I a woman? I have borne thirteen
> children and seen most of them sold off to slavery, and
> when I cried out with my mother's grief, none but Jesus
> heard me. And ain't I a woman? [9]

Women have been the doers of life-sustaining things, the "copers," those who have understood that the reception of the gift of life is no inert thing, that to receive this gift is to be engaged in its tending, constantly. I believe we have a very long way to go before the priority of activity over passivity is internalized in our theology and even farther to go before love, in our ethics, is understood to be a *mode of action*. In *Beyond God the Father*,[10] Mary Daly began the necessary theological shift by insisting that a feminist theism has no place for a God understood as stasis and fixity, that out of women's experience the sacred is better imaged in terms of process and movement. Her proposal that God be envisaged as Be-ing, as verb rather than as noun, struck a deep chord in her readers, and not merely in her women readers.

Even so, Daly's reformulation does not seem to me even to go far enough. Susanne Langer has rightly noted that philosophies of being — those philosophies that take the structures of nature as their starting point — have long since incorporated the notion that process is *the* basic structure of reality.[11] Process theologians rightly protest that Daly has not paid enough attention to, or given enough credit to, modern philosophy of religion for incorporating these new views of nature. However, not many process theologians — indeed, even Daly — recognize the further need to incorporate the full meaning of the human struggle for life into our understanding of God. It is necessary to open up the naturalistic metaphors for God to the power of human activity, to freedom not only as radical creativity but also as radical moral power. It is necessary to challenge the classic ontology of Be-ing even more deeply than Daly has done. Catholic natural law theologies, it has often been argued, fail to do justice to the fact that the power of nature passes through what Marx called "the species-being" of human nature. Our world and our faith are transformed, for good or ill, through human activity. A feminist moral theology needs to root its analysis in this realm of radical moral creativity. Such freedom is often abused, but the power to create a world of moral relations is a fundamental aspect of human nature itself. In my opinion, the metaphor of Be-ing does not permit us to incorporate the radicality of human agency adequately. *Do-ing* must be as fundamental as *be-ing* in our theologies. Both do-ing and be-ing are, of course, only metaphors for conceptualizing our world. Both are only "ways of seeing things." However, we can never make sense of what is deepest, "wholiest," most powerfully sacred in the lives of women if we identify women only with the more static metaphor of being, neglecting the centrality of praxis as basic to women's experience. We women have a special reason to appreciate the radical freedom of the power of real, concrete deeds.

To be sure, some male-articulated "theologies of praxis" have given feminist theologians pause on this point. Men often envisage the power of human activity under images that suggest that domination and control are the central modes of human activity, as though political or military conquest were the noblest expressions of the human power to act. Because of this, some women have urged that feminist theologies eschew historical categories and operate exclusively from naturalistic metaphors. I believe that such a theological move would have disastrous consequences. We dare not minimize the very real historical power of women to be architects of what is most authentically human. We must not lose hold of the fact that we have been the chief builders of whatever human dignity and community has come to expression. We have the right to speak of *building* human dignity and community.

Just as do-ing must be central to a feminist theology, so too be-ing and do-ing must never be treated as polarities. Receiving community as gift and doing the work of community building are two ways to view the same activity. A feminist theology is not a theology of either/or.[12] Anyone who has lived in "women's place" in human history has had to come to terms with the responsibility of being a reciprocal agent. Women's lives literally have been shaped by the power not only to bear human life at the biological level but to nurture life, which is a social and cultural power. Though our culture has come to disvalue women's role, and with it to disvalue nurturance, genuine nurturance is a formidable power.[13] Insofar as it has taken place in human history, it has been largely through women's action. For better or worse, women have had to face the reality that we have the power not only to create personal bonds between people but, more basically, to build up and deepen *personhood itself*. And to build up "the person" is also to deepen relationship, that is, to bring forth community.

We do not yet have a moral theology that teaches us the aweful, awe-some truth that we have the power through acts of love or lovelessness literally to create one another. I believe that an adequate feminist moral theology must call the tradition of Christian ethics to accountability for minimizing the deep power of human action in the work of or the denial of love. Because we do not understand love as the power to act-each-other-into-well-being we also do not understand the depth of our power to thwart life and to maim each other. The fateful choice is ours, either to set free the power of God's love in the world or to deprive each other of the very basis of personhood and community. This power of human activity, so crucial to the divine-human drama, is *not* the power of world conquest or empire building, nor is it control of one person by another. We are *not* most godlike in our human power when we take the view from the top, the view of rulers, or of empires, or the view of patriarchs.

I believe that our world is on the verge of self-destruction and death because the society as a whole has so deeply neglected that which is most human and most valuable and the most basic of all the works of love — the work of human communication, of caring and nurturance, of tending the personal bonds of community. This activity has been seen as women's work and discounted as too mundane and undramatic, too distracting from the serious business of world rule. Those who have been taught to imagine themselves as world builders have been too busy with master plans to see that love's work *is* the deepening and extension of human relations. This urgent work of love is subtle but powerful. Through acts of love — what Nelle Morton has called "hearing each other to speech" [14] — we literally build up the power of personhood in one another. It is within the power of human love to build up dignity and self-respect in each other or to tear each other down. We are better at the latter than the former. However, literally through acts of love directed to us, we become self-respecting and other-regarding persons, and we cannot be one without the other. If we lack self-respect we also become the sorts of people who can neither see nor hear each other.

We may wish, like children, that we did not have such awesome power for good or evil. But the fact is that we do. The power to receive and give love, or to withhold it — that is, to withhold the gift of life — is less dramatic, but every bit as awesome, as our technological power. It is a tender power. And, as women are never likely to forget, the exercise of that power begins, and is rooted in *our bodies, ourselves.* [15]

Our Bodies, Ourselves as the Agents of Love

A second basepoint for feminist moral theology derives from celebrating "embodiment." [16] A moral theology must not only be rooted in a worldly spirituality but must aim at overcoming the body/mind split in our intellectual and social life at every level. Feminist historical theologian Rosemary Ruether and, more recently, a number of male theologians have begun to identify the many connections between this body/mind dualism and our negative attitudes toward women. [17] Ironically, no dimension of our Western intellectual heritage has been so distorted by body/mind dualism as has our moral theology and moral philosophy, which is why a feminist moral theology is so needed. A number of male theologians — notably my colleague Tom Driver[18] — have begun to reenvisage a Christian theology that repudiates the mind/body split. However, fewer men in the field of Christian ethics have grasped the connection between body/mind dualism and the assumption many moral theologians make that we are most moral when most detached and disengaged from life-struggle.[19] Far too many Christian ethicists continue to imply that "disinterestedness" and "detachment" are basic preconditions for responsible moral action. And in the dominant ethical tradition, moral rationality too often is *disembodied* rationality.

If we begin, as feminists must, with "our bodies, ourselves," we recognize that all our knowledge, including our moral knowledge, is body-mediated knowledge. All knowledge is rooted in our sensuality. We know and value the world, *if* we know and value it, through our ability to touch, to hear, to see. *Perception* is foundational to *conception*. Ideas are dependent on our sensuality. Feeling is the basic bodily ingredient that mediates our connectedness to the world. When we cannot feel, literally, we lose our connection to the world. All power, including intellectual power, is rooted in feeling. If feeling is damaged or cut off, our power to image the world and act into it is destroyed and our rationality is impaired. But it is not merely the power to conceive the world that is lost. Our power to value the world gives way as well. If we are not perceptive in discerning our feelings, or if we do not know what we feel, we cannot be effective moral agents. This is why psychotherapy has to be understood as a very basic form of moral education. In the absence of feeling there is no rational ability to evaluate what is happening. Failure to live deeply in "our bodies, ourselves" destroys the possibility of moral relations between us.

These days there is much analysis of "loss of moral values" in our society. A feminist moral theology enables us to recognize that a major source of rising moral insensitivity derives from being out-of-touch with our bodies. Many people live so much in their heads that they no longer feel their connectedness to other living things. It is tragic that when religious people fear the loss of moral standards, they become *more* repressive about sex and sensuality. As a result they lose moral sensitivity and do the very thing they fear — they discredit moral relations through moralism. That is why the so-called "moral" majority is so dangerous.

By contrast, a feminist moral theology, rooted in embodiment, places great emphasis on "getting clear," on centering, on finding ways to enable us to stay connected to other people and to our natural environment.[20] Unless we value and respect feeling as the source of this mediation of the world, we lose this connection. To respect feeling is not, as some have suggested, to become subjectivistic. To the contrary, subjectivism is not the result of placing too much emphasis on the body and/or feeling. Subjectivism and moralism derive instead from evading feeling, from not integrating feeling deeply at the bodily level. This is not to suggest, however, that feelings are an end in themselves. We should never seek feelings, least of all loving feelings. Furthermore, the command to love is not now and never was an order to *feel a certain way*. Nor does the command to love create the power to *feel* love, and it was never intended to do so. Action does that. Feelings deserve our respect for what they are. There are no "right" and "wrong" feelings. Moral quality is a property of acts, not feelings, and our feelings arise in action. The moral question is not "what do I feel?" but rather "what do I do with what I feel?" Because this is not understood, contemporary Christianity is impaled between a subjectivist and sentimental piety that results from fear of strong feeling, especially strong negative feeling, and an objectivist, wooden piety that suppresses feeling under pretentious conceptual detachment. A feminist moral theology welcomes feeling for what it is — the basic ingredient in our relational transaction with the world.

The importance of all this becomes clear when we stop to consider the relation of our acts of love to our anger. It is my thesis that we Christians have come very close to killing love precisely because we have understood anger to be a deadly sin. Anger is not the opposite of love. It is better understood as a feeling-signal that all is not well in our relation to other persons or groups or to the world around us. Anger is a mode of connectedness to others and it is always a vivid form of caring. To put the point another way: anger is — and it always is — a sign of some resistance in ourselves to the moral quality of the social relations in which we are immersed. Extreme and intense anger signals a deep reaction to the action upon us or toward others to whom we are related.

To grasp this point — that anger signals something amiss in relationship — is a critical first step in understanding the power of anger in the work of love. Where anger rises, there the energy to act is present. In anger, one's body-self is engaged, and the signal comes that something is amiss in relation. To be sure, anger — no more than any other set of feelings — does not lead automatically to wise or humane action. (It is part of the deeper work of ethics to help us move through all our feelings to adequate strategies of moral action.) We must never lose touch with the fact that all serious human moral activity, especially action for social change, takes its bearings from the rising power of human anger.

Such anger is a signal that change is called for, that transformation in relation is required.

Can anyone doubt that the avoidance of anger in popular Christian piety, reinforced by a long tradition of fear of deep feeling in our body-denying Christian tradition, is a chief reason why the church is such a conservative, stodgy institution? I suggest, however, that while many of us actually hold out little hope for the moral renewal of the Christian church in our time, we are reluctant to face the cause of moral escapism in the church — namely, the fear of feeling and, more specifically, fear of the power of anger. We need to recognize that where the evasion of feeling is widespread, anger does not go away or disappear. Rather, in interpersonal life it masks itself as boredom, ennui, low energy, or it expresses itself in passive-aggressive activity or in moralistic self-righteousness and blaming. Anger denied subverts community. Anger expressed directly is a mode of taking the other seriously, of caring. The important point is that where feeling is evaded, where anger is hidden or goes unattended, masking itself, there the power of love, the power to act, to deepen relation, atrophies and dies.

Martin Buber is right that direct hatred (and hatred is anger turned rigid, fixated, deadened) is closer to love than to the absence of feeling.[21] The group or person who confronts us in anger is demanding acknowledgment from us, asking for the recognition of their presence, their value. We have two basic options in such a situation. We can ignore, avoid, condemn, or blame. Or we can act to alter relationship toward reciprocity, beginning a real process of hearing and speaking to each other. A feminist moral theology, then, celebrates anger's rightful place within the work of love and recognizes its central place in divine and human life.

The final and most important basepoint for a feminist moral theology is the centrality of relationship.

As a feminist moral theology celebrates the power of our human praxis as an intrinsic aspect of the work of God's love, as it celebrates the reality that our moral-selves are body-selves who touch and see and hear each other into life, recognizing sensuality as fundamental to the work and power of love, so above all else a feminist moral theology insists that relationality is at the heart of all things.

I am perfectly aware that our current preoccupation with "human relations," with "skills of relationship" is such that some have declared that our modern concern for relationship is merely trendy and faddish. It is true that, like everything else in late capitalism, "relationship" becomes transformed into a commodity to be packaged and exchanged at a price. To speak of the primacy of relationship in feminist experience, and to speak of a theology of relation, however, is not to buy in on the latest capitalist fad. It is, above all, to insist on the deep, total sociality of all things. All things cohere in each other. Nothing living is self-contained; if there were such a thing as an unrelated individual, none of us would know it. The ecologists have recently reminded us of what nurturers always knew — that we are part of a web of life so intricate as to be beyond our comprehension.[22] Our life is part of a vast cosmic web, and no moral theology that fails to envisage reality in this way will be able to make sense of our lives or our actions today.

In a recent, powerful, and pioneering work that lays the groundwork for a feminist theology of relationship,[23] Carter Heyward has made clear how far traditional Christian theism has wandered from the central concern with relationality that characterized the faith of the Israelite community and that was so central to Jesus' ministry. She stresses that the basic images of God that emerged in patristic Christianity were devoid of relationship. By stressing that God is "being itself" or is "the wholly other," the Christian tradition implies that a lack of relatedness in God is the source of divine strength. And this image of divine nonrelatedness surely feeds images of self that lead us to value isolation and monadic autonomy. In our dominant theologies and intellectual traditions, do we not think of ourselves as most effective, most powerful as moral agents when we are most autonomous and most self-reliant, when we least need anyone else's help or support?

In a brilliant work entitled *About Possession: The Self as Private Property*,[24] philosopher John Wikse notes the connection of the metaphors of self we use with the property metaphors dominant in the socioeconomic order. To be a free person, to be a self in this society, now, means "to possess oneself." We actually think of real freedom as "self-possession." Self-reliance and freedom from dependence on others is everything. Wikse argues, most plausibly, that it is now difficult to tell the difference between the way this culture's "ideal person" is supposed to behave and the way we have traditionally viewed the behavior of those who are idiots or suffer madness. The idiot, we had always assumed, is one cut off from relationship, one who does not share common meaning. Now, however, we also see maturity as involving the same freedom from relatedness; *self*-relatedness is now so much the highest value that we speak as if "being at one with oneself" were a condition for relationship to others rather than a consequence of it. The hope that we can control our identity from within fulfills a dream that we can live "beyond vulnerability" to others.[25]

Not surprisingly, Wikse sees an intimate connection between these ideals and the way in which one "grows up male" in this society. Learning this script of so-called "authenticity as self-possession" means being a *real* man. He illustrates how he learned to "take it like a man," how he got the hang of "hold(ing) onto oneself":

> I was taught that a real man is a masked man; the Lone Ranger. If others could see beneath the mask of self-possession, if they could know you in your real needs, they might reject you; a real man should not have needs. As a heroic stranger, a man performs a mission of salvation; problems are their problems, needs are theirs, not one's own. . . . I was . . . taught [in graduate school] that to succeed I must present a facade of invulnerability to other men, performing my work as a finished and perfect product, a performer immune to criticism and with no connection to the people with whom I work.[26]

I submit that a theological tradition that envisaged deity as autonomous and unrelated was bound over time to produce a humanism of the sort we have generated, with its vision of "Promethean man," the individual who may, if he chooses, enter into relationship. Where our image of transcendence is represented to us as unrelatedness, as freedom from reciprocity and mutuality, the experience of God as living presence grows cold and unreal. But even after such a God is long dead, the vision of the human historical agent as one who may, or may not, choose relationship lingers with us.

Such notions of love as also linger in a world like this — whether they are images of divine or of Promethean human love — are images of heroic, grand gestures of self-possessed people. It is an image of patronizing love, the love of the strong for the weak, or, conversely, the sniveling gratitude of the weak toward those stronger who grant "favors."

Never mind that none of us wants, or has ever wanted or needed, transactions with this sort of love. Never mind that we all know — unless our sense of self has already been twisted almost beyond human recognition by sadism and brutality — that the love we need and want is deeply mutual love, love that has both the quality of a gift received and the quality of a gift given.

The rhythm of a real, healing, and empowering love is take and give, give and take, free of the cloying inequality of one partner active and one partner passive.

I shudder to think how many times during my years of theological study I came upon a warning from a writer of Christian ethics not to confuse real, Christian love with "mere mutuality." [27] One senses that persons who can think this way have yet to experience the power of love as the real pleasure of mutual vulnerability, the experience of truly being cared for or of actively caring for another. Mutual love, I submit, is love in its deepest radicality. It is so radical that many of us have not yet learned to bear it. To experience it, we must be open, we must be capable of giving and receiving. The tragedy is that a masculinist reified Christianity cannot help us learn to be such lovers.

To dig beneath this reified masculinist idolatry is also, I believe, to move toward a recovery of a New Testament ethos of faith. Can Jesus' active embodiment of love be illumined by this image of mutuality? I believe it can. Orthodox Christological interpretations imply that somehow the entire meaning of Jesus' life and work is to be found in his headlong race toward Golgotha, toward crucifixion — as if he sought suffering as an end in itself to complete the resolution of the divine human drama once and for all.[28] I believe that this way of viewing Jesus' work robs it of its — and his — moral radicality. Jesus was radical not in his lust for sacrifice but in his power of mutuality. Jesus' death on a cross, his sacrifice, was no abstract exercise in moral virtue. His death was the price he paid for refusing to abandon the radical activity of love — of expressing solidarity and reciprocity with the excluded ones in his community. Sacrifice, I submit, is not a central moral goal or virtue in the Christian life. Radical acts of love — expressing human solidarity and bringing mutual relationship to life — are the central virtues of the Christian moral life. That we have turned sacrifice into a moral virtue has deeply confused the Christian moral tradition.

Like Jesus, we are called to a radical activity of love, to a way of being in the world that deepens relation, embodies and extends community, passes on the gift of life. Like Jesus, we must live out this calling in a place and time where the distortions of loveless power stand in conflict with the power of love. We are called to confront, as Jesus did, that which thwarts the power of human personal and communal becoming, that which twists relationship, which denies human well-being, community, and human solidarity to so many in our world. To confront these things, and to stay on the path of confrontation, to break through the "lies, secrets and silences" [29] that mask the prevailing distortions and manipulations in relationship and the power of relations is the vocation of those who are Jesus' followers.

It is one thing to live out a commitment to mutuality and reciprocity as the way to bear up God in the world and to be clear-eyed and realistic about what the consequences of that radical love may be. It is quite another to do what many Christians have done — that is, to rip the crucifixion of Jesus out of its lived-world context in his total life and historical project and turn sacrifice into an abstract norm for the Christian life. To be sure, Jesus was faithful unto death. He stayed with his cause and he died for it. He *accepted* sacrifice. But his sacrifice was *for* the cause of radical love, to make relationship and to sustain it, and, above all, to *righting* wrong relationship, which is what we call "doing justice."

Needless to say, in the best of times and under the most propitious of circumstances, it is risky to live as if the commonwealth of the living God were present — that is, to live by radical mutuality and reciprocity. Radical love creates dangerous precedents and lofty expectations among human beings. Those in power believe such love to be "unrealistic" because those touched by the power of such love tend to develop a reluctance to accept anything less than mutuality and self-respect, anything less than human dignity, anything less than authentic relatedness. It is for that reason that such persons become powerful threats to the status quo. As women have known, but also as men like Martin Luther King, Jr., and Archbishop Oscar Romero understood, as any must know who dare to act deeply and forcefully out of the power of love, radical love is a dangerous and serious business. Without blessed persistence, without the willingness to risk, even unto death, the power of radical love would not live on in our world. There are no ways around crucifixions, given the power of evil in the world. But as that poetic theologian of the gay liberation movement Sandra Browders has reminded us, the aim of love is not to perpetuate crucifixions, but to bring an end to them in a world where they go on and on and on! We do this through actions of mutuality and solidarity, not by aiming at an ethic of sacrifice.

Mark the point well: *We are not called to practice the virtue of sacrifice.* We are called to express, embody, share, celebrate the gift of life, and to pass it on! We are called to reach out, to deepen relationship, or to right wrong relations — those that deny, distort, or prevent human dignity from arising — as we recall each other into the power of personhood. We are called to journey this way, to stay in and with this radical power of love. When you do that for me, I am often overwhelmed by your generosity, and I may speak of the sacrifice you make for me. But we both need to be perfectly clear that you are not, thereby, practicing the virtue of sacrifice on me. You are merely passing on the power of love, gifting me as others have gifted you, into that power to *do* radical love.

Conclusion

There is much more to be said about the envisionment of the work of radical love within a feminist moral theology that takes its signals from what is deepest and best in women's historical struggle. Certainly, more also needs to be said about the depth of sin and evil in the world. It is important to remember that a feminist moral theology is utopian, as all good theology is, in that it *envisages* a society, a world, a cosmos, in which, as Jules Girardi puts it, there are "no excluded ones." [30] But feminist theology is also mightily realistic, in that it takes with complete seriousness the radical freedom we human beings have for doing good *or evil*. Since we acknowledge that we have, literally, the power to person-each-other into love — that is, into relationship — we can also acknowledge our power to obliterate dignity, respect, care, and concern for humanity from our world. All of that *is* within our power.

Far more than we care to remember, though, the evil that we do lives on, after us. The radicality of our vision of love gains its urgency from that very knowledge. The prophets of Israel were right to insist, long ago, that the sins of the fathers (and the mothers) live on in us, corroding and destroying the power of relation. This is why our human moral task sometimes seems overwhelming. We live in a time when massive and accumulated injustice, acted out over time, encounters answer in the rising anger of those whose dignity and life are being threatened by collective patterns of privilege that have to be undone. In a world such as this, actively pursuing the works of love will often mean doing all we can to stop the crucifixions, resisting the evil as best we can, or mitigating the suffering of those who are the victims of our humanly disordered relations. In the midst of such a world, it is still within the power of love, which is the good news of God, to keep us in the knowledge that none of us were born only to die, that we were meant to have the gift of life, to know the power of relation and to pass it on.

A chief evidence of the grace of God — which always comes to us in, with, and through each other — is this power to struggle and to experience indignation. We should not make light of our power to rage against the dying of the light. It is the root of the power of love. So may it never be said of any of us feminist theologians that we merely stood by, ladylike, when that power of love was called for or that we sought refuge in an Otherworld when we were needed here and now, in the line of march.

After Mary Daly lectures — on those somewhat rare occasions when men are invited to attend — it often happens that the first questioner is a man who inquires, in a befuddled way, "What about men? What does this mean for us?" Since I do not share Mary Daly's reverse Thomism[31] — that is, since I believe that the major differences between men's and women's behavior are rooted in culture and history rather than in a relatively fixed "nature" — I trust that my male readers will not at this point be suffering any confusion about what this essay means for them. It is not that it is wrong for any of us to ask: "What does all this mean for me?" That is a good question. But in a feminist moral theology, good questions are answered *by something we must do*. It is, I submit, urgent that men join women in doing feminist moral theology[32] — that is, acting to keep the power of relationship alive in our world — because men have more public power than women and because there is so much to be done.

But I do not wish to end on too sentimental a note about the relations of men and women in our world. Mary Daly had very good reasons for warning us women about the dangers of joining male-originated patriarchal processions. Since her diagnosis of the problem is so much on target, none of us must ever forget that, if we must join patriarchal processions in order to get on with the radical work of love, we had better be very sure that we invite a lot of our friends to come along.

SEXISM AND THE LANGUAGE
OF CHRISTIAN ETHICS*

Christian ethics, or Christian moral theology, is a much con-
troverted field. What is published in the discipline consists largely
of discussions, or debates, about the modes of reasoning appropriate to doing Christian ethics. Here, as in theology, feminists
often begin by criticizing the male gender monopoly in language
about God employed in Christian moral argument. Though I
share the objection to male gender exclusivity in all dimensions
of theological and moral reasoning,[1] a full appreciation of how
sexism has affected Christian ethics requires awareness that language about deity is but a special case of a deeper problem. Sexist gender assumptions inform and infect all dimensions of our
language and experience and condition our perception of reality
in far more subtle ways and at more inclusive levels than specific
gender referents reveal. Clarity on this point is critical for Christian feminist ethics because language about God is not the primary, direct discourse of ethics or moral theology. Christian ethical discourse is not, in the first instance, language about deity.
It is language about ourselves in relation to our world, our agency
or action in a social context, as that action is understood from
"the moral point of view."[2] To be sure, all ethical language is
informed by our theological assumptions, including particularly
our images, metaphors, and symbols of divine agency. Moral judgments are articulated always with reference to our basic experience of what is holy or sacred. Still, in feminist understanding,
"God talk" is only one dialectical element in a complex panoply
of Christian ethical discourse.

Not all Christian ethicists agree with our contention that
God language is only indirectly moral. Some persist in believing
that theological claims are also per se moral claims. This type of
Christian ethic is designated in theological ethics as a "Divine
Command Ethic." It presumes that to say that "God commands
x" constitutes adequate moral justification for accepting that "I

---

* This essay is a revision of a paper presented to the Task Force on Inclusive Language of the United Presbyterian Church in the U.S.A. in 1977. I was
asked to describe how sexism in language affected my discipline.

ought to do x." Here one moves logically and deductively from "God talk" to talk about what we as Christians *ought* to do. Many objections, logical and psychological, have been raised against this type of theological ethics.[3] I share many of these objections. At this point it is sufficient to note that it is relatively easy to track the effects of sexism in the God language of Divine Command Ethics. The male gender monopoly involved is a surface signal of male supremacy and moral legitimacy that is offensive not merely in itself but because it functions as a continuous reminder to aware people of the pattern of inferiority/superiority and power disparity that gender exclusion is designed to sustain. Half of the human species — women — are rendered quite literally invisible as we prattle on about the "nature of man" or discuss the requisites of *"mankind's* obedience to *Him* who creates *man's* moral sense." We will not correct this sort of invisibility of women manifest in such linguistic signals, however, unless we probe even more deeply the power dynamics this language is designed to keep in place.

Later I characterize briefly some of the negative effects on our conception of human agency resulting from this sort of Divine Command ethic. First, however, it is important to pursue my more inclusive claim that the problem of gender-exclusive language about deity is only a potent and symbolically loaded example of a more overarching issue. We must ask first how gender monopoly shapes our sense of power as human agents.

Sexism, the Language of Ethics, and Our Sense of Power

Ours is a world that has become fascinated with language. To be sure, the dialectic between language and human consciousness has long been acknowledged. What is distinctive about many of the recently emergent perspectives on human language, however, is that they focus on the critical role language plays in transmitting our experience of our social relations and social structure. Within the last two decades, representatives of every major tradition of social theory have "discovered" that language is the main bearer and transmitter of "social structure." Proponents of approaches to the study of society as diverse as neo-Marxian structuralists, critical theorists of the more idealist German Frankfurt School, such as Jürgen Habermas,[4] and even thoroughgoing neo-Kantian idealists, such as Thomas Luckmann, focus in varied ways on language as the major carrier of our sense of how the world is structured.

If it is so — and it seems to me incontestable that it is — that language is the ineluctable bearer and transmitter of all cultural and social patterns and all social relations, then language transmits not only a sense of the polis or political society we are born into but also conveys our sense of personal-relational power, or lack of it. Language encodes our sense of how we are positioned in our basic relations to and with others who make up our social world. This means that language teaches us, below the level of consciousness and intentionality, our sense of power-in-relation.[5] It also functions either to reproduce and reinforce existing social relations, thereby teaching us to accept the legitimacy of what is given, or to enable imaginative reappropriation or transcendence of the given. Language is not merely an "external" feature of reality. Appropriation of language either reproduces or reshapes our social relations. The potential of language, then, is either to expand human possibility or to function as a transmitter of subtle, and not so subtle, patterns of human oppression and domination. Language is through and through political, for it transmits the past to our present. The marks of past patterns of domination and of all that was not previously questioned in past social relations, of all that was merely taken for granted, are deeply embedded in our language.[6] A working assumption of a feminist ethic must be that we critically assess all language for its moral effects. We have a moral obligation[7] not to replicate language patterns that reinforce unjust social relations.

Male gender supremacy is ancient, so a critical feminist analysis must presume that power differentials along lines of gender have deeply affected all human social relations and institutions. Biological dimorphism is surely the first and the most universally experienced phenomenon of "difference" between the self and not-self. It is a "differentness" or distinction that all persons, across time, in all cultures, have experienced and learned. Before human beings recognized any other duality, or before any one group encountered physiological or cultural divergence, the distinctions that present themselves in external genital structure must have been obvious. How this experienced difference has been interpreted and patterned surely informs human perceptions of me/not-me and, at a later stage of individual development, self/not-self, in fundamental ways. If self/other polarity is informed, both sociohistorically and ontogenetically, by observable genital difference, then it becomes, at any early stage of human culture, not only a phenomenon to be explained or rationalized but a paradigm for interpreting all our other experience. No doubt, over time the human perceptual level itself has been shaped by it.

As a result, gender dualism surely provides not only a primitive historical dynamic but also an analogue for inherited evaluative dualisms reflected in language at every other level. This is a sweeping claim, but it is one that is now widely recognized within feminist theory.[8]

Such a contention must not be taken to mean that sexism is more pervasive, more destructive, or more evil morally than other patterns of human inequality, subjugation, or oppression. An adequate feminist theory does not rest on the claim that sexism is *the* primary form of social evil. After all, women are concretely the victims of *all* structural oppressions. One encounters sexism as a singular dynamic or pattern of subjugation only among a very few women, those who are not poor or women of color. Most women are doubly or triply victims of social oppression. Feminist theory should incorporate awareness that ancient gender oppression, actively interstructured through time with systems of racist control and economic exploitation, including cultural and political imperialism, shapes and distorts all social relations but is not per se the source of all oppression.[9]

In spite of the fact that male gender supremacy does not provide a full or adequate paradigm for human oppression, its ontogenetic and phylogenetic priority does mean that it patterns all human language structures as well. Given the diversity of social patterns of male supremacy, we should expect that all images, metaphors, and concepts that explain and direct human activity reflect not only the datum of physiological dimorphism but all the cultural meanings and values ascribed to presumed human biological gender difference.

As we know, the experience of duality is a fundamental dynamic of personal development. The me/not-me experience is critical to the entire process of self-differentiation, including cognitive and ego development.[10] If that were all there is to the matter, we might romanticize physiological dimorphism as a primary ground of human personhood and intelligence. But as I have observed, that is not all there is to the matter. We go from *duality* to *dualism*, from *difference* to *subordination* and *subjection*. Both gender dimorphism and ascribed gender valuations enter into and inform our basic interpretation of reality deeply and pervasively, yet we can hardly detect their impact. Maleness connotes power, strength, positive agency to the end that all dualism bears the mark of male gender supremacy. Most of the impact on our perception of value that is shaped by gender rests outside consciousness, at the very edge of our awareness.

Karl Marx had grave difficulty accounting for the shift in the evolution of society from the *differentiation* of the social functions of labor to the existence of *exploitation* of some human beings' labor by others. I find it even more difficult to "explain" the shift from gender differentiation to sexual exploitation and the pervasive and multifaceted historical development of male supremacy. What is clear is that, given the nature of the reproductive process, males would not have been able to ensure that a child was in fact their own progeny without "controlling" women and their reproduction.[11] But it is one thing to "explain" the historical genesis of all but universal patterns of social subjugation and quite another to account for it morally. This is one reason why we revert so frequently to religious myth to convey the reality of moral evil. From the standpoint of any genuine sensitivity, such evil is what Barth called a "surd,"[12] something that defies rationalization. Religious myths help us appropriate negative moral realities, whereas the causal, phylogenetic explanations of the social sciences can only abstract the human ugliness involved. So male supremacy and the greater value of all things connected with maleness, including male modes of action, remain an inexplicable, irrational evil that defies simple explanation.

Yet, even at the risk of overrationalizing the past, we need to insist that over time the substratum of biological dimorphism became a focal point for the dynamics of control between me/not-me, self/not-self, and a basic conditioning pattern affecting all our social relations. Through historical-social process, patterns of social interaction characterized by dynamics of gender inferiority-superiority were shaped, reproduced, extended, and, we may be sure, generalized into other institutionalized social relations.

That sexism is a dynamic aspect of all superior/inferior relationships characterizing human interaction is revealed by the way in which "feminization" is imputed to all oppressed males by the dominant culture.[13] When societies wish to punish or ostracize men, they portray them as deficient in masculinity, or as "feminine." What is less often noticed is how gender role inequality affects the way we learn to relate to basic patterns of social power. Roland Sampson is one political theorist who has observed that gender power dynamics in the family have widespread social significance precisely because we learn power relations so early.[14] How else, Sampson asks, do we acquire preferred patterns of human interrelationship if not from the dynamics of male/female relationship we encounter in our primary parenting figures, in infancy, well before we have outgrown childhood dependency? Recent feminist psychological analysis has illumined this process of early socialization in power relations in more precise detail.[15] Even so, few pause to wonder why so many in our culture find patterns of subordination and subjugation, not to mention overt coercion and violence, acceptable modes of human interaction. We have learned to accept, even to expect, these inequitable patterns of relation. That so many take them for granted surely derives from their familiarity. Such ways of relating "feel safe" to us precisely because they were the patterns that provided security when we were very young and dependent. Unjust social relations are reproduced in most families; yet we rarely pause to wonder why a sense of justice is so poorly developed in the sensibilities of people in society.

There is, I submit, a clear connection between our psychic tolerance for subjugation at the interpersonal level and the social, economic and political forms we tolerate or approve at the sociocommunal level. Our preferences for and styles of relationship between males and females learned well before we have any firm sense of personal identity are full of import for the shape of the subsequent moral sensibility we may develop. In short, what these "learnings" condition us to are basic "safe" patterns of relationship. This basic perception of power-in-relationship affects in turn both our feeling for what sort of world is possible and our sense of what ought to be, what is desirable. In sum, our sense of reality foundational to our moral development, what we may call our overall horizon of moral expectation, is shaped by gender patterns and our experience of gender relation. This means that there is more continuity between our personal experience in the family and our wider sociopolitical expectations than most Christian ethicists have acknowledged.

In fact, many modern Christian ethicists actually have denied any such connection. So celebrated an interpreter of Christian social ethics as Reinhold Niebuhr gained a following for predicating his entire social ethical approach on a presumed discontinuity between the dynamics of power existing in social, economic, and political life and the dynamics of power in interpersonal interactions, in face to face groups like the family. Like many a male ethicist, Niebuhr romanticized the family.[16] He characterized familial relationships as the sphere of human life in which mutuality and sacrifice can express themselves directly in human action. Niebuhr acknowledged that there had been some social injustice toward women,[17] a situation he believed had been largely overcome, and it never occurred to him that the "beatific" arena of interpersonal relations in families was maintained largely by a dualism of gender role expectations, values, and norms that was itself deeply unfair to women. Niebuhr, who is often cited as a critic of theological liberalism, was on this point a typical theological liberal.[18] He never questioned the dualism embedded in liberal political ideology between the "private" sphere, that is, the arena of those interpersonal, humane relations of the family, and the "public" sphere, those "impersonal relations" of institutions and collectivities. He did not notice that this private/public split legitimized both a capitalist mode of political-economic organization and female subjugation in personal or domestic life. That the broader social injustices toward women that he noticed at the collective level were only extensions of the dynamic operating in the supposedly blissful arena of the family never occurred to him. He celebrated "sacrifice," a characteristic in which he thought women excelled, and downgraded "mere" mutuality. Niebuhr was then also prototypical liberal male chauvinist.

Gender dualism and male supremacy condition the strongly dualistic and hierarchical character of much Christian ethics. Hierarchical dualisms, when we encounter them in moral discourse, tend to present themselves to us as alternative and exclusive patterns of action. Our moral language and moral vocabulary are filled with such implied irreconcilables, and, as a result, we experience our moral lives as characterized by exclusive alternatives. We Christians are taught that there are numerous life structures, norms, values, and patterns of action that Christians should experience as contradictory and fundamentally irreconcilable. On the one hand is self-interest or self-seeking; on the other is sacrifice or self-giving. There is *agape* — deep, disinterested love — and there is *eros* — usually defined as egoistic passion. We are taught that these are fundamentally different and unrelated forms of love and that they are in conflict, or at least that they stand in tension in our lives. Self-assertion and self-denial are portrayed not merely as polarities but as irreconcilable modes of being in the world. Persons are either realists or idealists morally. These attitudes represent diverse approaches to life — and we must choose between them. The ethical life is portrayed as a struggle involving a tangle of contradictions that inhere in our norms, our decisions, and our strategies of action.

These hierarchical dualisms not only are embedded in the language of Christian morality and ethical reflection but also characterize much secular moral philosophy as well. Consider, for example, the distinctions drawn between "ethics of consequences" and "ethics of intrinsic values." Again and again, we are informed that we must choose between such theoretical options or between norms that are irreconcilable or between modes of action and ways of being in the world that pose sharp either/ors for us. That we take for granted distinctions between mind and body, theory and practice, thought and feeling and give primacy to the side of these dualisms associated with males attests to the depth of the learned need to divide and superordinate reality in terms of inequity of power.[19] Such dualisms affect our perceptions of what our actions should be and even condition the modes of action we will attempt. In our Western industrial societies, where we mistakenly perceive ourselves as "activists," such rigidly dualistic conceptions reinforce a systemic, disastrous inability to act except through the mode of violence. The history of sexist practice is, I believe, a conditioning dimension to our astonishing blindness and speechlessness in terms of moral sensibility and to our inability to act constructively. "Decisive" action is invariably destructive action. The perspective we need to envision and the words we need to shape, our full human potential for holistic, integrated, and fresh human action, simply are rendered inconceivable by these rigid perceptions of the world.

Reconceiving the Basic Assumptions of Our Work in Christian Ethics

If it is true that the problem of gender dualism contaminates moral language so deeply, we have to begin with awareness that we have no language that is free of the power dualisms of domination. How are we to move beyond this dilemma, to transcend the historical effects of primal biological dimorphism that are so embedded? [20] Feminists, struggling to effect a praxis of full human power, participation, and justice have our work cut out for us at the level of feminist theory and also in terms of strategic formulations of the social policy we seek.

At the level of feminist theory, I believe we must begin by rejecting the notion that there is any *fundamental* dimorphism in human nature/being.[21] My assumptions about gender difference are at variance methodologically with versions of feminist theory that claim that women's experience, including women's spirituality, differs because of an "ontic" distinction between femaleness and maleness, a theory that parallels and sometimes claims to be grounded in presumed biological differences between men and women. The complexities of present feminist religious thought are reflected in the fact that this position is embraced both by some defenders of lesbian-feminist separatism[22] and also by apparent defenders of "normative" heterosexism.[23] Both seem to commend and support gender-determined views of human experience. By contrast, I believe that, given historical-cultural differences in male and female socialization, we must at the very least suspend any imputation of an irreducible difference between men and women rooted in biological distinctness. It is especially critical to avoid equating the cultural concepts "masculinity" and "femininity" with the concrete identity of women and men as individuals or as groups because the notions of femininity and masculinity are especially freighted with cultural stereotype.[24]

Gender is culturally and historically important but it is not of ontological significance. Gender is an infintely complex interaction of at least four biogenetic and three sociocultural systems.[25] The biogenetic systems themselves are so complex that it is doubtful that even the fundamental chromosomal distinction, at the XX/XY level, has major determinative force in social development. We know that genes do not control development in some cases where the hormonal system or internal sexual organs or external genitalia are at variance with chromosomal information.[26] We human beings differ in subtle, rich, and varied ways, but the differences between male and female are minute; only one of the forty-four chromosomes men and women carry diverge slightly in the genetic "information" they convey. Furthermore, the protoplasm that differentiates into male and female sexual organs, through the process of fetal development, is physiologically identical in males and females in early fetal life. It is time to recognize that men and women are far more alike than are any other two things in all creation. The designations "male" and "female" are actually "types," and types do not do justice to the infinite complexity and diverse possibility of any given person. Any typification is, at best, an approximation. If there are statistically significant psychological or physiological differences between men and women,[27] the moral question is "What are we to make of these differences in human history and society?" No conceivable biological or psychological differences can justify gender-based distinctions in social power, prestige, and wealth.

This does not mean, of course, that the distinctions between female and male *cultures* are insignificant. On the contrary, until very recently all societies were patterned on a strong division between male and female cultural systems and gender socialization. Still, these are historical differences and must be treated as such. To contend that maleness and femaleness constitute differences powerful enough to justify positing an essential or ontic difference is to incorporate, at the level of theory and therefore by definition, assumptions about what is possible for men and women to do or to be. From a moral point of view, we must be wary of such theoretical presumptions because, once made, they have the force of factual claims, and factual claims are less open to challenge and revision than any other aspect of moral argument. Since every existing concept, notion, and perception of masculinity and femininity and of "appropriate" gender difference is already suffused with an ancient and all but unbroken pattern of male supremacy, it seems clear to me that all assumptions of essential, or ontic, difference will be as tainted by past oppression as all our concepts and languages are. The history of the subjugation of women is a *social history* that must be changed. It is unjust, destructive of human wholeness, reinforcing and legitimating other dynamics of subjugation.

Getting our theory straight, however, does not enable us to escape the historical contradictions in which we stand. On the one hand, we women find ourselves having to celebrate, assert, and lay claim to that in ourselves, our experiences, and our culture which has been belittled, disvalued, and disavowed by the dominant male culture. We must embrace what is stereotyped as "female," even including what is characterized as "feminine." I have observed that we *can* do without the notion of "femininity" because it is a male construct and is always an ambivalent term, implying relinquishment of power or indirect or manipulative exercise of power. What we must protest is not neglect of femininity but the exclusion of concrete female experience, female modes of being, and women's culture. We must lose no opportunity to challenge the pervasive, if subtle, implication that what pertains to women concretely or to women's culture is of lesser value than male norms or is a lesser expression of the best reality of the human species.

When we attempt to do this, the social contradiction in which we live becomes obvious. As we affirm and celebrate femaleness, we seem to be embracing and reinforcing precisely the gender dualism that is itself the heart of the larger pattern of oppression that led to our disvaluation. Insofar as our sensibility remains dualistic, we will find ourselves impaled precisely on that either/or logic for which we have rightly criticized patriarchy. Some feminists have countered the ideal of patriarchy with romantic claims to matriarchy, reinforcing the principle of social rule or control by gender-defined groups. I believe such responses to our situation not only reinforce gender dualism but reinforce the "zero-sum" power perceptions that are distinctive to patriarchy, in which one gender must necessarily rule the other. Such proposed solutions to our situation are both source and symptom of our subjugation.

Most feminists are struggling mightily, recognizing the need to analyze our situation and celebrate women's concrete lives without lapsing back into gender dualism. We are attempting to find language that affirms the reality of our being, our experience, our stories, in ways that avoid reinforcing the power dynamics inhering already in the history of a world created and construed by patriarchy. Even so, finding our way beyond discourse that reinforces the dualistic social construction created by patriarchal power relations is no easy matter.

In the history of dualistic moral language to which I have alluded, no single dualism has consistently denoted male moral superiority. As many writers have forcefully reminded us, early Western traditions frequently identified the female with body, physicality, blood, and earth. Women were frequently said to be lacking in rationality. Yet other intellectual traditions feared, or even celebrated, females as especially intuitive, spontaneous, and ecstatic. Since nineteenth-century romanticism, the more modern pantheons of gender-stereotyped female virtues have symbolized the "feminine" far more complexly, usually in utterly contradictory ways. In Christian history, the split between the virgin — the selfless, "feminine" woman — and the "seductive," powerful whore discloses the ambivalence with which strong women are perceived. Women are said to be "more pure" than men but also dangerously unable to act rationally or "assume responsibility."

As I have observed elsewhere,[28] the split that developed in our value systems as a result of the development of an advanced capitalist industrial economy has caused the notion of "femininity" to become the dumping ground for all modes of being and doing that do not "work" or are not "functional" for success in the political-economic arena.[29] "Femininity" really has come to mean "lacking in public impact." Women are invariably expected to be and do whatever men cannot or do not wish to be or do and, above all, to provide personal emotional support for men. Male standards of "moral realism" incorporate what men do, or what they should be permitted to get away with, in the struggle for "success," politically, economically, and socially. "Realism" and "prudence" are strongly positive values for males to exemplify. In contrast, self-sacrifice and unflagging benevolence are the most valued norms for women. We are expected to be "idealistic" so long as it is our behavior that expresses the ideal. We are not to badger men morally! Here too the social contradiction in which many of us live is clear. Even as we celebrate what is female, we who are white and educated are giving voice, necessarily, to that matrix of goods and values that has already been rendered "unrealistic" and "unworkable" on the public side of the social world in which we live. What feminists demand, in terms of transcending hierarchy and correcting inequities of power and accountability, is seen as "unrealistic," an effort to bring personal values into the "impersonal" social sphere.

The burden that this places on women as agents of change and moral actors is immense. Is it any wonder that we are sometimes tempted to see ourselves as the potential messianic deliverers of the race[30] but at the same time experience ourselves as immobilized by the weight of heavy moral expectation we lay upon ourselves?[31] We must be aware that our present political economy places unprecedented moral, social, and economic demands on women while at the same time weakening the social bonds of women's culture that proffered support to women in past struggles. Is it any wonder that most women are fatigued by life?

One strategy that moralists have proposed to avoid facing the depth of sexism is to call for and affirm some need for "balance" in gender dualisms that are specious in the first place. Moralists such as Gordon Rattray Taylor, who has said some wise things about being human in light of the ecological crisis, can nevertheless propose, with a perfectly straight face, that what we need is a "balance" between "matrist" and "patrist" modes of being.[32] We are called on to embrace modes of being and doing characteristic of male and female existence because, it is claimed, we need to balance "being" and "doing." Such thinking perpetuates the patriarchal split between activity and passivity and between contemplation and action. Since process is foundational in a feminist vision, contemplation and passivity are not understood as inaction but as receptivity, and receptivity is itself an important mode of action. And all of us, female and male, need to possess the full power of agency and the full range of modes of action to survive together and live well.

Taylor, like other so-called scholars before him, extends his absurd thesis by classifying whole societies as either predominantly "matrist" or "patrist." Not surprisingly, he contends that imperial cultures like our own are "patrist," and (you guessed it!) he believes that it is especially important to balance matrist and patrist dynamics because our world *is currently overweighted in the direction of matrist values!* Never mind the threat of ecological destruction and nuclear holocaust or the vast military machine we have created to prevent movements for social justice from succeeding in our world. Ours is a matrist society that may be overwhelmed by female values![33]

Taylor's analysis exemplifies a clever counterattack on feminism. I first encountered this sort of reasoning many years ago from a male colleague who celebrated the importance of research of "the feminine." He won a considerable following from many women students for such research. Nevertheless, like Taylor, he blithely announced at every opportunity that "history proved" that the feminine becomes potent culturally only in periods of historical decline! Like Taylor, he also failed to make clear who or what was threatened or in decline when matters related to women came to the fore. The pseudo-objective use of the vague sexual dualisms "femininity" and "masculinity" always will reappear in a political counterattack against women's demands for full, uncompromised social, political, and economic justice, which is why "femininity" and "masculinity" are notions we must learn to live without.

In spite of these obfuscations, designed to place restraints on women's aspirations for justice, the goal of a feminist liberation ethic within Christianity must be the full, concrete emancipation of women in all societies. We have hardly begun to face the implications of male supremacy as it affects the lives of all women — black and other racial and ethnic women in the United States, the women of Bangladesh, rural Latin American women, women in the patriarchal cultures of Islam, to name only a few women whose suffering from oppression is much greater than our own. No one should be romantic about the meaning of feminism's moral goal or the length of the struggle involved.

Language About God and Its Effect
on Christian Ethical Analysis

It is time to return to the more specific issue of how male gender monopoly affects the modes of Christian theological ethics that attempt to move directly and deductively from language about deity to questions about human agency, what I have characterized as Divine Command Ethics. Practitioners of such ethics claim that they are doing "real" or "genuine" theological ethics because language about deity appears to set the frame directly for their thinking about human action. Actually, Divine Command enthusiasts are only invoking God's authority directly to legitimate their own indirect claims on our action. The not-so-subtle symbols of exclusive divine "maleness" have especially strong valence because when an action is urged because God commands it, the authority of the male both as God and as theologian stands between the agent (especially the female agent) and her own power of agency. The dubious consequence for Christians reasoning about our action is that Divine Command Ethics obscures the necessity of living into our responsibility. Divine Command Ethics fetishizes male symbols as "truly Godly," as powerful apart from relation to us, as untouched and unaffected by our action. Most traditional male Christian images for God derive, of course, both from the familial context and from the sociopolitical arena. Male images and male-derived concepts of God invariably incorporate the hierarchical principles embedded in both the *pater familias* — that is, male control of the household — and male control of the public order through monarchical or hierarchical political control. Thus all male images of a God convey divine-human relations as superordinate-subordinate relations, since both public and private male roles conjure power *over* others. The believer thus is "feminized." The impact of these images on our experience of God is formidable. Divinity is envisaged and experienced in relation — that is, metaphorically — to the experienced dynamics of our relations to fathers, patriarchs, kings, lords, sovereigns.[34] Such images function metaphorically to remind us of the disparity between our power and value and God's. The only thing that is sacred or holy is that which is above us or superior to us. We are profane: That which is human is lowly, and definitely not holy.

If we could stand far off from our own century and survey ourselves, listening to the most powerful theological voices in western Christianity, I believe we would find ourselves astonished at the extent to which our God language is power preoccupied while at the same time also fixated on human powerlessness. We are hardly ever aware that a power-preoccupied culture like our own has as its dominant "phantasie" of God, to use Dorothee Sölle's wonderful term,[35] symbols that deny our power and connote *His* prerogatives, power, control, and rule. It is true that in the twentieth century, such symbols of divine power were conjured to counter political totalitarianism. In the theology of Karl Barth, "the word of God" as sovereign freedom was posed in sharp distinction, and in opposition, to the "mere" words of men who were Fascist. But for Barth, the problem was not merely fascism. As he formulated his critique, employing masculinist universal generalization, the problem became for him all human self-assertion. All human power and achievement was "babel," idolatry.[36] Nothing in Barth's early theological protest acknowledged the irreplaceable power of human agency. Thus, increasingly powerful twentieth-century men embraced theologies denying their own power! The need for a feminist critique is manifest to prevent such madness (I speak literally here) from going further.

So this call "to obey God, not men," became the watchword of the mode of Christian ethics done by the most powerful men. It was aimed at creating resistance to unjust forms of social power, but it failed abysmally to do so because it countered totalitarianism in human society by calling us back to a totalitarian relationship to God. A Christian ethic continued to demand "obedience" to the Divine Word as its ethical watchword, but this obedience had no concrete political and social content. The totalitarian state had demanded obedience, but its obedience was concrete indeed. While the categories of this theology aimed to mobilize Christian resistance and intended to be critical, they turned out, in fact, to be merely reactive. Obedience to the Word remained abstract and formal. Without exception, this masculinist theology used terms that intentionally appropriated and directly endorsed social relations of superiority and subordination as ideal relations between humanity and deity. These images of God proclaimed that sacred power is control over us. God-relationship displaces and overwhelms images of human self-direction altogether. What we really needed, by contrast, was a new vision of *both* God *and* humanity, a vision of holiness or godliness and a vision of humanity as co-capacity-in-relationship.

Almost all of the theological ethics formulated in Protestant Christianity from 1920 until the present bears the stigma of this envisagement of God as all-controlling agent. The watchword for the Christian life and faith in this most modern Christian ethic remains "obedience" — the giving over of self-control to another.

I am sympathetic to the social circumstances that originally made the appeal to obedience to God rather than to human power an attractive alternative to theological liberalism. However, it was unwise then, as now, to counter obedience to unjust human authority with simple either/or claims to absolute divine authority. In terms of recent Christian ethics, the consequence of such a strategy has been a new and disastrous Christian conformity. Surely one of the reasons Dietrich Bonhoeffer's life and work hold such fascination for many is that he alone, among all the German Protestant theologians who reconstructed the tradition of the Divine Sovereign Word,[37] recognized, if only obliquely, the fundamental problem for ethics of this theological reformulation. He alone acknowledged the deep tension in Christian action between a morality of "freedom" and one of "obedience." At the time of the Synod of Barmen, in 1934, it was Bonhoeffer who recognized that the Barmen Declaration, aimed at resisting Nazism, was too cautious, too churchy! It was not adequate, he recognized, for the church to engage in resistance to the state only when the state directly threatened and inhibited the church's freedom. Rather, he understood that it must act to express direct opposition to any human oppression — in this case the oppression of the Jews. By the time of his imprisonment, under the sexist symbol of "man come of age," he signaled recognition that his own earlier theological formula of obedience was not conducive to mature human moral action.[38] We need to put the point more strongly — dependence on divine control and fear of self-direction is itself conducive to reproducing oppression. Bonhoeffer did not live to revision a theology adequate to a mature, nondependent

Christian ethic of liberation, but his romanticization by male theologians illustrates the paucity of mature alternatives to neoorthodox theology.

Ironically, in most subsequent twentieth-century Protestant theological ethical reconstruction, the pervasive emphasis on obedience to God did not lead even to shaping clear moral guidance in terms of resistance to oppression. In the ancient Jewish tradition, when the prophets called for people to be obedient to God, the content of that obedience was specified with reference to very concrete requirements of social justice in their community. In twentieth-century Christian ethics, "obedience" became not merely a free-floating but an empty category. For the early Barth, obedience to the divine command meant obedience to Christ's command of self-renunciation. By the later period of his life, Barth defined the divine command as giving us "permission" to embrace human freedom. Such "permissions," according to the later Barth, enable us to act beyond the limits of established human convention toward the goal of reconciliation with God. In his later work, Barth's insistence that reconciliation has already occurred in Christ simply overwhelms and obliterates the demand for action for justice.[39] And, in spite of all of the pages Barth wrote to elaborate his Divine Command Ethic, he still left us without any clear formulation of Christian criteria for right or good moral acts. Direct resistance to social domination has no clear normative place in his ethics. It is not too much to say that in terms of moral theory Barth was a christological "intuitionist" who assumed that Christians together would just somehow figure out what is right. Furthermore, while Barth contended that the command of God addresses the totality of life and brings all cultural forms, including religion, to judgment, frequently he sounded like a conventional biblical literalist or, even more, a conventional bourgeois pastor when it came to elaborating the meaning of a Christian ethic. He had to indulge in some tortuous, even silly, exegesis to prevent direct legitimation of the many traditional patterns of social domination, most especially in terms of the relations of men and women.[40] On gender relations, his ethic regresses into an eighteenth-century "orders of creation" argument that he elsewhere, pretentiously, denounced. An honest exegete,[41] reading his tortuous scriptural exegesis on voluntary female subordination to men must sense that Barth's entire ethic is an intellectual shambles.[42]

A fundamental problem with the modern renaissance of neoorthodoxy in Christian ethics, then, is that it reintroduced and replicated basic images of human subordination as morally right and theologically desirable forms of relationality, whether to God or to one another. Human subordination to God as faithfulness and human action as not properly within our own power remained hallmarks of a neo-orthodox view of the Christian moral life.

Nor did twentieth-century theological liberalism fare better in breaking the hold of this subordination motif on the Christian imagination. No more than Karl Barth did Rudolf Bultmann escape the fixation on obedience as the central paradigm for the practice of the Christian life. In Bultmann's hands, obedience to God became even more formalistic and fully vacuous morally. In his ethic, obedience to God took on a subjectivist, existentialist, and individualistic twist.[43] Obeying God turned out to consist largely in the willingness to *decide*, to *choose*, to *will* — personal authenticity — in short, to risk decision! Such "authenticity" is as empty of specific social content as was Barth's ethic, and it becomes even more psychologistic and subjectivist. Barth avoided psychologism by abstractly objectifying God or, rather, by denying the reality that all images of God are *our* images. Bultmann's theology remained characteristic of large sectors of liberal Protestant Christianity, and its problem, one that Barth had diagnosed, was its individualistic subjectivism. Bultmann jettisoned completely any connection between the personal and social worlds. In both versions of Divine Command Ethics, human attention is turned away from social relations and social structures to an abstract relation between God and selves. In Barth's neo-orthodoxy, our agency is mystified and lost. In Bultmann's liberalism, I, the agent, am central, but it is I, an isolated entity, whose "inner" attitude of "faith" becomes the central concern of theology and ethics. Concrete life and action disappear from view in either case and with them our very human morality. This is not surprising since moral relations *are* social relations.

Both liberal and neo-orthodox Divine Command Ethics move hierarchically from language about deity to human obligation. The theologians I have cited here are the best, not the worst, examples of those who have interpreted Christian agency under the symbols of powerful male agency, control, and obedience. The point, apropos of our topic, is that all such Christian ethics, though utterly innocent of any conscious intent to extend social subjugation, whether of women or of socially oppressed men, leads to the sort of Christian ethical discourse that in fact legitimates such oppression, especially the oppression of women.

It is time to insist that the notion of "obedience" itself is simply antithetical to what we mean by "ethics" or "the moral point of view." In the mid-nineteenth century, the Anglican-socialist theologian F. D. Maurice insisted that it was not possible to teach a child morality *and* obedience simultaneously.[44] Not surprisingly, Maurice was also the first and only mid-nineteenth-century Christian theologian who also *actively* protested the Christian legitimation of the subjugation of women; perhaps he was the only one to be conscious that the strivings of the nineteenth-century women's movement were of theological and moral significance.[45]

Given the implicit power dynamics that male gender supremacy teaches, obedience-oriented approaches to action also have a strong tendency to convey the implication that "good" action is a mode of "doing for" others rather than "acting with" them. In contrast, victims of oppression need an ethic grounded in images and concepts that affirm reciprocity in action. If our moral language is ever to interpret self/other duality in terms that affirm and embrace mutuality and support the whole spectrum of human fulfillment, autonomy, and as yet unrealized possibility, all of us must learn to envision all action as genuine *inter*action.[46] Theological images that portray God as Lord or King, even those that describe God as Mother/Father, teach us that holy power is not reciprocal power. By contrast, metaphors and images that locate and identify holiness in sister/brother relations teach us to long for a "Holy One" who is a companion, one not diminished by our growth, power, and fulfillment, one who does not need to rule by dictum.[47] Such images and metaphors teach us social relations of mutuality. God/ess does not replace us through substitution or render us subordinate but is flowing, alive with us, in the world.

My own deepest theological "phantasie" is of God/ess — One present who sustains us, gently but firmly grounding the fragile possibilities of our action, One whose power of co-relation enhances and enriches our acts aimed at human fulfillment, mutuality, and justice. In the web of life in which this lovely Holy One is enmeshed with us, personal fulfillment and mutuality are not inherently contradictions, irreconcilables. The social world that our antisocial corporate actions have constructed and sustained over time is now characterized by injustice, so now our interests often are set in deep opposition. But my well-being and yours are not inherently at odds. As relational beings, we need each other for our common well-being, and in our mutual relation we experience God/ess. Justice is a praxis that realizes conditions that make my fulfillment and yours possible simultaneously, that literally creates a common good. All moral goods are *inter*related possibilities. They seem irreconcilable to us because the world our freedom has constructed and construed is distorted by the heavy hand of privilege and domination. To say no to that is to say yes to this "phantasie of possibility" and, in the process, to encounter God as personal, living process and ground of relation.

I believe that any use of God language in our time is precarious. To speak of God is to participate in a much-needed poetic or imaginative act, but one that, given the scope of violence and injustice, may appear almost as naiveté or a form of madness. Consequently, we should choose all of our God language carefully. Through collective action we really get the power-in-relation we name! Much theological language perpetuates unjust forms of social relations enshrined in the past: Such images and concepts lead us to cling adamantly to an unjust world. They offer us an escape, a way to avoid change, to keep from having to be alive now, fully present toward the future. But there are also those forms of "phantasie" whose strangeness seems acute precisely because through them we encounter new possibility and a hope that refuses to die in the face of present dehumanizing reality. Such hope as any of us knows lives, and lives on, because there have been some who continue the sort of theological naming that presses us toward what is "impossible" or "unrealistic." "Don't try...it's impossible" is the state of mind that comes on us when we accept reality as structured by someone else's power — be it a ruler's, or God's. But creative power is yours/mine, ours, together. It is not dualistic. What is inherently dualistic cannot be resolved through fresh action. The Christian ethical challenge is precisely to discover new forms of cocreative action, new ways of being in the world, that forge fresh social relations and therefore break open new possibility out of existing contradictions. The aim is to shatter and transcend dualisms, to overcome the contradictions. To do this we need to be able to speak of One who is with us, who grounds such genuine possibility. Authentic "trust in God," in this sense, is all but dead because we do not believe that creative possibilities for action really exist among us. This means that the will to act is being extinguished among us as well. We need to be able to praise God in act once again.[48]

It is, I believe, this restoration of the power of action that we Christians celebrate in Jesus' life and death and resurrection. Even in death, another's power of action meets us and empowers us to continue the chain of just-making action. When we do, we join One who is our cocreator and coredeemer in the dance of redemption that is the created, material world.

Until our theological symbols have been revisioned, consistent with both this sort of moral horizon and a moral language forged to support the requirements of genuinely humane existence, Christian theological ethics will continue to reproduce social oppression. We will transmit and convey nonmutual, nonrelational and nonreciprocal images of God's power and action and diminish our own. The utter, unqualified reciprocity of neighbor love and love of God/ess must always be a hallmark of a feminist Christian ethic. Our knowledge of God *is* in and through each other. Our knowledge of each other *is* in and through God. We act together and find our good in each other and in God, and our power grows together, or we deny our relation and reproduce a violent world where no one experiences holy power. The task of a Christian feminist ethic is to undermine any morality of blind command and replace it with the process of moral reflection that comes from those who respectfully reason *together*.

THE EFFECT OF INDUSTRIALIZATION ON THE ROLE OF WOMEN IN SOCIETY*

The Social Amnesia About Women's History

Industrialization and its attendant processes of urbanization and technical acceleration are a preoccupation of western historical imagination, and for good reason. The shifts in personal, social, and cultural experience that follow upon industrialization are dramatic. Interpreters variously may relish such changes as the result of unprecedented upsurges in human creativity or judge them to be the latest of perennial demonstrations of irrevocable human perversity. But both in popular consciousness and in much presumed sophisticated intellectual analyses of industrialization lurks an unspoken assumption that the lived experience of women goes untouched by such changes. Subtle and not so subtle sexist assumptions keep in place presuppositions, patently false, that the lived world of female experience stands in unbroken continuity over time and that industrialization has had less impact on women's lives than on men's.

These assumptions, shrouding women's lives in a mystified ahistoric manner, serve well to legitimate theories of women's "special nature" and "special sphere of competence," theories that always mask the interest of those who, for whatever reason, wish to keep women "in their place." It is the central thesis of this essay that advanced industrial technological systems of production, developed under the aegis of private capital, weaken women's social role while supporting and strengthening ideologies of women's "special nature" and "special place" because these ideologies serve the smooth workings of these economic systems. This is not to say that those alternative economies — whether state capitalist, mixed, or socialist — will automatically find such ideologies dysfunctional. Even when ownership of the means of

---

* This essay is a revision of one that appeared in *Concilium, Sociologie de la Religion* III (1976) pp. 91–103. That issue of *Concilium*, on women, was not translated or published in English.

production shifts, acceleration of industrialization, when accompanied by centralization of production, bureaucratically administered social organization, and technical acceleration, brings social strains that reinforce women's "special role" and accelerate gender injustice. In the absence of a strong base of social, economic, and political power already developed by and for women themselves, there is no evidence that concern for the character and quality of women's lives will be given either attention or priority in any industrializing society. Modernization means the acceleration of women's social vulnerability and oppression because centralized production breaks down the gender-differentiated work systems in place in traditional society and entraps women in new ways within the domestic and wage-work systems.[1]

An effective way to demystify the interesting prevailing historical amnesia regarding the impact of industrialization on women is to identify briefly certain trends and patterns in women's lives that obtained in western societies prior to and during two centuries of rapid industrialization. This brief historical retrospective is not intended to suggest any "historical inevitability" regarding the impact of political and economic change on women's lives. To assume such inevitability would exemplify just that sort of reified "masculine" consciousness that is itself a part of the problem of patriarchy of which we feminists complain. Societies, struggling now to find patterns of socioeconomic development that can simultaneously break colonial economic dependency and maintain humane, premodern cultural traditions, may yet find paths to forms of socioeconomic organization that will have more humane consequences for the lives of women as well as men. Western women, aware of the results to ourselves of the political and economic system under which we live, have every reason to hope that this will happen. We do not wish to foreclose such possibility through premature cynicism, but no policy of social change will benefit women unless women themselves are given a central place in defining social well-being. We insist on this point because with respect to the social status of women, many nonwestern societies begin now at a point distressingly analogous to where western advanced industrial societies were at the start of their so-called political and economic modernization.

Two centuries ago, just prior to the rapid acceleration of industrial centralization, western women lived in an environment in which the dominant religious institutions and ethos functioned to legitimate a theory of women's "separate and special human nature" and in which a lack of a clear political and economic base relegated women's culture to the background of history. In the west, there had already been a break among intellectual elites with the dominant religious institutions and ideology. Even so, though the rising intellectual ethos supported the development of a secular consciousness critical of traditional religion, male intellectual elites resisted a break with the dominant religious interpretations of "female nature." Until women themselves found their voices through early feminism, there was little awareness of dissent from traditional gender "wisdom." Clearly, the cultural invisibility and social powerlessness of women served the interests of Enlightenment males just as it had served the system of ecclesiastical control broken by the Enlightenment. Even so, the aspirations for political self-direction the Enlightenment generated spread the hope of human liberation to some women themselves, much as contemporary struggles for liberation are spreading the aspiration for dignity and participation to women in nonwestern societies today. But in the west, the rising consciousness of women about their need for social justice proved to be too slender a reed to withstand the subverting dynamics of industrialization and urbanization.

In those parts of Europe where the industrial system evolved and differentiated slowly from the mercantile system, the impact of industrialization on women was slower. However, in those nations, such as England, where favorable political conditions enabled a rising middle class to generate rapid industrialization, the impact on women was more dramatic. In the United States, where chattel slavery, vast natural resources, and a weakly centralized political structure permitted economic forces to organize at will, the transition from a predominantly rural to an industrial society was achieved in a matter of decades, and the impact on women was traumatic. Reviewing the impact on women in England and the United States will go some way toward explaining the existence of a broad-based women's liberation movement in both nations today. The phenomenon appears to puzzle many from traditional societies because they take it for granted that the political and cultural emancipation of women is greatest precisely in the United States and Britain. Only when one understands the deeper impact of the dynamics of advanced capitalist socioeconomic systems on women's lives does it become clear why such a broad-based women's movement arose in the wake of these changes.

The Effect of Child-Centered Families on Women's Role

In Europe, as the mercantile system gradually generated a modestly affluent artisan and merchant class, the cultural foundations were laid for the root myth of women's "special nature" that has come to characterize the rhetoric of modern western society. The core of this myth is that women are "by nature" born to domicile and to the nurturance of children. It is important to stress that industrialization did not produce this myth *de novo*. Its ideological elements were in place in aristocratic romanticism and early chivalry. What the rising bourgeois class did was to lock the myth into western consciousness so deeply that the conceptions of women's experience as unchanging, as totally child-centered and domiciled became axiomatic. Most people actually believe that the single family unit has been a central social institution throughout human history — a seriously erroneous notion. As Philippe Aries — who reflects no specific feminist sensibility in his research — has demonstrated, the child-centered family in the west is the product of slow evolution that began in the thirteenth century.[2] What Aries terms "the discovery of childhood" became possible only when some adults began to have sufficient freedom from the pressure of basic economic survival to enable their progeny to contract out of the prevailing system of rural apprentice labor. Aries insists that the conception of childhood as a "phase" of life different from adulthood permeated Europe only very slowly. Ever so slowly did the family as a child-centered environment come to be the social ideal. Initially, the rural peasantry could hardly have aspired to such an ideal.

As Margaret Mead and other anthropologists have observed, in rural societies the functions of production and consumption are closely conjoined, and both men and women are producers.[3] In Europe, as in many preindustrial societies today, women as well as men were active both in agricultural production and in the barter economy, standard in precapitalist societies. Neither women nor men were strangers to cultivating fields or harvesting crops, nor to the marketplaces. Production and exchange involved both genders. No doubt the Protestant Reformation's embrace of the family unit as the proper locus for transmitting its conception of spirituality accelerated the hold of the child-centered domicile on European society. But it was several centuries — I place the date in the nineteenth century — before the social ideal of the child-centered home became even the normative social aspiration, not to mention a general reality. Only then did a social stigma come to be attached to poor women, either in rural areas or in cities, for "violating" that ideal. Women of all classes bore the children, of course, but the majority of babies were not born to "childhood," that is, to an extended life in a family-centered home. Poor women, even those who followed the protocols of legal marriage, lived on the edge of survival and did what they had to do —

whether behind a plow or in the marketplace — to survive or help provide wherewithal for young children. Only when the child-centered family was widely established did such women come to internalize the social disapproval that made any extra-domestic activities less than "feminine" and therefore the source of social stigma.

In much of Europe, the prolonged struggle between aristocracy and the rising middle class constrained the rapid accumulation of capital. Without the necessary freedom from political control to enable new economic ventures to accelerate, traditional gender systems changed slowly. In England, however, where the political power of the aristocracy had been partially broken earlier, the new middle class was under less constraint. Here the permutations on the ideology of "women's special place" that accompanied industrialization were especially clear-cut. The pervasiveness of class cleavage became obvious in the distance between the dominant ideology about women's lives — that is, the social ideal of bourgeois experience — and the actual condition of most women's lives.

Most nineteenth-century English women had to endure the trauma of enforced migration from rural lands to the congested cities. These women coped with life in the streets of London or other cities created by rural immigration, sought employment in the small but burgeoning factories, or, if they could find it, gratefully accepted domestic service in the homes of gentry or newly rich urban entrepreneurs. If they could not find wage labor, women, like men, fended as best they could through the remnants of the barter system. Failing that, many resorted to prostitution[4] — called, for good reason, women's "oldest profession."

In spite of these realities, the ideology of "women's special nature" accelerated, taking on ever more effete forms necessary to persuade newly affluent women to accept the new form of domesticity. The gap between the rising ideology and most women's actual experience was hardly noticed or commented on — not by the bourgeoisie, because it did not suit their interests to notice, nor by the rising urban proletariat, because survival rather than social commentary absorbed their energies.

The Rise of the Bourgeois Gentlewoman

The women of England's rising commercial classes had an interpretation of their "natures" constructed for them that was quite unprecedented in human history. Though born of strong identification with the aristocratic ideal, the new tradition of the "gentlewoman" was updated to take account of changed circumstance. The manor house of the aristocracy had been not a family dwelling but a complex setting for social life, political activity, and economic production and exchange. Women there had been involved in numerous and varied social functions. By contrast, in the homes of the rising urban bourgeoisie, "the woman of the house" was relieved of even the vestiges of social production that had previously centered in her domicile unit because servants were readily available from among the displaced rural population. The "cult of true womanhood" that now emerged, especially in England, was predicated on the assumption that the truly "genteel" woman could aspire to nothing higher than the contented practice of those "domestic arts" that graced the home. Interestingly enough, the nineteenth-century English social ideal, like the ideal of white women's lives on southern plantations in the United States, did not even require that the genteel woman have much direct transaction with the children that she bore. A bit of piano playing, perhaps, and needlework, and the capacity to preside, inconspicuously though handsomely, at tea or dinner were all that were required of her.

American sociologist Thorstein Veblen may well have been the first to observe that what was taken to be "the psychology of women" in the nineteenth century was in fact nothing other than the "psychology of the leisure class." [5] It should come as no surprise that the first strong wave of feminism arose as rebellion against the social powerlessness of the bourgeois woman. English feminists began to reject their vacuous fate, sustained by patronizing male consciousness, a fate that required them to live as leisured decorative objects, showcases of their family's economic success. The early English feminists rightly perceived that the tradition of the gentlewoman was utterly destructive to their personhood. Many of them, like their counterparts in the United States, educated themselves surreptitiously from the libraries of their fathers, brothers, or husbands and began to analyze their situations.

Two important consequences, already alluded to, resulted from this way of depicting women's nature. The new social ideal of "womanhood" involved unprecedented differentiation and separation from any productive economic function. As the earlier economic role played by the female gender system eroded, the ideology about what an individual woman "should be" expanded, and women's social power actually weakened. A second effect followed, as the new ideology about women that reflected the lives of women in the rising class increasingly was used to justify the moralization of class difference. The "good" woman came to be one who approximated rising bourgeois ideals, and those who could not were perceived as "failed" women.

It was characteristic of the rising class to define "freedom" from the standpoint of the already existing individual, apart from social ties. In the ideology of the early classical liberalism generated by the new bourgeoisie, the individual was portrayed as encountering the world *de novo*. The success or failure of one's encounter with the world came more and more to be seen as the fruit of personal "character" and "virtue." Since economic success enabled class mobility, that success became the index of personal moral rectitude. The tendency of such an individualized worldview to construe the "good woman" as the genteel woman came to full flower amid rising industrial affluence. Class difference took on an ever more stigmatic connotation that was doubly damaging to the vast majority of women. On the other hand, the pressure on the poor woman for direct participation in wage labor, if she could find it, increased.[6] Survival required that wherever possible she contribute wages or income, however small, to the livelihood of her extended or immediate household. At the same time, the onus of failure in the "arts of true womanhood" accelerated pressure to perform as the "respectable" homemaker and good mother as well. She continued to have to live by coping as best she could with the harsh economic necessities that the narrow margin of survival of an urban proletariat dictated. Yet she increasingly found her self-worth measured by her capacity to emulate the domestic arts of the middle-class woman, to raise children who would be judged by the standards of "character" dictated by the rising class. It is small wonder that many working-class women came to envy their richer counterparts, whose "easy" lives, free of the dehumanizing double bind of women's two roles, seemed extraordinarily humane. Many men and women of the working classes came to aspire to the middle-class sex role division and identified achieving it as an index of self-worth. This social contradiction between the daily experience of the majority of women and the class ideology of woman's "special nature" still functions today and continues to isolate women from one another, successfully undermining the possibility of cross-class solidarity among women in industrialized nations.[7]

The Effect of Industrialization on Women's Political Consciousness

Many nineteenth-century English feminists looked to the United States as a place where the heavy hand of tradition and social myth vis-à-vis women might be broken. There were solid grounds for these hopes, at least as they applied to women of European extraction. During the colonial period, European visitors often commented that under conditions of settlement in the wilderness, women in the new nation were called on to exhibit strength, endurance, and a wide range of skills that middle-strata women in Europe had ceased to express. After the United States gained independence from Great Britain, distinguished English feminists such as Harriet Martineau came to the United States to see firsthand the prospects for a "new woman" in a nation where sex role rigidities had weakened. Martineau's perceptions as an observer of life in the United States have led modern feminists to classify her as one of the first sociologists. Her observations here confirmed others' accounts of the extraordinary diversity of social roles played by women in the young nation.[8] However, she also signaled concern that two forces threatened positive change. She worried that both the low ratio of women to men and pressures on the rural frontier increased the trend toward a drastically lower marriage age for both men and women. Martineau recognized that this pattern of early marriage, with the resultant high rate of early childbirth, would offset the relative gains women in the United States had made in escaping the developed European bourgeois traditions of genteel womanhood.

In the United States, the social base of feminism varied from state to state and region to region. The seeds of the ideology that women are born to be homemakers and nurturers of children had been planted early in colonies founded by dissenting Protestant groups, but neither Puritans nor dissenters originally endorsed that distinctive and, later, urban-industrial cult of genteel womanhood and its sharply differentiated sex role divisions. This ideology did not subvert the more egalitarian roles of the rural frontier until capital accumulation created an extensive, new monied class. The factory system, accelerated by the Civil War, permeated where capital was concentrated, especially in the Northeast. As in England, the new myth of women's nature took hold precisely in the region where women were the first to work in the factories, illustrating again that this myth flourishes best where it is least apt.

The early factory system in the United States was even more dependent on the wage labor of women than was the English factory system because until immigration from Europe accelerated, labor was in short supply. Textiles and clothing were the core of early industry in New England, and women had the necessary skills for this work. Women, often lacking other modes of economic survival, also were willing to work for low wages. Resentment of women as laborers was a major factor in the slow development of an organized labor movement in the United States. Male industrial workers experienced women's lower wages as a menace to their demands for adequate salaries and better working conditions. Often male workers refused to organize with women or support the early strikes women initiated for better wages and working conditions. Masses of indigent European immigrants began to arrive in the newly industrialized United States. Those who did not find their way to cheap or free land on the frontier began to swell the industrial labor force, and women and children competed with men for extremely low-paying factory positions. The competition between men, women, and children for jobs was intense. Labor laws restricting children from factory work and limiting hours or setting special working conditions for them or for women were often supported by working men chiefly as a means of restricting competition for industrial jobs.

Even in the face of the grim reality of most women's lives, the capitalist centers of Boston and New York became the places where the bourgeois cult of true womanhood flourished. The locus of early American feminism took root elsewhere, in the Middle Atlantic region, where left-wing Protestant religion and the egalitarian conditions of small-town life had produced a feminism religious in its motivation and anti-elitist in its social orientation. In that milieu, women had actively scoffed at the thesis that they were, by nature, especially gentle and virtuous.

Slowly but surely this egalitarian feminism gave way to the accelerating pressures of the rising affluent ideal. By the time the women's suffrage movement became a widespread force at the end of the nineteenth century, many feminists themselves used the arguments of women's "special nature" as a reason why women should have political suffrage. Needless to say, by that time a few affluent women even hinted that genteel women would join their male counterparts in upholding "civilization" against the encroachments of the immigrant masses and black former slaves.[9]

In the southern United States, the social base of feminism was all but nonexistent. The dominant plantation system evolved, dependent on slavery for free labor. Since the legitimation of the slave system was a basic ideological requirement, interesting permutations in the prevailing ideology of "women's special nature" were required to sustain it. In the southern slave-holding states, a virulent pedestalism came to characterize the social myth of "women's nature," though of course "women" referred only to white women. The gap between the actual experience of even the plantation master's wife and this ideology was dramatic, however, as many historians have observed. Increasingly, white women were portrayed as asexual and chaste, in contrast to black women stereotyped to legitimate the frequent sexual liaisons forced on them by their white masters.[10] Since the black woman was fantasized as earthy, erotic, and promiscuous, the white woman was imaged as the opposite. Hence, the classic split in western male consciousness that projects women as either virgin or whore grounded the social mythologies that variously entrapped white and black women in the slave-holding states. The vast number of poor white women who were neither masters' wives nor slaves were all but invisible. They lived not only as rural poor women always have had to do, at the margins of survival, but they also labored under strong ideological constraints to identify with the master's wife, if only to avoid the fate of falling as low as the female slaves.

The ideology of "effete womanhood" in the industrially affluent northeastern United States and the schizophrenic ideology of "pure white womanhood" required by the southern slave system converged. It is little wonder that the efforts of newly conscious women, grounded in demands for religious, social, and political equality, fared badly in the wake of the rising tide of industrial affluence. Early "radical feminism" of the U.S. frontier, which espoused full personhood for women and which, if not revolutionary, was at least radically reformist and egalitarian in its social vision, gradually gave way to a more moderate, middle-strata congenial reformist women's perspective. Great freedom in dress, movement, and personal expression ensued, but these changes only masked the subtle erosion of the social and economic base of women's social power.

In the United States, as elsewhere, war has been a major force accelerating centralization and monopoly of the industrial system and of technological innovation. During wartime, women were needed in industrial production, but the postwar periods saw strong consolidation of the ideology of "women's place." Home and family life became ever more critical to those in a war-weary population, who now could afford to revert to private concerns. Note, however, that the line between the private sector and the public world clearly divided the family and the economy. The thesis some have advanced that the 1960s women's movement in the United States was the result of middle-class women being underchallenged in their spotless, mechanized kitchens fails totally to explain the broad-based structural reasons for women's dissatisfactions.

In the United States, as the gross national product skyrocketed, access to middle-strata existence appeared to be a panacea available to all who worked hard enough. Here, as in Britain, aspiration to middle-class status reinforced the hold of ideologies about what women should be. As always when the role of women is at issue, the reality of women's lives lay elsewhere. In the post–World War II period, women's role as housewives and mothers was everywhere celebrated. Some jobs briefly accessible to women during the early feminist period were largely closed after the war. In reality, increasing numbers of women were moving into the wage labor force out of economic necessity. Increasingly, women found employment only in castelike labor sectors that constitute "women's work"—clerical and stenographic positions, retail sales, and work that parallels domestic labor. The new, postwar technological professions required an expertise and psychological orientation that "privatized woman" had not acquired.

Those women who remained in the home began to experience the frustration attendant on their new economic role—that of being expert consumers. Those who worked, whether out of economic necessity or to escape the boredom engendered by the social powerlessness of the middle-strata home, found little respite from the powerlessness in the world of "feminine" work. These were the dynamics that engendered the feminist renaissance of the late 1960s and the 1970s.[11] Black women and other minority women, who have always carried either the double or triple jeopardy of racism, sexism, and class, moved to develop an analysis of gender equality more adequate to their lives than white feminists' interpretations. In spite of the ways that power and ideology separate and isolate women across boundaries of race and class, the social base for the rising consciousness of women is broad in the United States today.

Advanced capitalist industrial development needs the social myth of women's "special nature and place" to keep women out of productive work or, failing that, out of the labor movement, precisely as earlier political and economic systems needed women to stay in place as reproducers. To provide justice for women under advanced capitalist economies would require fundamental political and economic change. So far, postcapitalist systems of production, industrially centralized as capitalist systems have been, also have not redressed the injustices of women's dual role. In post-capitalist economies, men and women may have more equal access to wage labor, but women usually tend the home and children alone.[12] Women's political and economic powerlessness in all industrialized societies, then, is and will remain a deep source of social instability. Whether we are pressured to stay in the domestic sphere, as in capitalist modes of production, or encouraged to do both wage and domestic labor, as in some post-capitalist societies, advanced industrialized and centralized production double-binds us all.[13] Under these conditions women must either internalize a self-image of female impotence or bear the double load of social and domestic labor. In either case, the myths of female identity that are foisted on us are so remote from the reality of our lives as to force us to risk madness or begin to demystify the power relations under which we live. The evidence is growing that more and more women have begun the demystification process, which is why feminism is likely to remain a potent force no matter what resistance it meets.

THE ROLE OF SOCIAL THEORY IN RELIGIOUS SOCIAL ETHICS

Reconsidering the Case for Marxian Political Economy*

Where Has Economic Reality Gone?

A number of years ago, my distinguished teacher and professional colleague John C. Bennett issued an eloquent appeal to Christian social ethicists to focus our energies anew on the basic questions of economic justice.[1] His summons set me to thinking about why economic ethics remained so much at the margins of our work. Since then, the question has intensified because of two other divergent sorts of experiences. The first was my participation in a social ethics working group of the American Academy of Religion. This group took as its focus "the socialist question." After several annual meetings, I pointed out that our discussion never got further than asking whether Christians or religious people could consider socialism as an option. That particular group

---

* This essay is a substantive revision of a paper delivered to a social ethics working group of the American Academy of Religion in 1980. It was entitled "Some Notes on Alternatives in Political Economy." Readers of that original paper should observe that I have recast entirely the way in which I classify contemporary economic theory and ideology and have extended the discussion of how social theory is used by religious ethicists. The earlier draft was in some important respects misleading. Here I identify Adam Smith, David Ricardo, *and* Karl Marx as typical of "classical" political economists. Contemporary exponents of non-Marxian economics are treated either as "laissez-faire neoclassical" or as "welfare neoclassical." While there are two political ideologies employed by neoclassical theorists in contemporary public policy debate, all mainstream economists share the same so-called economic paradigm. The reputed "supply siders" of the Reagan administration or the followers of Milton Friedman may invoke "free-market" rhetoric, but neither are thereby repudiating the dominant working neoclassical macroeconomic paradigm they share with "liberal" welfare ideologists. My original essay obscured Karl Marx's rightful place as a "classical economist," but it also confused — as I here argue Christian ethicists tend to confuse — the "free-market ideology" some mainstream economists employ to legitimate their policy preferences with the actual paradigm they use, which is the same paradigm that welfare economists employ. Obviously, my understanding of the history of economic theory has deepened since I penned the paper on which this essay is based.

had been formed from a larger economic ethics circle precisely to get beyond that general question, to discuss specific economic alternatives. Yet at each gathering, discussion foundered over and over on a query as to whether socialist systems ever could be democratic. Thus, a group of self-identified critics of capitalism from the ranks of professional ethicists and theologians could not even take the first steps necessary to think beyond the presuppositions of the existing economic system. For that group, as for most in our field, the very term "socialist" had lost its historic definition and come to mean what capitalist neoclassical economists now mean by it: state centralized economic planning. Historically, in the tradition of radical social theory, a socialist approach to political economy *meant* economic democracy. It implied either shared resources or worker control of production and participation in determining the use of created wealth. All types of socialists addressed the specific alienations effected by separation of work and ownership.[2] In the wake of my experience in the social ethics group, I have pondered what it means for our work that we no longer even have terminology to discuss "going beyond" capitalism.

The other source of urgency about the marginality of economic ethics in religious ethics has been my teaching. For more than a decade, the finest students of social ethics with whom I have worked have been clear that their professional priorities needed to be shaped by the concerns of economic justice. Their intense and growing dissatisfaction both with the literature and with public discussion of economics in our discipline has had a consciousness-raising effect. I recall, in particular, the repeated incredulous query of one of these younger colleagues: "How can economic reality be so utterly invisible in Christian theological theory ... so *utterly* invisible?"[3] If, as I have come to believe, this invisibility is indeed deeply entrenched, what is its source? Increasingly it has become obvious that the problem is a methodological one, not merely the consequence of a pragmatic lack of interest in economic reality on the part of colleagues in the field.

What do I mean by identifying the difficulty as methodological? The methodologies appropriate to religious ethics demand that we integrate theological vision and commitment with moral and critical/postcritical historical and scientific modes of work. This makes our discipline a very high art form indeed. Some religious ethicists resist this reliance on several fields, protesting the magnitude of the interdisciplinary task and fearing that religious ethics will become too diffuse. Several recent methodological discussions proved less than optimally productive precisely because some argued that for the sake of coherence we must choose one disciplinary liaison. Urging exclusive use of either moral philosophy or social science/social theory[4] places a false dilemma before us that religious ethicists resolve at our peril. Such discussion about the one true "handmaiden" discipline for religious ethics should be consigned to our long list of "misplaced debates."[5] There can be no normative religious social ethics if we do not accept the multidisciplinary character of our work.

What has become apparent to me in light of the foregoing reflection about economics is the urgent need among us for a more focused discussion about the criteria we use for adopting both specific moral philosophical approaches and social theoretical options. Like theology, moral philosophy and the various social science theories are themselves diverse arenas of inquiry beset with their own internal debates. Critical decisions must be made about which moral philosophical and social scientific perspectives best serve theological-ethical sensibility.

These internal debates reflect the ideological conflict that divides each discipline. Whether we define ideology as commitment to a worldview or cultural gestalt on the one hand or as a politically mystifying conception of society on the other, ideological conflict pervades every humanistic field.[6] Its importance in religious ethics can hardly be overstated for ideology not only conditions how we interpret issues but also shapes several aspects of method.

Lack of ideological sophistication in religious ethics works itself out in many ways. Some may be led to an uncritical appropriation of theology as free of ideology, as if a theory of divine-human relations were not always simultaneously a theory of social and moral relations. Or insensitivity to ideology may result in a naively uncritical use of philosophical assumptions about moral reason that do not correlate with our sociohistorical theological assumptions and accountabilities. An ideological disposition also shapes the data we register as factual when describing a moral issue. To be clear and open about our ideological commitments is conditional to our ability to see and hear accurately and to be fair to those whose values we do not share. The pseudo-value-free ethos of some contemporary social science, philosophy, or theology serves only to obscure the ideological constraints that pervade these disciplines and makes more difficult the already complex conditions of objectivity.

All of this makes the discussion of criteria that lead us to adopt one or another moral philosophical or social-theoretical paradigm doubly important. Failure to appreciate the ideological conflicts that go on within disciplines may lead not only to our embracing valuations unawares but also to internal contradiction. Our methodological coherence depends on the consistency and convergence of presumptions obtaining in our theo-anthropological, moral, and social perspectives. The most serious threat of incoherence in religious ethics lies in the refusal to be self-conscious about how ideology shapes the social scientific and philosophical theory we incorporate into ethical reflection.

We religious ethicists agree that in the modern world no ethical issue can be analyzed without drawing on social scientific theoretical perspectives about what constitutes known social reality. For better or worse, social science and theory control the domain of "facticity." Social scientific models do not merely govern factual judgments however. They also condition conceptions of value and their relations to facts and, above all, shape perceptions of what social relations ought to be. It is these hidden normative assumptions in social science/theory that must be our focus when we seek criteria for interdisciplinary relations.[7]

I have become aware, in view of my preoccupation about economic reality in religious ethics in the United States, that we operate with ideological blinders in relation to social theory. In fact, we tend to ignore precisely that contemporary social theory that is most critical of our existing political economy. I believe it can be demonstrated that only in rare instances do religious ethicists read, or even know of, a vast range of social theoretical work done by social theorist/scientists on the left of the ideological spectrum. Even when the work such social scientists do has become central to discussion within their own disciplines, we tend to ignore it. The ideological constraints we have knowingly or unwittingly interjected into perceptions of our social world, its problems, and prospects, through the social theory we employ or fail to attend to, turn out to be dramatic indeed. To appreciate some of the reasons for this intellectual myopia, we need to retrace certain historical dynamics that contribute to this ideological captivity.

In the remainder of this essay I assess the ideological effects on religious ethics, more specifically on Christian ethics, of past choices many in our discipline have made vis-à-vis social theory/science. This discussion goes some way to explaining how our methodological decisions have muted our engagement with economic justice. Discussion of how we have appropriated moral philosophical theory is also relevant, but that is another large question that cannot be pursued here. The substance of this essay aims to assess the actual practice of religious ethicists in appropriating social theory/science and to trace some of the effects of that practice on our work, especially on the economic ethics that we do.

It is my basic thesis that we have employed social theories in our work that preclude a full reevaluation of economic life and a reorientation of our economic ethics. It is my further contention that radical or neo-Marxian social theory answers several important religious-ethical criteria in ways that other social theories widely used in our discipline do not and that failure to recognize this has precluded a more critical address to questions of economic justice.

The Antiradical Legacy of Social Theories Used in Christian Ethics: Reinhold Niebuhr

No account of the ideological blinders shaping the use of social theory in religious ethics can ignore the intellectual legacy of Reinhold Niebuhr. Over a period of at least four decades, Niebuhr's influence has conditioned both the practice and the ideological sensibility of religious ethicists. Niebuhr was widely regarded as the premier social ethicist American Christianity has produced, and in many quarters he still is so regarded. Even considerable dissent from his moral and theological theories has not dimmed confidence in the wisdom of his social ethics.[8] In fact, "veneration" is not too strong a term to describe the attitude of many toward his approach. As a result, it has been difficult to reopen any methodological question if Niebuhr's work is presumed to have closed it. It is particularly difficult to reopen the question of the use and ideological effects of social theory in religious ethics in the face of Niebuhr's legacy. Yet critical consciousness on this point is urgent to the intellectual health of our discipline.

Niebuhr's influence on the appropriation of social theory in religious ethics continues and is insufficiently challenged at two particular points. On the one hand, Niebuhr's choice of disciplinary liaison with political theory continues to enjoy privileged status among many ethicists. Some not only follow Niebuhr in relying exclusively on political science to inform their social theory but also look to the specific movement of political realism within that discipline to provide the key concepts for analyzing social change. While some limitations of political realism have been identified and a general protest lodged against its abstract and ahistorical conception of political power,[9] a thoroughgoing critique of its categories has not been developed. When "power" is conceived, as Niebuhr and other realists conceived it, as an inevitable dynamic of individual and group self-assertion endlessly reiterating itself, the particularity of historical process and the shifting history of institutions largely drops out of the picture. For those of us who believe that the centrality of historical method is a primary criterion for correlating religious ethics with a social theory, political realism's ahistorical treatment of power remains an insurmountable limitation. But many who profess the importance of historical perspective to theology appear not to notice this weakness of realist political theory.

Given the question before us, another obvious limitation of political realism as a social theory is its total inability to focus the role of economic activity in society, however one conceives that activity. Its imaging of human social relations simply leaves economic life out of account. Ironically, much of Niebuhr's early prestige derived from his awareness that economic power was an irrevocable dimension of social power.[10] However, this interest, never a clear analytic priority even in his early work, dropped out of the picture altogether in his mature writing.[11] "Communities" vaguely defined, and especially nation-states and imperial powers, come to be the central agents of Niebuhr's social world and ethics.[12] An overriding focus on political power as either self-assertion or national interest characterizes much of his work and correlates with an assumption that such power invariably keeps economic power in check. Niebuhr himself seemed never to notice that political realism arose historically to reflect and justify aristocratic class interests. He pressed realism into the service of a different ideology — one at the middle of the political spectrum — and made it serve as an analytic tool for reformist welfare liberalism. It should come as no surprise, however, that today neorealism in religious social ethics has relapsed into this original conservative ideological role. Today Niebuhr's name and theories are invoked most frequently by neoconservative writers who seek to reconstitute a moral rationale for the liaison between Christianity and capitalist economic order.[13] This direct baptism of capitalism would have distressed Niebuhr.[14]

The second point of Niebuhr's impact on religious ethicists' appropriation of social theory is, in my view, even more negative. It is the result of his ongoing polemic, even diatribe, against Marx and Marxist social theory.[15] Niebuhr's continued prestige as a critic of Karl Marx has left us a legacy of all but impenetrable closed-mindedness about any and all social theory influenced by this architect of dissenting, radical political economy. Since esteem for Marx, far from waning in contemporary social science/theory, has accelerated in the last four decades, penetrating every social science including mainstream historical research, the Niebuhr-engendered "marxophobia" of religious ethicists turns out to be an ideological impairment of staggering proportions. Because Niebuhr's evaluation of Marx is presumed to have been adequate, a chilling ideological mood operates in our discipline. Fully half of the ideological spectrum of modern social science/ theory is ignored by those who fancy that Niebuhr's "demonstration" of the weaknesses of Marxian social theory and its inadequacy for religious ethics is beyond dispute.

Many religious ethicists presume that Niebuhr assessed Marxian theory carefully, found it wanting on the basis of "profound" theological criteria, and definitely exposed its theoretical inadequacy from a Christian viewpoint. One frequently encounters lines of reasoning that invoke Niebuhr's name ritualistically as sufficient grounds to rule out discussion of Marxism a priori. Presumably to allow oneself to be influenced in any way by Marx is to have a superficial grasp of the modern history of Christian ethics.[16]

I wish to be counted as one student of Reinhold Niebuhr's who is convinced that we must learn to treat his evaluation of Marxist social theory both as misinformed and substantively inaccurate. I say this as one who first encountered Marx academically in Niebuhr's classroom. Even then, for all of my appreciation of Niebuhr and my then-total identification with his viewpoint, I was aware that he had read only a small part of the Marxian corpus. Since then, I also have concluded that he seriously misread Marx. I have had to unlearn much that he taught about Marx to appreciate what Marx was about and, perhaps more important, to comprehend the creative import of modern neo-Marxian social theory. In fact, Niebuhr's repudiation of Marxism is credited with a profundity, completeness, and irrefutability that it does not now and never did possess.[17] In my opinion, even some of Niebuhr's most thoughtful students and friends have contributed to an overestimation of Niebuhr's evaluation of Marx and Marxism.[18]

The truth is that Reinhold Niebuhr developed what knowledge of Marxism he possessed and much of his antipathy to it from his political activism and his aversion to the overpersonalized infighting of the Old Left. He absorbed the street-corner Marxism of political orators as serious Marxian social theory. Since Niebuhr was an idealist, he read Marx as an idealist. He misperceived Marx's methodology, distorting it in at least three ways critical to my concerns here. The result was a misinterpretation of what Marx was up to as a social theorist and where he fit into the history of social science.

First, Niebuhr portrayed Marx as an unqualified scientific positivist, one who believed that science gives us objective, non-relational knowledge that can be "applied" directly to gain "control" of social life. In fact, given the historical context of nineteenth-century debates about the proper method of political economy, Marx was *the* major critic of ahistorical positivism in social science.[19] On this point, Niebuhr all but reversed Marx's place in the history of the development of social science, missing entirely the double-edged character of his philosophical critique. Niebuhr acknowledged one side of it: Marx's attack on the philosophical idealist belief that ideas are, in themselves, autonomous historical forces. But Niebuhr ignored, or failed to grasp, Marx's assault on the belief that the study of political economy could mimic an abstract, objectivist model of natural science. Marx's satirical attack on the capitalist's "iron laws of the market" and the antihistorical character of some of his contemporaries' views of political economy and his insistence that human social institutions are the result of collective historical action were dismissed by Niebuhr because they did not fit his presumption that Marx was a scientific determinist. Marx's unrelenting demand for a rigorously historical conception of human life and political economy and his insistence that all economic patterns were open to transformation through intelligent collective historical action were reduced to the rantings of a rabid historical determinist who believed that he and his followers could change history through their "true science."

A fairer reading would recognize that Marx's goal was only to carefully characterize the concrete social relations of the particular historical epoch in which he lived. For Marx, the goal of social science was to provide a *critical description of what exists, not positive or predictive knowledge of what will be.* In Marx's view, critical knowledge is the sort of knowledge that actually enables agents to change what is, not in a technological manner but through political action. Niebuhr credited Marx with opinions about the inevitability of historical change through science that the latter actually energetically opposed. As a result, Niebuhr also ignored much of Marx's devastating analysis of the destructive effects of specifically capitalist modes of production on wider social and cultural relations.

Niebuhr not only insisted that Marx was a crass scientific positivist and historical-economic determinist, a misperception that still obtains widely among religious ethicists today, but he mischaracterized him in a second way critical to our project. He failed to notice that Marx objected to his contemporaries' way of characterizing the basic nature of human "economic" activity.

For Marx, the foundational economic activity of human beings is work or "sensuous labor," not exchange or business activity. Marx inveighed against the emerging theory of political economy of his time in part because he believed its reading of what it means to be "economic man" was so ideologically wedded to emerging bourgeois economic institutions. Only in a specifically capitalist political economy did economic activity become identified with the market exchange functions so central to bourgeois life. Marx denounced his contemporaries' paradigms because they posited buying and selling as the universal essence of economic life and predicted that the emerging so-called science of political economy would be nothing more than a legitimation of capitalist social relations, using the pretentions of science to mystify them as inevitable. While Marx's contemporaries sought the eternal "iron laws" of all political economy, he aspired only to grasp the "iron laws" of a capitalist mode of production — that is, the consequences of organizing life in a capitalist way and the negative effect of such "laws" on the social relations shaped by them. Marx actually looked where Niebuhr also looked for the source of constructive change — to political courage rather than "historical inevitability."

Niebuhr's third misrepresentation of Marx's social theory was his insistence that Marx's central intellectual project was the effort to construct a philosophy of history, and an inadequate one at that. This contention is simply erroneous. In fact, an aspect of Marx's rejection of idealism involved his denial of the possibility that a theory of history as a whole was possible. It was Niebuhr, not Marx, who insisted that we need such a philosophy.[20] Niebuhr's own theological-ethical synthesis is preoccupied with this question; Marx had no interest in it. Marx believed all such theories were the fruit of mystification and that we needed to learn to put aside such ahistorical rationalistic speculation.

Niebuhr's way of reading Marx chiefly as a philosopher of history further confirmed his confusion about what Marx's social theory entailed, and it allowed him to dismiss Marx's basic intellectual project as a quasi theology, a philosophy of history so "utopian" and "optimistic," so lacking in the dimensions of depth and tragedy that good religion required, that it should be rejected as bad theology. By characterizing the entire Marxian enterprise as "bad religion," Niebuhr avoided direct assessment of Marx's own critique of religion, a point of great importance for any interdisciplinary discussion of how the neo-Marxian tradition can be related to religious ethics. Whether and to what extent Marx's theories of religion limit or distort his theory of society is an interesting and important question, but it is not one Niebuhr even considered, much less answered. I share some of Niebuhr's reservations about Marx's analysis of religion, but not his assumptions about how much religion functions or his specific readings of where Marx "went wrong."

Today, the seeds of suspicion Niebuhr sowed toward Marxism are better placed at the foot of realism itself. It is political realism that has threatened a genuinely historical sensibility in our social ethics. Realists assume that all political struggle is reducible to the same core dynamic, that all agents inexorably are drawn to patterns of power seeking and self-aggrandizement mirrored at the macro-social level by the dynamics of nation-states. As a result, realists find little or no moral ground for choosing between sides in such struggles for power. To me, it has come to seem a great irony — one Niebuhr might appreciate — that the empirically oriented Niebuhr actually opened religious ethics to an anti-empirical, and probably the most antihistorical, social theory available in his time or in ours. When this paradigm is embellished with a passionate endorsement of capitalism that Niebuhr did not fully share, the historical awareness for which he pled has disappeared entirely.

Reinhold Niebuhr was also an acerbic critic of sociology, denouncing it along with Marxism as pretentiously positivistic social science. This evaluation of American empirical sociology — the only sociology he knew — was closely intertwined with his other great polemic against progressivism, especially against John Dewey and the pragmatists,[21] whose anti-idealism he understood as little as he understood Marx's. Fortunately, however, Reinhold Niebuhr's rejection of the sociological tradition did not have as much effect on religious ethics as did his realism and marxophobia.

The Ideological Bias of Weberian Sociology

Sociological and historical methodology has been slow in affecting the social theory. It was Reinhold Niebuhr's brother, H. Richard Niebuhr, along with James Luther Adams, who particularly cultivated these perspectives used in religious ethics. H. Richard Niebuhr was far more attuned than his brother both to historical methodology and to emergent sociological theory.[22] His early work and Adams's lifelong research incorporated the historical sociology of Ernst Troeltsch and Max Weber,[23] and these perspectives increasingly commended themselves to religious ethicists not constrained by realist categories. Furthermore, many of

H. Richard Niebuhr's students have demonstrated the helpfulness of historical sociology in clarifying the church's role as a social institution.[24] Work done from within the Weberian-Troeltschian paradigm has been strongly oriented to analyzing the impact of cultural and social movements and volunteer organizations on social change.[25]

All of the major theorists of historical sociology have enjoyed some influence on the work of religious ethics in the post–World War II period, though none has matched the impact of Weber's "verstehen sociology" precisely because of its explicit methodological commitment to a historical approach. This appeal of Weber's work also has been reinforced because he aspired to incorporate the viewpoint of historical subjects into his method[26] and sought to give due regard to cultural, including religious, factors in social process. Obviously the methodological commitment to analyze not only political and institutional dynamics but also, in principle, to do justice to religious forces made his method seem ideologically compatible with Christian theology. Historical sociology also presumed that multifactor causality is at work in the shaping of social life, and this assumption gives it an aura of antideterminism that commends it ethically.

To me, it is clear that Weber's impact on modern religious ethics has been, on the whole, constructive, especially by comparison with ahistorical political realism. Defining historicity as a minimal methodological necessity for a social theory and, by implication, for social ethics constituted a great step forward in non-Marxian social science.[27] While realist generalizations about the "structures of nations and empires," [28] without reference to the particularities of the wider global and temporal frame, has proved a ready handmaiden for neoconservatives in religious ethics, a Weberian-style sociology still characterizes the ongoing liberal center of the discipline.

At critical moments of historical change, however, it has been said that "the center does not hold," [29] and that adage appears to apply aptly to current religious ethics. Even some proponents of verstehen sociology close ranks with the neoconservatives to prevent radical reappraisal.[30] There are, I believe, several methodological reasons why Weber's style of work does not protect against political reaction, a point some social scientists seem to have appreciated more than religious ethicists have. Weber's work has been subjected to ideological analysis and challenged more perceptively among sociologists than among religious social ethicists. Not only has Weber's "value-free" conception of social science been related to his own ideological loyalties,[31] but very serious questions about the thoroughness and consistency of

Weber's own historical orientation have been raised. Forceful objections also have been formulated to Weber's thesis that "ideal typical" constructs offer an adequate method for dealing with the particularities of the historical process.[32] At the very least, such procedures obscure historical contingencies, making historical explanation deterministic in tone. Specifically ideal typologies are of no value in normative ethics because normative moral clarification requires careful attention especially to the particularity and contingency of human action and social-cultural experience, not merely to its general features.[33] However science is understood, moral reasoning is neither causal/predictive nor critical/descriptive, but evaluative/transformative; it aims to assess how our actions may affect a situation for the better, not how a historical process will proceed if no intervention occurs. When we "typify" social relations, we lose precisely the locus of historical contingency that gives moral questions their force.

In my opinion, however, the most serious limitation of Weberian social theory for religious ethics derives from the deeper theoretical evasion in his overall work, an evasion not unrelated to his own centrist ideological stance and interest. Just as Reinhold Niebuhr placed realism at the service of middle-of-the-road reform, so Weber used verstehen sociology to legitimate emergent liberal bureaucratic forms of social organization. Unlike Niebuhr, Weber was seriously interested in the interaction of cultural and economic forces, but he was no more predisposed than Niebuhr to focus sustained attention on emerging powerful economic interests of his own era. He exemplified the bourgeois fascination with the state and with formal political processes, and, like the mature Niebuhr, presumed that the political mechanisms of the liberal state would continue to constrain economic life.

While Weber's methodological concern for the interaction of "ideal" and "real" factors in social process commends his approach to theologically concerned students, it needs to be recognized that there is a lack of heuristic precision in his writings about these matters. Weber did not advance a hypothesis that has conceptual value in clarifying the interaction of cultural, political, and economic factors. Nor did he attempt to account for the way the interaction of these forces shaped his own historical epoch.

Weber's linguistic formulation about real and ideal factors itself participates in the idealist dualism he sought to overcome. Presuming the idealist split between "intellect" or "spirit" and "material" reality, he was eager to show that the former indeed had impact, but in his work at the macro-social level its role tended to disappear. He appreciatively described the "subjective" or ideational factors in earlier cultural eras, but in the end much Weberian sociology reinforced the deterministic conception of the social world it was presumably formulated to avoid. Its pre-occupation with dominant bourgeois social institutions and forces — particularly the state and its legal bureaucratic administrative structures — was marked. Weber's admiration for modern rational bureaucratic modes of social organization was obvious, yet he exhibited little interest in the interaction of state bureaucracy and economic institutions or in how their shifting relations would affect society.

It has long seemed to me that Weberian sociology enjoys a largely undeserved reputation for doing justice to the social microstructure, including intellectual life, in its theory of social change and society. While many religious ethicists presume that Weberian sociology is a truly humanistic, nonpositivist social scientific theory infinitely preferable to "deterministic" Marxist or radical theory, Weber's pretentions to value-free inquiry suffuse his work with a positivistic tone.[34]

Apparently Weber's methodological preoccupations regarding subjective factors resulted from his belief, similar to Niebuhr's, that Marx was an economic determinist who denied culture any role in social change. He misread Marx's place in social theory much as Niebuhr did. Like Niebuhr (and most philosophical idealists), Weber construed Marx's polemic against idealism as leading inevitably to crass materialist causation in social science. Marx's perpetual denunciation of the *nondialectical* materialism advanced by some of his opponents was as much ignored by Weber as by Niebuhr. Both imagined that Marx's theory of social change involved reducing all aspects of life to economic processes. Neither placed Marx in the broader traditions of eighteenth- and early-nineteenth-century thought or emergent social science.

As ideological centrists, Weber and Niebuhr shared the bourgeois confidence that economic forces could be checked by the sort of politics their liberal worldviews endorsed. The political sphere, as defined by liberalism — the legal and administrative functions of the state — fascinated both, and both presumed that formal legal political democracy would always guarantee a proper balancing of social interests to control economic power. Confidence that liberal political constraints would hold economic forces in check pervades their work. Power is defined in both models as it always is in a bourgeois context, as a function of political "interests" and of political parties who, it is imagined, control the state. Both rejected as preposterous Marx's contention that the historically specific dynamics of a capitalist mode of production shape society so as to place antagonistic social relations at its heart and predispose formally democratic legal and political institutions to serve ruling-class interests, thus betraying the promise of the bourgeois political revolution itself.

The Disciplinary Impact of an Antiradical Legacy

Today Niebuhr's realism and Weber's scientific "multifactor indeterminism" both ideologically reinforce those theories of society that assume the benign character of any political system that has the trappings of parliamentary democracy. Neoconservatives use realism in the service of a conservative ideology that would be distasteful to Niebuhr himself, while the center uses "indeterminate determinism" to support a moderate liberal ideology of reformist politics. The important point for my topic is that neither seriously integrates the historical dynamics of economic life into its paradigm of social process. Neither offers a critical heuristic for appreciating what is distinctive about the historically concrete state of our present economic situation; by virtue of that failure, I insist, both embrace a valuation of the arrangements of a capitalist political economy as normatively desirable, even optimal morally. Genuinely critical economic questions simply do not emerge or make sense in either paradigm.

Both analyses of our social relations are inadequate because the entire fabric of the current global market system and other distinctively capitalist economic institutions are invisible within them.[35] Both theories, and their attendant ideologies, presume that economic activity *is* business, or buying and selling, the exchange of goods and services. Both presume that liberty is widespread in our system while completely absent in postcapitalist systems. In a global context where dozens of the largest corporations and financial institutions control more wealth and command more resources than all but a few nation-states and where the state apparatus of advanced capitalist nations and corporate structures are managed by the same inner circle, this image of "politics" as the "free" clash of interest groups, including business, all of whom presumably are otherwise "private" and "apolitical," creates a picture of existing social relations remote from reality. Neither addresses the actual interaction between the state and modern economic institutions. In sum, the particular social theories most employed in religious ethics, whether informed by a neoconservative or a liberal ideology, mask the very existence of the modern economy. This situation is particularly appalling precisely at a time in history when the accelerating power of advanced capitalist economies is changing the face of our world. Is it any wonder then that Christian social ethics seems remote from reality?

While the modes of discourse used in Christian social ethics shield us from awareness of economic reality altogether, discussions of public policy questions in the wider society are ever more shaped by economic considerations and by economic discourse. In fact, such public discussions hardly any longer incorporate perspectives from the "soft" social sciences such as historical sociology. Nor is the reigning social theory of such public discussion any longer political realism, although realism is still invoked in foreign policy debate. The discourse of contemporary public life is governed by the presumed "hard" science of capitalist business theory — neoclassical economics. Whether neoclassical theorists *are* ideologically conservative, presuming that the rules of capitalism are "iron laws" of exchange, or welfare-liberals who prefer a regulated market system is beside the point. Currently all public policy decisions are constrained by the assumptions of the version of "the dismal science" that have prevailed since Alfred Marshall succeeded in operationalizing "utility at the margins" as the theory of choice governing consumption as well as production.[36] Today few object when policy discussion presumes that the true science of society is neoclassical economics. Without a critical perspective on *this* social theory, it is literally not possible to challenge most public policy presumptions.

The ideological overdetermination of Christian ethical approaches to social theory comes home to roost in its most destructive form precisely here. Not only is the silence of religious ethicists on economic justice issues deafening and economic reality invisible in our discourse, but we are mute in the face of most public policy debate because that debate can be entered critically only by taking seriously the very social theory we have already, a priori, ruled out — namely, neo-Marxian political economy.

The scope of our discipline's ideological entrapment also can be measured by a closer look at what today passes for "economic ethics" among us. Two types of work are done under this rubric, and — not surprisingly, in view of the foregoing — neither is considered of central import in the work of religious ethics.

One type of current economic ethics is "business ethics," [37] reflection on the presumed dilemmas of choice within existing economic institutions. A major subspecies of business ethics today is designated corporate responsibility ethics.[38] The wider inquiry of both business ethics and corporate responsibility ethics is constituted by the ideological boundaries of capitalism. The former addresses some of the questionable moral features of business activity and seeks to ameliorate them by bringing moral norms to bear on practices that occur within the business firm. The critically minded in our discipline frequently acknowledge that business ethics is of limited interest because so much of its focus turns on whether or to what extent moral norms are at all relevant. If one does not challenge neoclassical economic "science" at its base, moral norms *are* beside the point in business. Neoclassical theory posits utility-maximizing activity as the basic, truly rational behavior of "economic man." [39] Utility maximization, on the production side of the neoclassical market model, is, in a word, profit-making; on the consumption side, it is getting the most for one's money. Since moral considerations, however defined, fall outside this definition of rational economic behavior, the moralist appears in any discussion of business activity as an outsider, intruding extraneous concerns into a discussion where rational economic behavior is already predefined. If the moralist counsels altruism, which, by definition, is at least not optimally utility-maximizing, such urging can be shunted aside as irrelevant to what business is about. Is it any wonder that business ethics seems boring? One may succeed in justifying minimal standards of honesty in business behavior, but efforts even to formulate moral questions about the wider social effects of business practice will be dismissed as the moralism of people intrinsically hostile to economic activity altogether. Or more sophisticated liberal students tutored in neoclassical economics will acknowledge that while such moral concerns are valid in their place, they are not the proper province of the businessperson doing business, since such "problems" are — again, by definition — "exogenous" to the economic system.[40]

Corporate responsibility ethics has managed a slightly more sustained critical dialogue in economic ethics. By focusing on the behavior of concrete corporations, many ethicists have successfully raised questions about corporate moral culpability in environmental pollution, apartheid, and other evils.[41] The impact of such massively powerful institutions has been difficult to obscure, even in the face of the narrow normative account of economic rationality that neoclassical theory proffers. Nevertheless, the more successful the corporate responsibility ethicists are in pressing their questions, the more obvious it becomes that the moral problems they identify cannot be resolved within the presuppositions of the existing "rules" defining action in the institutions they study. Corporate responsibility analyses either adopt the corporation's definition of the problem, fitting it to the scope of difficulty the corporation allows, or end up challenging the corporate system itself.

The other genre of economic ethics exemplified in contemporary religious ethics purports to offer a more substantive and structural critique. It focuses on the moral evaluation of economic systems as such and seeks to determine how such systems should be evaluated morally. These religious ethical evaluations of economic systems as a whole frequently employ Weberian ideal analyses. Those who do economic ethics this way presume that existing economic systems represent a number of ideal types, usually four. Typically they include laissez-faire capitalist systems, democratic-capitalist systems, democratic-socialist systems, and Marxist or communist systems.[42] The goal of this sort of ethical analysis is to determine whether and why these presumably discrete economic systems are morally acceptable or unacceptable from the standpoint of theological ethics. It is assumed either that there is such a spectrum of actually existing systems or that each type might come to exist. No historical developmental pattern or interrelationship of economic systems is acknowledged.

The limitation of this type of economic ethics is revealed precisely in this assumption. Historically, it is debatable whether a laissez-faire economic system ever actually existed. Certainly there was a period of economic activity relatively unconstrained by government, but that historical period is not the same as the "pure" notion of the "free market" that was the hypothetical ideal of right-wing neoclassical economics.[43] Furthermore, a theoretical notion of a "free market" is not an existing system. In any case we may be sure that given advanced capitalist economic conditions, there will never again be an economy unregulated by the state. Laissez-faire ideology lingers, but all existing capitalist economies are highly regulated. In addition, in capitalism as a whole, corporate concentration is intense, and monopoly, not "free" exchange, is the goal of business.[44] Today, capitalist corporations depend on the state to maintain the conditions of political stability they require, and the concentration of corporate power in liaison with the state proceeds apace within every capitalist system. Even laissez-faire rhetoricians such as Milton Friedman are selective in the government restraint they recommend.[45] Chiefly, they wish to restrain the state only when it challenges corporate power, not when it supports it. Today capitalist empirical reality and ideological rhetoric are remote from one another. By and large, however, religious ethicists are without the intellectual resources to observe this hypocrisy, and many of us speak as if a return to early capitalism were actually possible.

At the other end of the presumed spectrum of economic systems, the ideal-type ethicist classifies economies such as the Soviet Union's as Marxist or communist, oblivious to the fact that Marx's theory was not a theory of communist economy or for that matter of socialism. No model for a postcapitalist economy is, in any technical sense, Marxian, and to define any existing economy as Marxist or communist is to misunderstand what Marx did on the one hand and what the economic goals of the communist political movements are on the other.[46] Again, a historical viewpoint is needed.

Furthermore, it is debatable to what extent the first efforts of nations committed to developing postcapitalist economies could even be said to approximate the genuine conditions of a socialist system. Evaluations of such systems must take into account that each non- or postcapitalist economy has had to forge its economic policies within an all-encompassing and powerful global capitalist system. All raw materials, monetary policy, credit, and access to and terms of trade are conditioned by this global capitalist system. Under such circumstances, what does it mean to go beyond capitalism economically? A serious ethical evaluation of economic systems like those of the Soviets or Chinese also would have to be based on careful comparison of performance of these economies with capitalist ones under analogous historical conditions. It seems to me that only the most obdurate ideologue could fail to acknowledge some remarkable economic accomplishments of both the Soviet and Chinese economies, given the past history of economic life in Russia and China. China's achievement in erasing the massive poverty of one-quarter of the world's population in thirty years surely must count as morally relevant. The debate as to whether the Soviet system itself is best classified as socialist or as state capitalist needs also to be considered in this connection.

In fact, the national economies of all the technologically advanced nations now differ only in the relative degree to which they permit the market to shape production. State regulation and state maintenance of production increase in all economies. Under capitalist regimes, state social welfare mechanisms have expanded rapidly because so-called free markets do not provide many of the services people need. Under capitalism, the state has slowly taken over those service sectors of economic life that do not provide capitalists with attractive enough profit margins. Conversely, when the so-called socialist economies have failed to provide their citizens with the most urgent consumer goods, some features of markets have been retained or reintroduced. (Socialist citizens do not face bankruptcy over health care or the acquisition of housing, but their shops are drab.) The economies of both the United States and the Soviet Union are highly centralized and highly controlled by the state. Both governments protect existing productive units. Both are shaped internally by the dynamics of defense and war production and are remote from the concrete needs of their people. Many morally sensitive mainstream economists today acknowledge that the positive economic features of market systems may not outweigh their negative social costs and that market reliance may not be possible or wise for every nation.[47] Given these facts, is this sort of moral evaluation of economic systems really acceptable "ethics"?

We must underscore that these discussions among religious ethicists of the ethics of economic systems do not touch on these or other concrete considerations. If one looks closely at what is being evaluated in this genre of ethics, it becomes apparent that the moral quality of the system turns on the formal presence or absence of bourgeois political rights, not on the performance of the economy itself in relation to human well-being. Invariably, the conclusions reached in these studies is that either democratic capitalism or democratic socialism is morally acceptable. Democratic capitalism turns out to describe our own political economy, while democratic socialism refers to alternatives such as Sweden's. The moral imprimatur is thus extended to the economies of western Europe, North America, and Japan. The economies of rich nations, precisely those that now control the global political economy, are "approved" because these nations have the formal political constitutions of bourgeois democracy. Economic functions such as the production and distribution of food and housing or shelter, the eradication of illiteracy, the effectiveness of health care delivery, education, or other essential goods and services are irrelevant to this discussion! In religious circles, the "ethics of economic systems" can be done without reference to these matters. So long as the formal political rights associated with the earlier bourgeois revolutions are present, or appear to be — if "free" elections, freedom of speech and the press, and freedom of religions are *formally* guaranteed — the economy is morally approved, whatever basic material conditions it sustains or effects.

Certainly there is a historical connection between a nation's capacity to maintain conditions of political democracy and its ability to move out of poverty or economic dependency, but the relation is probably the reverse of that implied in this sort of moral evaluation. The formal conditions of political democracy are sustainable only where certain foundational conditions of economic justice prevail and not the reverse. Dare we rest easy when Christian ethicists evaluate national economies by political criteria reflecting their own nation's historical successes but do not bring into play those criteria by which their own nations might be found wanting? We do well, I believe, to question whether this way of evaluating economic systems even deserves to be counted as serious economic ethics. What some religious ethicists have been doing under the rubric of economic ethics is evaluating the political ideologies used to defend economic systems rather than assessing concretely the capacity of these systems to meet the physical needs of their people or evaluating their impact on the environment, other nations, or the longer-term prospects of life on this planet.

John C. Bennett's plea, referred to earlier, that Christian ethicists give a central place to economic justice has not lost its urgency in the intervening years. The neoconservative political ideology of late capitalism tells us that we live in the best of all possible worlds and that we will continue to do so if only we give unqualified allegiance to the U.S. political economy. This is a promise that many citizens of advanced industrial economies appear to trust at the moment, particularly those who are white and in the middle strata of these societies. As neoconservatives invite us to ideological complacency about the state of the global and the U.S. economy, however, deep and fateful structural changes are going on here and abroad, changes that will greatly increase the economic suffering of most people on the planet. As military budgets escalate and class lines between rich and poor become sharper within and between nations, dissent from dominant ideology will rise globally and eventually at home.[48]

The needed renaissance within our religious communities of ethical reflection on economic life will probably not come quickly and, I submit, will not come at all unless we are prepared to take with new seriousness the tradition of radical social theory. To do this we must also regain a critical historical perspective on the history of political economy itself. We need to comprehend the story of how the "dismal science" of economics became detached from the concerns that informed the work of the classical political economists, including Marx.[49] Such economists focused on social conflict and the concrete dynamics and human effects of social change and looked to political economy to illumine these realities. To understand how the "science" of economics came to its current self-conception as a predictive model describing the internal relations of "the economy," abstracted from wider social processes, requires us to understand how positivism triumphed. The prestige of contemporary neoclassical theory rests in its presumed ability to be highly accurate at predicting "micro-level" economic behavior, the behavior of individual markets and firms. All concede that it is predictively weak at the "macro level" — the level of the economy as a whole — because here "exogenous" factors like politics or natural disaster tend to muddy the elegant waters

of the abstract paradigm. Fortunately, many neoclassical economists let their analyses be muddied, but that is because their personal morality is better than the "scientific" paradigm they use.

The humanly valuable economic research done today by
economists is largely the work of mavericks, many of whom are
influenced by the presumably discredited "radical" tradition of
political economy. Competence in political economy is coming to
mean a thorough grounding in both — the neoclassical *and* the
Marxian — traditions at least in some of our better graduate
schools of economics.[50] Only those who press questions that the
"pure" neoclassical model does not enable us to entertain can
help refocus the questions proper to a serious ethics of economic
life. At the same time, academic reputations in economics are
made for econometric refinements of the pure model whether or
not such refinements clarify any actual economic issue.

The Theological and Moral Viability of Radical
Political Economy Compared with Neoclassical Theory

If we are to resist the neoconservative tide sufficiently to initiate
a genuinely critical economic ethics, we will also have to declare
a moratorium both on red-baiting and on knee-jerk marxophobia
in our discipline. Not only must we place Marx more accurately
in the history of social science and the traditions of radical social
thought in the ways already indicated, but we must come to terms
with the breadth, diversity, and liveliness of the current movements in radical social theory indebted to him.[51] It is difficult to
generalize about the massive and growing body of work that is
contemporary neo-Marxian political economy, precisely because
of its enormity. The torrent of literature emerging from this tradition exemplifies a range of sensibility and is fraught with important internal debates.[52]

The character of any new dialogue between radical political
economy and the various streams of Christian theological ethics
will turn on two key issues. From the side of radical social theory/
science, much will depend on how fully a given social theorist
has broken with the positivist spirit still characteristic of some
academic philosophical Marxism.[53] On the theological side, much
will turn on the extent to which a given theological stance accepts or repudiates the powerful body/spirit dualism so characteristic of dominant, right-wing Christianity. Those of us who share
a feminist Christian liberation hermeneutic are likely to find a
genuinely dialectical materialism more congenial to an adequate
Christian theological ethic than the body- and matter-denying

spiritualism of contemporary neo-Fascist Christianity. Since for us *the* arena of divine/human relations is this very mundane, flesh and blood world,[54] we have no problem with the assumption that sensuous labor and bread are even more foundational to the life of the spirit than is prayer. However, we are no less critical of vulgar or mechanistic Marxism than we are of the anti-embodiment spiritualism of right-wing religion or bourgeois academic idealism. We affirm the possibility that a liaison between Christian theory and neo-Marxian political economy can deliver Christians from the strong lingering vestiges of an antimaterialist, world-denying spirituality that remains the complex legacy of Christianity's identification with male gender stereotypes and imperial political power. We also affirm that an adequate theological moral vision can deliver Marxists from the strong lingering vestiges of rationalistic scientism and cultural insensitivity that Soviet elites and European male academics have bequeathed their tradition.[55] For feminist liberation theologians like myself, such mutual conversion is devoutly to be wished.

For those who reject this feminist vision of Christianity, the claim that radical social thought is more congenial to normative Christian theology than are other available theories of society may be far from obvious. Yet I believe that serious attention to criteria for employing social theory to our work will clarify the value of neo-Marxian social theory in comparison with realism, historical sociology, and, above all, neoclassical economic theory. Here I can mention only four general and related features of radical theory that correlate well with the needs of a theological ethic.

The first of these is the attention radical theory gives to concrete conflict and suffering. The three greatest classical political economists — Adam Smith, David Ricardo, and Karl Marx — shared a concern that a theory of political economy actually illumine the growing social conflict of the rising economic system. Each acknowledged that class antagonism was a discernible and accelerating hallmark of capitalist economic development. While both Smith and Ricardo's agitation about this reality became muted as their interest in defending the rising economic system increased, Marx kept central his attention to social conflict and the concrete effects of this conflict. He stressed that the study of political economy must aim not only to clarify class antagonism but also to enable human action to transcend the social exploitation that generated it.

Stereotypically, Marx and his social scientific followers often are treated by theologians as those who "urge" or "commend" class conflict.[56] This charge is based on an ideological assumption that conflict is not already endemic to society but happens only when "fomented" by radicals. A radical social theory, in contrast, presumes the actual existence of widespread social exploitation and has as its goal the analysis of this exploitation so that effective opposition to it may occur. Concern for specific human suffering is explicit. In this context, I must stress again that radical social theorists do not aspire to produce a blueprint for socialism. For them, a social science could never yield simple positive or technological knowledge for changing history. The path beyond the exploitation of a given political economy must rest in the creative capacity of historical agents to forge alternative modes of production. Genuine radicals seek to overcome a central source of exploitation, to ensure that those who work will have a voice in the surplus value their labor generates.[57] Nor does a radical view of class antagonism suggest that what workers need most is a bigger share of the existing pie. Marx said nothing about the capitalist mode of distribution. He argued that a capitalist system could never adequately resolve distributional injustice and, more important, could not bring together labor power and worker control of wealth produced. To modify the capitalist system so that political control of economic decisions is lodged in the hands of those whose work and labor create the wealth that the economy produces requires us to go beyond the mere "redistribution" of wealth on which bourgeois ethics focuses.[58]

We religious ethicists must at least learn to acknowledge the humane and democratic concerns that animate radical theory. Marx's authentic radical political economic heirs do not seek to foment violence but to expose its existence so as to enable people to increase the self-direction of their lives. In this respect, I submit, radical social theory is far more congenial to theological and moral presuppositions than are the reductionist, economist assumptions of the neoclassical paradigm.

In connection with my polemic against the misreading of Marx common in our field, I have already identified implicitly a second characteristic of radical social theory that meets a criterion central to theological ethics: its unequivocal methodological requirement that the political economy be understood as sociohistorical reality that is, in principle, transformable. A radical political-economic theory not only presumes the historical character of all social institutions but carefully traces the historical shifts in that most basic institution, the organization of the mode of production.

This is the political economist's task — to trace and assess these historical dynamics. Furthermore — and this is another much misunderstood point — radical theory incorporates an appreciation for many positive historical aspects and consequences of capitalism. Following Marx on this point, most radical economists presume that capitalism creates the necessary conditions for economic democracy by productive innovation. Economic democracy, in this view, is a possibility that emerges as much because of capitalism's success as because of its failures. Contrary to stereotypical readings, radical political economists do not treat capitalism as irrevocably evil, but they do insist that its pattern of exploitation must be transcended historically.

A further implication of this historical method constitutes a third way in which radical theory correlates with the sort of theological insight that ethicists require. Because its methodology is historical, radical social theory is more likely than mainstream social science to hold itself answerable to and to accept responsibility for concretely illuminating the experiences of everyday life.[59] In this circumstance, an actual dialectic between theory and critical political practice can operate. While many orthodox Marxists have behaved much like orthodox Christians in their anti-empirical dogmatism, a consistently radical social theory, like a consistently critical theology, aims constantly to test its theory by its practice. In sum, if we are finally to transcend the reductionistic anti-ethical effects of both social scientific positivism and religious authoritarianism, our social theories and our theologies must present social history to us not as inexorable or predetermined and resistant to change but as responsive to our agency. Since moral perspective becomes relevant only to those ranges of human life that are open to self-direction and decision, those that can be shaped broadly by options and alternatives, we can develop an adequate theological ethical perspective on political economy only if we break the mesmerizing hold of all scientific and theological assumptions that render forms of social life "inevitable."

We need to appreciate the superiority of the radical paradigm on this point as well as on the other points identified here. Concern for the basic material well-being that is at the heart of an adequate economic ethic can become a matter of moral urgency as we escape a mood of economic determinism. The "rational economic man" of the bourgeois era and the ideal agent of its reigning social theory, one who acts only as neoclassical theory presumes, "wisely" optimizing his utility before all else, is today a dangerous, dehumanized agent. "He" is the conceptual product of a social science that justifies such behavior by predicating economic rationality on decisions and policies that are not morally accountable and that rule out most actual questions about human well-being as "undue" interference in this sort of economic activity. The moral myopia of the dominant political economy can be displaced only by a thoroughgoing historical-critical perspective.

A fourth and final characteristic that should commend radical political economy to those who work from a theological ethical perspective is, I submit, its emphatic perception not only that the political economy is one integrated whole but that all economic activity is intrinsically and directly related to the overall cultural and institutional matrix of human social life. To affirm that all dimensions of political-economic life are interrelated in a social whole — that "everything is interconnected" — is hardly a novel insight, and many neoclassical economists concur in intention. However, it is *not* a theoretical postulate of the dominant economic theory. In fact, neoclassical theory presents us with a picture of the social world as segmented into differing "spheres" of activity. Economic behavior is presumed limited to the processes of production and exchange central to capitalism, while political, aesthetic, and religious activity are discrete and differing arenas of action. The result is a "science" that cannot analyze problems holistically.[60] We need a theory of political economy that posits economic activity as a basic, integrated aspect of the life of individuals, groups, and society as a whole and that does not endorse the sort of institutional segregation characteristic of bourgeois theory. Insofar as we rely exclusively on neoclassical economics to discuss public policy, we collude in masking the way the massive political-economic structures of late capitalism shape social problems such as racism, sexism, or classism and we allow these powerful institutions to continue to be unresponsive to the social consequences of their actions. The presumption that human activity is divided into sectors, each optimally shaped by a logic and rationale unrelated to any other, and that economics, politics, morality, and religion are in no intrinsic way related or answerable to the logic of the needs of the whole social order is lingering ideology of the capitalist humanism of the Enlightenment, and it must be transcended.

In sum, the track record of radical social theorists in clarifying the concrete, historical impact of political economy on everyday life is impressive. Some neo-Marxian political economists have placed a priority on doing economics not for banks or for government agencies but for grass-roots groups, aiming to clarify political and economic issues for precisely those usually bypassed in discussions of economic policy.[61] Placing their work at the service of those adversely affected — workers, racial and ethnic people, and women who seek gender justice — many of the new breed of radical economists take seriously the need to enable action among

the people actually hurt by the social policies mainstream economists usually endorse. It is the goal of radical economists to translate the presumed mysteries of political economy, to help people
understand what is going on and how it affects their lives.

A critical test of an economic theory, then, is whether it enables an "ah-hah" experience not unlike the moment of religious
transcendence. When a social theory helps people experience
their presumed private troubles as actually grounded in the way
the social world works, that theory is theologically and morally
apt. A holistic radical social theoretical perspective actually functions this way as a compass or road map that enables people to
get their bearings and to feel a bit less crazy about the way the
world is going. Too often, work done in the reigning "dismal
science" constricts our view of actual dynamics and leads us,
more and more, to adapt our lives to the "mysteries" of the business cycle. The capacity of a theory to critically break open our
experience is, I submit, a criterion of its theological usefulness,
and in this respect radical theory is demonstrably superior to neoclassical theory.

To identify some of the general features of a social theory that
make it compatible with a theological and moral perspective is
not, of course, to endorse all theses or specific conclusions that its
proponents advance through its use. Social scientific studies and
analyses have to be weighed and assessed on their own terms and
in relation to relevant standards of accuracy and evidence as well
as in relation to the theoretical presuppositions that shape them.
Yet when the issue before us is ethical, involving evaluation of
our lives as social beings, these general features of our social
theory are fully as important as are our theological presumptions.
For many centuries, various Christian perspectives on life, the
world, and nature were shaped by a dialogue between the concrete traditions of the Jesus community and the presumptions of
the philosophical systems of the day. Theological anthropologies
were a compound of both. In the twentieth century, that dialogue
has shifted, and our theological anthropologies — those conceptions of who we are as human-species beings — are now irrevocably hammered out between the discourse of concrete faith
communities and the social theories that increasingly shape our
self-perceptions. The assumptions of our social theory shape our
anthropologies today much as philosophic systems once did.[62]

Obviously, if practitioners of religious ethics are to make human economic well-being a central animating passion of our ongoing work we must reject the notion, all reports to the contrary
notwithstanding, that the "socialist question" has been laid to
rest. Serious deliberation is urgent about moving beyond the high

and ever-inflating moral costs of our current political economy. *Sustaining a centralized global advanced industrial capitalist system is bringing death to all but a few on our planet.* Genuine, deep, authentic economic democracy is an urgent need — so urgent, in fact, that without it we will live to see the eclipse of those valued political rights we white, affluent Christians have too readily presumed secure.[63] Enabling people to understand this reality and to recover a capacity to long for economic justice[64] as deeply as we desire political justice is the task of religious ethics today.

II

FEMINIST SOCIAL ETHICS

Social Policy and the Practice
of the Churches

The essays in this section are based on Harrison's view of what justice requires in the area of sexuality, procreative choice, the place of our elders, the Equal Rights Amendment, and energy conservation. These topics are included not because they are the only issues relevant to women's lives but as responses Harrison has made to urgent issues facing our society and requiring moral reflection in the formulation of policy. They are examples of a feminist social ethicist at work.

These essays serve as case studies about what happens when one asks what justice requires from the point of view of the people on the underside, those who bear the brunt of the organization of society in a particular manner: older people, the poor, lesbians and gay men, women in general, and also those who are pregnant against their will. They illustrate several important characteristics of the way Harrison analyzes social problems and social relations in addition to attending to how those disadvantaged and negatively affected experience the situation. We are to ask what are the historical and social roots of the wrong social relationships or the failure of justice. We are to investigate what interests keep these patterns of injustice in place. And we are to ask what patterns of institutional relations must be confronted and transformed before right relationship can be achieved.

Harrison in these selections consistently marks the complicity of the churches in maintaining patterns of injustice. There are two recurring responses of religious institutions, the Christian churches in particular, that are unfaithful to their own norms and that must be challenged. One is the claim that the churches should not be involved in the political arena to influence social policy because the task of the churches is spiritual. They, in so saying, are pretending no involvement, but they leave in place irresponsible social power that is heedless of the concrete conditions of human social well-being. The second duplicitous response of the churches is to exempt an issue from moral reflection altogether, particularly if it relates either to sexuality or to the distribution of wealth. Issues of sexuality and the social allocation of goods affect everyone, and to leave them unexamined is to give assent to unaccountable power. The practice of the churches in mystifying injustice is therefore a consistent theme in these selections, as is Harrison's calling the churches to account to engage the project of making right relationships.

SEXUALITY AND SOCIAL POLICY*

The Contradictions of Liberal and Conservative Theological Approaches to Sexuality

In our present society, and far too frequently in our churches as well, persons of very different theological and political persuasions — conservatives, liberals, and radicals — coconspire to keep in place assumptions about human sexuality, ethics, and social policy that block a much-needed rethinking of how our human capacity for intimacy and love and our aspirations for a just social order coinhere. Taken at face value, this claim may seem incredible. Surely, the conservative who longs for clear and precise normative rules about the rights and wrongs of sexual acts on the one hand and who wishes to keep religion out of social policy or politics on the other appears to have little in common with theological liberals or radicals. After all, the latter usually put concern for the justice of social institutions squarely at the center of their religious commitment and are quite likely to take the position that the ethics of sexuality is merely a personal issue and a matter of relative indifference compared with the "grave" issues of social justice. The fact is, however, that both positions accept a set of assumptions about our human personhood that badly need to be challenged. For both, the personal and the political are sealed off from each other, and the dynamics that make for social and personal well-being are not deeply interconnected. The conventional wisdom that sustains this split is precisely what needs to be challenged, I believe, if we are to rise to a major responsibility in our time: rethinking our understanding of human sexuality to appropriate a sexual ethics deep enough to clarify the relation between our capacity for interpersonal love and our ability to struggle effectually for social justice in our common life.

Without a better grasp of the intimate connection between personal and social well-being, our sexual ethic will simply reinforce a growing trend toward privatism and the churches' withdrawal from social engagement. But equally problematic would

---

* This essay combines social policy material prepared for discussion in the Consultants Panel of the Sexuality Study of the United Church of Christ and a related article prepared for the *Journal of Current Social Issues*, 1978.

be any renewed concern for social justice that is devoid of aware-ness of how our social passivity is rooted in the dynamics of our interpersonal, primary relationships. The churches are always tempted to avoid altogether the volatile questions of human sexu-ality, abandoning people in the confused struggle to find more adequate paths to personal fulfillment and human intimacy. What we Christians evade is the connection between our silence on sexuality and our general conventionality toward social relations. Even our presumed "social action" often suffers from lack of cre-ativity and imagination.

That we need a new understanding of the dialectic between love and justice is obvious from the way that both conservative and liberal ideologies within Christianity lead to obvious contra-dictions in the actions and strategies of their respective proponents. For their part, many Christian social activist liberals are perplexed at a growing political apathy in the churches and seem unable to find ways to mobilize social conscience except through the meth-ods of rhetorical moralizing, which were the very means deplored as overindividualistic in the past. At the same time, conservatives who have long cried out for clear-cut standards of right and wrong in personal sexual ethics and who always have insisted that a rigid line be drawn between religion and ethics on the one hand and politics and economics on the other find themselves mobiliz-ing politically to change the direction of social policy to prevent further changes that they deem immoral. So religiopolitical move-ments against the defeated Equal Rights Amendment and against legal abortion and the civil rights of homosexuals flourish. That many who support these efforts are violating their own deeply held convictions against government interference with or regula-tion of individual liberty only underscores the inability of estab-lished social theory to encompass our lived-world reality.

The complexity of the relation between sexuality and social order becomes clear when we observe how little impact such largely successful political mobilization has on our culture's pre-occupation with human sexuality. Legislators can gain support by turning back permissive social policies, but our fascination with genital sexuality and explicit sexual themes seems to increase. We even see the emergence of groups, such as the Total Woman Movement, that combine a celebration of heterosexual genital sexual liberation in marriage with a militant reassertion of tradi-tional notions about "woman's place" in home, family, and so-ciety. Evidently, the pleasures of genital-sexual eroticism are here to stay, whatever the outcome of social movements aimed at jus-tice for women. This trend is further confirmed by the response of several television networks to complaints about gratuitous physical violence during prime-time programming. In a number of cases, detective shows and adventure stories have given way to situation comedies that feature a new and presumably "daring" explicitness about sexuality. Since the television media often know more about our collective tastes and attitudes than we ourselves do, the substitution of the titillations of explicit sex for the presumed excitation of physical violence suggests that we are a long way from any shift back toward more traditional sexual reticences.

The fact is that explicit sexuality is very big business in this nation, and our fascination with the technologies of sex, with sexual therapies, and with the paraphernalia of sexual experimentation is flourishing. Those who cry out for a tightening of sexual standards notwithstanding, "sexual liberation," in its tawdry, commercial guise, will not abate until the profit wanes. The anomaly of our situation can be measured by the way in which sexuality is becoming part of the performance- and achievement-oriented ethic characteristic of a business society. We appear so preoccupied by sexual performance that some commentators wonder whether capacity for sexual pleasure may not be giving way to ennui and boredom. If greater sexual genital expression were, in itself, a panacea for what ails us, we would expect clear evidence that a sense of personal well-being was on the rise in our society. In fact, there is no indication that we are experiencing a reduction in loneliness, isolation, competitiveness, or alienation from community.

In the face of all this, the trivialization of sexuality by those whose concerns are presumably focused on the "more substantive" questions of social justice is understandable. Such people consider preoccupation with sexual concerns and sexual pleasure to be a cause of our social malaise. There has been much loose talk about a "new narcissism," turning to self-preoccupation that presumably threatens our capacity to take the reality of other persons seriously. The problem with much of this sort of social diagnosis is that it does not probe deeply enough to lead to a reintegrated sense of how interpersonal well-being interacts with the wider social realities that shape our experience. The analysis of our presumed narcissism too often confuses "cause" with social "symptom." [1] The almost desperate search for physical pleasure and personal intimacy that pervasively characterizes our culture is much more a symptom of the lack of humanly fulfilling opportunities in work and frustration at depersonalized, bureaucratic institutional patterns that suffuse our life than a cause of our social ills. And the tragedy is that the simple pleasures of sex, while real, are not a sufficiently powerful antidote to the wounds to self-respect we endure elsewhere. Genital sexuality, narrowly conceived, is simply too weak a reed to bear the overloaded expectations that people in our society are encouraged to place on it. What is most needed is an approach to sexuality that aims to be holistic, that sets what we know of ourselves as sexual persons in the broadest possible context of our lives within our existing social order.

Sources, Principles, and Priorities for a More Adequate Ethics of Sexuality

The time is ripe for a reappraisal of our understanding of sexuality, ethics, and social policy, in spite of the controversy such reappraisal engenders. There are two salient and appropriate pressures for a reevaluation in contemporary society, and both provide resources for recovering a deeper, holistic understanding of the nature of our sexuality. The first of these pressures derives from the emergence of basic paradigm shifts in social scientific conceptions of the nature of gender difference and "normal" sexuality. What we are discovering today is how little we really have ever understood about ourselves as sexual persons. The new paradigms of psychosocial development make clear that the meaning of our sexuality involves the integration of many levels of biological and social determinants. More and more, we are coming to realize the full range of possible healthy sexual development that characterizes human life. New knowledge per se does not yield new ethical awareness, but the emerging paradigms are themselves more open to humane value questions.[2] These newer scientific perspectives afford us opportunity to appropriate a more adequate sense of human diversity in sexual development and expression. They correlate well with the best insights of our religious and moral tradition about the interrelationship of human freedom and moral responsibility.

However, Christians have as yet been reluctant to embrace an ethic of maturity where sexuality is concerned. In many dimensions of our life as human agents, Christian ethicists have insisted, explicitly, that we must both accept our power as agents and learn to express that power responsibly, without recourse to unexceptional rules. In relation to our actions as sexual beings, however, there remains a lingering fear of affirming any genuine capacity of moral agents to live responsibly apart from largely prohibitive and constricting action guides.[3]

The second pressure and resource for reappraisal of sexual ethics come from the fruit of women's efforts to achieve full social recognition as persons. In our time, it is the women's movement and, more recently, the gay and lesbian liberation movements that have called into question many of the traditional views formerly held to be "scientific." At the deepest level, the insights of contemporary feminism lead to reappropriation of the meaning of our sexuality, which runs counter to the narrow "sexual liberation" fixation on genital sexuality.

What women have discovered, signaled in the phrase "we are our bodies, ourselves," is that in the absence of freedom to understand, control, and direct our own sexuality, our power as self-regulating moral agents does not develop. Numerous feminists have formulated telling critiques of traditional erotic patterns, insisting, for example, that our modern romantic ideals of love between the sexes involve the celebration of dehumanizing seduction and conquest on the male side and feminine passivity and denial of pleasure on the other.[4] A clear break with male myths regarding female sexuality has enabled women to recognize to what extent such myths have been generated to keep women obeisant to the social function of procreation. The religious dictum that the only moral expression of sexuality is that which is at least open to the possibility of procreation has been a source of many women's inability to achieve a self-defining role in relation to their bodies. Many women have denied their own needs for bodily pleasuring as the cost of being "good" women. Conversely, when women have been sexually active or self-initiating, society has defined them as "whores" or "deviants." In the positive reappropriation and appreciation of ourselves as embodied persons, women are regaining the capacity to celebrate our sexuality as inherent in our own embodiedness. But the experience of genuine embodiedness also leads to rejection of the view that sexual pleasure is limited to genital contact or that women's sexuality is passive, mediated exclusively through active relationships with men. The feminist insight is that sexuality is mutual pleasuring in the context of genuine openness and intimacy. That such communication is of "ultimate value" only when it is shaped by procreative potential or procreative intent — the Christian teaching, at least as it applies to women — is simply lingering male supremacist doctrine that reinforces male control of women's self-definition.

The social criticism generated by feminism also has led to a fresh analysis of the way in which sex role patterns in the family operate destructively in relation to women's self-esteem. These sex role expectations have subtly conditioned us, men and women alike, to accept inequities of power and differing capacities for self-direction between men and women in the broader society.[5]

It is one thing, however, for groups of women — and, increasingly, for sensitive men — to begin to diagnose the destructive aspects of sex role socialization as they affect the lives of individuals and the broader community; it is another to begin to reverse these powerfully ingrained patterns of traditional gender socialization in society.

The women's movement and the gay and lesbian movements are resources and pressures for change, but they do not provide a simple blueprint that enables us to prioritize issues relating to sexuality and social policy. Insofar as these movements are limited by theory or practice to the reality of white experience or fail to address the dynamics of class, identified priorities will be inadequate. In addition, public knowledge of feminism and gay and lesbian liberation movements is filtered through and conditioned by the mass media that aim to minimize offense to some presumed "general public" and therefore also aim to mute serious systemic criticism. This means that it is mostly the priorities for social policy change that resonate with already existing "public opinion" that are called to our attention. The full implications of a serious feminist social policy are rarely understood in public debate.

The corrective for uncritical acceptance of media-interpreted priorities of these social movements, however, is deeper listening and involvement and a greater effort to respect the principles underlying the specific priorities of all social justice movements. For example, in the women's movement, the principle of bodily self-determination underlies the emphasis on the need for accessible contraception and the availability of legal abortion. The same principle, applied in the context of the existing race and class dynamics of this society, requires equal attention to the abhorrent social practice of developing contraceptive devices through medical experimentation on poor and nonwhite women and the too frequent practice of forced sterilization, especially of poor and nonwhite women.[6] Yet the media focus only on the former issues, leaving concern for the latter, widespread in the women's movement, undiscussed as a serious social evil. The fundamental social attitude toward women — that our competence as moral agents vis-à-vis our bodies and reproductive capacities is not trustworthy — inevitably results in divergent patterns of social control across race and class lines. Many middle-strata white women experience social deprivation only when they insist on self-determination that flies in the face of traditional female roles. They may count on family and community support and personal affirmation if they choose childbearing and function as "good" mothers and homemakers. Only when they

resist conformity to these conventional roles does their environment grow hostile or suspicious of them as women. Poor and
working-class women, by contrast, suffer more acute deprivation; they have neither easy access to prevention of pregnancy
nor support for their exercise of women's "traditional" role. Racism and poverty function as coercive pressures against even traditional fulfillment through procreation.

The point is that the social policy priorities of groups aiming
at liberation from the various forms of sexual oppression are adequately liberating only insofar as these priorities are defined by
how they touch the lives of persons on both sides of the institutionalized and interstructured patterns of race and class oppression. Andrea Dworkin has put this point forcefully:

> The analysis of sexism . . . articulates clearly what
> the oppression of women is, how it functions, how it is
> rooted in psyche and culture. But that analysis is use-
> less unless it is tied to a political consciousness and
> commitment which will totally redefine community.
> One cannot be free, never, not ever, in an unfree world,
> and in the course of redefining family, church, power
> relations, all the institutions which inhibit and order
> our lives, there is no way to hold onto privilege and
> comfort. To attempt to do so is destructive, criminal,
> and intolerable . . .
>
> The analysis [of sexism] applies to the life situa-
> tions of all women, but all women are not necessarily
> in a state of primary emergency as women. What I
> mean by this is simple. As a Jew in Nazi Germany, I
> would be oppressed as a woman, but hunted, slaugh-
> tered as a Jew. As a Native American, I would be op-
> pressed as a squaw, but hunted, slaughtered, as a Na-
> tive American. *The first identity, the one which brings
> with it as a part of its definition death, is the identity
> of primary emergency.* This is an important recognition
> because it relieves us of a serious confusion. The fact,
> for instance, that many Black women (by no means all)
> experience primary emergency as Blacks in no way less-
> ens the responsibility of the Black community to assim-
> ilate this and other analyses of sexism and to apply it
> in their own revolutionary work. [Emphasis mine] [7]

This same insight must be extended to gay and lesbian analyses
and sensibilities. The social priorities of gay men do not always
adequately incorporate the needs and sensibilities of lesbians or
of black people or the poor. In the churches and in the wider

gay movement, white gay men are often those who specify the agenda for change in relation to heterosexism. Setting adequate priorities for just social policy in relation to human sexuality will occur only if we learn to ask How do the matters that are central to my liberation touch the lives of those who are doubly or triply oppressed? We must learn to shape our formulation of sexual justice with this question and these persons in view. No sexual ethic will be adequate unless it incorporates a full appreciation of the interstructuring of social oppression. For example, economic justice as access to and genuine participation in the production, distribution, and determination of the use of a society's wealth is also a condition of genuine sexual freedom. All distortions of power in society reveal themselves in the inequity of power dynamics in interpersonal life. An adequate normative sexual ethic will be predicated on awareness that where people (men, women, *and* children) are socially powerless, they are vulnerable to irresponsible and inappropriate — that is, nonvoluntary and/or nonmutual — sexual transactions. The goal of a holistic and integrated sexual ethic is to affirm sexual activity that enhances human dignity, that entails self- and other-regarding respect and genuine communication. Such an ethic must challenge actions that degrade, disempower, and reduce oneself's and others' esteem or that aim at control, objectification, or manipulation of another.

The basic theological and moral principles implicit in the feminist and gay liberation movements — the affirmation of the goodness of sexuality as embodiment, the respect for bodily integrity, and the appropriateness of self-direction and noncoercion in expressing sexuality — are constitutive of everyone's human dignity. They are foundational to all claims for human well-being, as fundamental to the eradication of racism and ethnic oppression as to women's and gay men's historic emancipation. As such, they are criteria for a sexual ethic that genuinely affirms personal freedom, community, and responsibility.

Difficulties of Constructive Social Change
in Relation to Human Sexuality

Another awareness that must inform our efforts to translate social policy priorities into strategy is a recognition of the difficulty of finding effective loci for social change in this society. Genuine implementation of change in relation to our well-being as sexual persons is difficult to achieve. Liberal social reform efforts tend to focus strategies for change primarily through government, aiming chiefly at legal reform and government administrative change. Neither legal nor administrative reform can be neglected in efforts to implement new policies with respect to gender and sexual justice. But it is important to be clear about the role, and also the limits, of law and procedural reform. Liberals frequently misunderstand the role that law plays in strategies for change. In our society, fundamental legal change (including constitutional change, as, for example, the Equal Rights Amendment) or the achievements of administrative fairness are always as much a response to already partially realized conditions for justice as they are initiators of such change. The initiation of conditions for social justice always begins with social movements. Legislation is important because without it or without administrative fairness, the relevant conditions for sustaining justice will never approximate "normalcy" in the wider society. Reversion to repressive policies is always easier if the requisite legitimations in law and administrative procedure have not been realized.

Nevertheless, it is critical to be aware of the actual dialectic between such legal change and wider social change. Genuine change is always the result of hard-won struggle from below. Some groups and some institutions must begin to shape a liberating praxis within the society before there is sufficient pressure to actualize humane conditions as a legal norm. Theological liberalism has misunderstood this fact, which is why liberal church activism for justice has been so inept. Tragically, liberal Christians who aver that the church should avoid controversy until issues are respectable and who refuse liaisons with social movements and activist social policy groups are those who ensure that Christianity will never play an active role in shaping policy development within our society. To "get involved" only when consensus about positive legal change has developed means that such Christians are never influential in the process of change. Social movements are the means whereby any positive change emerges, and the politics of mainstream theological liberals are never engaged enough to interact with such movements.

In sum, double focus on change at the cultural and legal levels offers the best hope for transforming the split between what is presumed to be political or public and what is held to be merely personal or private, a split that reinforces and legitimates our widespread moral schizophrenia and keeps sexual oppression in place. The potential for "radicalizing" people's broader awareness of the importance of social justice by integrating their sensibilities to sexual justice lies precisely here. It is worth emphasizing again that the conventionality of our religion is maintained by our fear of honestly and openly facing issues of human sexuality.

The Role of Liberal Churches in Social Change

If exclusive reliance on the power of government to initiate change is one fallacy of much liberal social strategy, the tendency to overestimate the capacity of formal education to transform personal values is another. "Public" education (and, by default, most "private" education as well) is in a weak position to challenge the dominant or established understandings of human sexuality that are transmitted powerfully in our society. "Sex education" in our schools can at most challenge the miasma of misinformation, fear, and prejudice with respect to human sexuality. Furthermore, what actually goes on in the name of "sex education" has some way to go to reach even this minimum standard of effectiveness and moral adequacy. The truth is that our so-called public schools are often rendered educationally ineffectual because of fear of conflict. With respect to sexuality, as at so many other points, this fear often results in an educational strategy that postures a reductionistically "scientific" approach. Sexuality is dealt with from a physiological stance in which human reproductive biology is taught abstractly, in an environment where discussions of values are avoided to evade conflict.[8] The result is a bland conventionality that is more devastatingly effective in reinforcing the status quo than a more explicitly reactionary stance would be.

A strong case can be made that on this issue, at least, the liberal churches (regretfully, by default) have a genuine opportunity to serve the social good by a humane educational approach to human sexuality. Yet because of sexism, that is, the disvaluation of women, and fear of sexuality, the churches are not better equipped than other institutions for this task. Liberal churches, in particular, need a critical perspective on their own past social praxis in relation to public policy. Most of the public utterance of liberal churches vis-à-vis social policy questions has taken the form of voicing support for "the rights of individuals" against state intrusion on those rights. Even the most liberal of our churches have gone only so far as to ground support for sexual liberation in statements that affirm individual civil liberties. Some liberal churches have urged the state to avoid heavy-handed enforcement of sexual morality; they have affirmed women's individual freedom of conscience in seeking access to legal abortion; they have accepted the appropriateness of civil liberties for gay people. Such a posture and such policy positions have been legitimated with reference to a theology that is not substantively social. The bottom line for the liberal churches has been to oppose policies in relation to sexuality that deny status and dignity to the individual within the "public" sphere. These policy positions have helped to reduce pressure from other, more reactionary quarters for more oppressive public policies, but they lack moral vision. We need to recognize that a more adequately social theology would provide a substantive positive political rationale that would go beyond this individualistic bottom line. As it is, liberal Protestant churches have a public policy stance that suggests that it is acceptable for us to be "political" only if and when individual rights have been demonstrably violated. Whether or not the social system itself is just appears, from this perspective, to be a matter of indifference.

The very fact that we resort to such individualistic justifications — supporting individuals' civil rights rather than embracing positive and substantive moral principles rooted in an adequate vision of social justice — bespeaks the disorder of the churches' theological approach to sexual ethics. Because this is so, such defensive, "individual rights" policy stances are ineffectual. They appear to the wider society as hypocritical because they are predicated on a moral double standard that all the world reads (and reads properly) as Christian double-talk. Gay people, we claim, deserve "civil rights," but they do not receive full human affirmation and respect in the churches. Women should have the "civil right" to elect legal abortion, but abortion continues to be viewed as, at best, morally dubious, an evil necessity. The churches have not affirmed people's sexual well-being as basic to their personal dignity. The state is not charged to *support* citizens' sexual well-being but simply to desist from meddling. Because the churches do not embrace theologically the positive, nonfunctional good of human sexuality or affirm the positive principles related to sexual well-being as substantively moral, our "liberal" stance is dismissed as mere accommodation to modern culture. Because we do not accept the mandate to active solidarity with those who are the victims of sexual oppression, our social policy positions appear equivocal. We deny our own best understanding of the inherently theosocial nature of persons and community, and speak instead as individualists whose message to society is that it must adopt a moderate tolerance of human sexual expression, a moderate tolerance that we, within the churches, are not even willing to exemplify in our own community.

There is a long roster of social policy concerns that come into view when we actually embrace a positive, holistic understanding of sexuality. In addition to the policy issues I address here, this roster should include the question of how children and the sexual well-being of the differently abled can be protected and how sexual manipulation of inmates of "total institutions" can be prevented. Here I have limited my discussion to analyzing the way in which an adequate view of human sexuality requires us to take an inclusive view of women's lives and to identify some of the needed social policy concerns affecting men, gay men and lesbians, and families.

As I have already made clear, any identified social policy issue has an economic aspect. Among other things, this means that the matters I address here gain their urgency as social policy questions from the fact that they hold no "priority" in the regular, day-to-day workings of our present political economy. Serious social vulnerability in this society rests on economic marginality; hence, children and older people, all women and gay males, as well as nonskilled males (mostly, though not exclusively, nonwhite) are vulnerable as groups, which also makes them especially susceptible to sexual exploitation, violence, or forms of "benign neglect." Since the capacity to produce income and to accumulate wealth (not to be equated with wages) is *the* measure of personal worth in this society, anyone who does not participate in money-making will also be a priori a victim vulnerable to sexual oppression or to being treated as a nonperson sexually. The elderly or physically handicapped, for example, are frequently characterized as "beyond sexuality" for just this reason, a point that I develop in the essay "Older Persons' Worth in the Eyes of Society" later in this collection.

In keeping with the principles identified earlier, we need always to ask how these policy matters affect persons differently, how the dynamics of class and white supremacy intersect with the social dynamics of human sexuality and gender difference.

Women's Sociosexual Oppression

It is not easy to develop the sensibility to recognize how many social policy changes related to women's lives are morally required. Recent discussion by feminists has stressed that a genuine feminist social policy agenda must incorporate changes of policy in two directions. Changes must come both in the division of labor in the family and in relation to women's access to the workplace.[9] In all industrial societies, more and more women are engaged in both domestic and wage labor, a change generated not by feminist ideology but by structural shifts in the economy that make two incomes necessary for minimal freedom from poverty for a low- to middle-income family — the statistically typical U.S. family. The need for change in both domestic and wage labor sectors is made clear by the experience of socialist societies.

Even where women are more justly treated in the workplace, as in socialist nations, changes in women's lives have been insufficient precisely because change in the domestic sphere has been neglected.[10]

The single most powerful source of women's sexual subjugation remains women's lack of deep and genuine economic equality because economic inequality goes well beyond the need for "equal pay for equal work." Among other things, there must be a transformation of the castelike character of the work women are allowed to perform in the economy for wages.[11] Current employment patterns segregate groups of women into low-paying job categories. For example, racial and ethnic women work in the lowest-paying jobs as domestics, piece workers in industry, as maids or attendants.[12] The vast majority of all women, white and racial ethnic, are dead-ended in the work force in pink collar, sex-segregated jobs that parallel women's domestic role in the home. Women work chiefly as waitresses, laundresses, nurses, cooks, and retail salespersons for smaller goods — cosmetics, small housewares, clothing, and the like. Women function as secretaries, typists, file clerks, or performers of other routine labor, completing the pink collar pattern. A twofold social policy change is required.[13] Gender segregation by job category must end, but in addition the wage rates of pink collar job categories must be raised to equal the rates in comparable male job categories.

Second, we must cease to treat domestic labor in the home as socially nonproductive labor. At present, housework and child care are not in any way recognized as value-adding labor. At the level of minimum reform, we need to provide social security coverage for full-time homemakers, male or female. Those who do housework and raise children deserve to be counted among those doing socially valuable labor, and "wages for housework" may be a key to such value in our money society. The realists among us will note immediately how wildly utopian such a proposal is under existing political and economic arrangements. Yet there never will be genuine economic justice for women until greater justice prevails between domestic labor and labor outside the home.[14] The fact remains that women's psychic and social vulnerability is so deeply conditioned economically (and some women's reputed "conservatism" follows from this) that only this two-pronged strategy will begin to affect women's lives deeply. Sexual politics will not be eradicated until and unless this sort of social change occurs.

Needless to say, the presumed resistance of many men to economic justice for women might shift if there were wage compensation for work done in the home. As it is, some men resent women's competition in the workplace precisely because they have dependent spouses and imagine (usually wrongly) that other women could choose to stay at home as well. Resentment of both women's economic dependency and the threat of increasing numbers of women in the workplace increases men's hostility to women. The psychological dynamics of male-female and female-female relationships also might improve if the trade-offs between domestic work and wage labor in the workplace were different. At present, the relation of dependency flows from those who work at home to those who labor in the workplace. Therefore, the domestic sphere is disvalued. If housework carried financial remuneration, it would be more respected by society and recognized for the difficult and socially necessary labor that it is. Conversely, any relative reduction of women's actual economic dependence on men would enhance homemakers' expectations for fair and respectful treatment from men. Women who have been least identified with a feminist analysis, namely housebound women who concur with their husbands that they should not work, often understand that if they did work, the jobs open to them would involve an additional dose of drudgery just like that done at home. If the two sources of economic injustice for women are linked, these women may come to understand how an adequate feminist agenda touches their lives.

It is, of course, extremely naive to imagine that the conditions for economic change at this level will come suddenly or that prospects for any such substantial changes are bright. Recent Department of Labor statistics signal an accelerating overall downward trend in the average per capita income of women in relation to men.[15] A few women have gained access to better-paying work, but as the proportion of women in relation to men in the labor force continues to increase, so does the number of women entering the job market at the lower end of the wage scale. Females from racial ethnic communities, such as Hispanic women, are overrepresented among the newly employed women in the work force and make up a substantial proportion of the new working poor population.[16] In addition, the competition between women and nonwhite men for skilled middle-wage and low-paying, low-skilled white collar jobs is a dramatic feature of the present economic scene. Tensions between nonwhites and white women may well increase unless our analyses adequately clarify what is happening and why. Michelle Russell has reminded us that

in contemporary America we experience at least as many varieties of subjective human alienation as there are job categories in the system. Our immediate impulse as individuals fighting for self-respect is to legitimize only our particular form of victimization. But that simply isn't enough. We unfurl the flag of our separate and personal situation and make that our morality.[17]

Small gains made in the last decade around all issues of gender justice are jeopardized in large part because overall economic inequity is increasing so rapidly. This is why we must always count economic justice as a foundational consideration to the sexual well-being of women and men in society. Economic marginalization of groups struggling for sexual justice reduces social pressure for contructive change, unless the disadvantaged organize collective resistance.

Other, more explicitly sexual issues continue to mobilize the energy and the anger of large groups of women because direct sexual exploitation is on the increase. More and more women are learning to recognize the connection between controlling one's own body and one's self-respect. As I have already observed, the broad principle of self-determination and control of our own procreative power remains critical, though women's understanding of what policies really create such self-determination vary in relation to class and frequently in terms of race.

Leo Kanowitz has contended[18] that laws relating to sexual conduct continue to be a primary source of legal discrimination against women. For example, laws against prostitution most often control and penalize women prostitutes more than their male customers. Patterns of law enforcement further reinforce the bias of such laws. Rules of evidence and legal requirements for rape convictions are especially stringent, and married women are not protected against marital rape or abuse in most states. Furthermore, women are more likely to be stigmatized and penalized for active sexuality. Women are likely to lose custody of children if sexual "misconduct" can be proved.

Access to legal abortion, the prevention of sterilization abuse, adequate women's health care, including the availability of safe contraception, must be integrated into any political strategy for procreative choice. Accelerating efforts to prohibit the use of Medicaid and other federal funds for abortion continue to affect poor women's lives, and other ways of blocking access to abortion continue to be discovered,[19] so organized efforts to secure procreative choice for women must continue. The scandal of the sexual politics of reproduction is revealed in a "catch-22" situation in which political pressure against safer and more reliable means of birth control escalates simultaneously with efforts to secure antiabortion legislation. Clearly, the aim of many in this society is to return women to a place of "necessary" childbearing. Funds from all sources expended for research on biological fertility have steadily declined since 1972; and U.S. government funding continues to decline in the face of the Roman Catholic bishops' and right-wing Protestant groups' mounting opposition to federal funding for such research.[20] In spite of the widespread recognition that all but the least effective "barrier" methods of birth control involve probable serious side effects, there is little public pressure for funding additional contraceptive research. In fact, it is probable that the amount of monies expended in activity against abortion far exceeds the funds invested in medical research to prevent unwanted pregnancies.

The other side of this "catch-22" situation also falls on women. Nearly all experimentation to test birth control technologies has been carried out on largely unknowing populations of poor and predominantly nonwhite women here and abroad. Such practices are characteristic of the wider dynamics of class and race oppression, for by some estimates 80 percent of all medical experimentation in the United States is carried out on poor subjects. Several male interpreters of scientific research have acknowledged the existence of the serious abuses in contraceptive research.[21] The paucity of women researchers and the lack of female participation in the development of experimentation policy and practice are also well documented. Certainly this public policy pattern, along with the practice of dumping unsafe contraceptive technologies on so-called third world nations, accounts in large part for the widespread suspicion among poor and nonwhite people that "family planning" functions in the dominant white community as a euphemism for genocide toward nonwhite people.[22] The not uncommon practice of sterilization by tubal ligations or hysterectomies, used as a means of birth control particularly in medical facilities that treat poor women, is another source of hostility because, more often than not, women of color are the victims of these practices. Some public health groups believe that the rate of hysterectomies in training hospitals is related to the "need" to provide surgical experience for medical residents and that other, reversible means of birth control could be used. Sterilization has been and continues to be a principal "means" of birth control in Puerto Rico, where a frequently cited figure indicates that 35 percent of childbearing-age women are sterilized. A similar rate is claimed among American Indian women. The failure of "liberal" people to appreciate the elements of coercion operating here is illustrated by the *Family Planning*

Digest, published by the Center for Family Planning Services, which in May 1972 was still heralding unequivocally the growing importance of sterilization as an effective contraception without any awareness of these abuses. Not all of these unnecessary hysterectomies qualify as forced sterilization, but such estimates imply the magnitude of pressures against women's gaining self-direction vis-à-vis their bodies.

Women's sexual emancipation further rests on the ability, of all of us, to face our culture's dubious legacy of confusion between sexuality and violence. Rape is usually conceded to be the violent crime most on the increase in the United States. We think of it erroneously as a sexual crime. Though data are admittedly imprecise, it appears that we are witnessing both an actual increase in the frequency of rape and women's more frequent public reporting of what has always been a frequent crime. If, as I believe, the absolute number of rapes in relation to the female population is rising dramatically, such that violence against women is on the increase in all social classes, we need to ask why this is happening. A new variation of the old theme that women are somehow "responsible" for rape and other violent acts against them emerges in the argument that this increased violent "acting out" toward women is the result of women's "greater aggressiveness" because of "women's lib." Like other forms of our cultural proclivity to "blame the victim," [23] this explanation confuses cause and consequence of social change. The largest increase of reported rapes is occurring in just those populations of women least affected by the women's movement: the elderly and the poor, frequently the most reticent and vulnerable among women. There has been a significant increase of reported rape among black and other racial ethnic women.

Though some efforts have been made by law enforcement agencies and hospitals to eliminate the crassest and most insensitive responses to rape victims, many of these efforts now are threatened, as in New York, by budget cuts and personnel layoffs. Arrest rates for rapes committed remain low, with convictions even lower. The majority of rape victims know or have had some previous contact with their assailants, which often means women are rarely believed when they deny provocation. And marital rape is not even a crime in most states. Though massive efforts have been made by women's groups to build support for rape victims, to encourage women to come forward to charge offenders, and to testify against their attackers, the prospect for increased successful prosecution for rape, given the condition of our criminal courts and social ethos, is not encouraging. The ordeal that women must go through to press such charges and sustain their cases has not abated. As a result, rape remains a largely unpunished crime in this society, and rapists know that.

Analysis of the sociology of rape has sharpened awareness that it is not an isolated "sex crime" — the result of erotic attraction — but a long-established and legitimated institution of male control and punishment of women.[24] Among women there is now a growing awareness that we must remove rape from the legal category of sexual offense. Rape is not a sexual act but a particularly heinous form of criminal assault, aimed at humiliating the victim. Rapists are not moved by erotic desire. Rather, they act out a socially accepted pattern whereby women (or powerless men who are perceived as "feminine") are "put in their place." Male contempt for women is ritualistically expressed through rape, usually by males who themselves feel powerless and otherwise exhibit low self-esteem. Often men use rape to express resentment toward other men; females are perceived functionally as "belonging" to men, as their extensions. Yet nowhere is rape classified as a nonsexual offense. Legal reform will be necessary to alter the machismo image of the rapist, who deserves to be viewed not as one having sexual prowess but as a thug. Several years ago, San Francisco newspaper columnist Charles McCabe made this point well by proposing to women who had been raped that they charge their assailants with indecent exposure. In so doing, he argued, women would be denying the rapist the sanction of male approval and would appeal to the widespread machismo prejudice of law enforcement officers. A charge of indecent exposure, he reasoned, would assure disdain for the rapist rather than identification with the rapist's behavior as sexual prowess. Sadly, McCabe's tongue-in-cheek proposal is on target. Indecent exposure, though only a legal misdemeanor on first conviction, becomes, in some states, a felony after a second conviction. The growing gravity of the problem of rape and the entrenched prejudice that makes it so difficult to mobilize social pressure to stop it may make such strategies, proposed in jest, a serious option for women.

Rape does not, of course, exhaust the spectrum of violence against women in the guise of sex. As more women gain the courage to talk about their personal lives, the magnitude and extent of violence and coercion via sexuality becomes clear. Violence in marriage increasingly appears to be as much the rule as the exception, including those forced genital assaults not even counted as rape.[25] Sexual harassment in the workplace and in academia is widespread, taking overt and covert forms. Many women tolerate physical advances, verbal exploitation, and inappropriate intimate behavior from men out of fear of economic and professional reprisals, failing grades, or professional or academic badmouthing. As Marilyn Frye has observed, men often presume access to women's bodies and emotions as the rightful legacy of socially sanctioned male supremacy.[26] While some of the connections between male supremacist ideology and social violence have begun to be explored, much more analysis is needed. To appreciate how deep the ramifications of our culture's confusion about eroticism and violence are, we must make the connections between our emotive attachments to relations of domination, or superior/inferior power, and pervasive fear of relations of equality and intimacy. Sadomasochistic human relationships, whether subtle or openly violent, permeate our society and our social institutions.[27]

Two related issues profoundly affect female sexuality in this culture. Pornography and prostitution are pervasive social realities, and what to do about them is hotly debated among feminists. There are strong disagreements about what evaluations are to be made of prostitution and what strategies are appropriate to contain pornography. A much debated issue is how law and legal enforcement should shape public policy on prostitution and pornography. With respect to prostitution, feminists are well aware of the antifemale effects of enforcement of antiprostitution laws. Furthermore, enforcement of antiprostitution laws falls unequally and most heavily on the poor and nonwhite prostitute, who most often works the street rather than the "social club." Prostitutes are usually women, and while, from one point of view, they do "sell" their bodies as commodities of exchange and live by this "sale," feminists recognize that women's exchange of sex for economic security is a general characteristic of female existence, given patriarchy, and is hardly limited to female prostitution. Self-righteous stigmatization of prostitutes is hardly in order if we acknowledge that throughout history women have had to "sell" themselves as sexual beings into marriage or long-term sexual liaisons to survive. For considerable segments of socially marginated females, women's "oldest profession" often has also been women's *only* profession. To comprehend the dynamics of sexual politics is to be rightly reluctant to join the social censure of the female prostitute.

Even so, feminist social policy discussion about prostitution divides concerned women.[28] Most feminists agree in opposing a shift to *legalization* of prostitution. Such policy stamps the seal of public approval on purchasing women's sexual services or paying for the "use" of women's bodies, and invariably places prostitutes themselves directly under state licensing and control. Women are required to "register" to practice their "profession" and must submit to regular medical examinations. Many feminists argue for a social policy of *decriminalizing* prostitution; removing all laws and regulations that either prohibit or sanction the practice. This mitigates the double stigma women who are prostitutes bear. The decriminalization of prostitution does nothing to reduce its social functionality because the institution is deeply rooted in sexism, including those deeply ingrained patterns of economic exploitation of women already analyzed. Furthermore, the line between legalization and decriminalization seems not to work in practice. Nevada has claims to "decriminalize" prostitution, but tight governmental supervision creates a de facto situation of "legalization," by placing prostitutes under tight state control. In any case, those negative public dimensions of prostitution such as pandering and aggressive, offensive street solicitation are better controlled by vigorous enforcement of public nuisance ordinances and financial penalties than through criminal law.

What constitutes constructive social policy in relation to pornography poses far more difficult issues and has bitterly divided feminists.[29] There is, inevitably, a fine line between what constitutes appropriate, sexually explicit material, or erotica, on the one hand and obscene or pornographic material on the other. Determinations of criteria for distinguishing erotica and pornography are difficult at best. Under current law, especially, the distinction is distressingly unclear. Recent Supreme Court rulings on the matter make no attempt at a principled solution. It is now left to local communities to determine what is "obscene," which opens the way to a crazy-quilt diversity of criteria across the country. What is obscene in one area is considered appropriate artistic expression in another. Our situation is an inducement to ambitious local politicians to cultivate and cater to repressive local political pressures. In the midst of this, feminists have mobilized to protest the sort of hard-core pornography that makes women the masochistic objects of male sexual sadism. Pornography is a vast, growing, high-profit sector of our economy, and antipornography feminists rightly contend that current pornography broadcasts the message that women exist to be used by men and actually enjoy male exploitation and control. In spite of controversies about how much exposure to this sort of pornographic material actually affects people's behavior patterns, it is incontrovertible that pornography on a grand scale feeds a social ethos of violence and exploitation of women. It is also true that current law has opened the way for ambitious politicians and law enforcement officers to harass pornography producers and distributors. Legal action is taken arbitrarily, closing or bankrupting some pornography entrepreneurs while ignoring the activity of others. Civil libertarians, including many feminists, have serious reservations not only about current Supreme Court policy but also about other feminists' failure to recognize that some strategies against pornography can set precedents for government censorship that could be turned on feminists.

For those who believe that the role of the state with respect to sexuality should be less directed at imposing uniform personal moral standards on adults than at adjudicating competing claims and interests, pornography poses vexing issues. No one should obscure the fact that pornographic material does encourage exploitation, especially of women and children, but there are those who seek access to it nevertheless. In any case, feminist efforts to clarify differences between erotica and obscenity should target our objections to pornography in terms of violence and control, not at the explicitness of sex acts or genitalia. Materials can be offensive to purported "community standards" for both reasons. It is the sadism of pornography — the imposition and enjoyment of another's suffering — that is morally reprehensible, not the explicitness of sexuality. Feminist efforts to resist and discredit hard-core pornography must be carefully conceived, in full awareness that strong traditions of respect for the constitutional liberty of free speech is much needed by such "radical" women as ourselves. We cannot summarily dismiss such concerns. It would be naive to assume that any dubious legal tactics aimed against pornographers would not subsequently also be used against us.

I believe that feminists should expose publicly the names of those who control and profit from the pornography industry, that we should boycott pornography in selected instances, and that we need well-conceived public demonstrations to make people aware of women's objections to the pervasive pornography of this culture. We need to know who profits from porn and identify the celebration of domination that it is transmitting. However, we also need a vivid sense that there is a difference between erotica and porn and avoid antisexual or antisensual attitudes. Our awareness must be keen that efforts to erode "rights to privacy" threaten social radicals whenever it suits those in power to discredit political opposition.

Men's Lives and Social Policy

Men, *qua* male, do not suffer from the range of sexual inequities before the law that women do. Except in those cases where an earlier "soft-feminism" led to changes in marriage, divorce, and custody laws that extended compensatory favors to women, the legal and social disadvantages men suffer are related to race and poverty rather than to gender. Two areas most often singled out for legal reform by men are provisions for alimony that do not take into account a woman's capacity to earn a living and child custody laws that presume the mother possesses "natural" competence in childrearing that fathers do not share. These are areas in which injustices sometimes do occur, though it also needs to be observed that changes in men's favor here often have been more rapid than changes in areas where women are disadvantaged. Furthermore, even where child support and alimony settlements are made formally in women's favor, enforcement of these settlements is notoriously weak. Women usually have to rely on men's voluntary cooperation.

Our sexist presuppositions about sex roles, including presumptions about women's special responsibility for parenting, do not encourage men to exercise genuine responsibility for children's continued economic well-being after divorce. Therefore, until and unless women's broader economic vulnerability in society is rectified, most women will continue to support the "favoritism" implicit in divorce and child custody laws as compensation for the objective economic disadvantage that looms so large in our lives. Many women's only alternative to alimony and child support is the welfare system, with all the personal degradation it entails, or low-paying work, the only sort of employment available to the growing number of female single-parent heads of households. As a result, divorce and child custody are both acrimonious issues that are difficult to resolve by legal reform. Only if support for men's claims to justice in family law are balanced by unwavering commitment to improving women's disadvantaged economic situation and to changing men's parenting roles in the family can we avoid a further deterioration in women's situation by legal reform in this area.

The key to constructive change in family policy lies in the direction of redefining the meaning of parenting in society. For men to accept full and equal responsibility as parents, broad-based changes must occur. Of special importance are changes in the structure and organization of the work men do. At the very least, men should have paternity leaves when needed and be able to limit claims on their time made by employers or clients. The current expectation that men's lives are to be immersed totally in work thwarts and undermines voluntary male change. Male professionals, including clergy, often are the worst offenders in neglecting their families or refusing shared parenting because their social functions imply "total access" for their clients. Both men and women need to be able to adjust work schedules to permit some flexibility in sharing the care of children. In principle, professional people often have the advantage over wage earners because the latter are constrained by a regular and rigid work day. Social pressures, however, do not encourage men in any social stratum to reorient actively their lives toward parenting. Upward mobility in corporations and professions increasingly requires that family life be neglected and that one parent, usually the woman, take on childrearing full time. Only a sustained reorientation in the organization of work in our dominant economic and social institutions could alter this dynamic. Many couples now are seeking genuine role-sharing, including "shared parenting," [30] but because their efforts cut against the institutional grain, such couples often must make economic sacrifice and positive life changes only by dint of extra energy. No social or institutional support exists to facilitate these conscientious and constructive efforts of sensitive people.

Those of us concerned with Christian ethics need to underscore the extent to which the church is a serious offender in relation to shared parenting. As institutional employer, the church requires its clergy "professionals," men and women alike, to be "totally available." Invariably such expectations operate to the detriment of the family life of clergy. Religious organizations need to be reminded that they bear much responsibility for long-standing "modeling" of this morally dubious pattern. It is not an overstatement to say that male clerical parenting has long expressed itself as a form of active child neglect. The time has come for the church to rectify such disastrous practices. Criteria of ministry for married persons should presume that professional competence entails the capacity for responsible parenting so that married clergy with children come to be expected, always, to make childrearing a personal-professional priority.

Heterosexism and Social Policy vis-à-vis Homosexual Persons

There are, of course, numerous dimensions of social policy that must be addressed if we are to extend justice to nonheterosexuals and to the prevalent experience of homoeroticism. Because of the strength of institutionalized heterosexism in this society, including in the workplace, gay men and lesbians are subject to continuous and arbitrary discrimination. Legal protections to ensure the civil liberties of gays and lesbians, even when these exist, do not usually touch the depth of active homophobia. Like nonwhite persons, gays and lesbians are subject to subtle or vicious and direct retributions, to which heterosexuals can remain oblivious. No address to social policy questions in light of heterosexism as a system of social oppression can ignore the varied and widespread injustices gay men and lesbians endure.

The public policy stance of liberal religious groups in support of the civil liberties of homosexual persons is, as indicated, equivocal and frequently halfhearted. The public policy positions of such groups are easily dismissed in the public arena because of the exclusion of gays and lesbians from ordination and from other indices of full participation in the life of the churches. The tepid and reluctant entry of churches into public debate about gay civil rights is greeted with contempt by mature gay men and lesbians who do not wish to be patronized and who rightly refuse the church's feeble "charity." Homophobia is so deeply rooted in ecclesiastical culture that facing its depth requires painful self-awareness.

At the public policy level, two areas for legal change are often targeted by gay men and lesbians seeking to overturn those laws that have most destructive consequences. Many gay men and lesbians object to the lack of legal protection afforded to their relationships, which makes mutual care between them and their lovers difficult. Second, a prejudicial legal pattern jeopardizes lesbians' and gay men's custody rights to their own children or makes it difficult for them to choose to adopt or bear children.

For heterosexual couples and families, the legal status of marriage conveys some rights and protections and much moral legitimacy. Gay and lesbian couples committed to each other have none of these legal protections, even when the lived-world character of their partnership has exactly the same qualities as the heterosexual marital arrangements so celebrated and sanctified by religious communities. Without access to the prerogatives and protections of legal marital status, gay and lesbian couples can be prevented from carrying out their commitments to each other in numerous ways. In the event of injury to one partner, the mate cannot easily provide the health care benefits or continuing economic security that heterosexual partners take for granted. The death of one leaves no economic security to his or her mate as does the death of an insured heterosexual man or woman. Often lovers are not permitted to participate, as family members automatically are, in decisions regarding potential medical treatment of their closest loved one or to intervene in case of medical emergencies. It seems to me that the most minimal claims of justice require legal reforms that can enable gay men and lesbians to define a same-sex partner as a "spouse." To be sure, not all gays and lesbians seek or want such relationships, but those who do should have equal protection under the law and legal sanction of the commitments they make.

Obviously, a related question for religious communities concerns whether they will recognize, sanctify, and celebrate "marriages" or partnerships between same-sex persons regardless of the state's responsiveness or lack of it to claims of equal justice before the law. It is ironic that religious people frequently criticize gay men and lesbians for their "promiscuity" and "laxity" while adamantly refusing to support committed same-sex relationships as they support heterosexual coupling.

Heterosexism and discrimination against gays currently falls especially hard on lesbians in custody battles involving children. Reputed homosexuality is one of the few "accusations" that all but guarantees that a woman will be judged incompetent as a mother before the court. But gay men are also penalized in this regard. Beneath these social practices lurks a deep-seated, though mistaken, view that homosexuality is "contagious," along with the vicious and erroneous belief that lesbians are less capable than nonlesbians of extending positive nurturance and healthy support to children. Perhaps a majority of lesbians do marry and bear children prior to clarifying their own mature emotional needs, but most are highly competent nurturers precisely because of their hard-won level of self-awareness. Decisions about parental competence must be made for all persons — male and female — on actual performance, not on stereotype or social phobia. Until the moral dubiousness of treating homoeroticism as a "problem" is recognized, along with the questionableness of extending automatic, uncritical moral endorsement to so many loveless, graceless heterosexual relationships, Christian moral teaching on sexual relationships is not likely to gain the respect of any but the socially conventional. If heterosexuality and heterosexual mating continue to be given uncritical religious and moral sanctification and legitimation simply because they are heterosexual, how can we teach anything morally normative about what constitutes humane interpersonal relationships? So long as heterosexual coupling continues to serve as a major operative exclusionary principle and structural constraint in our religious communities, we will perpetuate an uncritical, even conventional, sexual ethic rather than an active and emphatic ethic of interpersonal love and responsibility. Meanwhile, in the wider society, the movement for gender justice and for gay and lesbian self-respect and rights will continue to be pressed at the public policy level by those wounded by traditional Christian teaching. As our society's understandings of human sexuality become ever less stereotyped, the gap between church teaching and mature human experience will widen, reducing further the credibility of the churches' presumed "ethic" of sexuality. By marginating themselves from constructive and humane social struggle, religious communities become not more righteous but more rigid and less alive to movements of the Spirit.

Families and Selected Aspects of Marriage
That Require Social Policy Review

The problematics of existing social policies affecting families and the institution of marriage are so complex that I can touch on only a few obvious issues here. It should be clear that I do not believe that a sexual ethic can any longer give direct, or even indirect, support to the notion that living one's life in the heterosexual, lifelong family unit places one in a status of special moral merit or that this lifestyle warrants superior theological legitimation. Long-term, committed relationships do provide a strong environment for personal growth and for childrearing, so there is good reason to insist that social policies support rather than constrain people's option for this sort of family relation. We must not imagine, however, that what some have called the "crisis of the family" — that is, the growing rate of divorce — is altogether negative morally. Nor should we assume that the growing numbers of failed marriages are caused merely by changing individual attitudes toward the family, as if the divorce rate were chiefly a result of personal inability to make a "go" of family life. Social institutions and political-economic structures operate on the family, locking it in or changing it. The family pressures that children, women, and men find dehumanizing are generated from changes in the wider social structure, which in turn occasion the "crisis" of the family. In the broad segments of our society where genuine economic security is lacking — among the poor, among semiskilled poor wage laborers, among all persons vulnerable to marginality, many of whom are nonwhite — the current dynamics of the economy and some public policies actually operate directly to destroy the family unit. Public welfare payments, limited to dependent children and their mothers, drive fathers out of the home, reward so-called illegitimacy, and encourage family breakup. Among the working poor, where wives often *must* work, provision for adequate day-care facilities for children is very rare, yet a mother's wages are critical to the continued economic viability of the family unit. No one should imagine that the need for adequate day-care programs is a "woman's issue." Adequate day care is basic to the well-being not only of whole families but of society itself.

Younger people who understand some of the positive possibilities of new lifestyle alternatives place increasing emphasis on living with another person prior to marriage as a means of testing the long-term viability of a relationship. I believe that such "trial relationships" should be encouraged as positive and ethically appropriate. At the public policy level we need to ask whether such living arrangements and covenant commitments that fall short of the "death-do-us-part" intentions of traditional marriage should be extended some legal standing. Extending civil legitimacy to such arrangements would lower the pressure and stigma against them. As long as the state regulates marriage at all, it is probably wiser to provide for dual-level legal relationships between couples. Couples might enter into a simple legal status, easily dissolved, unless or until they were prepared to function together as a childbearing, childrearing unit. The first level, an easily dissolvable, legal contractual relationship, would not involve all of the current common-law assumptions about the "one-person" status of a married couple. This first-level "marriage" would permit couples to designate, by contract, those areas of joint standing under law that they agree to assume. Such arrangements could vary somewhat from couple to couple. The second-level, more inclusive legal marriage provision involving common-law precedents could come into play only when couples wished it or when couples agreed to have children.

Such a social policy direction certainly carries attendant problems. One might be the possible increased complexity of litigation surrounding marginal circumstances not explicitly covered by the first-level law. The proliferation of marriage law could mean a proliferation of the legal services needed to cope with such laws unless continued progress is made to simplify legal procedures for interpersonal coupling. Another might be the reinforcement and extension of the social norm of coupling as the expected lifestyle in our society. On the other side of the question, though, we need to acknowledge that current social policies penalize and often stigmatize responsible persons who perceive that they are not yet ready to enter into marriage as currently defined by law but who have accepted some of the mutual responsibilities of relationship and cohabitation. Just as the unavailability of married status penalizes many same-sex couples who live a paired lifestyle, so our all-or-nothing approach to marriage works to discourage mature, step-by-step relational commitments.

Recent legal reform has established a trend in marriage law that deserves continued support. Many states have moved to institute no-fault divorce law provisions. While the form of these laws varies considerably from state to state, most aim to open the way for couples who have mutually agreed to end their marriages to do so without harassment or great legal expense. These new laws no longer require one party to accept the divorce and the other to assume "blame" for the failure of the marriage. The end of a marriage is always painful, at best, and most often debilitating to both parties involved, whatever their circumstances. Reform that facilitates the process of securing a divorce by removing the power of the court to adjudicate blame and that maximizes the competence of partners to deliberate the conditions of the dissolution of their marriage represents highly desirable change. In matters of intimacy, social policy should involve the least amount of intrusion by the state that is commensurate with the dignity of the persons involved, with the well-being of their children, and with the greater social vulnerability of women in cases where that applies.

To cease giving overriding direct and indirect ethical sanction to lifelong heterosexual monogamous marriage would not, I submit, encourage us to antifamily attitudes or to opposition to lifelong relational commitments between two persons. We need to recognize that marriage is not for everyone. At the same time, we can and should affirm, celebrate, and support all covenantal relationships that deepen our capacity for intimacy, creative work, and joyful community, whether or not they accord with the current legally permissible definitions of marriage. Since marriage in our society is primarily a legal relationship, we should make marriage as amenable as possible to the life situations of mature adults. Religiously and morally, we need to differentiate more sharply the legal institution of marriage from the religious relationship of covenant between persons that our religious ethics and theology embrace as normative for human well-being. Simultaneously, though, we need to acknowledge the reverse reality: Where the legal status of marriage is not available, long-term committed relationships are harder to sustain within our social order. We need to support legal efforts to create the conditions that sustain them.

A fundamental rethinking of the ethics of marriage and family life, a reconsideration that delivers us from confusing existing social institutions with ethically and theologically envisioned standards of relationship, is, to say the least, long overdue. A profound ethic of sexuality could help us gain a more adequate perspective on the diversity of failures that characterize committed human relationships. Broken covenants, terminated marriages and primary relationships frequently involve moral fault, but not always. Some divorces, or relational closures, are the result of positive moral growth and courage.[31] We need to be able to help people recognize that there are moral reasons as well as morally dubious ones for ending relationships. Few efforts have been made in religious ethics to identify positive justifications for such termination. And even when moral failure is involved, such failure surely should not lead to the condemnation or exclusion of the persons who have failed. It is ironic that we Christians, who profess to be a community of sinners in need of forgiveness, often are unable to help persons in our own midst accept, live through, and learn from primary relational failures in a way that enables them to experience forgiveness, healing, and growth.

Conclusion

Many of the thorniest questions of social policy in relation to sexuality will continue to pose dilemmas for morally concerned persons whatever happens in the future. Even if we succeed in deepening our awareness of the connections between personal intimacy patterns and the sociopolitical and economic forces that mold our lives, the constructive shaping of our personal-social relationships is a challenge that does not admit easy solutions. How societies should function, through government, to influence individual behavior is always a difficult question. How and in which ways sexual behavior should be shaped is, perhaps, the hardest question of all.

Efforts to regulate sexual conduct between consenting adults are notoriously difficult and, as I have observed, are fraught with potential for the abuse of state power. Enforcement of laws regulating sexual conduct are more the exception than the rule. The temptation of government authorities to use techniques of police entrapment to catch "sexual offenders" seems inexorable, and the tendency toward corrupt use of public authority in enforcement is strong. This state of affairs is probably inevitable because sexuality involves intimate spaces — where we sleep, dress, and retire for privacy. Given our dominant value patterns, such enforcement will always catch the poor, relatively powerless, socially marginated offenders, while more privileged lawbreakers go free. Conversely, sexual entrapment can always be used against those whose political views are unpopular. Nothing can reduce the tension between those provisional rights to privacy that we all need and initiatives to use law to encourage a positive moral climate regarding sexual conduct because monitoring sexual conduct requires intrusive observation. As a result, our presumptive stance should be that restrictive law needs to be used sparingly where sexuality is involved. In the face of this fact, all of us should exercise caution in looking to government for simple redress of grievances because others' sexual conduct offends our personal moral sensibilities. In spite of considerable social pressure on the churches to demand legal action to curtail "dubious" sexual behavior, we need to exercise critical sensibility and a healthy dose of skepticism as to what such laws actually accomplish.

How a society may best live with this tension between the diverse personal sensibilities of adults and the need for a degree of public order will always be subject to debate. I have already made it clear that we would be well served by considerably "desexualizing" our criminal codes. Morally evil behaviors that are frequently classified as sex offenses — molestation or exploitation of young children, rape, publicly intrusive pandering of sexually explicit or obscene material, and the offensive hawking of sexual devices, including solicitation for prostitution — are wrong, in different degrees, not because they involve genitally explicit activity but because they express morally inappropriate power relations between people — physical and psychic assault or obvious insensitivity to the dignity of another person's rights and capacity for self-direction. The most heinous of these so-called sex crimes are not more "especially wrong" than other acts of violence, unjustified coercion, or manipulation, though in a sex-phobic society "sex crimes" are experienced as especially "dirty" or polluting. These acts are wrong because they involve the harassment or the abuse and degradation of persons who are relatively powerless to resist. Such acts *intend* humiliation or control. Genital or sexual intrusion is perceived as the best way to express contempt or to establish power over another person. Legal changes that desexualize criminal law while strengthening legal sanctions against any bodily harassment or assault toward children or nonconsenting adults might go a long way toward helping us disentangle our fears of sexuality from our fears of being humiliated by other persons through contemptuous physical abuse aimed at the most vulnerable areas of our bodies. No unjustified violence toward another's body, against that person's will, should ever be construed as a sign of positive erotic capacity or mature action. Rather, such actions are usually rooted in fear of closeness and mutuality. They express a need for control and a disordered incapacity for relationship over an appropriate capacity for interdependence. Victims of so-called sex crimes often are more stigmatized than the perpetrators of the crimes because such offenses stereotype victims as sexually "impure." It is time to recognize that those who are recipients of violent "sexual" acts are *not* sexually polluted; they have been victimized by ugly acts of human retribution, evil because of the contempt for persons they express rather than the genital contact they involve.

If acts of coercion and violence involving genitals are "desexualized" and understood as crimes of assault and bodily intrusion, it may be possible to see more clearly why minimal regulation of sexual conduct between consenting adults by the state is desirable, even a positive moral good. If there is any "zone of privacy" that requires, seriously, to be sacrosanct and respected, it is a person's right to bodily integrity. Our body-selves, the zone of body-space we possess by virtue of our being embodied persons, deserve explicit protection from arbitrary interference and unjustified coercion. "Consent" at this level is a condition of having a moral relationship. From a moral point of view, embracing "consent" as a criterion is not to deny a norm or to be merely "permissive." In our most intimate, interpersonal relations, consent or self-direction is a critical condition of human well-being. Space in which it can be expressed is a social good. Those who govern with regard for the conditions of a just society do well to respect this reality. Honoring the decisions regarding sexual expression between consenting adults is not a negative moral norm but a positive moral value. We ought to possess the conditions for nonconstrained expression of intimacy.

We must not be romantic about the quality of sexual communication that characterizes our society. We are sex-preoccupied but neither genuinely sensual nor genuinely pleasure-oriented. Because much that passes for sexual liberation is only a blend of alienated technological consciousness with the most puerile notions of what good male/female eroticism involves — notions, alas, often imitated in same-sex eroticism — we have no reason to celebrate the actual "quality" of the presumed new "sexual liberation" overall. Nevertheless, there are hopeful indications that through "our bodies, ourselves," some of us are learning to ground our capacity for personal fulfillment and for genuine mutuality. The affirmation of our capacity for giving and receiving pleasure and for appropriating our self-worth in and through our bodies has also begun to lead to an important demystification of our sexuality. The ancient idea that sexuality itself is an irrational, alien, even evil power, deeply foreign to our personal integrity and outside the range of our self-direction, is giving way to new integrations of psychosexual identity with socially fulfilling action. The fact that some can now celebrate sexuality as an important, albeit not all-controlling, aspect of selfhood, having learned to value it as a deep mode of communication, is a great step forward. Sexuality involves pleasure and erotic intensity, but it also expresses playfulness, tenderness, and a generalized sense of well-being.

Our culture expresses simultaneously an animalistic affirmation and prim denial of sexuality. We do not yet see clearly that our capacity for caring, for expressing and receiving deep feeling, for reaching out to others is grounded in and through our bodies or not at all. Given this insight, the way is now open for us to affirm genuinely what we have long given lip service to in our theologies — that our sexuality is a gift of God. Positive affirmation of our sensuality leads to the understanding that when we abuse our sexuality, it is not because we have been too free or too permissive or too spontaneous. Rather, it is because our capacity for intimacy and sensual communication has been twisted and distorted by manipulative and nonmutual patterns of relationship. If we cannot tolerate mutually respectful and mutually enhancing erotic communication, if we prefer relational patterns of conquest or subservience, sadism or masochism, or if we are stuck in compulsive, inappropriate, and repetitive patterns of action, it is because we have failed to find the positive power of our own being as sexual persons. If this is so, no repudiation of sexuality, as such, will deliver us. Rather, what we need is a deepened and more holistic sense of ourselves that will enable us to grow sexually, to celebrate, and to respect our own sexuality and that of others. Today no Christian ethics of sexuality can straddle the fence or hedge positive affirmations with qualified Victorian bets of modified prudery. Too many have learned to celebrate the wondrous gift of our created being to want to go back on the discovery.

THEOLOGY AND MORALITY
OF PROCREATIVE CHOICE*

With Shirley Cloyes

Much discussion of abortion betrays the heavy hand of misogyny, the hatred of women. We all have a responsibility to recognize this bias — sometimes subtle — when ancient negative attitudes toward women intrude into the abortion debate. It is morally incumbent on us to convert the Christian position to a teaching more respectful of women's concrete history and experience.

My professional peers who are my opponents on this question feel they own the Christian tradition in this matter and recognize no need to rethink their positions in the light of this claim. As a feminist, I cannot sit in silence when women's right to shape the use of our own procreative power is denied. Women's competence as moral decision makers is once again challenged by the state even before the moral basis of women's right to procreative choice has been fully elaborated and recognized. Those who deny women control of procreative power claim that they do so in defense of moral sensibility, in the name of the sanctity of human life. We have a long way to go before the sanctity of human life will include genuine regard and concern for every female already born, and no social policy discussion that obscures this fact deserves to be called moral. We hope the day will come when it will not be called "Christian" either, for the Christian ethos is the generating source of the current moral crusade to prevent women from gaining control over the most life-shaping power we possess.

Although I am a Protestant, my own "moral theology" [1] has more in common with a Catholic approach than with much neoorthodox ethics of my own tradition. I want to stress this at the

---

* This essay was adapted from articles appearing in the July and September 1981 issues of *The Witness* (vol. 64, nos. 7 and 9) and in Edward Batchelor, ed., *Abortion: The Moral Issues* (New York: Pilgrim Press, 1982). The reluctant author could not face a further revision of this essay, so its greater clarity is a result of Shirley Cloyes's collaboration. For a fuller discussion of these issues, see Beverly Wildung Harrison, *Our Right to Choose: Toward a New Ethic of Abortion* (Boston: Beacon Press, 1983).

outset because in what follows I am highly critical of the reigning Roman Catholic social teaching on procreation and abortion. I believe that on most other issues of social justice, the Catholic tradition is often more substantive, morally serious, and less imbued with the dominant economic ideology than the brand of Protestant theological ethics that claims biblical warrants for its moral norms. I am no biblicist; I believe that the human wisdom that informs our ethics derives not from using the Bible alone but from reflecting in a manner that earlier Catholic moral theologians referred to as consonant with "natural law."[2] Unfortunately, however, all major strands of natural law reflection have been every bit as awful as Protestant biblicism on any matter involving human sexuality, including discussion of women's nature and women's divine vocation in relation to procreative power. And it is precisely because I recognize Catholic natural law tradition as having produced the most sophisticated type of moral reflection among Christians that I believe it must be challenged where it intersects negatively with women's lives.

Given the depth of my dissatisfaction with Protestant moral tradition, I take no pleasure in singling out Roman Catholic moral theology and the activity of the Catholic hierarchy on the abortion issue. The problem nevertheless remains that there is really only one set of moral claims involved in the Christian antiabortion argument. Protestants who oppose procreative choice[3] either tend to follow official Catholic moral theology on these matters or ground their positions in biblicist anti-intellectualism, claiming that God's "word" requires no justification other than their attestation that divine utterance says what it says. Against such irrationalism, no rational objections have a chance. When, however, Protestant fundamentalists actually specify the reasons why they believe abortion is evil, they invariably revert to traditional natural law assumptions about women, sexuality, and procreation. Hence, direct objection must be registered to the traditional natural law framework if we are serious about transforming Christian moral teaching on abortion.

To do a methodologically adequate analysis of any moral problem in religious social ethics it is necessary to (1) situate the problem in the context of various religious communities' theologies or "generative" stories, (2) do a critical historical review of the problem as it appears in our religious traditions and in the concrete lives of human agents (so that we do not confuse the past and the present), (3) scrutinize the problem from the standpoint of various moral theories, and (4) analyze existing social policy and potential alternatives to determine our "normative moral sense" or best judgment of what ought to be done in contemporary society. Although these methodological basepoints must be addressed in any socioethical analysis, their treatment is crucial when abortion is under discussion because unexamined theological presumptions and misrepresentations of Christian history figure heavily in the current public policy debate. Given the brevity of this essay, I will address the theological, Christian historical, and moral theoretical problematics first and analyze the social policy dimensions of the abortion issue only at the end, even though optimum ethical methodology would reverse this procedure.

Abortion in Theological Context

In the history of Christian theology, a central metaphor for understanding life, including human life, is as a gift of God. Creation itself has been interpreted primarily under this metaphor. It follows that in this creational context procreation itself took on special significance as the central image for the divine blessing of human life. The elevation of procreation as the central symbol of divine benevolence happened over time, however. It did not, for instance, typify the very early, primitive Christian community. The synoptic gospels provide ample evidence that procreation played no such metaphorical role in early Christianity.[4] In later Christian history, an emergent powerful antisexual bias within Christianity made asceticism the primary spiritual ideal, although this ideal usually stood in tension with procreative power as a second sacred expression of divine blessing. But by the time of the Protestant Reformation, there was clear reaffirmation of the early Israelite theme of procreative blessing, and procreation has since become all but synonymous among Christians with the theological theme of creation as divine gift. It is important to observe that Roman Catholic theology actually followed on and adapted to Protestant teaching on this point.[5] Only in the last century, with the recognition of the danger of dramatic population growth in a world of finite resources, has any question been raised about the appropriateness of this unqualified theological sacralization of procreation.

The elevation of procreation as the central image for divine blessing is intimately connected to the rise of patriarchy. In patriarchal societies it is the male's power that is enhanced by the gift of new life. Throughout history, women's power of procreation has stood in definite tension with this male social control. In fact, what we feminists call patriarchy — that is, patterned or institutionalized legitimations of male superiority — derives from the need of men, through male-dominated political institutions such as tribes, states, and religious systems, to control women's power to procreate the species. We must assume, then, that many of these efforts at social control of procreation, including some church teaching on contraception and abortion, were part of this institutional system. The perpetuation of patriarchal control itself depended on wresting the power of procreation from women and shaping women's lives accordingly.

In the past four centuries, the entire Christian story has had to undergo dramatic accommodation to new and emergent world conditions and to the scientific revolution. As the older theological metaphors for creation encountered the rising power of science, a new self-understanding including our human capacity to affect nature had to be incorporated into Christian theology or its central theological story would have become obscurantist. Human agency had to be introjected into a dialectical understanding of creation.

The range of human freedom to shape and enhance creation is now celebrated theologically, but only up to the point of changes in our understanding of what is natural for women. Here a barrier has been drawn that declares No Radical Freedom! The only difference between mainstream Protestant and Roman Catholic theologians on these matters is at the point of contraception, which Protestants more readily accept. However, Protestants like Karl Barth and Helmut Thielicke exhibit a subtle shift of mood when they turn to discussing issues regarding women. They follow the typical Protestant pattern: They have accepted contraception or family planning as part of the new freedom, granted by God, but both draw back from the idea that abortion could be morally acceptable. In *The Ethics of Sex*, Thielicke offers a romantic, ecstatic celebration of family planning on one page and then elaborates a total denunciation of abortion as unthinkable on the next.[6] Most Christian theological opinion draws the line between contraception and abortion, whereas the *official* Catholic teaching still anathematizes contraception.

The problem, then, is that Christian theology celebrates the power of human freedom to shape and determine the quality of human life except when the issue of procreative choice arises. Abortion is anathema, while widespread sterilization abuse goes unnoticed. The power of man to shape creation radically is never rejected. When one stops to consider the awesome power over nature that males take for granted and celebrate, including the power to alter the conditions of human life in myriad ways, the suspicion dawns that the near hysteria that prevails about the immorality of women's right to choose abortion derives its force from the ancient power of misogyny rather than from any passion for the sacredness of human life. An index of the continuing misogyny in Christian tradition is male theologians' refusal to recognize the full range of human power to shape creation in those matters that pertain to women's power to affect the quality of our lives.

In contrast, a feminist theological approach recognizes that nothing is more urgent, in light of the changing circumstances of human beings on planet Earth, than to recognize that the entire natural-historical context of human procreative power has shifted.[7] We desperately need a desacralization of our biological power to reproduce[8] and at the same time a real concern for human dignity and the social conditions for personhood and the values of human relationship.[9] And note that desacralization does not mean complete devaluation of the worth of procreation. It means we must shift away from the notion that the central metaphors for divine blessing are expressed at the biological level to the recognition that our social relations bear the image of what is most holy. An excellent expression of this point comes from Marie Augusta Neal, a Roman Catholic feminist and a distinguished sociologist of religion:

> As long as the central human need called for was continued motivation to propagate the race, it was essential that religious symbols idealize that process above all others. Given the vicissitudes of life in a hostile environment, women had to be encouraged to bear children and men to support them: childbearing was central to the struggle for existence. Today, however, the size of the base population, together with knowledge already accumulated about artificial insemination, sperm banking, cloning, make more certain a peopled world.
>
> The more serious human problems now are who will live, who will die and who will decide.[10]

A Critical Historical Review of Abortion: An Alternative Perspective

Between persons who oppose all abortions on moral grounds and those who believe abortion is sometimes or frequently morally justifiable, there is no difference of moral principle. Pro-choice advocates and antiabortion advocates share the ethical principle of respect for human life, which is probably why the debate is so acrimonious. I have already indicated that one major source of disagreement is the way in which the theological story is appropriated in relation to the changing circumstances of history. In addition, we should recognize that whenever strong moral disagreement is encountered, we simultaneously confront different readings of the history of a moral issue. The way we interpret the past is already laden with and shaped by our present sense of what the moral problem is.

For example, professional male Christian ethicists tend to assume that Christianity has an unbroken history of "all but absolute" prohibition of abortion and that the history of morality of abortion can best be traced by studying the teaching of the now best-remembered theologians. Looking at the matter this way, one can find numerous proof-texts to show that some of the "church fathers" condemned abortion and equated abortion with either homicide or murder. Whenever a "leading" churchman equated abortion with homicide or murder, he also *and simultaneously* equated *contraception* with homicide or murder. This reflects not only male chauvinist biology but also the then almost phobic antisexual bias of the Christian tradition. Claims that one can separate abortion teaching into an ethic of killing separate from an antisexual and antifemale ethic in the history of Christianity do not withstand critical scrutiny.[11]

The history of Christian natural law ethics is totally conditioned by the equation of any effort to control procreation with homicide. However, this antisexual, antiabortion tradition is not universal, even among theologians and canon lawyers. On the subject of sexuality and its abuse, many well-known theologians had nothing to say; abortion was not even mentioned in most moral theology. An important, untold chapter in Christian history is the great struggle that took place in the medieval period when clerical celibacy came to be imposed and the rules of sexual behavior rigidified.

My thesis is that there is a relative disinterest in the question of abortion overall in Christian history. Occasionally, Christian theologians picked up the issue, especially when these theologians were state-related, that is, were articulating policy not only for the church but for political authority. Demographer Jean Meyer, himself a Catholic, insists that the Christian tradition took over "expansion by population growth" from the Roman Empire.[12] Christians opposed abortion strongly only when Christianity was closely identified with imperial state policy or when theologians were inveighing against women and any sexuality except that expressed in the reluctant service of procreation.

The Holy Crusade quality of present teaching on abortion is quite new in Christianity and is related to cultural shifts that are requiring the Christian tradition to choose sides in the present ideological struggle under pressure to rethink its entire attitude toward women and sexuality. My research has led me to the tentative conclusion that, in Protestant cultures, except where Protestantism is the "established religion," merging church and state, one does not find a strong antiabortion theological-ethical teaching at all. At least in the United States, this is beyond historical debate.[13] No Protestant clergy or theologian gave early support for proposed nineteenth-century laws banning abortion in the United States. It is my impression that Protestant clergy, usually married and often poor, were aware that romanticizing nature's bounty with respect to procreation resulted in a great deal of human suffering. The Protestant clergy who finally did join the antiabortion crusade were racist, classist white clergy, who feared America's strength was being threatened because white, middle-class, respectable women had a lower birth rate than black and ethnic women. Such arguments are still with us.

One other historical point must be stressed. Until the late nineteenth century the natural law tradition, and biblicism following it, tended to define the act of abortion as interruption of pregnancy after ensoulment, which was understood to be the point at which the breath of God entered the fetus. The point at which ensoulment was said to occur varied, but most typically it was marked by quickening, when fetal movement began. Knowledge about embryology was primitive until the past half-century, so this commonsense understanding prevailed. As a result, when abortion was condemned in earlier Christian teaching it was understood to refer to the termination of a pregnancy well into the process of the pregnancy, after ensoulment. Until the late nineteenth century, when Pope Pius IX, intrigued with the new embryonic discoveries, brought the natural law tradition into consonance with "modern science," abortion in ecclesiastical teaching often applied only to termination of prenatal life in more advanced stages of pregnancy.

Another distortion in the male-generated history of this issue derives from failure to note that, until the development of safe, surgical, elective abortion, the act of abortion commonly referred to something done to the woman, with or without her consent (see Exodus 22), either as a wrong done a husband or for the better moral reasons that abortion was an act of violence against both a pregnant woman and fetal life. In recent discussion it is the woman who does the wrongful act. No one would deny that abortion, if it terminates a pregnancy against the woman's wishes, is morally wrong. And until recent decades, abortion endangered the woman's life as much as it did the prenatal life in her womb.

Hence, one premodern moral reason for opposing abortion was that it threatened the life and well-being of the mother more than did carrying the pregnancy to term. Today abortion is statistically safer than childbearing. Consequently, no one has a right to discuss the morality of abortion today without recognizing that one of the traditional and appropriate moral reasons for objecting to abortion — concern for women's well-being — now inheres in the pro-choice side of the debate. Anti-abortion proponents who accord the fetus full human standing without also assigning positive value to women's lives and well-being are not really pressing the full sense of Christian moral tradition in the abortion debate.

Beyond all this, the deepest moral flaw in the "pro-life" position's historical view is that none of its proponents has attempted to reconstruct the concrete, lived-world context in which the abortion discussion belongs: the all but desperate struggle by sexually active women to gain some proximate control over nature's profligacy in conception. Under the most adverse conditions, women have had to try to control our fertility — everywhere, always. Women's relation to procreation irrevocably marks and shapes our lives. Even those of us who do not have sexual contact with males, because we are celibate or lesbian, have been potential, even probable, victims of male sexual violence or have had to bear heavy social stigma for refusing the centrality of dependence on men and of procreation in our lives. The lives of infertile women, too, are shaped by our failure to meet procreative expectations. Women's lack of social power, in all recorded history, has made this struggle to control procreation a life-bending, often life-destroying one for a large percentage of females.

So most women have had to do whatever we could to prevent too-numerous pregnancies. In societies and cultures, except the most patriarchal, the processes of procreation have been transmitted through women's culture. Birth control techniques have been widely practiced, and some primitive ones have proved effective. Increasingly, anthropologists are gaining hints of how procreative control occurred in some premodern societies. Frequently women have had to choose to risk their lives in order not to have that extra child that would destroy the family's ability to cope or bring about an unmanageable crisis.

We have to concede that modern medicine, for all its misogyny, has replaced some dangerous contraceptive practices still widely used where surgical abortion is unavailable. In light of these gains, more privileged western women must not lose the ability to imagine the real-life pressures that lead women in other cultures to resort to ground-glass douches, reeds inserted in the uterus, and so on, to induce labor. The radical nature of methods women use bespeaks the desperation involved in unwanted pregnancy and reveals the real character of our struggle.

Nor should we suppress the fact that a major means of birth control now is, as it was in earlier times, infanticide. And let no one imagine that women have made decisions to expose or kill newborn infants casually. Women understand what many men cannot seem to grasp — that the birth of a child requires that some person must be prepared to care, without interruption, for this infant, provide material resources and energy-draining amounts of time and attention for it. The human infant is the most needy and dependent of all newborn creatures. It seems to me that men, especially celibate men, romanticize this total and uncompromising dependency of the infant on the already existing human community. Women bear the brunt of this reality and know its full implications. And this dependency is even greater in a fragmented, centralized urban-industrial modern culture than in a rural culture, where another pair of hands often increased an extended family unit's productive power. No historical interpretation of abortion as a moral issue that ignores these matters deserves moral standing in the present debate.

A treatment of any moral problem is inadequate if it fails to analyze the morality of a given act in a way that represents the concrete experience of the agent who faces a decision with respect to that act. Misogyny in Christian discussions of abortion is evidenced clearly in that the abortion decision is never treated in the way it arises as part of the female agent's life process. The decision at issue when the dilemma of choice arises for women is whether or not to be pregnant. In most discussions of the morality of abortion it is treated as an abstract act[14] rather than as a possible way to deal with a pregnancy that frequently is the result of circumstances beyond the woman's control. John Noonan, for instance, evades this fact by referring to the pregnant woman almost exclusively as "the gravida" (a Latin term meaning "pregnant one") or "the carrier" in his A Private Choice: Abortion in America in the Seventies.[15] In any pregnancy a woman's life is deeply, irrevocably affected. Those such as Noonan who uphold the unexceptional immorality of abortion are probably wise to obscure the fact that an unwanted pregnancy always involves a life-shaping consequence for a woman, because suppressing the identity of the moral agent and the reality of her dilemma greatly reduces the ability to recognize the moral complexity of abortion. When the question of abortion arises it is usually because a woman finds herself facing an unwanted pregnancy. Consider the actual circumstances that may precipitate this. One is the situation in which a woman did not intend to be sexually active or did not enter into a sexual act voluntarily. Since women are frequently victims of sexual violence, numerous cases of this type arise because of rape, incest, or forced marital coitus. Many morally sensitive opponents of abortion concede that in such cases abortion may be morally justifiable. I insist that in such cases it is a moral good because it is not rational to treat a newly fertilized ovum as though it had the same value as the existent, pregnant female person and because it is morally wrong to make the victim of sexual violence suffer the further agonies of unwanted pregnancy and childbearing against her will. Enforced pregnancy would be viewed as a morally reprehensible violation of bodily integrity if women were recognized as fully human moral agents.

Another more frequent case results when a woman — or usually a young girl — participates in heterosexual activity without clear knowledge of how pregnancy occurs and without intention to conceive a child. A girl who became pregnant in this manner would, by traditional natural law morality, be held in a state of invincible ignorance and therefore not morally culpable. One scholarly Roman Catholic nun I met argued — quite appropriately, I believe — that her church should not consider the abortions of young Catholic girls as morally culpable because the Church overprotected them, which contributed to their lack of understanding of procreation and to their inability to cope with the sexual pressures girls experience in contemporary society. A social policy that pressures the sexually ill-informed child or young woman into unintended or unaware motherhood would be morally dubious indeed.

A related type of pregnancy happens when a woman runs risks by not using contraceptives, perhaps because taking precaution in romantic affairs is not perceived as ladylike or requires her to be too unspontaneous about sex. Our society resents women's sexuality unless it is "innocent" and male-mediated, so many women, lest they be censured as "loose" and "promiscuous," are slow to assume adult responsibility for contraception. However, when pregnancies occur because women are skirting the edges of responsibility and running risks out of immaturity, is enforced motherhood a desirable solution? Such pregnancies could be minimized only by challenging precisely those childish myths of female socialization embedded in natural law teaching about female sexuality.

It is likely that most decisions about abortion arise because mature women who are sexually active with men and who understand the risk of pregnancy nevertheless experience contraceptive failure. Our moral schizophrenia in this matter is exhibited in that many people believe women have more responsibility than men to practice contraception and that family planning is always a moral good, but even so rule out abortion altogether. Such a split consciousness ignores the fact that no inexorable biological line exists between prevention of conception and abortion.[16] More important, such reasoning ignores the genuine risks involved in female contraceptive methods. Some women are at higher risk than others in using the most reliable means of birth control. Furthermore, the reason we do not have more concern for safer contraceptive methods for men and women is that matters relating to women's health and well-being are never urgent in this society. Moreover, many contraceptive failures are due to the irresponsibility of the producers of contraceptives rather than to bad luck.[17] Given these facts, should a woman who actively attempts to avoid pregnancy be punished for contraceptive failure when it occurs?

In concluding this historical section, I must stress that if present efforts to criminalize abortion succeed, we will need a state apparatus of massive proportions to enforce compulsory childbearing. In addition, withdrawal of legal abortion will create one more massively profitable underworld economy in which the Mafia and other sections of quasi-legal capitalism may and will profitably invest. The radical right promises to get the state out of regulation of people's lives, but what they really mean is that they will let economic activity go unrestrained. What their agenda signifies for the personal lives of women is quite another matter.

An adequate historical perspective on abortion recognizes the long struggle women have waged for some degree of control over fertility and their efforts to regain control of procreative power from patriarchal and state-imperial culture and institutions. Such a perspective also takes into account that more nearly adequate contraceptive methods and the existence of safe, surgical, elective abortion represent positive historic steps toward full human freedom and dignity for women. While the same gains in medical knowledge also open the way to new forms of sterilization abuse and to social pressures against some women's use of their power of procreation, I know of no women who would choose to return to a state of lesser knowledge about these matters.

There has been an objective gain in the quality of women's lives for those fortunate enough to have access to procreative choice. That millions upon millions of women as yet do not possess even the rudimentary conditions — moral or physical — for such choice is obvious. Our moral goal should be to struggle against those real barriers — poverty, racism, and antifemale cultural oppression — that prevent authentic choice from being a reality for every woman. In this process we will be able to minimize the need for abortions only insofar as we place the abortion debate in the real lived-world context of women's lives.

Abortion and Moral Theory

The greatest strategic problem of pro-choice advocates is the widespread assumption that pro-lifers have a monopoly on the moral factors that ought to enter into decisions about abortion. *Moral* here is defined as that which makes for the self-respect and well-being of human persons and their environment. Moral legitimacy seems to adhere to their position in part because traditionalists have an array of religiomoral terminology at their command that the sometimes more secular proponents of choice lack. But those who would displace women's power of choice by the power of the state and/or the medical profession do not deserve the aura of moral sanctity. We must do our homework if we are to dispel this myth of moral superiority. A major way in which Christian moral theologians and moral philosophers contribute to this monopoly of moral sanctity is by equating fetal or prenatal life with human personhood in a simplistic way and by failing to acknowledge changes regarding this issue in the history of Christianity.

We need to remember that even in Roman Catholic natural law ethics, the definition of the status of fetal life has shifted over time and in all cases the status of prenatal life involves a moral judgment, not a scientific one. The question is properly posed this way: What status are we morally wise to predicate to prenatal human life, given that the fetus is not yet a fully existent human being? Those constrained under Catholic teaching have been required for the past ninety years to believe a human being exists from conception, when the ovum and sperm merge.[18] This answer from one tradition has had far wider impact on our culture than most people recognize. Other Christians come from traditions that do not offer (and could not offer, given their conception of the structure of the church as moral community) a definitive answer to this question.

Even so, some contemporary Protestant medical ethicists, fascinated by recent genetic discoveries and experiments with deoxyribonucleic acid (DNA), have all but sacralized the moment in which the genetic code is implanted as the moment of humanization, which leaves them close to the traditional Roman Catholic position. Protestant male theologians have long let their enthrallment with science lead to a sacralization of specific scientific discoveries, usually to the detriment of theological and moral clarity. In any case, there are two responses that must be made to the claim that the fetus in early stages of development is a human life or, more dubiously, a human person.

First, the historical struggle for women's personhood is far from won, owing chiefly to the opposition of organized religious groups to full equality for women. Those who proclaim that a zygote at the moment of conception is a person worthy of citizenship continue to deny full social and political rights to women. Whatever one's judgment about the moral status of the fetus, it cannot be argued that that assessment deserves greater moral standing in analysis than does the position of the pregnant woman. This matter of evaluating the meaning of prenatal life is where morally sensitive people's judgments diverge. I cannot believe that any morally sensitive person would fail to value the woman's full, existent life less than they value early fetal life. Most women can become pregnant and carry fetal life to term many, many times in their lifetimes. The distinctly human power is not our biologic capacity to bear children, but our power to actively love, nurture, care for one another and shape one another's existence in cultural and social interaction.[19] To equate a biologic process with full normative humanity is crass biologic reductionism, and such reductionism is never practiced in religious ethics except where women's lives and well-being are involved.

Second, even though prenatal life, as it moves toward biologic individuation of human form, has value, the equation of abortion with murder is dubious. And the equation of abortion with homicide — the taking of human life — should be carefully weighed. We should also remember that we live in a world where men extend other men wide moral range in relation to justifiable homicide. For example, the just-war tradition has legitimated widespread forms of killing in war, and Christian ethicists have often extended great latitude to rulers and those in power in making choices about killing human beings.[20] Would that such moralists extended equal benefit of a doubt to women facing life-crushing psychological and politicoeconomic pressures in the face of childbearing! Men, daily, make life-determining decisions concerning nuclear power or chemical use in the environment, for example, that affect the well-being of fetuses, and our society expresses no significant opposition, even when such decisions do widespread genetic damage. When we argue for the appropriateness of legal abortion, moral outrage rises.

The so-called pro-life position also gains support by invoking the general principle of respect for human life as foundational to its morality in a way that suggests that the pro-choice advocates are unprincipled. I have already noted that pro-choice advocates have every right to claim the same moral principle, and that this debate, like most debates that are morally acrimonious, is in no sense about basic moral principles. I do not believe there is any clear-cut conflict of principle in this very deep, very bitter controversy.

It needs to be stressed that we all have an absolute obligation to honor any moral principle that seems, after rational deliberation, to be sound. This is the one absolutism appropriate to ethics. There are often several moral principles relevant to a decision and many ways to relate a given principle to a decisional context. For most right-to-lifers only one principle has moral standing in this argument. Admitting only one principle to one's process of moral reasoning means that a range of other moral values is slighted. Right-to-lifers are also moral absolutists in the sense that they admit only one possible meaning or application of the principle they invoke. Both these types of absolutism obscure moral debate and lead to less, not more, rational deliberation. The principle of respect for human life is one we should all honor, but we must also recognize that this principle often comes into conflict with other valid moral principles in the process of making real, lived-world decisions. Understood in an adequate way, this principle can be restated to mean that we should treat what falls under a reasonable definition of human life as having sanctity or intrinsic moral value. But even when this is clear, other principles are needed to help us choose between two intrinsic values, in this case between the prenatal life and the pregnant woman's life.

Another general moral principle from which we cannot exempt our actions is the principle of justice, or right relations between persons and between groups of persons and communities. Another relevant principle is respect for all that supports human life, namely, the natural environment. As any person knows who thinks deeply about morality, genuine moral conflicts, as often as not, are due not to ignoring moral principles but to the fact that different principles lead to conflicting implications for action or are selectively related to decisions. For example, we live in a time when the principle of justice for women, aimed at transforming the social relations that damage women's lives, is historically urgent. For many of us this principle has greater moral urgency than the extension of the principle of respect for human life to include early fetal life, even though respect for fetal life is also a positive moral good. We should resist approaches to ethics that claim that one overriding principle always deserves to control morality. Clarification of principle, for that matter, is only a small part of moral reasoning. When we weigh moral principles and their potential application, we must also consider the implications of a given act for our present historical context and envision its long-term consequences.

One further proviso on this issue of principles in moral reasoning: There are several distinct theories among religious ethicists and moral philosophers as to what the function of principles ought to be. One group believes moral principles are for the purpose of terminating the process of moral reasoning. Hence, if this sort of moralist tells you always to honor the principle of respect for human life, what he or she means is for you to stop reflection and act in a certain way — in this case to accept one's pregnancy regardless of consequences. Others believe that it is better to refer to principles (broad, generalized moral criteria) than to apply rules (narrower, specific moral prescriptions) because principles function to open up processes of reasoning rather than close them off. The principle of respect for life, on this reading, is not invoked to prescribe action but to help locate and weigh values, to illuminate a range of values that always inhere in significant human decisions. A major difference in the moral debate on abortion, then, is that some believe that to invoke the principle of respect for human life settles the matter, stops debate, and precludes the single, simple act of abortion. By contrast, many of us believe the breadth of the principle opens up to reconsideration the question of what the essential moral quality of human life is all about and to increase moral seriousness about choosing whether or when to bear children.

Two other concerns related to our efforts to make a strong moral case for women's right to procreative choice need to be touched on. The first has to do with the problems our Christian tradition creates for any attempt to make clear why women's right to control our bodies is an urgent and substantive moral claim. One of Christianity's greatest weaknesses is its spiritualizing neglect of respect for the physical body and physical well-being. Tragically, women, more than men, are expected in Christian teaching never to honor their own well-being as a moral consideration. I want to stress, then, that we have no moral tradition in Christianity that starts with body-space, or body-right, as a basic condition of moral relations. (Judaism is far better in this regard, for it acknowledges that we all have a moral right to be concerned for our life and our survival.) Hence, many Christian ethicists simply do not get the point when we speak of women's right to bodily integrity. They blithely denounce such reasons as women's disguised self-indulgence or hysterical rhetoric.[21]

We must articulate our view that body-right is a basic moral claim and also remind our hearers that there is no unchallengeable analogy among other human activities to women's procreative power. Pregnancy is a distinctive human experience. In any social relation, body-space must be respected or nothing deeply human or moral can be created. The social institutions most similar to compulsory pregnancy in their moral violations of body-space are chattel slavery and peonage. These institutions distort the moral relations of a community and deform a community over time. (Witness racism in the United States.) Coercion of women, through enforced sterilization or enforced pregnancy, legitimates unjust power in intimate human relationships and cuts to the heart of our capacity for moral social relations. As we should recognize, given our violence-prone society, people learn violence at home and at an early age when women's lives are violated!

Even so, we must be careful, when we make the case for our right to bodily integrity, not to confuse moral rights with mere liberties.[22] To claim that we have a moral right to procreative choice does not mean we believe women can exercise this right free of all moral claims from the community. For example, we need to teach female children that childbearing is not a purely capricious, individualistic matter, and we need to challenge the assumption that a woman who enjoys motherhood should have as many children as she and her mate wish, regardless of its effects on others. Population self-control is a moral issue, although more so in high-consuming, affluent societies like our own than in nations where a modest, simple, and less wasteful lifestyle obtains.

A second point is the need, as we work politically for a prochoice social policy, to avoid the use of morally objectionable arguments to mobilize support for our side of the issue. One can get a lot of political mileage in U.S. society by using covert racist and classist appeals ("abortion lowers the cost of welfare rolls or reduces illegitimacy" or "paying for abortions saves the taxpayers money in the long run"). Sometimes it is argued that good politics is more important than good morality and that one should use whatever arguments work to gain political support. I do not believe that these crassly utilitarian[23] arguments turn out, in the long run, to be good politics for they are costly to our sense of polis and of community. But even if they were effective in the short run, I am doubly sure that on the issue of the right to choose abortion, good morality doth a good political struggle make. I believe, deeply, that moral right is on the side of the struggle for the freedom and self-respect of women, especially poor and non-white women, and on the side of developing social policy that ensures that every child born can be certain to be a wanted child. Issues of justice are those that deserve the deepest moral caretaking as we develop a political strategy.

Only when people see that they cannot prohibit safe, legal, elective surgical abortion without violating the conditions of well-being for the vast majority of women — especially those most socially vulnerable because of historic patterns of oppression — will the effort to impose a selective, abstract morality of the sanctity of human life on all of us cease. This is a moral battle par excellence, and whenever we forget that we make it harder to reach the group most important to the cause of procreative choice — those women who have never suffered from childbearing pressures, who have not yet put this issue into a larger historical context, and who reverence women's historical commitment to childbearing. We will surely not reach them with pragmatic appeals to the taxpayer's wallet! To be sure, we cannot let such women go unchallenged as they support ruling-class ideology that the state should control procreation. But they will not change their politics until they see that pro-choice is grounded in a deeper, tougher, more caring moral vision than the political option they now endorse.

The Social Policy Dimensions of the Debate

Most people fail to understand that in ethics we need, provisionally, to separate our reflection on the morality of specific acts from questions about how we express our moral values within our social institutions and systems (that is, social policy). When we do this, the morality of abortion appears in a different light. Focusing attention away from the single act of abortion to the larger historical context thrusts into relief what "respect for human life" means in the pro-choice position. It also illuminates the common core of moral concern that unites pro-choice advocates to pro-lifers who have genuine concern for expanding the circle of who really counts as human in this society. Finally, placing abortion in a larger historical context enables proponents of pro-choice to clarify where we most differ from the pro-lifers, that is, in our total skepticism that a state-enforced antiabortion policy could ever have the intended "pro-life" consequences they claim.

We must always insist that the objective social conditions

that make women and children already born highly vulnerable can only be worsened by a social policy of compulsory pregnancy. However one judges the moral quality of the individual act of abortion (and here, differences among us do exist that are morally justifiable), it is still necessary to distinguish between how one judges the act of abortion morally and what one believes a societywide policy on abortion should be. We must not let those who have moral scruples against the personal act ignore the fact that a just social policy must also include active concern for enhancement of women's well-being and, for that, policies that would in fact make abortions less necessary. To anathematize abortion when the social and material conditions for control of procreation do not exist is to blame the victim, not to address the deep dilemmas of female existence in this society.

Even so, there is no reason for those of us who celebrate procreative choice as a great moral good to pretend that resort to abortion is ever a desirable means of expressing this choice. I know of no one on the pro-choice side who has confused the desirability of the availability of abortion with the celebration of the act itself. We all have every reason to hope that safer, more reliable means of contraception may be found and that violence against women will be reduced. Furthermore, we should be emphatic that our social policy demands include opposition to sterilization abuse, insistence on higher standards of health care for women and children, better prenatal care, reduction of unnecessary surgery on women's reproductive systems, increased research to improve contraception, and so on. Nor should we draw back from criticizing a health care delivery system that exploits women. An abortion industry thrives on the profitability of abortion, but women are not to blame for this.

A feminist position demands social conditions that support women's full, self-respecting right to procreative choice, including the right not to be sterilized against our wills, the right to choose abortion as a birth control means of last resort, and the right to a prenatal and postnatal health care system that will also reduce the now widespread trauma of having to deliver babies in rigid, impersonal health care settings. Pro-lifers do best politically when we allow them to keep the discussion narrowly focused on the morality of the act of abortion and on the moral value of the fetus. We do best politically when we make the deep connections between the full context of this issue in women's lives, including this society's systemic or patterned injustice toward women.

It is well to remember that it has been traditional Catholic natural law ethics that most clarified and stressed this distinction between the morality of an individual act on the one hand and the policies that produce the optional social morality on the other. The strength of this tradition is probably reflected in the fact that even now most polls show that slightly more Catholics than Protestants believe it unwise for the state to attempt to regulate abortion. In the past, Catholics, more than Protestants, have been wary of using the state as an instrument of moral crusade. Tragically, by taking their present approach to abortion, the Roman Catholic hierarchy may be risking the loss of the deepest wisdom of its own ethical tradition. By failing to acknowledge a distinction between the church's moral teaching on the act of abortion and the question of what is a desirable social policy to minimize abortion, as well as overemphasizing it to the neglect of other social justice concerns, the Roman Catholic church may well be dissipating the best of its moral tradition.[24]

The frenzy of the current pope and many Roman Catholic bishops in the United States on this issue has reached startling proportions. The United States bishops have equated nuclear war and the social practice of abortion as the most heinous social evils of our time.[25] While this appallingly misguided analogy has gained credibility because of the welcome if modest opposition of the bishops to nuclear escalation, I predict that the long-term result will be to further discredit Roman Catholic moral wisdom in the culture.

If we are to be a society genuinely concerned with enhancing women's well-being and minimizing the necessity of abortions, thereby avoiding the danger over time of becoming an abortion culture,[26] what kind of a society must we become? It is here that the moral clarity of the feminist analysis becomes most obvious. How can we reduce the number of abortions due to contraceptive failure? By placing greater emphasis on medical research in this area, by requiring producers of contraceptives to behave more responsibly, and by developing patterns of institutional life that place as much emphasis on male responsibility for procreation and long-term care and nurturance of children as on female responsibility.

How can we reduce the number of abortions due to childish ignorance about sexuality among female children or adult women and our mates? By adopting a widespread program of sex education and by supporting institutional policies that teach male and female children alike that a girl is as fully capable as a boy of enjoying sex and that both must share moral responsibility for preventing pregnancy except when they have decided, as a deliberative moral act, to have a child.

How would we reduce the necessity of abortion due to sexual violence against women in and out of marriage? By challenging vicious male-generated myths that women exist primarily to meet the sexual needs of men, that women are, by nature, those who are really fulfilled only through our procreative powers. We would teach feminist history as the truthful history of the race, stressing that historic patterns of patriarchy were morally wrong and that a humane or moral society would be a fully nonsexist society.

Technological developments that may reduce the need for abortions are not entirely within our control, but the sociomoral ethos that makes abortion common is within our power to change. And we would begin to create such conditions by adopting a thoroughgoing feminist program for society. Nothing less, I submit, expresses genuine respect for all human life.

MISOGYNY AND HOMOPHOBIA

The Unexplored Connections*

The Dualisms That Shape the Problem

Some years ago, philosopher Dorothea Krook observed that ecclesiastical statements regarding sexuality exemplify an antisensual ambivalence. Citing the Anglican bishops' *Lambeth Report on Sexuality*[1] as evidence of her thesis, she pointed out that the bishops begin well enough by criticizing any "false dualism" that makes it impossible to affirm physical love unequivocally. Then, however, their affirmation of sexuality is hedged, and finally they vigorously disapprove of any sexual expression outside of marital sexual relations. Krook concludes,

> In spite of their statements to the contrary, sexual love for the bishops is, it seems, physical, unspiritual, "carnal," or "sensual" in a way that parental and pastoral love are not.[2]

The body, we may note, simply is not understood as mediating spirituality directly. The bishops' statement clearly reflects two differing and contradictory attitudes toward sexuality.

To grasp the connections between misogyny and homophobia, we need to examine this problematic tendency of Christian theological tradition to neglect, ignore, or denigrate the body. This tendency is not characteristic only of the dominant traditions of Christianity; it is expressed in the spiritualities and official ideologies of dominant groups in every society, and more especially those of males who rule over and represent the masculinist norms of those societies. Such spiritualities sacralize mental activity or consciousness as "higher" than the rest of physical existence. Thus we are conditioned by religious and philosophical orthodoxy, or the official doctrines of the elites, to view the body and bodily needs as "lower," "animal" modalities of existence that have to be tamed or in some way overcome and transcended

---

* This essay is a revision of one that was published in *Integrity Forum* 7:2 (1981), pp. 7–13, and excerpted and republished in *Church and Society* (November/December 1982).

by a higher and loftier power that is "really" rational and spiritual. This assumption of a tension between what is most deeply "spiritual" and our physical embodiment and physical needs runs so deep in Christian culture that accepting the priority of mind over body, as if mind is not a function of body experienced in a certain way, or the "transcendence" of spirit over nature, is often held to be the essence of religious conviction. "To believe" comes to mean believing such nonsense. To be religious then involves living and acting as though a split between lower "nature" and consciousness were part of fundamental reality. The connections between homophobia and misogyny are sustained by the depth of this anti-body, antisensual bias of dominant Christianity. While these anti-body attitudes do not fully explain our society's revulsion from homosexuality or any sexual "deviance," they are an important part of the story. The fear of the power of, and revulsion from sexuality itself is an important element in homophobia. Homosexuality, in our social and cultural context, represents a break with the strongest and most familiar control on sexuality — compulsory heterosexuality — and thus is a break with that strong social patterning which, because it is familiar, makes sexuality seem safe and conventionally channeled. Homosexuality then becomes a strong metaphor for active, freely expressed sexuality. Many imagine that we have moved beyond the Christian legacy of affirming sexuality only within marriage, for the purpose of procreation, but these ancient constraints on our behavior live on in a generalized uneasiness about "loose" or unchanneled sexuality as dangerous. Any demand that homoeroticism be accepted as "healthy" therefore calls us to recognize that sexuality itself is good not merely when channeled in "reputable" and well-patterned ways but good per se.

One of the many reasons to celebrate James Nelson's fine book *Embodiment: An Approach to Sexuality and Christian Theology*[3] is that it is among the first theological treatments of sexuality to grapple deeply and frankly with this anti-body dualism in the Christian tradition. Even more important, however, is Nelson's recognition of another and related dualism that has shaped and distorted Christian history vis-à-vis sexuality. Nelson rightly connects this other dualism — male/female dualism, predicated on the view that male and female are fundamentally different, even "opposites," and that maleness is superior — with the rejection of the body.

The value accorded female "being" varies somewhat from society to society, but all existing societies are in some degree male supremacist, so male nature is held to be expressive of full humanity while female nature is held to be different from and of less value than male human nature. Male "nature" also is perceived as more complex and subtle because it is characteristic of genuine, full humanity. Whatever the value of femaleness in a given dualistic culture, women were believed to lack some ingredient necessary for the full range of ideal human functioning. In contemporary western culture, most often, women are perceived as lacking the full range of what we mean by rationality. As a result, many "feel" safer when men are "in charge."

An interesting variant of this ideology aimed at assuring male control was developed in the nineteenth century to prolong male dominance in the wake of the first organized women's movement and early feminism. It came to be believed then that women have a different sort of rational capacity than men have. We were said to be more "genteel" and to possess deeper "feeling," to be more sensitive morally. Such pedestalism was nothing more than a last-ditch effort to keep women in "our place," for this presumed distinctive "femininity" (a notion invented only in the nineteenth century) was never presumed to be important at the centers of power or decision making in society. Where commerce or the arts of statecraft were practiced, such qualities were dismissed as "sentimental" and "weak," much as they were being praised wherever women gathered. Unfortunately for Christianity, this sentimentalized pedestalism was adopted and eventually even "proclaimed" by Christian churches as a second-rate substitute for feminist justice. The result was a sentimentalized church, not transformation of women's lives.

We will never get the morality of male/female relations straightened out within Christianity until this pattern of male supremacy comes to be recognized for what it is — misogyny, or the hatred of women. Like all historical oppression, the practice of male supremacy over time breeds real hostility to women, hostility that runs deeper in this society than most people — especially Christians — wish to acknowledge. Since men and women live in such proximity, hostility toward women often takes on masked, mystified, or covert forms. Often it presents itself as patronizing superiority toward women's "foibles" or is expressed in slightly contemptuous humor. It will take the form of contemptuous downplaying of "women's concerns" or the effort to trivialize. A major unrecognized index of hostility against women is the degree of indirect manipulation of women's actions, use of flirtation or seductive patterns of control aimed at making sure that women respond "sweetly." The hostility toward women as a group, implicit in the pedestalism or the romanticization of the "good" (read "unassertive") woman, is rarely perceived but is powerful nonetheless. The real face of misogyny is exposed clearly only when a woman, or groups of women, behave in strong, to-gether, assertive ways. In fact, we can identify the true measure of misogyny only by noting how strong and independent women are received. Strong women are invariably perceived and described as "aggressive" and "hostile." Where a woman, or a group of women, are competent and self-reliant, not easily controlled, oth-ers will be threatened and they in turn will project *their* hostility onto that woman or group. Rage toward women is pervasive, and invariably it is the women who point this out who become its most conspicuous victims.

It is an error to imagine that in a misogynist society anti-woman feelings are learned only by men. All of us, male and fe-male, learn antiwoman feelings and attitudes, just as all of us, whatever our erotic practice, learn antihomosexual feelings and attitudes. Women express such antiwoman feelings by acts and attitudes of self-abnegation and by refusing to value ourselves and/or other women as much as we value men. But it is also true that women cooperate with misogyny to avoid the rage that non-compliance looses. As long as women cooperate in our subjuga-tion, as long as we are gently unassertive or relatively undemand-ing, male hostility toward us expresses itself only in gentler forms. But as the massive, sustained, and universal patterns of violence toward women in this and other societies makes clear, rage to-ward women lies just beneath the surface of all of our social relations and our institutional life. Women's "weakness" is, often, women's unnamed terror of this reality.

Only a genuine feminist analysis, one that advocates women's well-being, can clarify why anti-body, antinature dualism has had such a powerful hold on our traditions. These dualisms are irre-ducibly related core theses in the ideology of control developed by the ruling male elites of a patriarchal social system to keep their power in place and women in theirs. In fact, the anti-body dualism of Christian culture is so tenacious precisely because it sustains the other dualism — the male/female dualism — which in turn grounds male superiority and privilege. Patriarchal ideol-ogy idealizes disembodied rationality and the disinterested and detached modes of experience characteristic of the way of life of dominant male groups. A feminist moral theology, by contrast, affirms the bodily grounded experience and struggle of women and nonruling groups of males and seeks to demystify and expose "spiritualistic" theories of human nature generated to perpetuate male dominance. Only when we begin to recognize that the fem-inist analysis is correct, that *social control of women as a group has totally shaped our deepest and most basic attitudes toward sexuality,* do we comprehend the full social functionality of enforcing compulsory heterosexuality on both women and men. The only "respectable" alternative to compulsory heterosexuality in our culture is, of course, asexuality or celibacy.

Toward an Understanding of the Historical-Cultural Connections Between Homophobia and Misogyny

We need a clearer historical appreciation for the ways in which the long-standing and deeply rooted antipathy toward women in western, Christian tradition interacted with and became entwined with anti-body, antisensual attitudes if we are also to understand why we have reached the place where the stigma of homosexuality incorporates and encompasses all of the power dynamics of misogyny. Until we develop such an analysis, we will not even begin to appreciate why homophobia is such an intense madness among us or why homophobic frenzy thrives so in the churches. Feminists and a few others have begun to pursue the concrete historical connections between the antisexual phobia that came to characterize large sectors of Christendom and the antifemale bias so strong, continuous, and as yet untranscended in Christian history.[4] Such speculation is, as yet, very provisional. Much further investigation is needed to give precision to these matters. A feminist critique must reopen fully a Pandora's box of issues. Not only must we reconsider sex role definitions, that is, what is held to be the proper province of male and female activity, but we must also examine the entire range of assumptions and definitions that mapped socialization into what was accepted as "normal" gender identity in all of its aspects, including notions of what has constituted "normal eroticism"[5] in various cultures and epochs. Historians such as John Boswell have begun to identify some evidence to describe the diversity and pluralism of attitudes toward sexuality and male homosexuality in Christian history,[6] but a full picture will require examining the development of compulsory heterosexuality as a social institution and its social and political enforcement.

Neither of those ancient cultural traditions usually considered to have nurtured Christianity — the early Israelite, or Hebraic, and the classic Greek — reflected an antisexual bias that came to characterize Christian history. Ancient Israelite culture was a physically oriented culture, one in which sexuality, at least in its heterosexual expressions, was not only affirmed but celebrated. John Boswell, among other exegetes,[7] has also provided evidence for an appropriate skepticism about the once widely accepted view that Israelite culture was antihomosexual and homophobic. Hel-

lenic culture was neither antisexual nor antihomoerotic. It celebrated eroticism and basically affirmed sensuality. Some have
claimed that classical Greek culture was strongly antifemale and
predominantly homoerotic. Certainly some of the great philosophers of the Greek tradition were antifemale, and the status of
male-female relations in that culture is a much-disputed question.
In any case, though, what is astonishing is how readily Christian
tradition became antisexual and, simultaneously, misogynist and
homophobic, given a twofold cultural heritage that was neither
antisexual nor sharply homophobic.

Most current evidence suggests that misogyny is a far more
consistent trend in Christian history than homophobia. Even in
periods when homophobia was not intense,[8] there was still a
strong pattern of disvaluing things associated with females. Given
some of the reigning "scientific" assumptions, thoroughly imbued with patriarchal prejudice, males usually were viewed as
sexually active "by nature" and females were held "by nature" to
be passive or receptive. It appears that some male homosexual activity came to be despised because one male was understood to
play the passive role, that is, was penetrated. One stigma of homosexuality, then, was that it "reduced" some men to the role of females.[9] Similarly, the intensity of much contemporary homophobia confirms this continuing element in the revulsion against
male homosexuality. Homoerotic men are perceived as failed
men, no better than females. The widespread but empirically mistaken equation of male homosexuality with effeminacy is further
evidence that the stigma of male homosexuality involves association with females and the "feminine." Though any connection
between homoeroticism and "effeminate" personality characteristics has been totally discredited through social scientific research, the stereotype persists tenaciously in the nongay community.

The truth is that all nonwhite males, or males of cultural
groups not endorsed by the dominant culture, are also seen in
some degree as "effeminate." Sometimes this involves the accusation that one is controlled by feeling or is less "rational" than
males of dominant racial and cultural groups, or more animalistic,
rhythmic, or childlike. The depth of the hatred toward women is
clearly reflected in this projection of female stigma onto any males
who need to be distanced from dominant norms of "real manhood" for purposes of social control. Not surprisingly, the consequence is that men in oppressed groups who internalize this oppression often "answer back" to ruling-class men by acting out
super-macho patterns of relationships to women in order to "dis-
prove" any deficiency in their manhood. Some homosexual men

also appear to attempt "expiation" of this female stigma by adopting super-macho patterns of sexual relationship. Male homosexual culture bears obvious marks of such compensation and the fear that male homosexuality may really be some sort of failure in "real" manhood.

The force of homophobia in the church and in some sectors of society is such that even the long-standing symbolic superiority of "maleness" does not appear adequate to explain it. Clearly, we are dealing with something even more highly charged than a simple male chauvinism and its convoluted consequences. Feminist historical scholarship leads us to suspect that the force of homophobia rests in yet a deeper social contradiction. To understand this contradiction we must connect two historical developments. First, we need to recognize that the hierarchicalization and centralization of the Catholic tradition of Christianity, including the solidification of power in priestly orders and in a centralized hierarchy, was the result of an active attack on the growing role of women in early Christianity.[10] We feminist theologians now believe that the development of "orthodoxy" in theology and church order was the result of an active effort to disempower women in early Christianity. Those groups within early Christianity that we viewed as deviant, heterodox, or "sectarian" turn out to have been those parts of the Christian community in which women played an extensive and strong role. The centralization of power within, and the creation of, a Catholic Christian tradition controlled by a male hierarchical elite rapidly engendered the rise within Christian theology of myths of feminine evil and images of woman either as temptress or perpetual Eve, as virgin or harlot. What this means is that a concrete power struggle over the definition of and the control of Christianity took place in the church and that the "male dominance" party won. As a result, a dominant Catholic hierarchy of Christianity, over time, became a male homophile organization, one of the most successful such organizations in human history. Whatever the historical details, the fact is that the priesthood and hierarchy of Catholic Christianity evolved as institutions predicated on and sustained by a powerful impulse of male bonding. Unless this is understood, the traumatic and sometimes bizarre reactions to the ordination of women and of gay men in the dominant churches will make no sense.

My own experience and that of other self-aware women attest that we literally can "feel" the visceral power of male/male bonding and the powerful energy sustaining such bonds when we enter a room full of men wearing clerical collars or ecclesiastical garb. Furthermore, when we listen to the rhetoric of bishops referring to their obligations to keep solidarity with "brother" bishops (by, for example, not supporting women's ordination) or hear them attest the "spiritual unity" of the church embodied in the community of bishops and priests, the power and depth of this male bonding are obvious. It is not too much to say that the feelings conveyed are deeply erotic.

This historical dynamic is, however, conjoined with another that conspires to forge the depth of the historical contradiction in which Christianity is trapped and, therefore, to generate the full force of its hysterical response to homosexuality. Not only is Christianity an institution characterized by deep male erotic bonds, but it is also the dominant institutional legitimizer of society's gender system of compulsory heterosexuality. The pressure to provide the ideology for maintaining compulsory heterosexuality and to sustain male homophile bonding creates chasms in consciousness. In such an institution, where actual relational patterns of male/male contact and regard run so contrary to the publicly endorsed, and therefore publicly permissible, patterns of eroticism, strictures *against* homosexual eroticism become almost violent and compulsive. Homosexuality *and* females both, simultaneously, threaten the uneasy balance of psychic forces and ideological functions that create the "security" of the institutional elite.

The fact is that in Christianity, considerable numbers of celibate male clergy and bishops are closeted homosexuals. This is surely one reason for the powerful resistance to sacrificing the exclusivity of male bonding through the inclusion of women in priestly orders. Often, closeted homosexual priests, those who embrace "celibacy" to cover their own sexual orientation and/or practice, lead the attack against the ordination of women. These same priests often join the attack not on homosexuality but on *gayness* — that is, on the act of being a *self*-affirming and *self*-respecting person who insists that homoeroticism is good and who wants to live a life of integrity, demanding respect that any person has a moral right to expect. In the Christian churches today the sexual sin is to wish to have your "public" and "private" lives integrated. The deepest rage is aimed not against the fact that there are homosexuals in the church but against the presence of gay men and open lesbians. Homosexuality is tolerated if homosexual persons observe secrecy and practice hypocrisy!

The viciousness of what is going on in the churches around homosexuality is that many clergy are choosing to live lives of active duplicity with the church's public encouragement while large numbers of closeted homosexual clergy to seek acceptance in the church actively attack women and gay men. All of this threatens the spiritual integrity and lifeblood of Christianity.

Closeted priests are not per se the problem. In a homophobic church and culture, no homosexual or lesbian should be expected to "come out of the closet" unless that person's personal or professional integrity or survival requires it. No one ever should be pressured to come out. What I am talking about is the *active* misrepresentation of the truth about human sexuality and the character assassination and moral blackmail that closeted homosexual male clergy are wreaking on women, especially lesbians, and on self-affirming gay male clergy. This situation is a scandal, and it is eroding the soul of Christianity.

Where human beings do not deal honestly and directly with their own sexuality, sexual anxiety rises and begins to mystify and obscure the basic power dynamics of the community. People live in fear of being exposed, and as a result they capitulate to corrupt power, giving away their own power of intellectual and moral judgment to a presumed higher "authority," without regard to the moral value of that "higher power." In addition, when basic issues of sexuality are too threatening to face, repression occurs and the source of all our energy is suppressed. As a result, the spirituality of a community becomes a vacuous, empty formalism, filled with effete and eccentric religiosity and ritual. The power of embodiment — of flesh and blood energy to live and grow — is lost.

It is time for male clergy and bishops to own how deeply male bonding runs, how contemptuous clerical males are of women and how fearful of all but dependent and "obedient" women. Whether male clergy or bishops' own erotic preferences are homosexual or heterosexual is irrelevant here. What is relevant is how all clerical males, and powerful lay men, relate to women, most especially to strong, self-respecting women. The test is whether they can relate to women fully as peers whose basic worth and way of being in the world are recognized as fully valuable as men's. It is also time for men to acknowledge, appreciate, and respect the fact that many women are living or choose to live homosexual lives, actively preferring the support and intimacy of female/female relations, including erotic relations. For many women, lesbianism is less fate than choice, and many women choose lesbian relations because more and more women have moved beyond male dependency and will *not* accept intimate relations that lack mutuality.

Male clergy and bishops must also face how deeply angry they are with gay men, men who are open about their erotic bonding to other men and who demand self-respect for who they are. It is precisely these men who are often able to hear a feminist analysis of sexuality and who join us in making the connections between homophobia and misogyny. What generates rage against gay men is that, by coming out, they signal that they will no longer co-operate in refusing to rock the ecclesiastical boat: They join women in expecting the church, finally, to come of age regarding human sexuality.

Implications for Ministry and for Reformulating an Ethic of Sexuality

Since I am a moralist by profession, I cannot resist spelling out some of the implications of this analysis for a theological ethic of sexuality and for Christian ministry. Nothing is more critical at the present moment than for the dominant traditions of Christianity to recognize and begin making the connections between the dehumanizing and ancient patriarchal attitudes toward women and our present ideological entrapment in relationship to human sexuality. Contrary to popular assumptions, it happens to be the case that an adequate response to the present global political and economic crisis actually turns on a more honest and adult confrontation with these issues. Our society's fears regarding human sexuality and the widespread, confused, and phobic anxieties about same-sex eroticism, together with the disordered relations between men and women generated by deep inequalities of power and respect, are a major source of our inability to tolerate diversity and difference in this world. Because we are uncertain and vulnerable to terror in terms of our fear of sexuality, these issues provide a perfect foil for the new political right, which uses them to silence people. Homophobia functions to mask real, deep, and growing social and economic inequity. Gay men, lesbians, and women who insist on their procreative rights or who press for full standing as citizens are joining the poor, and nonwhite women and men, as groups that became society's chief scapegoats. We are accused, preposterously, of "destroying traditional values," whereas the erosion not only of "traditional values" but of all moral concern is rooted concretely in a political-economic system that makes every human consideration except the maximization of profit irrelevant. Late advanced monopoly capitalism not only erodes traditional values but is eroding the functional capacity of all of our liberal institutions. While traditional "family values" were never adequate morally to women's situation, the political forces attacking women and gay men seeking justice have no real concern for any sort of intrinsic moral value. Right-wing groups demand women's acquiescence to traditional "family values" only because they are astute supporters of the existing economic system that cannot accommodate genuine claims to economic equity.

Since women as a group are the largest systematically disadvantaged group, the new right understands perfectly well that any efforts to realize full human equality for women must be discredited along with all other claims to social justice, especially claims for racial equality. The pressure now is great to revert to some presumed conventional wisdom, to take a more traditional stance, but not because the right wing really values "tradition." Socioeconomic pressures on families will continue to escalate whatever happens; should the rate of divorce drop, it will be only because economic pressures force people to remain in unfulfilling marriages. The economic crisis of late advanced capitalism is so deep that any group's claims that require reallocation of social power and resources must be silenced. People must be pressured to accept a social system that can no longer buy off discontent by "trickling down" modest benefits to those in the middle and at the bottom of the system.

If the formerly liberal churches now fall into line with the expectations of the new right regarding "traditional" values of sexuality, the result hardly will be a sudden increase in moral sensibility or lessening of dissolution of family life. The massive violence now characteristic of the American family will increase as long as social justice is denied. As economic pressures increase, we may count on it that violence, including spouse and child abuse, will continue to escalate. If churches buy in on the antifeminist, homophobic line of the new right, the few precarious and as yet not well established strides toward justice for women and the more mature attitude toward sexuality made by whole generations of liberals, including liberal Christianity, will be wiped out. What has happened recently in the churches is that former liberals, frightened of change largely because they could not simultaneously become critical of Christianity's role in gender oppression and also become more self-aware and self-accepting of their own sexuality, have collaborated with neoconservatives to stop constructive change.

A Christian community in the grips of homophobia is unable to grapple with the subtle challenges of ministry in the present. To have a role in the real healing of people today, to contribute to the genuine empowerment of people, to express radical love in a social context of right relationship (justice), the church must continue to walk the long road of transforming its mores of sexuality. Once and for all, the Christian community must overcome its sex-phobic fear of eroticism as a foreign and evil power that wars with positive spiritual energy. We Christians must come to recognize that our sexuality is a foundational aspect of our total, integrated bodily well-being. It is the root of our personal integrity and it must be integrated holistically into our lifestyles and value commitments if we are to possess a deep capacity for intimacy, for powerful communication and rich interaction with others.

All of this means that the churches are going to have to acknowledge that, contrary to popular opinion and customary wisdom, *Christianity has not yet developed an adequate ethic of sexuality.* The ponderous rhetoric of the Lambeth statement on sexuality and other ecclesiastical utterances notwithstanding, a new mood of modesty about the wisdom of Christian tradition is urgently required. What most historians of Christian ethics have missed completely is that the present confusions and disagreements around the issues of human sexuality in the church parallel earlier debates on political or economic ethics when a "taken-for-granted" church monopoly on moral wisdom held sway. Precisely at the point when the church could no longer simply dictate political policy, a new moral debate had to occur. When the church could no longer dictate the meaning of science, a similar conflict ensued. When traditional Christianity is no longer viewed as possessing a monopoly on or able simply to dictate the moral meaning of an aspect of life, conflict escalates. So today we are in conflict because consensus has been lost about the meaning of sexuality. Our past sexual mores are inadequate to integrate the new insights we need.

Traditional Christianity has persistently confused sexual mores with genuine morals, assuming that earlier patterns of practice continue to have value for their own sake, quite apart from our need as rational beings continuously to justify past norms and practices in light of new conditions. In a world where women will no longer accept inferiority, where overpopulation threatens, and where new and nonexploitive patterns of communication and intimacy that sustain genuine human dignity are needed, we must, perhaps for the first time, articulate, in a self-aware and responsible way, criteria for expressing our sexuality that are not based on institutionalized relations of male hegemony, control, and possession or on social myths about our sexual "natures" that do not correlate with the experiences that actually empower our lives. Values operative in earlier social orders may have made some sense when mere physical survival of the species was a major issue,[11] but those patterns of human practice sacralized unjust power relations and are no longer justifiable. Our sexuality, like everything human, is a historical reality and as such undergoes genuine change. Patterns of human sexual expression have always varied from culture to culture, and they have altered over time. Since sexual mores, like all mores, change, there is the possibility that the moral quality of our social-sexual relations can also deepen over time.

In the past, the Christian ethic kept women "in our place" by confining us to procreation, but it also included the simultaneous demand that males limit erotic contact only to such less-valued creatures as women. Christian cultures have had to fetishize heterosexuality to enforce contact with women on men whom it was also teaching to disvalue women. Enforced heterosexism, in the form of the assumption that heterosexuality is "natural" sex, is the ideology of a culture that simultaneously encourages and disguises its hatred for women, seeks to extend its male supremacy, and must force males to "do their duty" by "inferior" women.

If our sexual behavior were really determined "by nature," we would, of course, need no ethic of sexuality. Human beings do not need morality to deal with what is determinate or, in an older worldview, "natural." Ethics begins where necessity, or predetermination in creation, leaves off. From an adequate theological viewpoint, we need to say bluntly that traditional Christian sexual standards are too rigid to be healthy or conducive to human well-being. The newer efforts to "take thought," to "do ethics" in relation to the meaning of sexuality, are a sign of genuine faith and hope in the church. Happily, those whose lives are twisted and thwarted by society's strongly patterned "compulsory heterosexuality" are finally speaking up, no longer willing to accept social stigma for sexual expression and personal relationships that have intrinsic value. The communal process of shaping criteria for an adequate morality of sexual-social relations must be informed by the wisdom of those who have learned to affirm their sexuality in the face of society's oppressive negations.

We need also to remember that we live in a world where persons come to puberty earlier and earlier but where the young come to adulthood later and later. Our sexual ethic must come to terms with these dynamics. The prolonged period of young adulthood means that condemnation of sex outside marriage increases pressures for early and premature marriages. Today, people have double the life expectancy and nearly double the years of reproductive fertility as did persons only a few centuries ago. In a society like ours, lifelong monogamous sexual relations mean something quite different from what they once did, and the traditional Christian ethic, continuously reiterated, has some quite unprecedented negative effects.

To disavow, once and for all, that sexuality per se is dirty or wrong will enable us to "put sex in its place" as an important, though neither all-powerful nor traumatic, dimension of our lives. It is clear that many of our society's sexual fixations and preoccupations are connected to and interrelated with our sexual repressions. Only a society so sex-preoccupied could be so sex-phobic. Because sexuality is experienced chiefly as a means of controlling others rather than as a means of deepened communication, it is often joyless, boring, and fixated! And not surprisingly, we seem to be a culture as bored by sex as we are obsessed with it!

A Christian moral reevaluation of sexuality must be posited on the sober fact that our sexual relations, broadly considered, are a problem, but it is *not* the problem envisaged in the traditional Christian sexual ethic — that is, too much or too "loose" sex. Rather, we must acknowledge that it is through our socialization to sexuality that we begin to learn "fear of equality" and either to feel "strong" by lording it over others or to feel "safe" by being controlled by them. By conforming rigidly to "masculine" or "feminine" [12] roles, we learn, at a foundational level, to tolerate inequality. Through our earliest experience of family power relations we learn whether superiority or inferiority makes us feel safe.[13] We may be sure that there is a direct connection between this preferred form of psychic security and what "turns us on" erotically. The awful truth is that most heterosexuals, and a lot of homosexuals too, get turned on only by those who either are more powerful than they or by those dependent on them — the sort of person for whom they otherwise can easily feel contempt! The tragedy of our so-called sexual morality is that mutual respect and eroticism are utterly separated in the lives of most people. Ours is a culture where sadomasochistic relations are the most typical forms of sexual relations and the Christian traditionalist ethic is a major source of legitimation of sadomasochism.

Many seem to confuse erotic feeling with feelings of control, finding violence "more exciting" than mutual erotic expression. Ironically, violence apparently makes many feel safer and stronger than does passionate mutual sexual exchange. Violence *is* as American as apple pie, and it is the displacement of mutality and spontaneous consent by coercion. Evidently, people prefer control to the more vulnerable and spontaneous experience of eroticism. A people who lack a genuine power of eroticism will indeed assuage their emptiness by controlling others.

When we accept that our sexual problem is fear of genuine intimacy and mutuality and security born of having others under our control or at bay, we will also accept our responsibility for teaching an ethic that supports such norms. That loveless control of another can be viewed as morally acceptable sexual expression by current Christian standards simply because it falls within the province of "normal" heterosexual marriage is a scandal. The search for an adequate Christian ethics of sexuality can begin in earnest when we face this level of truth.

A feminist moral theology requires that we ground our new ethics of sexuality in a "spirituality of sensuality." [14] Our energy — literally, the gift of life — is body-mediated energy. Our sexuality does not detract from, but deepens and shapes, our power of personal being. Our bodies, through our senses, mediate our real, physical connectedness to all things. Our sexuality represents our most intense interaction with the world. Because this is so, it is also a key to the quality and integrity of our overall spirituality. Our body-space is literally the ground of our personhood and our means of communicating the power of our presence to and with others. How we deal with our own body-space and how we relate to others' provides a paradigm for all our moral relations to the world. Furthermore, touch is the most powerful and effectual means of human interaction; we resort to it when words and gestures are not powerful enough or do not suffice to convey what we need to communicate. We use touch either to control others or to convey bonds and feeling. Hence, sexuality is indispensable to our spirituality because it is a power of communication, most especially a power to give and receive powerful meaning — love and respect or contempt and disdain.

Because traditional Christian ethics held that communication through genital touch should be limited only to those relationships where nonphysical intimacy and an exclusivity of personal commitment prevailed, the primary, direct power of body communication has been largely denied. Genital contact and touch was viewed as less valuable in itself, morally inferior to other modes of communication. To the contrary, the intensity of touch, which warrants its tender use, is the source of its spiritual power. The idea that genital sexual expression, except within the confines of a lifelong, committed, monogamous relationship, is dirty or wrong does not stand scrutiny for many who have long since learned that sexual touch often opens the way to other dimensions of human intimacy. Orgasm, as an expression of vulnerability and receptivity to the world, is a powerful metaphor for spiritual blessing and healing.

A holistic approach to sexuality, free of the body/mind dualism that sustains patriarchy, will yield a rather simple ethic, one foundationally grounded in mutual respect. The giving and receiving of touch, the sharing of erotic pleasure, is a powerful bonding with another. Sexual communication, at its best, mutually enhances self-respect and valuation of the other. The moral norm for sexual communication in a feminist ethic is radical mutuality — the simultaneous acknowledgment of vulnerability to and need of another, the recognition of one's own power to give and receive pleasure and to call forth another's power of relation and to express one's own. The sexual ethic of patriarchy — our present operative ethic — has ownership as its formative value. We are to possess total right of access to and control of another's body-space and the fruits of the other's body, if the other is female. A norm of control prevails, which is why so-called marital fidelity really means only sexual exclusivity for the female spouse.

Many fear that giving up the ethics of patriarchy will result in the emergence of a sexually normless, "promiscuous" world, a world in which any and all sexual activity is all right if it "feels good and if nobody gets hurt." It is difficult to respond to the fears people have about presumed "promiscuity," since these fears are often based on the projections or unfulfilled sexual fantasies of those who are not at all at home with their own sexuality and who therefore worry that if sexuality is more fully expressed it may "explode" or get out of hand. A feminist Christian sexual ethic, by contrast, rejects as inappropriate all sexual relations or any dynamics of human relationships characterized by inequities of power and lack of mutuality. "Nobody gets hurt" is a negative standard. A more adequate ethic insists that in sexual communication our sense of self-worth should be enhanced. Power and the quality of caring are the key issues in assessing when the criterion of mutual respect obtains. Incest is wrong, for example, because it involves sexual activity between needy, vulnerable, and psychologically dependent children and parents lacking the appropriate power or capacity for adult self-control. Power inequity and the adult's inability not to exploit dependency, not its character as a genital act, make the sexual exchange wrong. A feminist moral norm in sexual relations also would rule out hard-core (that is, not playful) seduction of one person by another or any sexual relationships or acts based on manipulation and ego aggrandizement of one person at the expense of another. But such an ethic never condemns, a priori, a sexual act or a sexual relationship where equality and respect prevail.

Human intimacy relations are complex, and those that include genital sexual relations are often the most complex of all. Because many of us are at our moral worst in our closest relationships, we frequently use sexual exchange, or its withholding, as a weapon to wound, punish, or reward. We need to ask honestly why this is the case. Why do we, in fact, usually "hurt the ones we love"? Why are we most uncaring and insensitive to those with whom our life relations run deepest? A feminist moral theology has a clear answer to this question that a traditional sexual ethics does not even ask, much less answer: We are most loveless in our closest personal relations because we have studied in the patriarchal school of life, learning security in intimate patterns of inequity. It is hard to repent of lessons so early and subtly learned. Few of us ever experience the healing power of eroticism rooted in mutual dependency. How we feel about ourselves most deeply, and therefore how we feel about those whom we claim to care for most, begins at our birth and is learned before we know enough to reject the lesson. If our sexuality is in trouble, we need to be perfectly clear that what has gone wrong is already embedded in the traditional patterns of family life, in our socially enforced sex role socialization, and in gender relations. These inadequacies are embedded in our traditional ethic itself. The sexual disorder of the present is itself glaring evidence that our traditional sexual mores do not deserve acceptance as an adequate morality of sexual relations. The search for a moral-theological ethic of sexuality that encourages genuine, radical love has had to await the challenging of the ancient oppression of misogyny. A world in which gender relations are deeply unjust is not a world whose traditional sexual norms should be commended. To do so is to defend the historical oppression of women and the pervasive ideology that has sustained that oppression, "natural" or compulsory heterosexuality. Homophobia will give way only when misogyny is recognized as a pathological source of human sexual disorder.

THE OLDER PERSON'S WORTH
IN THE EYES OF SOCIETY*

The Social Point of View in Theology and Ethics

It is obvious to anyone who lives in the United States that "growing old" has a strong negative valence in this society and that older persons are devalued and marginalized. This means that as we grow older we not only lose power but most of us lose relationship to what makes people count, that is, to what "gives power." Only a concrete sociohistorical analysis will enable us to probe the social-structural sources of the negative patterns, dynamics, and valuations of older people that lead to a systemic "ageism."

To speak of the older person's worth in the eyes of society requires one to ask "Who speaks for society?" My presupposition is that we all speak in and out of our social relations. Each of us is in society as we speak about it. A perceptive Protestant theologian of the last generation, H. Richard Niebuhr, insisted that we modern Christians need to internalize our historicity more adequately because "we are in history as a fish is in the water." [1] Niebuhr devoted much of his life energy to ensuring that theologians appropriate a historical point of view, learning what it means always to speak from a standpoint *within* history. Much Christian theology has assumed that we can speak as though we were outside of society and historical process, but Niebuhr understood that we cannot do that. To envisage a transhistorical or transsocial viewpoint is still to think from within history and from within society. What Niebuhr called "the social point of view" was a correlate of the historical point of view, and following the German theologian Ernst Troeltsch, Niebuhr described the sociological point of view as "literally a new way of seeing things" [2] and a new dimension of human self-understanding. It is

---

* This essay is remotely based on one that appeared originally in *The Older Person's Worth: A Theological Perspective*, published by Interdenominational Ministries with the Aging, New York, 1980. I have retained the original title assigned, even though, as the introduction to the essay suggests, it was a misleading one for purposes of a theological-ethical analysis.

an awareness that there is a world of sociocultural historical relations, pregiven, into which we are born. We internalize this social
world of meaning and it shapes our ways of seeing things long before we have any fully individuated selfhood or way of construing
our world. "Society" is in us before we are in society. Knowledge
itself is socially constructed; we know nothing of ourselves, our
world, or God, that is not socially constructed knowledge.[3]

There were anticipations of this sociological way of seeing
things long before nineteenth-century European intellectuals began to comprehend the importance of our preconscious sociality.
In fact, this social viewpoint was a sorely needed recovery of
older insights in European cultural history. Awareness of basic
sociality had been lost through an individualizing trend in Reformation and Enlightenment Christian culture. Aspects of ancient
biblical culture give testimony to the presence of a sociological
viewpoint because in Hebraic scripture the world and God are
known through community, never through merely isolated "rational" beings. Even so, H. Richard Niebuhr was right that Christians need still to be challenged in our time to more fully appropriate a historical and social way of seeing things in our theology
and ethics. To do both is a major constructive intellectual challenge because of the heavy individualistic bias of dominant Christian theology and ethics. This bias manifests itself theologically
in the notion that individual persons have a direct connection to
divine revelation, not mediated through social experience. Or, to
put it another way, experience is perceived as something "I"
have, not as "interaction with." Experience is always misunderstood if it is characterized as a "possession" of a self rather than
as an interaction between persons. There is no "experience" alone.

This means with respect to our topic that none of us experiences aging in isolation from the complex social interrelations —
cultural, institutional, historical — in which our lives are set.
Since all assessments of the older person's worth are themselves
social evaluations, what is of ethical or moral interest is not the
question "What does society say about the older person's worth?"
That is a rather abstract question to which the only answer is
either "Society does not speak; people do" or "Society says many
things." Morally, our question should be "What are the dominant
evaluations of older persons' worth in this society, and how do
these evaluations hold up under ethical scrutiny, that is, in terms
of our best considered standards for human well-being?" Since
everything that is right and everything that is wrong about the
way older persons are conceived, envisaged, and called to live life
in this society is a social product, we must ask which social evaluations are morally justified and which we should reject on moral

grounds. The point is not to "get beyond" social evaluations or society but to determine which social judgments are morally justifiable and to ask what we can do to strengthen them and embody them in concrete social relations.

We Christians have no business treating society's viewpoints as something we can avoid sharing. We are in society, and if there is a problem with the ways society interprets reality, we are a part of that problem. Our critical task as Christians, however, is to act and assess our own and others' social evaluations from an adequate theological-ethical standpoint.

The dehumanization of older people is simultaneously a moral and a theological issue. Dehumanization implies that those who share our cohumanity are less than "one of us," which is a moral issue. It is a theological issue insofar as it violates the triadic structure of our simultaneous relations to God-in-neighbor and the neighbor-in-God. A theological ethic that has, in Niebuhr's words, adopted the sociohistorical way of seeing things never attempts to abstract God and neighbor relations from each other. We do not love God if we deprecate our neighbor.

A sociohistorical theological ethic must also presume that any immoral or sinful (to use ethical and theoethical terms, respectively) evaluation of older persons is itself the result of wrong or evil sociohistorical processes enacted over time. The deepest tragedy of human life is that evil, the wrong that we do each other under God, plays itself out and is felt over time in the very ways social systems develop. The old Hebraic lament "Our fathers have eaten sour grapes and the children's teeth are set on edge" [4] expresses the moral wisdom of a properly social ethic. Human alienation and sin live on so ferociously from one generation to the next because evil, injustice, or wrong and distorted social relationships are patterned or institutionalized over time. Social structure, the patterned ways communities and groups relate to each other, generates dynamics of power that shape our communal and personal identities, including our sense of self-worth and self-esteem. When social inequities, structured over time, continue, the result is great disparities of power between persons and groups and the violation of one group by another.[5] Evil is the consequence of disparities of power because where disparity of power is great, violence or control by coercion is the predominant mode of social interaction. Evil, in this reading, is the active or passive effort to deny or suppress another's power-of-being-in-relation. When power disparities are great, those "in charge" cease to have to be accountable to those less powerful for what they do. Societies in which relationships of power are unequal, that is, in which some groups have vast and unchecked power and others are denied even the power of survival, are unjust societies. In such societies, powerful groups need not answer to those affected by their power, and violence, whether covert or direct, prevails. A society where power inequity prevails perpetuates deep woundedness in the lives of its members. Those who are "outsiders" to the predominant power base and values of that society are seen to be, and therefore often experience themselves as, worthless.

Cross-cultural analysis can make us aware of how "modern" and "untypical" is our society's contempt for aging, but only a concrete grasp of the development of our dominant political-economic institutions will enable us to appreciate why we are not dealing merely with "unfortunate attitudes" but rather with substantive social-institutional power interests. The attitudes and human values that make us despise growing old are held in place by the dominant power system operating in the society, and the forces that support the injustices done to older persons must be understood concretely. The sources of alienation and dehumanization operating on the lives of those who are older are political, economic, and cultural, not merely symbolic or psychological.

The Mythologies That Obscure the Sources of Ageism

Our basic myths are contained in the stories we tell ourselves about the distinctive meaning of our society. These myths set the parameters of how we evaluate and judge ourselves and our life activities. This society's basic social myth is that ours has been the greatest social experiment in human history and that here the possibilities for human fulfillment have come to fruition as never before. The code words we use for human fulfillment are "opportunity," "success," and "freedom." We are, most of us imagine, a society where everyone who *really* works at it will make it, successfully improving his or her lot. It is public heresy of the first order to challenge the notion that opportunities are there for everyone. This myth provides a touchstone for how all of us feel about our lives. Racial and ethnic people and the very poor do not buy into it quite as readily as middle- or upper-strata groups. But no one escapes its effects totally. Individuals' lives are measured by the myth, whatever their social realities may be.

Because of this, social inequities and objective disadvantages between persons and between groups are obscured and repressed. We all tend to view ourselves and our society in a way that involves denial of any experience of failure. Since we do not acknowledge any basic unfairness in the system, we even take upon ourselves responsibility for the discontinuity between our actual lives and our "real success." In our personal lives, we can meet failure both with denial and with self-loathing. There is evidence that many Americans live out strategies for coping with the pain of disappointment and lack of fulfillment they do not even know they experience.[6] We all live our lives within a social system marked by astonishing inequalities of wealth and privilege,[7] but since our pervasive social mythos denies that this is the way it is, we come to fear the gap between the realities of our own lives and social expectations. This gap, we secretly imagine, is a true measure of *our* failure. Imaginative sociological research has begun to help us understand how persons attempt to come to grips with thwarted hopes, dreams, and expectations that result from discontinuity between the way society actually functions and the way we are socialized to *believe* that it functions. The result of all of this is split consciousness. At one level we perceive ourselves as failures, while on another level we blame others for the pain and frustration we experience.[8] There are many strategies for "keeping face," and much of the presumed materialism of our culture is related to these compensatory strategies.[9] What we lack is a perspective to analyze and grasp what is really wrong. Our dominant myth directs our attention away from the social structure and the effects it has on our lives. This invisibility is hardly accidental.

A social structure, or a society, is strongly shaped by two interlocking social systems, the reproductive and the productive. We human beings depend on a complex system to perpetuate ourselves biologically and provide for the socialization of our young into the community. Efforts to reproduce and socialize the young, all that constitutes the "reproductive system," go well beyond the mere biological requisites of birth because the human animal is the most helpless of all creatures at birth. A newborn baby has no capacity whatsoever to survive on its own. It is totally dependent on its community. Unless that community responds by providing full care and protection, survival is impossible. To become a fully functioning human, massive learning must take place, including the acquisition of language and other means of communication. Human beings die if there is no one available to provide intense socialization. Among human beings then, the reproductive system is absolutely basic and critically important. For purposes of ethical analysis we must appreciate that the human reproductive system is not merely a biological system, as some social scientists and theologians suggest. It is a *moral* system, that is, a system of embodied values predicated on our mature self-directing capacity as culture creators to care for and value each other. The organization of this system depends not only on existing conditions for biological survival but on our capacity to become the sorts of persons we can be as complex cultural beings. It is through the reproductive system that we come to grasp what our life is about, who our people are, and what life and death mean to our community. The reproductive system, then, is the basic and initial transmitter of cultural values.

The other foundational social dynamic in society involves the productive system, which is determined by how we organize ourselves to produce goods and services for survival out of the material resources available. Until quite recently in recorded history, the productive systems of most societies were intertwined or even subsumed under their reproductive systems. Whatever the basic interrelationship, these two systems — the one that provides socialization into the common culture and the other organized to meet basic needs for food, shelter, and other survival goods — interacted closely to shape the life of a society. In modern societies, however, especially since the development of a distinctively capitalist mode of production,[10] the power of reproductive and cultural systems to shape society has been displaced by the overriding power of the productive system, which now generates change and overrides the values of the intimacy system. This creates incredible strains in society — *incredible* strains.

The Productive System: Overriding Cultural Values and Shaping Ageism

Given the impact for change of a now global capitalist productive system, economic production and exchange strongly dictate cultural values rather than the reverse. Work life in this society is arranged so that human activity is divided into homogeneous segments and sectors. Most people function in their work life as cogs in a machine.[11] We are not expected to function as or to be whole persons in our economic activity. All of this is deeply alienating and dehumanizing to people. We work not for intrinsic gratification but to earn money to survive.[12] The connection that once existed between the reproductive and productive systems now has been severed.[13] All except productive values are doomed to be shunted aside until and unless there are effective checks on economic power such that production can be shaped by social need, not social need by production.

When a person passes a certain presumed point of productivity in work, he or she is adjudged marginal and dysfunctional. These basic dynamics in which "worth" comes to mean "ability to generate money" are exacerbated by the advertising mania on which capitalist consumption depends. "Staying young" sells, and the value of youthfulness is canonized to lure us to spend more.

The culture of capitalism escalates the powerlessness of the no longer young and reinforces their bias against growing older in myriad ways. The passing of young adulthood, symbolized as the high point of life's pleasures and joys, as *the* time when sex appeal and physical prowess reach their zenith, is met with dread. In spite of evidence to the contrary, most people perceive themselves as less capable of sustaining loving sensual relationships as they grow older. The wisdom most cultures associate with maturity — open-mindedness, tolerance, tenderness, and gentle humor — are not the qualities most of us associate with aging.

Even before retirement, people in this society begin to feel old. Work itself often involves a psychological debilitation process. By and large, people suffer through their work. They grow dispirited over time with the processes of earning a living. Much energy is lost as well as the capacity for creativity and productiveness. Resignation to aging, the acceptance of a loss of energy and self-direction, often is a result of alienation over time in the workplace. Much of the economic system's structure causes people to become psychologically weary so that they long for retirement and even for the marginalization that goes with it. The prospect of leisure lures them, but the reality of marginalization further debilitates them. Our technological advances have created the conditions for living longer, but the technological modes of organization we adopt in the workplace also ensure that we will become marginal producers earlier and become psychologically less alert in the process.

An advanced capitalist, technologically oriented system of production values those labor skills that involve the proficiencies of youth — quick performance, adept memory, capacity for repetition. The abilities associated with young adulthood and early middle age are optimized through technological change. If and when one falters in high productivity, the system can do without you. Unemployment is becoming a massive problem, and fewer and fewer workers have seniority protection to enable them to keep their jobs if their "productivity" in this new sense drops. All sorts of explanations regarding current rates of unemployment are offered, but an economic system in which profit or productivity defined this way is the sole consideration is inevitably one in which the number of jobs will give way if means can be found to replace workers with machines. "Efficiency of production" remains the single "rational" index of "intelligent" economic behavior. The trend of our current economic system is toward fewer and fewer jobs per capita, higher technological requirements of those jobs at the higher echelons, and fewer and fewer meaningful jobs at the bottom of the spectrum.

Our system cannot absorb the productive labor of the unskilled young, and it cannot absorb the productive labor of older persons. Currently, of course, battles have been waged against mandatory retirement, with some success. Legislation that allows people to work beyond age sixty-five has passed in several states. However, we should not be surprised if enthusiasm for this trend wanes and if such laws are enforced or applied only in selected work sectors. Most progressive social legislation passed in the United States in the last fifty years is being systematically dismantled and undone. Nonmandatory retirement as one "progressive" gain will, I predict, turn out to protect only one group — upper-middle-income white male professionals. Older people should not be naive as to how broad-based or secure are any gains won so far. Neither the young nor older persons count as productive members of this sort of society. If you are not in the productive labor force, whether because you cannot get in at the usual entry point or because you have been pushed out at the other end, you are stigmatized and rendered objectively powerless.

The concept of "profit" under capitalism is one that most of us do not understand very well. Those who defend "profit" as a rational basis for economic activity usually do so on grounds that it is a measure of "efficiency" in economic activity. I would argue, however, that in late monopoly capitalism, there is little or no connection between profit and efficiency of production.[14] Furthermore, there is now an inverse relation between what is profitable and what makes for human well-being. Under late capitalism, so-called private capital supports only those activities — whether productive or service activities — that realize a high rate of return over cost. Goods and services that do not have high profitability in this sense fall under "public" funding, that is, they are paid for by the state. Everything that ceases to provide high capital return is turned over to the state. Since our society is organized to ensure that everything that can be done with monetary profit will be done by so-called private enterprise and everything that cannot be turned into profit will be funded by the state, and underfunded because it is not profitable, it follows that the well-being of children and older people who are not rich will be increasingly the province of the state and will be underfunded. So-called private enterprise, that is, capital not controlled socially, will not support what is not profitable. All costs of human well-being that are not covered by wage labor become "welfare." It is very important to realize what all this means for the situation of older persons in this society. All except the wealthiest of older persons, and everybody else who does not or cannot amass capital, is becoming a part of the "welfare problem" by default. The state is becoming a battleground between the capitalist group — those who are in a position to amass capital in the form of either moderate or huge profits — and everybody else — middle-income people, the working poor (whose numbers are growing dramatically), and those outside the wage labor system altogether. However, both political parties obscure these dynamics by denying the diametrically opposite interests of the wealthy and middle-income group. The Republicans show more active contempt for the poor than do the Democrats, but neither party challenges the basic and pervasive policy of government protection of the rich.

When middle-strata people criticize the "welfare system," they are talking about only the smallest aspect of the total welfare system that is our huge federal budget, the tiny sector of government spending that redirects small amounts of income to unemployed or unemployable people. If, however, we understand the entire federal budget as the sum of our public welfare expenditure, we can see how public money is actually being expended to shape human welfare and security. Nothing in the private sector is spent for well-being, except the well-being of those who can use wealth to create wealth. Welfare economists sometimes portray the role of the state as that of "redistributing" wealth. The problem with this characterization is that, given tax policies, the redistribution is from the wage labor of middle-income people to the corporations via policies that favor capital formation, the military budget, highway expenditures that serve business, and so forth. Public perception is that redistribution is from the upper-middle sector to the poor, but this is a palpable falsehood.

The public welfare recipients who in fact get the lion's share of direct government aid are corporations that produce arms, the energy companies, so-called private enterprises. We should not be deceived that public welfare in this society consists only of transfers made to the very poor.[15] The federal budget is one vast welfare network through which all activities afflicted by the falling rate of profit endemic to capitalism are bailed out. As the human services are neglected, people are pitted against each other for them. We come to perceive each other as the "enemy," as rivals for limited public resources, as "freeloaders" who are doing less than their just share of social labor. The number of older persons in this society is increasing rapidly. It is safe to predict that more and more older persons will be resented by those in the prime of life. And the truth is that a smaller and smaller percentage of older persons will be able to live out their lives in the modest affluence many have come to aspire to in retirement. The aged poor, especially women, are dramatically on the increase in this society.

The Reproductive System: No Room for Our Elders

In less than two centuries, the whole globe has been caught up in processes of change that have eroded traditional interpersonal life, driven myriads off the land, out of extended families and into urban settings. Not only have families and all groups within the broader face-to-face community been affected by the dramatic and accelerating changes in capitalist economy but the Christian church has been transformed by these forces as well. Contrary to some mindless theological analyses, these changes are the result of the growing power of political economy to control our lives, not the result of changing ideas or some dangerous, if abstract, "loss of traditional values."

Even so, for the alienated worker, family life and intimacy relations take on great symbolic importance and become an arena of "compensatory dignity." Many of us expect "interpersonal relations" to enable us to offset the alienation and dehumanization occurring within our work life. However, those who do not even have a place within the productive system as it currently functions are doubly marginalized and considered to be "social problems." And such persons are doubly "problems" if they do not conform to the dominant pattern within the reproductive system — the nuclear family. It is obvious that most older persons in our society are "outsiders" on both counts. They either have left or, in the case of women who were homemakers, never entered, the productive system, and they frequently are "deviants" — that is, "non-nuclears" in the reproductive system. And so the mindset so pervasive in our society is that older people are "a social problem." From an ethical point of view, of course, human beings are never problems. Our real problem — the moral one — is that we have a social system that cannot accommodate the well-being of real, living people, a system that shunts people aside if they do not "fit" *its* needs. Often we Christians participate in an immoral misdiagnosis of this "problem" by supporting the patronizing notion that the help older people need is pity or charity to ameliorate their pain rather than liberation through systematic change.

Another aspect of Christian complicity in ageism derives from the church's subtle but uncritical sanctification of the family, especially the modern nuclear family, which is equated naively with God's will. The nuclear family is a recent invention in human history, and it is in fact not a very strong social unit for coping with the pressures of modern life. Our basic way of patterning intimacy relationship — coupling in households — is in deep trouble because it too has become the victim of the way we organize our productive life. The theologians and church leaders who moralize about "weakening family values" fail completely to grasp the relation between these strains and the functioning of the political economy. The loss of family values is presumed to derive from changing attitudes of women toward traditional roles of subordination.[16] Again, those most vulnerable to the system are blamed for forces that they have little or no power to change.

The same dynamics that have produced and threatened the nuclear family also shape the family relations that condition the experience of the value of older persons. The nuclear family as a consumption unit survives more and more on two incomes, since women increasingly work for economic reasons. Where the family has broken down, women and their dependent children live on the meager income of the working mother. It becomes extremely difficult for persons in their "productive prime" to maintain older family members' full participation in the family intimacy system. Few have either the flexibility of time or resources to provide such maintenance fully within the family unit. The primary family system has to cope with pressure created by both an ever-extended period of pre-adult life or "youth," and an ever-longer period of "postproductive" old age.

We celebrate youth in this society, and more particularly young adulthood, as the cultural ideal. However, children, the very young, are perceived as a problem just as older people are.[17] Those who have not yet entered economic productivity or who are no longer needed within the economic system are problematic. Between coping with the needs of the young and the pressures of the workplace with all its alienation, adults in their prime also live under tremendous pressure. So much time and energy, and so much of a family's resources, are required to raise children that the aging person becomes the interloper to be shunted aside and isolated from the family system when things get hard. Not surprisingly, many older persons resign themselves to this fate, to having their basic needs overlooked, as if such treatment were punishment for growing older. Such resignation is reinforced as older people are treated in patronizing ways and their passivity constantly reinforced. Not surprisingly, self-pity and stoicism about the processes of aging and dying are widespread among older people.

The danger of reinforcing passivity among older persons is obvious to those who work with them, but what is not so obvious is the way reinforcement of the alienation of ageism is conditioned by and builds on patterns generated by the productive system. Older people's experience of powerlessness is objectively structured by their marginality.[18] They enter the mainstream of ongoing social life only when they are *brought* in — only on special occasions. Grandparents come for holidays, but they are not a part of an ongoing system of intimacy relations. Such marginalization is a particular burden for older persons who are single. Subjectively, then, a major burden of older people is coping psychologically with actual marginalization, real loneliness, being forgotten, except on special occasions. Is it any wonder, then, that depression is the major psychological impairment of persons in this society as they grow old? Is it surprising that older persons so often live in the past, are filled with nostalgia, and are embittered by their fate?

Over a decade ago, a social scientist living and working in the East who had grown up in California returned there after an absence of many years. Addressing a group about changes he observed since his childhood, he described California as a bastion of conflict between the young, who were the first full generation of Californians born and raised in the state, and the old, many of whom had grown up elsewhere and retired to California. He sensed a pitched battle going on between these groups such that the respective social aspirations of both were canceling each other out. What he described of California has become characteristic of the dynamics of other regions of this society. Currently, older persons often see others who require public resources for education or social services as a threat to their well-being. Some older citizens are quick to blame youth or poor or racial ethnic people as a threat to society. Conversely, the young often fail to understand the vulnerability of older persons. It is time for all of us to recognize that here, as elsewhere, our political economy denies actual interdependence and disguises our mutual victimization. It creates woundedness and disempowerment in the lives of all but a few.

The Church's Ministry with Older Persons

What does all of this mean for the church's ministry with and among older persons? Only ministry understood not merely as service to or for but work in solidarity with them can be justified in the present. The image of ministry as empowerment is especially crucial when this ministry is with older persons because, as we have seen, passivity reinforces aging, and our "help" negates wholeness for those who will be trapped by our paternalism. We cannot condemn society for marginalizing older persons while we ourselves relate to them paternalistically, for paternalism is a passive and nonmutual relation. Anything done to or for older persons that does not mobilize them to enhance their self-direction and increase their solidarity with others to organize for their rights increases their victimization. The first criterion of adequacy of any church ministry with older persons is its effectiveness in motivating them to active political engagement.

A second requirement of adequate ministry is that congregations take responsibility for not reproducing alienated patterns of relating to older persons in the internal life of the church itself. H. Richard Niebuhr argued that the appropriate starting point for Christian ministry is always transforming social patterns within the church.[19] Churches often are not aware of the subtle ways in which they perpetuate negative images of older people in the ongoing structure of congregational life. Many congregations are structured to marginalize older persons at every turn. Furthermore, insofar as the churches teach and reinforce a "sensuality-denying spirituality," insofar as they convey a body-denying antisensuality, they participate deeply in the dominant sexual stereotypes that stigmatize older persons. Those who learn to affirm their sensuality can also affirm their natural finitude. Acceptance of positive embodiedness also enables us to accept the natural processes of aging and death.

Unless we learn to overcome our historic negativism toward embodiedness and learn to celebrate sensuality, we will continue to perpetuate the isolation, exclusion, and devaluation of those no longer young in another way. Older persons are, more often than not, disenfranchised sexually.[20] Often those most deprived of touch and sexual expression are persons institutionalized in the facilities owned and run by the churches! Since the human need for touch and physical intimacy does not lessen as we get older, deprivation of touch and sensuality increases the rapidity of the aging process. To break the church's deep complicity in perpetuating the myth of older persons' asexuality is a major priority.

Our uncritical sanctification of the nuclear family, already discussed, shapes the way congregations organize themselves, and this in turn further reinforces the older person's sense of failure, deviance, and aloneness. Nearly all congregations appear to assume that the nuclear family is both the statistical and the moral norm for all persons in society. The nuclear family surely is no longer the statistical norm in the United States, that is, it is not the living unit of most people in our society.[21] More and more of us question whether it should be the moral norm, so it is surely time to assess whether traditional patterns of congregational life make sense.

Many urban congregations, at least those struggling most, have had to learn through hard experience that the nuclear family is neither statistically typical nor to be uncritically celebrated. However, in the more affluent urban churches or in suburban and many rural churches, one has only to participate in worship observing what is said and done through the eyes of the single older person to sense how "foreign" and outside the norm the older person is made to feel. So much preaching and teaching takes for granted the nuclear family, heterosexual marriage, and parenting as everyone's daily experience. Little except public worship is cross-generational, and children and youth are as segregated as older people because they too are considered a "special problem" for ministry. The single person of any age, including the single older person, is particularly made to feel like an outsider.

Nor is this issue a source of discontent only in liberal churches. Several years ago, I was asked to lead a workshop on patterns of congregational life at a conference attended by many theological conservatives. I asked them to identify the forms and patterns of church life that they found alienating. Much to my surprise I was suddenly confronted by a very angry group. Far from being uncritical of the church, this group of very pious, largely over-forty and many over-sixty Presbyterians expressed outrage at the family-centered biases of their congregations. Self-designated "evangelicals" from a very conservative region, these people were every bit as disaffected as any group of liberals might be about the rigidity of the churches on this question. I was amazed at the depth of feeling expressed about their experience of being outsiders because they were single or older or both. As we analyzed these patterns together, the presumed theological differences between us fell away, and all of us agreed that a total reorientation of parish life is needed if human wholeness and well-being are to be served.

For any of us to be who we are intended to be in God's image, we must all experience the communality of human solidarity. None of us is a full person in isolation, and a ministry of empowerment in our time means calling people to be who they are under God, to own their power of personhood as the power of shared life. The devastating consequence of a social system that disvalues older persons is that we all become more alone, more isolated, and therefore less engaged in the fullness of life as we grow older. "Life" here is not an abstract virtue. It is given to be engaged, actively. We can move toward the end of our lives, into death, without fear only if our lives have been deeply lived. Ministry as the work of empowerment is a challenge among older persons precisely because so much in their environment conspires to subvert their active engagement in life.

Older persons do need to hear the call of others to struggle to express their power, their creativity, their ongoing strength to live fully as God's people. With the wisdom of maturity, we ought to experience new dimensions of freedom in our lives. From an adequate theological perspective, freedom is not just liberty or even possessing a range of options; it is the power of self-expression and the ability to respond to and richly interact with the society of living beings. Older persons can be free — uniquely free — to respond to life in new and deep ways. Even though aging involves real loss of physical power and a foreshortening of some life options, it need not involve despair or isolation. To accept the appropriate forms of dependency that come with growing old need not mean loss of dignity. In fact, the transitions aging requires depend on this well-grounded sense of dignity. Older persons can learn the lessons of artful living toward death if we are really *with them* as they do. We need to be present to older persons in ways that never discourage their own resourcefulness in using their continuing power. In challenging them to exercise power over their lives, we also call on them to minister to us, because we genuinely need their modeling as witness that the fullness of life is possible even into death. The process of aging is, after all, a cross-cultural universal phenomenon. Any of us blessed to reach maturity experience it. All of us are getting older and we all need to learn the art — and courage — of aging. We need the help and experience of older people.

Obviously, then, we all have a stake in resistance and struggle against the dominant evaluations of aging in our society. It is one of the burdens of life in the culture of late capitalism that none of the nobility, none of the reverence, none of the awe that other cultures have associated with growing older obtains for us. To reclaim aging as a miracle of life, a beautiful process that is part and parcel of abundant life, will take a united effort at subversion of the dominant political economy and its culture. To share this subversive work is the serious business of ministry in our time.

THE EQUAL RIGHTS AMENDMENT

A Moral Analysis*

The proposed Twenty-Seventh Amendment to the U.S. Constitution, the Equal Rights Amendment, has gone down to defeat, and it may well be a long time before a strong political effort can again be mounted to ensure women full and unambiguous standing as citizens in this nation. That women's inequality before the law continues in manifold ways is obvious.[1] Even the ERA would have changed that reality only slowly.[2] Retrospectively, what was surprising was the ease with which the anti-ERA forces prevailed, especially given the fact that there was little morally informed opposition to the ERA. The feebleness of the victors' moral case was paralleled only by their political acumen.

During the entire ERA debate it was difficult, even distasteful, for me to have to spell out the moral claims that grounded the case for the Equal Rights Amendment. The truth is that as a woman and a feminist — one committed to the full emancipation of the majority of the human race — I grew weary of taking seriously persons who questioned the moral rightness of the ERA. Those who still have reservations about the ethical appropriateness of including women in society's constitutional framework of justice seem to me to be on such shabby ground morally that further discussion seems pointless. I realize that those people who fear having gender excluded from categories that legitimate inequality before the law are still numerous, and I recognize that there are many such persons among my own professional peers in the ranks of scholars of religion. However, I simply do not give such persons high status as moral reasoners, much as I take seriously their power as moral agents. Having won the last round of the political battle confirms their political clout but says nothing, I am persuaded, about their moral competence.

One of the primary tasks of moral analysis such as this is to

---

* This essay is adapted from a presentation made at a plenary session on the ERA at the American Academy of Religion in New Orleans, November 1978.

envision morally salient reasons for supporting or objecting to the
public policy under discussion. Yet what reasons for opposing
the ERA deserve moral standing? The Senate committee that referred the ERA to the Senate for consideration in 1972 stated its
legal theory (or, in nontechnical terms, its constitutional intent)
concisely: "that the Federal government and all state and local
governments treat each person, male and female, as an individual."[3] Since the provisions for equal protection of the law contained in the Fifth and Fourteenth Amendments to the Constitution have never been interpreted consistently to prohibit all
discrimination against women as a class, the Twenty-Seventh
Amendment would have prohibited such discrimination, if and
when that discrimination had been shown to be predicated simply on one's being a woman. While the full meaning of the ERA
would have been sorted out and sifted only through years of judicial decision, its legal theory was simple, and, in terms of our
legal and moral traditions, noncontroversial: Gender, per se, is
not to be an impediment to full standing as an individual before
the law. Such theory is, quite literally, of the essence of both
nineteenth- and twentieth-century liberalism, hence of twentieth-
century conservative and liberal ideology. What possible moral
reason could one find for objecting to it? I am inclined to think
that persons who believed they were morally justified to oppose
the ERA either (1) do not understand what a moral category, especially the moral category of rights, is or (2) do not believe that
women deserve basic status vis-à-vis the category "human person."

With respect to the first possibility — the failure to understand the moral category of rights — one can only point out to
such ERA opponents that they themselves cannot claim as
"rights" anything they deny to others in the same morally relevant group as themselves. Many moral philosophers have pointed
out that on logical grounds no one can claim anything as a human moral right — a right that obtains even in the absence of
entering a specified contractual arrangement — without granting
that such a claim belongs generally to all who fall into the category "human."[4] If any of us is prepared to invoke anything as a
human moral right on our own behalf, that very act implies the
existence of a similar claim for every other member of our species. Furthermore, a right is not a mere liberty. That is, it is not
simply a demand to be unencumbered or to be left alone. A right
is relational and implies my claim to legitimately interfere with
others should they attempt to restrain my action in certain specified ways. I cannot reasonably assert that it is rightful to restrain
others under specified conditions without acknowledging others'

similar right to restrain me if my action comparably infringes on them. Opponents of ERA who are legal positivists, ruling out moral considerations as irrelevant to constitutional discussion, can ignore such considerations, but anyone who acknowledges the relevance of the moral category of rights at all must, I believe, find this consideration about their reciprocal and relational nature persuasive. None who claims a right to discrete personal standing — that is, as "an individual" — before the law could, on moral grounds, deny such standing to others of the same category.

The only other line of moral opposition to the ERA requires its adversaries to make explicit and defend the thesis that male and female do not share a common human nature. The question here is not whether there are any differences between men and women but whether gender is so basic a distinction that it is legitimate morally to treat females as a fundamentally different category from males. Many people believe that men and women differ greatly. But are there valid reasons for believing that gender differences should translate into a normative moral difference? I most emphatically do not believe that there are.

The most powerful and emotionally effectual warrants for a "double human nature" view of male and female have been engendered by and transmitted through our major religious traditions as well as by these traditions' secular counterparts and progeny — certain so-called scientific teachings about biological or natural gender determinism.[5] I recognize, of course, that some women who share my feminist commitment also advocate a "two human natures" theory of gender difference, reversing, however, the traditional view of male supremacy. While I disagree strenuously with some of my feminist sisters on this matter, the argument between us is not strictly relevant to the ERA debate since the present legal arrangement of this society favors men, and feminists who advocate the superiority of female nature do not support the prevailing state of affairs any more than I do. We are united in support of the ERA, as we are united in finding any "male superiority" line of argument preposterous. I will no longer expend energy refuting notions of the supremacy and normativeness of male humanity in any form, nor do I think that attempts to refute it will be fruitful. Such opinions, like all bigotry, go untouched by reason, hence by morality. Like most feminists, I simply prefer to allow my own life to bespeak the absurdity of such belief. The time has long passed when I will ask or encourage any other woman to ask anyone's permission — least of all any male who views me as inferior to him — to count myself as a full member of my species or my society. Such intellectually vacuous nonsense, though still held in some benighted circles to be an intellectually serious claim, is a twentieth-century equivalent to a pre-Copernican worldview.

If my initial thesis is accepted — that the ERA is clearly morally justified social policy and that its defeat had nothing to do with the legitimacy of women's moral claims to equality before the law — the question that looms large is this: "Why, given the clear intent of the Twenty-Seventh Amendment to formally establish specific personhood as grounds for equal treatment before the law, did the ERA fare so badly?"

Let me reiterate that I am under no illusion that passage of the ERA would have established the legal equality of men and women in this nation. There are clear limits to the power of law, even of constitutional law, to effect social change. I am keenly aware that "equal standing before the law" for men has not meant actual legal equality between men. The massive social deformations of race and class privilege, the inordinate power of wealth and institutional status in this society are such that the formal requisites of legal equality are rendered inoperative at many relevant points. In fact, by asking why the ERA fared so badly, we are confronted by precisely the same social constraints that continue to prevent functional equality before the law among males.

Some interpreters have considered it a sufficient answer to the question of why the ERA failed to argue that it was a victim of the complex process of ratification of constitutional amendments handed down to us by the founding fathers. It goes without saying that there is some truth to this contention. It *is* true in large part because the founding fathers did not really desire a deeply egalitarian society, some of their rhetoric to the contrary notwithstanding. The procedure they mandated for constitutional change and extension of the meaning of legal rights is so complex that the burden of proof, always and overwhelmingly, is placed on those who seek change in an egalitarian direction. Yet the constitutional process, per se, did not defeat the ERA.

We need to remember that among all of the proposed social policy changes ever placed before the nation, the Equal Rights Amendment was not only among the most morally compelling but, in terms of public opinion at this point in our history, among the *least* controversial. A very substantial majority of Americans actively favored it. We should remind ourselves of how rarely such widespread public consensus is achieved for a social policy change before its passage if there is well-organized and well-financed political opposition to it. The states that ratified the ERA included within their boundaries well over 75 percent of the population of this nation — a demographic three-quarters, if not three-quarters of the actual number of states. Furthermore, in many states whose legislatures militantly opposed ratification — for example, Louisiana — black and/or female support for the ERA created a massive base of approval that white male reactionary legislatures simply refused to heed.

The thesis that complex constitutional amendment procedures accounted for the protracted nature of the struggle and defeat of the ERA is, therefore, only a half-truth because it ignores the political interests affected. An adequate analysis of why the ERA languished must specifically identify whose interests are at stake in the status quo. Unless we understand that some very concrete privileges are protected by women's disadvantaged legal status, we will never appreciate the sheer power of mobilized resistance to this positive moral change favored by the majority. The deeper question, then, is not only who stands to gain but who really stands to lose from the legal equality of women and men in this society. Here, the ERA is only the symbolic tip of the iceberg. A real culture of equality between men and women, as between white and nonwhite persons and as between rich and poor, would require very deep, fundamental changes in the way resources and benefits are distributed in this society. It was, I submit, the possibility — not the certainty, but the possibility — that resources and benefits would be equalized that was the deepest threat.

The assault on the ERA was only one prong of a broad-based political counterattack against all claims to equality still being advanced in this nation; but gender equality, a seemingly innocuous demand on a one-to-one basis, has, given our numbers, radical implications because women are *not* a minority. Female equality is more dangerous to established interests than it looks because continued organized political pressure by women would eventually portend very basic shifts in the distribution of goods and services. The individuality of the legal theory underlying the ERA means that such pressure would mount only slowly, but the aspiration to equality is catching. Remote as the direct threat to the political-economic macrostructure seems, some powerful sectors of the economy were quick to anticipate its possible relevance. Most conspicuously, a vast sector of corporate capitalism — the insurance industry — was the first to sense the potential danger. ERA-based legal challenges surely would arise against the insurance industry's practice of using gender-based actuarial tables to determine policy payoff rates. Anticipating such a threat, this industry invested millions of dollars in the defeat of the Twenty-Seventh Amendment.

The insurance industry may have been right to fear the ERA,

but it is unlikely that litigation based on the amendment would have legitimated immediate change toward economic justice given the present make up of the Supreme Court. This court construes economic rights to adhere only to corporations, and citizens' "political" rights to be narrow indeed. However, the feminization of poverty proceeds apace,[6] and this would mean continued mobilization of pressure for gender justice at every economic level over time. Every ERA-based victory would encourage further challenge and perhaps bring closer the day when such provisions as social security for homemakers might be demanded. Even that "minor" change would have staggering implications for redistributing income, and such changes would also increase pressure for other changes, such as wages for housework, that is, remuneration for women's vast amount of now unpaid labor in the home. Any or all economic redress further encourages women to expect to be treated justly economically — an expectation few women have, as yet, even acquired. Does anyone doubt that the ERA would fuel rising female expectations for justice?

If the defeat of the ERA demonstrates anything, it reveals how impervious our dominant political economy is to the moral will of citizens. Political democracy has, in fact, ceased to function when corporate economic interests are threatened. The ERA went down to defeat in spite of the fact that no one found any good moral reason to oppose it! Opposition to it was rooted in specific economic interests, wrapped in vague ideological innuendo to the effect that the ERA would be a "dangerous" step toward loss of "traditional values." The truth is that what is really feared is greater democracy at the economic level, for that would threaten the basic patterns of ownership and control that now endanger our political rights, including our right to count as individuals before the law. Ironically, the defeat of the ERA not only is evidence that women are *not* full citizens but is also graphic evidence that these citizenship rights no longer operate well for men as individuals. No matter how many of us individually affirm our need for equality, it will not happen if profits are threatened. Unless we move toward economic democracy, we are at the end of political democracy in this society. The rising cultural counterattack against changes in women's role is tied to the rising tide of protectionism of existing economic privilege.

The lack of commitment to the ERA, particularly among moderate, well-educated, more-or-less liberal males (and some females) in academia is, for this reason, deeply disturbing. In the absence of good reasons for objecting to the ERA — moderates strongly share what Michael Lewis has called "the person-as-central-sensibility" — many in academia did not actively oppose it.

Precisely because no one could actively oppose it and sustain their moral credentials, such persons merely dragged their feet. Moderates and liberals are adept at giving tepid support to causes whenever their morality and their interests are at odds.

Even more distressing, given the intellectual vacuum on the anti-ERA side, were the numbers of academics who attempted to make the "two natures" theory of gender intellectually respectable once again. Neoconservatives such as George Gilder, Michael Novak, Bruno Bettelheim, and even Christopher Lasch have been "discovered" and have provided desperately needed fresh intellectual buttresses and legitimations against gender justice.[7] The novel mystifications these intellectuals have offered give their claims to male supremacy a modern twist. In Gilder's case, this even involved the strategy of embracing male inferiority to ensure male supremacy. Even so, neoconservative proponents of gender dualism would make a disastrous mistake if they imagined that their newfound intellectual respectability and status reflect *either* any recovery of reverence for intellectuality *or* respect for traditional masculinist elitist values of "merit" among society's rulers. These intellectuals are being welcomed to lend respectability to what, given the inroads of liberalism, has now become a highly distasteful enterprise in the United States — giving direct intellectual legitimation to "the culture of inequality."[8] Neoconservative intellectuals are the hit men of the new corporate ruling class. The latter are as ideologically flexible as they are morally mercurial, all in the service of sustaining their control.

In light of all this, what those of us in learned societies of religion owe ourselves is acknowledgment that we have been among the most reluctant professional academic groups in accepting responsibility for advocating the justice of the ERA. We need to ask ourselves why so many of us professors of religion — with numerous clergy in our ranks — were so slow to acknowledge anything morally important at stake in the passage of the Equal Rights Amendment. Have *we* come so far in separating morality and religion that a moral claim no longer implies anything about our religious responsibilities? Our silence and begrudging response to the ERA bespoke a distressing lack of concern about whose interests and values our intellectual labor actually serves. The ERA is, for the time being, dead. It falls to those of us who care about the integrity of the enterprise of religious studies to name the moral, spiritual, and intellectual mediocrity of the performance we professors of religion managed in its behalf before it died.

THE POLITICS
OF ENERGY POLICY*

The Requirements of an Adequate
Theological Ethic of Ecojustice

Our theological and moral perspectives must accommodate the deepened sense of human interdependence that we gain when we place ourselves and our societies in an emergent ecological perspective. Such a perspective enables us to envision, more radically than ever before, our relationship to the full cosmos. We human beings and our societies are an interlocking and interdependent part of a wider environmental system. We no longer dare perceive nature merely as something inert, "out there," capable of whatever "use" we may choose to make of it. Our ravenous use of fossil fuel resources is the most dramatic expression of our insensitivity to the limits imposed by this environmental system, which increasingly asserts itself as a living part of "our bodies, ourselves." [1] The finitude of those resources and the values of a high energy consumption society pose a fundamental religious and moral challenge to human beings on this planet.

The ecologists have taught us that the demands we make on our natural environment "answer back," and the ecosystem — as the totality of our relationships and interactions with nature through society — responds to our intervention in intricate ways, with consequences uncalculated in the best-laid schemes of human historical agents. To use a traditional ethical metaphor not usually extended to inanimate or nonhuman entities in earlier moral philosophy, our environment turns out to impose moral claims on us. These claims, if ignored, may dramatically influence our destinies and not only limit our own historical options but deeply affect the lives of others on this planet and also the prospects of any surviving heirs.

From an ecological perspective,[2] our use of energy is the most dramatic of the many transactions we enter into with the totality of our environment. Painful as it may be to recognize the fact, it

---

* This essay is an adapted version of one that appeared in Dieter Hessel, ed., *Energy Ethics: A Christian Response* (New York: Friendship Press, 1979).

is now all too clear that established patterns of energy use have been developed heedless of the consequences of our actions for our own and others' well-being as parts of the wider ecosystem.

It is not surprising that women, and feminists in particular, who insist on a holistic, relational approach to nature, culture, history, and society have embraced this ecological perspective as a basepoint of feminist theory.[3] "Reweaving the web of life"[4] stands in feminist theory as a metaphor not only for eradicating violence but for reintegrating corelational respect for nature into all our moral agency. Such expanded moral sensibility requires a new, nonexploitative attitude toward the natural environment and to ourselves as creatures whose well-being is intertwined with the rest of nature. It involves a dramatic reorientation in our sense of power-in-relation to nature, including the other members of our species. The feminist insight that power is enhanced when shared, reciprocal, and constrained by the limits that respectful interrelationship imposes has been widely, and properly, invoked over against other and more typical images of social power in our western intellectual traditions. "Power" has long connoted the capacity to control others. Furthermore, power as a social resource has been interpreted primarily as a fixed and static "zero sum" that can only be traded off, coerced, or seized. Contrary to some feminist analysis, I believe that in situations of genuine conflict of interest, power does take on a zero-sum dynamic, but it is the goal of a genuinely transformative social ethic to identify social policies that will enhance shared, reciprocal, accountable social power so as to press beyond zero-sum power toward more inclusive shared power and participation.[5]

Current debates over energy policy are not merely confrontations between those who acknowledge the limits and contraints imposed by moral relations to the ecosystem and those more confident that further technological breakthroughs will deliver us from such constraints, though this confrontation is important. If the controversy about a public energy policy simply expressed this particular value conflict, there would be reason to hope that eventually (and perhaps sooner rather than later) the human wisdom of a conservation ethic[6] would commend itself to all concerned. The more troublesome dimension of the public policy debate around energy production and consumption is that the interests and values that shape the debate are frequently masked, and information controlled, by those who have the least to gain by any genuine conservation approach or any reorientation of consumption values. The energy corporations' accounts of what our energy problems are and what ought to be done about them preempt other, more critical and perceptive voices.

The Need for Social Analysis

Clarification of the theological and moral foundations of the energy issue is but a first step in determining what public policy an optimal theological social ethic would commend. One of the serious failures of much theologically informed energy ethics has been a tendency to envision a "salvific ethic" [7] without consideration of the actual conditions for, and consequences of, implementing that ethic at the level of public policy. It is not enough merely to envisage an energy ethic adequate to the insights of Christian theological tradition and appropriate to a well-considered sense of our moral obligations.

Determining a just public policy regarding energy also requires us to analyze the existing social arrangements that form the institutional matrix through which an energy policy must be formulated. To put the point another way, a feminist approach must incorporate sensitivity to power in the institutional matrix. From a moral point of view, it is insufficient if our analysis of power deals exclusively with its expressive aspects, that is, with the capacity of persons and groups to realize shared goals and values, to attain common social ends. Social policy always is forged in an institutional context in which power is inequitably distributed between groups of persons and between organizational systems. Therefore, clear awareness of who gains and who loses from any particular social policy option among the ecologically attuned public is critical. The challenge is to gain political support for morally viable social policies. Any energy policy will bear the mark of existing social arrangements, and it will have consequences for the lives of persons that can be identified only through analysis of how the political and economic dynamics of the existing social system will work on that policy.

We are political beings — those who pursue our own and our community's interests — not because we are "fallen" or are sinners but because we live in a finite world where, at least hypothetically, we cannot be sure that even our legitimate and well-considered interests will be accommodated. Politics as the process of seeking the realization of our interests in society, then, is inherent in our existence as finite, or creaturely, social beings. Power becomes a finite resource — a zero-sum quantity — because some goals and interests cannot be accommodated if other interests conflict with them. In society, some gain their interests at the expense of others. In politics, power takes on the character of the capacity to set limits to others' pursuit of their interests.

Such abstract, theoretical considerations about power and the nature of society do not clarify fully the major barriers to implementing our moral norms through a morally adequate public energy policy. Since every proposal for social change emerges in situations where certain organizations and groups are already in the ascendancy with respect to shaping public policy and determining what interests that policy will serve, a social ethic must incorporate analyses of these power realities and their ongoing dynamics. An adequate theological-ethical analysis must convey this sort of concrete sense of existing power dynamics that work to prevent the realization of a just public energy policy.

Justice in a Theological Context

From the standpoint of Christian theological ethics, not only is "justice the first virtue of social institutions," [8] but it is also the central notion of what constitutes all rightly related communities under God. In the context of biblical theology, our commitment to justice is understood as *the* expression of our covenantal relationship to God. The people of God live under a stringent expectation of communal right relationships in which the meaning of justice is discerned particularly by the way the community deals with those who are most marginated or are not well placed to defend their own needs and interests.[9] In biblical terms, the righteous community — the one rightly related to God — is the community that expresses its fidelity to God through concern for the least well-off persons and groups. Jesus expanded this prophetic theme of justice in praxis and teaching by identifying God's continuing presence with the presence and solidarity of those who were especially victimized by society's existing arrangements.[10] A theologically based Christian ethic of ecojustice cannot aim at anything less than a social policy that takes special account of the effects of that policy on those already most disadvantaged in society.

Nor can a theologically grounded sense of justice allow us to rest content with procedural definitions of justice. Those who define social justice primarily as requiring concern for "treating like cases alike" or for optimizing procedural fairness in society, important as these considerations are, often evade the question of whether justice involves a substantive conception of what is good for human persons.[11] A biblical sense of justice focuses on concrete human need and is therefore substantive, not merely procedural. Our sense of justice requires us to make direct address to real, lived-world inequities and to critically scrutinize and protest against institutional arrangements that pervasively perpetuate and deepen social inequities. Without a clear sense of how policies impact the lives of those already vulnerable and disadvantaged by current social relations, a "conservation ethic" could increase human suffering unawares. No theological ethic can avoid facing the politics of energy policy or overlook the deep-seated barriers that block the way to a radical, relationally inclusive standard of social justice in the production and use of energy resources.

The Difficulty of Securing a Just Energy Policy

Much that has occurred in the initial process of developing a national energy policy for the United States illustrates the difficulty of surfacing fundamental questions of justice in public policy debate. Neither corporate energy producers nor those who perceive their interests to be very different opposed former President Jimmy Carter's original effort to develop a national energy policy. This fact might be considered surprising in a nation where most business interests and a sizable sector of the public espouse a social philosophy that the least government is the best government. But a superficial consensus about the need for a national energy policy masks the fact that there is little agreement about the nature of the energy crisis. Few are prepared, even now, to discern how deeply divided we are as a people on the question.

One of the reasons why no one objected to the development of a federal policy is that the federal government has long been involved in energy policy in several important ways: (1) at the regulatory level,[12] (2) in providing tax incentives that have shaped the previous course of energy development,[13] and (3) in massive direct financial support for research and development of certain lines of energy supply, most especially nuclear power.[14] Because the government is already deeply involved, no one on any side of the energy debate could plausibly argue that it was in the national interest for the government to take a more passive role. Moreover, in the face of mounting evidence that ad hoc approaches to energy policy could result in dislocation of energy supply, with severe repercussions to the economy and increased political tensions domestically or internationally, no serious argument against a national energy policy was possible. The important point, however, is that all sides in the public policy debate recognized that formation of a more coherent national public policy held out promise of shaping that policy in a way congenial to their long-term interests. From the outset, then, a wide range of conflicting interests converged to support the momentum for national policy.

Carter's energy policy efforts make an interesting case study of the way in which intentions to fairness become eroded by the inequity of power between competing interests. In his initial appeals for public support for the development of a national policy, Carter especially stressed the need to recognize the dangers of profligate use of limited fossil fuel resources and tried to heighten public awareness of the dangers to our national security of extreme dependence on imported oil. Out of this analysis he identified as the primary goals of his program the conservation of energy resources and production shifts that would increase our independence of foreign sources of supply. In addition, he pledged as a basic policy goal fairness in distributing the costs and hardships of the policy itself. Nearly twenty months later, Congress enacted an energy package that did not reflect in any substantive way these originally stated presidential goals and priorities. Furthermore, the American people became more confused than before about the nature of the energy crisis. This confusion among the general public about the nature of "the crisis" was a sure sign that the superficial consensus on the need for a national policy obscured more than it revealed.

The Power Monopoly

The original national energy policy debate dramatically illustrated the inordinate existing disparities of power (in the zero-sum sense) that operate in the formation of an energy policy. With the immense power of corporate energy producers arrayed against him, Carter and his major energy policy advisers had to concede at the outset that the chief strategy in curbing energy (particularly oil) consumption would be use of market pricing mechanisms, with tax write-off incentives as a second strategy for encouraging conservation and redistributing the costs of the policy. A third policy option, the use of direct grants to lighten the cost burden on certain segments of the population and to encourage more rapid shifts toward renewable energy sources, was not envisioned as a major strategy because of presumed pressures against "inflationary" government expenditures.

As a candidate for the presidency, Carter had said some brave things about the massive power of the major oil corporations and had spoken sympathetically of the need for government action to curtail the corporations' monopoly power to restore freer market conditions so that the public would not pay excessively for its energy supply. He did not endorse vertical divestiture — the effort to limit corporate control to one of several stages of the oil production process, such as extraction, refining, transportation, or marketing. But he had supported horizontal divestiture, the effort to prevent the trend toward monopoly control by a few corporations over production of differing types of energy — oil, coal, nuclear power, and so on. This should have meant an effort to curb the accelerating expansion of the major oil corporations into production of other forms of energy.[15]

By the time Carter unveiled his initial energy proposals, he had backed away from *any* initiatives in the direction of horizontal divestiture. This decision not to take any action in restraint of growing concentration in the energy production field, combined with the decision made at the outset of the debate to rely on pricing and tax incentive mechanisms to implement energy policy, meant that the executive branch was unwilling to mount serious pressure to offset the massive power of energy producers, whose interests are always protected in Congress. The Carter administration's refusal to challenge the interests of the oil corporations has accelerated since the Reagan-led shifts in the makeup of Congress.

Energy legislation passed under Carter authorized closer monitoring of the financial operations of the energy producers, but those who know the history of such previous efforts to monitor the activities of the oil corporations could not be optimistic about such activities.[16] Given the weakness of control mechanisms mandated by the national energy legislation, there was no reason to expect that the government would inhibit expansionist dynamics toward monopoly control of energy production. Such skepticism was confirmed under Carter, and the Reagan administration's policy actively encourages such monopolization. Because the National Energy Act of 1978 drastically centralized governmental decision making and administration of government policy, public oversight of government monitoring activities in fact became more difficult[17] even before the Reagan administration's effort to undermine the program altogether. The initial congressional debate over energy policy largely ignored the well-documented reality of monopoly power in energy production and continues to do so.[18] The only critical questions asked in Congress came from a coalition of "consumer advocates" in the House and Senate, and their efforts focused on a losing struggle to extract some compromises on energy pricing mechanisms, especially in the area of natural gas production.[19] Today, most senators and congressional representatives take monopolization of energy for granted.

The Producers' Interpretation

During the entire period of previous debate on energy legislation, the American people were treated to an unprecedented campaign of propaganda initiated by energy producers. Through television advertising and the print media, we were subjected to unrelenting industry "interpretation" of the energy crisis. Mobil Oil and other major oil companies became the main educators about the nature of the crisis. The spectacle of the most powerful interested parties in the national policy debate spending large sums from their vast corporate resources to shape public opinion, under the guise of presenting the only "economically sound" approach, raises the question of whether points of view other than those of the multinational corporations will ever again get equal time in national public policy discussions.[20] Small wonder that the American people were more confused than ever about the character of the energy crisis after this legislation passed. The corporate line, as exhibited in the Mobil pedagogy, was bound to confuse. For example, the public was informed that our high energy consumption was due to the government's previous efforts at price regulation! We were told that because our political leaders had opted for "popular" solutions such as price regulation in the past, we had indulged ourselves in natural gas usage. These misguided regulatory efforts, we were assured, had been made "in . . . the guise of helping the consumer, punishing certain 'villains,' or providing an instant 'answer' to a pressing problem."[21]

The oil industry's "solution" for achieving the needed conservation of energy (this stress on conservation was a new value in the Pandora's box of corporate "concerns"), was, of course, a return to what Mobil called "free market" pricing mechanisms. But in advanced industrial capitalism such appeals to a presumed "free market" mean only that pricing is to be left to the discretion of the corporate producers. By appealing to a purported "free market" dear to the value systems of many Americans who have little technical understanding of the massively monopolistic conditions currently existing in the energy field, the industry attempted to dispel widespread suspicion, now confirmed, about the role of the corporations in accelerating the rise of oil and gas prices. Mobil warned the public, in soberest terms, that such "free market" conditions, while encouraging a climate of conservation, would not be sufficient to avert a crisis. If our "total environment" — by which Mobil meant our present standard of living — was to be maintained, we must rapidly increase the production of alternative fuels — gas, shale, *and* nuclear energy.[22] Not surprisingly, these are the alternative energy sources in which oil companies have long since made major investments and where incursions of oil corporation capital have been heavily centered. Mobil shied away from direct attack on environmental interest groups by lumping environmentalists with those who seek "popular" and "short-term" solutions.[23] They also acknowledged the probable eventual importance of solar, geothermal, and other renewable energy sources, thereby projecting an open image while offering comforting assurance that we could solve this real and genuine crisis with a minimum of social dislocation and discomfort. What observers of the major oil corporations have come to call the "private government of energy" so thoroughly controlled information flow to the public and interpretation of the causes of the energy crisis that public awareness of corporate monopoly of energy production appears to be less vivid today than it was before public policy debate began.

We ended the first round of development of a national energy policy, then, with the most powerful of the interested parties in the debate unscathed. Reagan's election to the presidency merely accelerated the concentrations of power and centralization in energy production and supply. A few major corporations will continue to control the future course of energy policy unless the public comes to understand the problem more clearly and to act accordingly. Public insensitivity to the negative consequences of this state of affairs will be reinforced not only by continuance of corporate "educational" efforts but by the active collaboration of the Reagan administration in increasing corporate monopoly.

Congressional debate on energy is always cast as a confrontation between the interests of producers and consumers — with all lines converging on one or the other side. What this state of affairs illustrated is that all "interests" are now construed by the market system. In late capitalism, the interests of the corporations and the interests of those of us who understand the common welfare differently are all reduced to market calculations. We are merely consumers, and our interests are only "consumer" interests. No other questions of public well-being can be brought into focus in such a state of affairs. Concessions to "consumers" may be made, especially as politicians face elections, but concerns for our common and personal well-being that do not fit the existing dynamics of production cease even to enter the discussion except as "consumer discontent." Insofar as the public interest has been reduced to "consumer concerns," there is no room for substantive questions of social justice and ecological well-being in the ongoing process of shaping and implementing public energy policy.

The Least Well-Off Are the Ongoing Losers

To construe the American public merely as an abstract collection of consumers who are assumed to have nothing more at stake in energy policy than concern for pressure on their pocketbooks is worrisome enough. It means that our national energy policy tends less and less to take account of how that policy affects already existing inequities in the American economic system and the total environment. But equally, construing the interests at stake in the political process in this way will make it increasingly difficult to focus on how U.S. policy affects inequities between our nation and other nations, especially nations that are currently disadvantaged in terms of the dynamics of the global economic system.

While the questions about a just energy policy on a global scale are too complex to be treated in this essay, we do need to observe how adversely existing patterns of inequity between nations are affected and reinforced by the energy situation. In this respect, the power dynamics of the world market system repeat themselves globally, as they do at home; however, poor nations have even less power in policy trade-offs than do the disadvantaged in the United States. For those of us who are citizens of the rich advanced nations, all of our productive activities, including those aimed at our fundamental survival needs (food, shelter, clothing), those aimed at enhancing the quality of our lives, and those that are mere luxuries,[24] involve the high consumption of energy. The poorest nations are those where increased energy resources are needed even to begin to meet the fundamental survival needs of their people.

The world market system is such that our globe is divided roughly between advanced industrial systems with diversified economies, whose world market exports include a range of excess manufactured goods to sell abroad, and those nations whose economic systems are not so diversified and whose major source of capital in world trade comes from the sale of their natural resources. These often must be sold at low commodity prices to buy other natural resources and needed manufactured goods. Manufactured goods are extremely costly in relation to the income these nations receive from selling basic commodities. This global class system has been intensified because high world market prices for energy have devoured the meager resources of the market-disadvantaged nations and have made capital formation for economic development even harder. Poor nations' efforts to address the basic survival needs of their people have been set back, and even nations that have no wish to duplicate the questionable patterns of "economic development" of the advanced industrial systems have been forced into greater dependency on the rich nations, with attendant loss of political autonomy. Such nations also have been forced to open their doors to foreign corporate capital that deeply skews their development away from policies that give priority to the survival needs of their own people. The only exception to this state of affairs has been some of the cartel of oil-producing nations, who were for a time able to accelerate capital formation due to the rising demand for oil. But most of the nations in the world do not have sufficient natural resources or capacity for capital formation to allow them to avoid a downward poverty spiral that energy dependency worsens. Only fundamental changes in the global economic order and a loosening pressure on fossil fuel consumption in the industrial nations can help them.

Conservation and shifts away from fossil fuel consumption in the rich world are urgent morally not only because nonrenewable energy is finite but because poor nations must compete with rich nations for energy supplies. The problem is exacerbated by the fact that until now the only alternative to fossil fuels given priority by industrial nations has been the development of nuclear power. Increasingly, as evidence mounts that reliance on nuclear energy has long-term disastrous consequences ecologically and that the social and economic costs of a plutonium economy are staggering, the nuclear solution is being rejected by citizens of the advanced industrial societies. Still, the governments (including our own) continue to spend vast sums in support of nuclear power and encourage the poorer nations to follow the nuclear path. Meanwhile, developing alternative energy supplies from renewable sources is given less than central priority in the energy policies of the rich nations. All of this increases the numbers of countries that are being made poor by energy dependency and the dynamics of the so-called free-market system.

Similar dynamics repeat themselves at the domestic level. Former President Carter's original goal to distribute the added costs of energy policy fairly was both good politics and good morality. The public was unlikely to support any policy that required sacrifices that did not appear to be well distributed in the society as a whole. The problem, however, is that even without the accelerating cost of energy, the economic vulnerability of most people in American society is increasing. Ours is also a society where deep economic disparities are mystified and frequently not even understood to exist. Because of our collective affluence and because disparities of economic wealth are less apparent in a society where the vast majority have access to basic needs, most of us fail to realize that the total economic wealth of our nation is distributed as unevenly as is the wealth of a nation such as India.[25] Furthermore, much of the wealth in this society (wealth is not merely income but also the means to produce income) is controlled by a very few affluent white males. Racial and ethnic minorities and women of all groups not dependent on this small wealth-holding elite grow daily more vulnerable economically. Furthermore, our ideology of success discourages persons from acknowledging and protesting their increasingly disadvantaged economic position.

It has long been recognized that at least one-fifth of our population exists as a poverty subculture outside direct participation in the productive economy.[26] Nonwhite Americans, women, the elderly, the handicapped, and persons living in economically underdeveloped regions of the country are all dramatically overrepresented in this subculture in proportion to their numbers in society at large.[27] In addition, as our population grows older, this subculture will grow even if unemployment rates drop for other reasons. Nor is *unemployment* ever likely to be reduced without vast increases in the economic growth rate because our ever more technologically oriented modes of production are yielding fewer and fewer jobs in the productive center of the economy in proportion to the number of persons who need work in the society as a whole.

We are witnessing a growing differentiation between skilled and unskilled labor. While the wages of skilled labor in the private sector of the economy may increase in some rough relation to increasing costs of living — because some sectors of organized labor have been effective in protecting the position of those who are skilled — the real wages of public sector employees and the growing proportion of unskilled and low-skilled workers will not do so. Where jobs are funded by taxes — and this includes workers who deliver services funded by government at all levels — we are seeing large cutbacks and heavy pressure for wage restraints that will move many workers to lower positions on the income spectrum. Persons who are entering the job market are finding that the most readily available work is in the less-skilled and lower-paying end of the job spectrum or that the best job markets are in parts of the country where organized labor is weak and not in a position to provide counterpressure against wage restraints. Competition for access to high-income work, especially professional and professional-managerial positions,[28] is growing more intense as students are warned away from the middle-income service positions, funded through the public sector of the economy, especially teaching, social work, and the like. It is precisely these service professions where women are employed and where racial ethnic groups have made most employment gains in the recent past.

These shifts are the structural basis for the economic pressures now being experienced by the great majority of Americans.

Inflation, which usually gets the blame for the misery many are experiencing, is not really an independent economic variable. Rather, it is both a cause and an effect of all these shifting economic patterns: Inflation results from the high costs of energy,[29] from rising profit margins, and from the high level of "cost" producers, including energy producers, that charge against profit levels for "research, development, and capital expenditures." The level of loss of real income that so many citizens experienced slowed but did not deter the Carter administration's efforts to effect energy conservation through pricing mechanisms. Furthermore, it was a purported threat of a taxpayers' revolt that served as a justification for refusing more extensive use of direct grants to shape energy policy in fairer ways. Monies allocated to be spent on direct grants through the Energy Act of 1978 were extremely small, too small to have much effect on redistributing the costs of the new energy policy or to encourage genuine conservation. Loan funds for the middle-income elderly fared better in Congress than did direct grant proposals, but in the end only tax credit strategies were widely used, and most of the tax credit benefits went to businesses rather than directly to family units.

The problem with tax incentives as an instrument of public policy is that they work, if at all, only for those who are now at least moderately affluent. Low-interest loans expand the social base of tax incentive programs and increase the numbers of those who can take advantage of tax provisions, but one must have a margin of resources above survival needs to benefit from such loans. Even though, until 1982, increased energy costs were reflected in rising prices at every level, those increases most affected persons whose income and financial resources stretched only to cover basic survival needs. While oil prices have dropped slightly in the meantime, these shifts are due to the depressed state of the global economy, not to any well-established trend toward conservation or to any lessening of price manipulation.[30] Furthermore, deregulation of natural gas, a goal of the Reagan administration, has resulted in substantial increased costs of energy in many areas, and the escalating costs of nuclear power are also creating economic hardship. Nor will lower costs of crude oil result in a commensurate drop in refined fuel. Prices are too much set by monopoly factors for any sustained downward trend in energy costs.

An adequate assessment of how much more drastically the poor, including not only those outside the productive economy but also millions of working poor, have been affected by the rising costs of energy is not possible here. The seriousness of the situation can be illustrated, though, by noting what rising home fuel costs did to citizens classified as poor by official government standards. In 1976, middle-income families were spending 4 to 7 percent of their income for fuel. By comparison, low-income households were using only half as much electricity and a quarter less natural gas than were middle-income families, but this smaller usage cost between 15 and 25 percent of the total income of these families. Even before Reagan's election in 1980, commentators contended that in some areas 30 to 50 percent of total income of poor families was going to such fuel expenditures.[31] Obviously, for such persons, belt tightening does not mean foregoing luxuries or enhancement needs. It means cutting essentials such as food and clothing. Given this context, it is easy to see why the Carter-initiated tax incentives were of no help to those already least well-off. Poor people do not have the capital to pay for conservation measures in the first place, and loans, even low-interest loans, are just as irrelevant, since they cannot qualify for or repay them. Because the primary relief mechanisms of government energy policy implementation cannot work for them, the poor are made worse off by such policies.

Government energy policy also distributes costs inequitably in the direction of the poor and lower-middle-income groups at several other important points. In a society without adequate public transportation, addicted to the automobile culture, lower-income persons, especially the working poor, expend a higher percentage of their incomes for transportation than do those who earn more. Many persons in this nation simply must have automobiles if they are to work at all, since alternative transportation frequently is not available and the best jobs are often located at some distance from centers of population or in areas where housing costs are high. The National Energy Act of 1978 made no effort to wean us from our dependency on the automobile; national transportation policy has yet to be coordinated with a national energy policy.[32] The Energy Act imposed some tax penalties on persons who purchased gas-guzzling automobiles, but those who need the automobile to stay in the job market, not the wealthy, are hit hardest. The working poor cannot always avoid gas guzzlers, since they must often buy cheaper secondhand vehicles, which often are fuel-inefficent. Those who have discretionary income for luxuries (and who are the major proportionate consumers of gasoline in any case) are not much deterred by higher gasoline prices and taxes on fuel-inefficent cars. Those who use the automobile chiefly for access to jobs and for related survival needs are hard hit indeed.

Only the most well-off in this society can afford to disregard the consequences of energy policy in two other important areas

of human well-being — its impact on creating jobs and its consequences for human health. Here low- and middle-income Americans can find common ground in support of policies that serve
their mutual interest. But to appreciate why there is so much common ground in terms of what is good for poor and middle-strata
people in this society, we must help people understand how misleading are the energy industry's scenarios of what is at stake.

The threat of unemployment has been perhaps the most
powerful factor in the federal government's repeated acquiescence
to corporation ideology in many areas of public policy, and the
politics of energy policy has been no exception. Many took at face
value the energy producers' claims that any shift in existing priorities for new energy production from nuclear power would result in escalating unemployment and economic dislocations. Some
still believe this despite mounting evidence compiled by public
interest groups showing that the energy policies that would best
address our unemployment ills are those that are most benign in
terms of health and safety. Serious conservation efforts would
create new jobs, as would the rapid development of a decentral-
ized solar industry and the development of other renewable energy sources.[33] The jobs created by such policy options would be
scattered across the country rather than located at energy boom
sites, where fossil fuel extraction or nuclear power–related jobs
are concentrated. Many energy boom sites, including those that
will be created by increased reliance on coal and shale, are located
in what are now sparsely populated areas. The social costs of these
developments must be recognized to include the costs of building
new communities, of expanding services for the boom towns, and
of moving workers and their families to the sites. Nuclear power,
a high-technology industry, produces relatively few jobs in relation to the massive capital expenditures required for its development. And the use of nuclear power and coal carries the hidden
social costs of serious health hazards to employees and to the
public, especially those who live near extraction or production
locations.[34]

No one can assess precisely all the indirect costs or the wider
environmental damage that will occur from our growing reliance
on high-technology energy production, but there is no doubt that
industry projections of the costs of energy production include
none of these. It is time we learned that such social costs will be
paid not by the industry involved but by citizens, who will shoul-
der the price of remedial government services to victims and of
most environmental reclamation that occurs. For example, the
estimated minimum cost to taxpayers for cleaning up the West

Valley nuclear waste storage site in Upstate New York was $600 million.

No government administration, least of all the Reagan administration, has calculated such costs in the formation of public policy. The hard-won environmental restrictions maintained by the Carter administration have been seriously undermined, and all departments of Reagan's administration conspire to strengthen the growing monopoly control of corporate America. Discretionary government regulatory powers over corporations are no longer used. Even so, coalitions of persons and groups deeply concerned about the effects of a national energy policy on jobs and health continue to challenge the conventional data generated by and propounded through the energy industry to exacerbate largely misplaced fears that sound energy policy would be detrimental to the total economy.[35] They can be made to appear to be detrimental because corporations have such unconstrained power to pollute, move, or control supplies that, if they carry out their threats, disorder could follow. How to make such unaccountable power more accountable to broader public well-being is the single most urgent political and moral question this nation faces, but we must not delude ourselves into imagining that what we face are "inexorable market forces." What we are encountering is irresponsible social power that is heedless of the concrete conditions of human suffering.

Conclusion

The politics of energy policy does not permit us to be hopeful that our government will quickly become responsive to fundamental standards of social justice. In spite of massive grass-roots activity aimed at shaping energy policy in a direction that acknowledges the interconnections between the quality of life and fairness or substantive justice, what has been accomplished so far at the national level is the reinforcement of massive power of control of monopoly energy producers. Even so, we have no option but to work to increase the public's growing sophistication about what a just social policy would look like, and this effort must be made in the face of massive "educational" efforts by those who claim that our ecojustice perspectives are "utopian," "socialistic," and dangerous. Far too much is at stake for all of us, including future generations whose interests can only be represented through our moral sensitivity, to allow us to abandon efforts to reassert a conception of a genuinely public interest in relation to energy. As

Christians we have no choice but to accelerate our involvement, working together with coalitions of persons engaged in these concerns.[36]

Our churches must become centers for reexamining our personal and institutional values and lifestyles but must also become places where *countereducation* on energy policy questions occurs. Otherwise the public debate will continue to be thrashed out within parameters that cut us off from critical information. We must speak out and act politically to press the claims of the least well-off in society, pointing to the rapidly escalating disparities of wealth and privilege that characterize our nation. We must also call our government to account for its persistent failure to address the seriousness of the global crisis of inequities between rich and poor nations. Unless these trends are reversed, a privileged minority will continue to undermine the very conditions of human survival on this planet. In societies and between nations riddled with social inequities, the rich themselves can survive only by turning their world into an armed camp in which privilege prevails, if it does for a while, through the barrel of a gun.

III

CHRISTIAN HISTORY, COMMUNITY, AND THEOLOGY AS A CONTEXT FOR FEMINIST ETHICS

In this section, Beverly Harrison integrates two approaches exemplified in earlier essays, the historical and the analytical, with a third, the personal narrative, to clarify the way her experience shapes her normative perspective theologically and morally.

Using the historical approach, Harrison traces the roots of the nineteenth-century reform and women's rights movements and draws this conclusion: The root of nineteenth-century abolition and women's rights movements was the suffering of black people and the disenfranchisement of white women together with faithfulness to an evangelical mission to meet God's requirements for justice. White clergy isolated the women who became activists in abolition and suffrage just as they isolated freed slaves. As a consequence, many of those white women who had made the connection between religious fidelity and social justice left the churches. The clergy's response to movements for human fulfillment has been replicated through the years, says Harrison, as the churches play the role of justifying the status quo. While some of us assume the churches have usually played a role in maintaining existing social structures and are prepared to hear this history, we must not lose sight of the second point, that there is a message preached in the churches that faithfulness to God requires right relationship among everyone in our society. That message has been a source of the moral vision of liberation when it has been heard within the context of a collective struggle against dehumanizing forces.

In Harrison's autobiographical statement "Keeping Faith in a Sexist Church," she relates her process of appropriating the norm of justice for herself as a white woman from the middle strata in the United States. Parallel in important ways to the movement she traces in "The Early Feminists and the Clergy," Harrison came to political awareness of her own alienation within the context of a church that preached justice, not anticipating that she would

191

ever ask what justice requires for herself. As Harrison faced her personal/social alienation, the women around her helped her ask that question. They provided the supportive environment to grow into the painful realization that to be a woman in this culture is to be despised or discounted. The norms for liberation from oppression are in her religious heritage, but the purveyors of that tradition never intended her to claim them for herself. Women growing to love themselves push that claim. Having made that claim her own, Harrison then self-consciously retells the Jesus story as a story that affirms the dignity of women.

Harrison's analytic voice, well exemplified in the final essay, "Theological Reflection in the Struggle for Liberation," likens the process of doing feminist theology and ethics to the process of other oppressed people's coming to the liberating word and deed. She universalizes women's claims, that is, she annunciates the connection between women's struggles to selfhood and worldwide movements for liberation. This annunciation accompanies a denunciation of the various ways progressive movements trivialize the feminist movement.

"Theological Reflection in the Struggle for Liberation" is perhaps the single article in this book that relates all the other efforts into a methodological whole. In this essay, Harrison lifts up the step-by-step process of coming to moral and theological consciousness. Here is the most explicit treatment of the source of feminist norms: How do feminists know that embodiment, mutuality, equal regard, as examples, are required for liberation? It is in evaluating our theological heritage against our lived-world experience, and it is in assessing our concrete reality against our theological vision, in the company of our neighbors with whom we move into transforming action, that we test our norms. After reading this article, I recommend rereading "The Power of Anger in the Work of Love" for the full impact of Beverly Harrison's vision of the dignity of women and our agency. We have here an ethic conducive to a responsible worldly spirituality.

THE EARLY FEMINISTS AND THE CLERGY

A Case Study in the Dynamics of Secularization*

The Record of the Churches on Women's Rights

By the early 1870s, the activism of women in Protestant Christian denominations in the United States had reached such proportions that a widespread concern was being voiced. The suspicion was abroad that the "Woman's Rights Movement" had begun to "infect" the church. R. Pierce Beaver quotes an unnamed, "eminent Methodist minister" of the time: "Some of the most thoughtful minds are beginning to ask what is to become of this Woman Movement in the Church." In the face of the question, this particular clergyman maintained equanimity. Possibly, he was so deeply convinced of the truth of the conventional wisdom that women were "by nature" more fragile and delicate than men that he could not share others' sense of doom and foreboding at what was occurring. In any case, while acknowledging the depth and range of concern about the matter, he counseled his readers to take the long view: "Let them alone, ... all through our history like movements have started. Do not oppose them, and it will die out." [1]

The source of this quotation from the ecclesiastical press is not on record. Hence, we can only speculate on the author's full meaning. Admittedly, exegesis in such circumstances is precarious. We cannot know with certainty what the author meant by "our history." It is possible, though not probable, that he was re-

---

* This essay was published originally in *The Review and Expositor*, vol. 72, no. 1 (1975), pp. 41–52. It is typical of several early essays reflecting my efforts to situate U.S. feminism historically vis-à-vis the churches, and it reflects my broader thesis that failure to place a hermeneutic of justice at the center of Christian life and praxis always has the effect of driving creative Christians out of the churches and of deforming dominant Christian teaching in the direction of denial and sentimentality.

ferring to the long span of Christian or western cultural history. From time to time over the centuries, there had been outbreaks of such "movements" by women, and most had indeed "died out." But even the educated and well-informed American clergyman of the nineteenth century was not likely to have had any awareness of these movements, for on that point the learned historical treatises of the period were completely silent. More likely, then, what he had in view was the nearer span of Anglo-American history, perhaps reaching back nearly a century.

Any person concerned for public issues would, by 1870, have been well aware that there had been ripples of "discontent" among "the ladies" over the span of a century.[2] Those active in the many reform organizations of the time — and our eminent Methodist cleric may well have been thus involved — would have heard of the tensions and controversies set off by "the woman question" in these organizations. And even without a national press or mass media, there had been sufficient coverage of certain odd gatherings called "woman's rights conventions" during the period between 1848 and the Civil War to enable awareness that the issue, raised in the 1870s, was hardly "new."

To be sure, so far as the vast majority of persons in the United States were aware, nothing with respect to women had much changed in the meanwhile. A woman, standing in public to speak in a "promiscuous assembly" (a meeting where both sexes were present), caused almost as much general consternation in 1870 as she had in 1837,[3] when the Calvinist clergy of Massachusetts unleashed their anathema on the dangers to woman's nature engendered by such goings-on as the public appearances, in abolitionist meetings, of the Grimké sisters, Sarah and Angelina, of South Carolina.[4] Consequently, it is understandable that our commentator, retrospectively, might make the judgment that "the woman thing" always had a tendency to die out. But there appear to have been two assumptions underlying his viewpoint that were deeply erroneous. The first was that the "cause" for the demise of these supposed "sporadic" outbreaks of a women's movement had been "benign neglect." The actual causes of the temporary waning of women's organized efforts had been, first, the turmoil and social chaos surrounding the Civil War and, second, the real but disruptive tensions about priorities within the various reform movements.[5] A second mistaken assumption was that the women's movement had, in fact, been met with equanimity and disinterest by the churches at an earlier time. Clearly, our anonymous editorialist was no student of the early history of the "woman movement." Though he did not know it, it was, in fact, far too late for his counsel. The pattern of churchly response to the women's rights movement had already been well established and was hardly one of neglect, benign or otherwise.

In the nineteenth century, of course, "the response of the churches" was equivalent to "the reaction of the clergy." By the 1830s, thanks to the impact of the Second Great Awakening[6] and the spirit of reform, "woman's rights" had their advocates among the clergy.[7] When women finally began to organize to seek those rights a decade later, they lost no opportunity to call on such support. But the more usual response of the clergy was not support but adamant denunciation, as careful scrutiny of the documentary history of the women's rights conventions attests.

It is seriously misleading to identify the nineteenth-century "woman movement" merely with its organized expressions in the women's rights conventions. Subtle changes were taking place in the lives of women more generally, changes that had deep social and cultural roots.[8] However, focusing on these formal gatherings, aimed to mobilize women in their own behalf, enables us to see how clerical response affected the early activist women — women who, by 1870, were widely viewed as involved in matters hostile and inimical to the well-being of the church.

When, in 1848, four women issued a "call" to the first women's rights convention, to be held in the Methodist chapel in Seneca Falls, New York, it was already clear to them that their grievances were in part religious. The purpose of the meeting was "to discuss the social, civil, and religious condition and rights of woman." [9] The signatories of the convention "call" included the renowned Quaker leader Lucretia Mott and her sister, Martha C. Wright, Mary Ann McClintock, and the still young woman who would, during the next fifty years, come to represent the greatest intellectual force behind the women's rights struggle, Elizabeth Cady Stanton.

Those who gathered at Seneca Falls did give voice to religious grievances, but their grievances were not then their central preoccupation. Somewhat ironically and good-humoredly, they seized the rising "theological" argument[10] that conceded women's "moral" superiority to men and turned it to their advantage. One of the least controversial of the resolutions passed at Seneca Falls declared:

> That inasmuch as man, while claiming for itself [sic] intellectual superiority, does accord to woman moral superiority, it is preeminently his duty to encourage her to speak and teach, as she has opportunity, in all religious assemblies.

Another resolution affirmed:

> That woman has too long rested satisfied in the cir-
> cumscribed limits which corrupt customs and a per-
> verted application of the Scriptures have marked out
> for her, and that it is time she should move in an en-
> larged sphere which her great Creator has assigned to
> her.

Like most of the resolutions, both of these passed unanimously.
The dramatic controversy at Seneca Falls was unleashed by the
resolution that declared that "it was the duty of the women of
this country to secure to themselves their sacred right to the elective franchise." [11] That resolution survived by a few votes, thanks
only to the eloquent support of newspaper editor and former
slave Frederick Douglass and to the persuasiveness of Stanton,
who with great pain and anguish had earlier managed her first
public address.[12]

Obviously these activists, female and male, did not expect
the hostile response from the clergy and the press that actually
greeted the Seneca Falls Declaration, nor did they imagine the
depth of the struggle that lay ahead. They had confidently resolved to "enlist the pulpit and the press in our behalf." They
did not expect instantaneous success, of course. They acknowledged that they would encounter "misconception, misrepresentation, and ridicule" for their resolve to press the issue of equality
for women. But the depth of the storm that broke over them was
a shock. The women must have trembled when even some of
their loyal friends, among them evangelist-abolitionist Theodore
Weld, began to urge caution lest their actions jeopardize the other
concerns of the Great Reform.[13]

As the fragmentary records of their subsequent meetings —
beginning only two weeks later in Rochester, New York — make
clear, after Seneca Falls their every gathering was attended by
hostile critics who came to monitor their actions and to debate
them. Without exception, the most vigorous critical spokesmen,
there to warn them of the evils of their ways, were members of
the clergy. It evidently became harder and harder to find a cleric
to begin their conventions with prayer, so they quickly learned
to provide their own.[14]

From the standpoint of much so-called secular historical interpretation, the story of the interaction between the formal
women's rights movements and the churches has been deeply
neglected. In part, this is because the women's rights story is reconstructed through the perceptions of the activist women themselves, who at a later point were far more "secularized" and no

longer hoped for any sympathetic support from clergy. But it is also because many contemporary historiographers view the religious sympathies of these early "radical" feminists as the fruit of social conventionality that they assume these women to have easily and rapidly shed. Such an interpretation is misleading.

The Social Origins of the Women's Movement

In discussing the social roots of the women's movement, it is standard procedure to stress the dramatic difference between the European feminists of the eighteenth and nineteenth centuries and their American counterparts. The former, already deeply imbued with Enlightenment-rationalist sentiments, were for the most part disdainful not only of clericalism and ecclesiastical establishment but of Christianity itself. They were individual intellectuals, unsupported by any "movement." Like most intellectuals of the time, they had passed through the crucible of skepticism, moving from distrust of clerical and ecclesiastical power to distrust of all religion.[15]

With the exception of Margaret Fuller, the American-born feminists had a different history and a quite different orientation to religion. It is traditional to lump them, somewhat derisively in contrast to their European contemporaries, as "moral crusaders." Except Fuller, all of the American-born feminists, it is said, were profoundly "conservative and moralistic."[16] Such generalized characterization is misleading. The "conservatism" and "moralism" of many, even most, of the early feminists was of a character that cannot be understood apart from appreciation of the utopic character of a profoundly Christian evangelical impulse. To be sure, there was an element of class conservatism and sexual prudery in the outlook of many.[17] Still, we should not discount the pervasive evangelical confidence that made others willing to press for changes that, by the standards of their time, were deeply "shocking." Even their temperance passions are easily misunderstood by secular interpreters, who forget that in the nineteenth century many European secular socialists were also adamant temperance supporters. Certainly, by comparison with their other middle-class contemporaries, their "moralism" had nothing of the character of that prim and brittle propriety that the rising "cult of true womanhood" demanded of women. They did indeed often profess shock and outrage, but that was because they were looking with freshly opened eyes at the conditions of their society. Given their previously limited experience, what shocked them was to their everlasting credit. For example, armed with little else than a thorough familiarity with scripture and a sensitivity to human cruelty, the Grimké sisters had managed to discern some of the basic underlying psychological and social dynamics that made the slave system destructive to master as well as to slave.[18] Others, assigned to investigate the conditions of women in the rising factory system, quickly perceived the sort of shame and hypocrisy surrounding the "cult of true womanhood" in a society where the factory system was evolving chiefly on the cheap labor of women.[19] Even their attitude toward prostitution was exceptional by the standards of their day. They had deep sympathy for the prostitute; they aimed their antipathy to that double system of morality that allowed a man to participate in commercial sex without penalty while the woman involved was socially ostracized. They rightly identified the economic subjugation of women as the major source of prostitution as a social system. (The very young, usually rural and impoverished women who became prostitutes in nineteenth-century America were not the "happy hookers" of twentieth-century renown.)

As a group, the early feminists were candid, compassionate, full of "common sense," with a ready capacity for laughing at themselves. There is ample testimony that outside observers were astonished at the lack of class and status distinctions at early women's rights gatherings and at the lack of racial consciousness, much less racial superiority, they manifested.[20] It must always be remembered that the picture of the white Protestant middle-class American woman — rigid, moralistic, and proper — comes to us through the dynamics of late-nineteenth-century life. The patronizing spirit of the middle class in these later decades was the fruit of a vastly changed society. The early feminists were closer to their sisters of the colonial period, who had astonished many in Europe by their strength, courage, and endurance on the frontier[21] and who had been regularly celebrated by European feminists as living evidence that current European social stereotypes about female fragility were nonsense.[22]

The fact is that the social origins of the women's rights movement in America will not be fully or adequately understood nor the early feminists rightly appreciated until the connection is duly acknowledged between the women's movement and left-wing Reformation evangelicalism in America. It is to Alice Rossi's credit that she was one of the first contemporary feminists to identify a connection between the Second Great Awakening, in which Charles Finney himself was moved to support women's right to pray and testify, and the emergence of the women's rights movement.[23] However, the full connection between U.S. feminism and evangelical reform may never be reconstructed because the evidence is so fragmentary. How Mistress Anne Hutchinson's challenge to and persecution at the hands of the Puritan theocracy in Massachusetts in the 1640s or the full participation of women preachers among the Free Baptists of New England in the late eighteenth century[24] is related to nineteenth-century developments among feminist evangelicals is not clear, but it invites speculation. There *is* a clear relation between the evangelical spiritualism of the Quakers and the emergence of powerful, articulate Quaker feminists like Lucretia Mott, who deserves even more credit than she is usually given for the early rise of the women's movement.

The Moral Passion of Early Feminists

In evaluating the early feminists, it is important to distinguish between the sort of moralism born of self-righteousness and that moral passion born of the conviction that injustice must be rectified. What characterized the early feminists was a confidence that they and other women had the capacity, and would find the courage, to act effectually in behalf of the emancipation of women. They had precisely that form of equanimity, so unlike complacency, that comes from confidence that one's cause is just. Lucretia Mott put it best, if characteristically, at the Rochester Convention, when she countered a "well-written" speech by a male supporter who had evidently celebrated mightily the moral superiority of woman. She set aside his rhetoric with a word: "Woman is now sufficiently developed to prefer justice to compliment." [25]

Clear evidence that the deep-seated religious appeals of the early feminists deserve to be taken seriously can be found in their early speeches and in the actual structure of events that transpired at the women's rights conventions. To be sure, early feminists represented a wide spectrum of theological viewpoints. Much of the way that they have been interpreted religiously derives from the central role played in later years by Elizabeth Cady Stanton, who was atypical. Before she became a feminist, she had shed her youthful Presbyterian orthodoxy in favor of a highly sophisticated philosophical deism, informed by New England transcendentalism.[26] Hers was a gentle but, through the century, growing skepticism about doctrine and scriptural authority. Even she, however, remained of divided mind on the point.[27] She never lost the conviction that it was the will of the Creator that women be recognized as "full moral persons." [28] Hers was clearly an ambivalent, not a hostile, relationship to religious tradition.

The initial theological stance of the women's rights movement, one that was maintained even when clerical denunciation reached scatological proportions, was that the religious source of women's oppression was due to the suppression of the Christian gospel by "priestcraft." Here again, Lucretia Mott was prototypical in her insistence that a whole gospel must be wrested from the clerical tendency to confuse conventional practice with gospel truth.[29] While not movement activists, the Grimké sisters, whose intellectual influence was considerable,[30] professed that their vision of full human solidarity in Christ had come as the fruit of studying the scriptures and teaching the gospel to slaves. Antoinette Brown, the first woman ordained to the ministry in a church that had a professional clergy, and Lucy Stone, younger members of the early circle, were initially of similar persuasion.

While the records of the various women's rights conventions are fragmentary, the proceedings that can be reconstructed lead us to an interesting conclusion. With the presence of hostile clerics now always assumed, the agendas of the early meetings regularly evolved into extended debates on biblical authority and theological doctrine. Initially, it fell to Lucretia Mott, who was, after all, an experienced preacher, to articulate the defense of women's cause in light of scriptural and doctrinal denunciation. Others, such as Brown, Stone, and Matilda Gage, quickly became competent debaters on these matters, however. It was clearly important to these women not to be cast as infidels who were undermining Christian faith, for initially they understood their own vision to be grounded in that faith.

We need to remember that early in the nineteenth century the scriptural injunctions employed against women's role changes were more varied than those used today. New Testament quotations admonishing women to keep silent in church and obey their husbands were, of course, invoked. But equally, the shadow of Eve's role as temptress and inaugurator of the Fall was at the time lively and vivid doctrine, widely preached. Even so learned a divine and self-professed friend of women as the Reverend Mr. Asa Mahan, president of Oberlin College (at the time one of two institutions of higher learning in the United States to admit women), thought nothing of invoking the sin of Eve against the feminists. He sat through the entire session of the Third Ohio Woman's Rights Convention in 1852 to head off what he deemed to be strategic errors and misconceptions on the part of the women. The Seneca Falls Declaration had offended him. He took special offense that in it women had laid the blame for female degradation on men. That, he insisted, was nonsense: "Now I assert that it is chargeable on woman herself; and that as she was first in man's original transgression, she is first here."[31] One sympathizes with Antoinette Brown and Lucy Stone, who complained of the hostile attitude toward women at Oberlin during their years of study there!

In the face of such comments and far more exasperating invocations of scriptural "authority," these women maintained not only equanimity but at times good humor. Lucretia Mott led the way in a form of debate that never fell lower than gentle sarcasm. She usually began by affirming her devotion to scripture and urged her protagonists to themselves take the full Pauline teaching, especially with respect to Christian freedom, charity, and the power of the spirit of Christ, with greater seriousness. If a speaker persisted in fetishizing Paul's advice to first-century Christian congregations, she would then remind him of his obligation to follow *all* of Paul's advice. Why, she would ask, had the gentleman himself married when he knew Paul's judgment that the single life was the preferred state of Christians? Her arguments often reappeared, reformulated by other women.

At the Seneca Falls meeting, none of the women participants either had the courage or believed in their own capacity to chair the meeting, so they asked James Mott to do so. At Rochester, two weeks later, Lucretia Mott and Stanton still voiced doubt about a woman being elected president of the convention.[32] Fortunately, they were outvoted. Given this fact, it is startling that from that point onward all of the varied gatherings on women's rights were chaired by women. The level of civility and order achieved was, given the provocation, incredible. Other reform gatherings had been known to break into open riot if even one woman presented herself for participation.[33]

These women's patience and endurance, I submit, can be accounted for only by their wish to persuade their fellow Christians and to make good on their resolve to reach the pulpit and the press with their message. Only slowly did they finally heed the early advice of men like Horace Greeley, who had been exasperated beyond endurance by their willingness to enter into discussions of scriptural authority and doctrine. Their patience, however, had clearly waned by the 1870s, when the now divided women's rights movement began once again, slowly, to gain momentum. By then it was a "secular" movement and the resolve to persuade the pulpit largely had faded. By 1870 more cautious advocates hoped, at best, to avoid giving offense to the clergy sufficiently to prevent grave setbacks to their cause.

Individualistic or personalistic historiography could, I suppose, credit the waning religious concern of women's rights activists to a lack of genuine fervor in matters of Christian faith.

Such an interpretation would, however, fail to acknowledge the actual and vital dialectic between Christian faith and practice. The personal pilgrimages of some of the younger feminists of the early period, such as Antoinette Brown, make clear the agonizing process of disillusion with the church and finally with evangelical theological interpretation that followed a deep and genuine struggle to be heard. Responsibility for the disillusion of such women can more plausibly be laid to the insensitivity of the clergy to the claims, motivated by evangelical confidence, for justice for women than to any presumed weakness in subjective faith on the part of the individual women.

The Role of the Churches in Secularizing Activists

Few movements for social justice in the modern world have origins so intimately and dialectically related to Christian faithfulness as does the "woman movement" in the United States. There are clearly some analogies here to the black civil rights struggle and to Latin American liberation movements. For the most part, though, movements for social and economic justice in dominantly Christian cultures have lost any connection to a theological heritage. Most persons who are the victims of injustice now assume that Christianity is inimical to such claims for social justice. Our complicity in defense of the status quo gives broad legitimacy to this assumption. Originally, the early feminists thought otherwise, but they were slowly driven to a more "secular" viewpoint.

Certain "theories of secularization," both theological and sociological, have permitted us too easily to imagine that "secularization" is some sort of inexorable social process, born either of "religious specialization" or the displacement of an "outmoded" religious worldview by a "scientific" one (this in spite of the fact that deep religious commitment and rigorous intellectual and scientific honesty often characterize religiously committed persons). Such theories teach us, too quickly, to accept as inexorable what is in fact the fruit of real, lived-world moral interaction. Such interpretations tempt us to a fatalistic and dehumanized view of history. Secularization, in its varied forms and species, need not and would not now involve such adamant repudiation of the meaningfulness of religious faith if it were not for the actual history of Christian complicity in suffering and injustice. An ideological use of scripture and theology as a buffer against social change is part of that complicity.

By crushing the evangelical spirit of early feminism, what the clergy accomplished was not to "stop" the women's rights movement. As I have elsewhere argued, the "radical" feminist vision of full human possibility for women was suppressed in the churches.[34] This suppression did nothing to turn back the impact of women on the churches. What it did was to determine the form that that impact would have.

The fact is (and it is a lesson to be writ large in contemporary theological discussion) that the church has always been, and will always remain, in a responsive position with respect to nonecclesiastical cultural movements. Regretfully, the misconceived way in which much recent neo-orthodox theology stated the problem of Christian faith and culture has deeply obscured this fact. Neo-orthodox theologians applied the biblical symbols of "Word" and "World" uncritically to "Church proclamation" and ecclesiastical culture on the one hand and to all other forms of culture on the other. Many speak as if Christian faith can exist in "noncultural" forms and in isolation from other cultural movements. The watchword for a theology that misconstrues the dynamics of faith and culture is always a "pure gospel" standing in tension with and above "culture."

If we are to use the term "culture" in relation to "gospel" at all, we have no choice but to acknowledge the meaning that the term "culture" has in contemporary parlance. To think or speak of being "above culture" in the modern sense of the term is a contradiction in terms. By anthropological definition, all human activity is substantively "culture." Christians, when we speak of being "above culture," are simply demonstrating that we do not understand the basic constructs of modern social science.[35]

Churches cannot avoid "cultural entanglements." Our choices are threefold. We can support, and help give birth to, cultural change that is humanly enriching; we can support change that is humanly destructive; or we can, with lack of awareness, seek to prevent change altogether by reinforcing existing convention and practice. But change happens, and as a distinguished Protestant theologian frequently observed, if you continue with conventional action and the social situation changes, it may turn out that you are doing the opposite of what you intended.[36]

This is precisely what happened to the churches with respect to the "woman movement." Protestant Christianity has long celebrated its role in raising the status of women.[37] Actually, however, by driving out a "radical" feminist witness, what the churches did was to legitimate and become the chief cultural buttress of the rising "cult of true womanhood." That ideology was only a last-gasp cultural barricade against constructive change that was threatening.

Women in the churches have been accused of sentimentality and moralism. When that charge is made, it is hardly ever noted that it was not women who decided what doctrine about women would be preached or which female voices would be given support by the churches. To stay in the church, one had to become a "soft feminist," one who accepted woman's "special virtue." Even so, by the end of the century, those women on the move in the churches who were less "radical" had come to accept much that the earlier feminists had taught.

In 1985, even the most cautious and frightened "Christian" woman in this nation celebrates what those early women demanded and accomplished. Few disagree that women should receive equal pay for equal work, though the idea was "radical" in 1848. And the "awful" thing that women pledged to secure then — female political suffrage — is not now denounced even by those who anticipate the deepest doom to follow on full human equality for women. Things that were widely proclaimed as "abnormal" and "unwomanly" by nineteenth-century opponents of the "radical" women are today taken as matters that are required precisely because women are "special." Few contemporary critics of the women's rights movement, for example, are aware that its first victory was gaining the legal right of a widow to inherit her husband's property.[38] Imagine contemporary female opponents of "women's lib" having to return to a status in which they would not have the economic security of inheriting their husband's money, should he die first! Or imagine their reaction if they had to return to the prevailing practice of the nineteenth century with respect to child custody in case of divorce. In those states where divorce was permitted, it was then *unheard of* for a divorced woman to gain custody of her children. These examples are but a few of the dozens of "victories" that women finally won because a few were outspokenly courageous in opposing conventions of their time. Those feared and denounced as "radical" are, more often than not, the chief agents of social conditions few would relinquish once they are achieved.

Even the accomplishments of soft feminism in the churches cannot be gainsaid. For example, at the 1976 General Convention of the Episcopal Church, the media made it a point to give wide coverage to laywomen delegates adamantly opposed to the ordination of women to the priesthood. It is an obvious historical anomaly that women who have voice and vote as lay delegates because of struggles of earlier "radicals" should now be used to check the women's movement. Advances by women in the churches could not be turned back fully because their energy and sacrifice (especially monetary sacrifice) made them indispensable even to those most resentful of change.[39] The earlier hostile response to feminism did not stop cultural change. It merely ensured that churches would preach the Victorian culture's doctrine of the "special virtue" of women as "pure gospel" and "scriptural truth." Even the earlier stress on women's special responsibility for sin had to be abandoned in deference to the ladies, God bless 'em.

No social institution, least of all the church, can return to the past, though there can be a "recovery" of the authentic spirit of faith. But evangelical faith is far removed from that spirit that wishes to reinforce present convention in the name of "pure" religion. Given the rebirth of the women's movement, it would be wise for the churches to abandon the ideology regarding women that it teaches but that is really the "pure doctrine" of nineteenth-century middle-class morality. To continue such teaching as theologically sound and as "biblical" and as a weapon against further constructive change is silly. The consequences, however, will not be laughable. Continuing such nonsense, tragically, will accomplish what it has always accomplished — the further discrediting of Christianity among just those persons whose mature human sensibility to the requirements of genuine love and justice are, in our own time, the keenest.

KEEPING FAITH IN A SEXIST CHURCH

Not for Women Only*

The Personal Context of My Christian Feminism

"Keeping Faith in a Sexist Church" is a matter about which I can claim expertise quite apart from the research and work I have done in feminist studies. I am one of a handful of women who has had continuous experience as a working professional in the church and in Christian institutions over a period of three decades. Unfortunately few other women have had the options and opportunities that opened to me. I speak as a veteran of the struggle to know what it means simultaneously to "keep faith" *and* keep my integrity.

I am of a generation of women in the Protestant churches who aspired to enter the ministry after World War II. Ours is largely an untold story.[1] In the 1950s, when I was first a seminary student, there were nearly as many women enrolled at my seminary, Union Theological Seminary in New York, and in other ecumenical seminaries as there were in the late 1960s when I joined the Union faculty as an administrator and teacher. Most of us who attended seminary in the 1950s were drawn to theological education by the theological renaissance of the post–World War II period. Many of us sensed a vague call to study theology; some, like myself, were even drawn to ministry and to the work of the churches. Most, however, experienced little support, were overwhelmed, and eventually disappeared quietly from the ranks of the professionally employed. I was a survivor among this much larger group. An equally large number of women who graduated from seminary in the 1950s and early 1960s, very often

---

* This essay incorporates, in substantially revised form, two lectures and a panel presentation. The first, from which the title is taken, was given at United Theological Seminary in New Brighton, Minnesota, in 1977. The second, entitled "Feminism and Ministry," was delivered to an Interchurch Center Retreat for Women Church Executives and was circulated in 1979 by Church Women United.

with excellent academic records, did not even attempt to work professionally at the time. Why did these things happen?

Importantly, most of these women, like myself, were born after 1930. I was born in 1932. Throughout most of my childhood and into my college and post-college years, the only important awareness I had about my birthdate was that it fell in the midst of the Great Depression. This was indeed an important fact about my life. But what I did not understand until well over three decades later was that being born in the 1930s or 1940s was also a very fateful reality for a girl child in this society. I had been born into a white, middle-strata family in a small midwestern town, where women's roles were firmly fixed and where the influence of feminism had hardly permeated. By 1930, the impact of many decades of ferment in women's lives had subsided even in urban areas of the country. By most indices, I was born into that period in U.S. history when the ideology of women's "traditional" roles was reasserting itself strongly. Economic crisis, then as now, had precipitated efforts to discredit feminism systematically. Those who know something of recent research about women in American history are aware that a much-debated point in contemporary feminist historiography is how successful the effort was to suppress change in women's roles from the 1920s through the 1950s. Certainly many of the gains of nineteenth- and early-twentieth-century feminism were not overturned.[2] And yet, in the world to which I was socialized, justice for women was never articulated as an issue. So far as I was aware growing up, no such reality as feminism had ever existed. I was to come to adulthood and enter a career without the least awareness that there had been a hundred and fifty years of struggle in this society for gender justice, a struggle that achieved minimal, and costly, victories. I now believe it was an unspeakable impoverishment of my life to grow up and live so long without *any* knowledge of the critique and struggle that courageous and strong women had launched for women's full humanity. How much easier my life would have been had I known of this earlier challenge to the social conventions that enshrouded my life, conventions that taught me that I was by "nature," by virtue of my genitals, especially suited to be a wife and mother, that my "femininity" meant that professional work, if I did it at all, should and would be only a transitional or secondary phase of my existence.

Like all of my generation, I was unknowingly an heir and debtor to the first wave of feminism. I was utterly without awareness of, and hence gratitude for, the struggles of sisters who had preceded me. They had created the space I came to occupy, but I had no appreciation of that fact. I did not know that feminism had been a powerful collective force that defenders of the status quo belittled to hold off demands for genuine economic and political change in the society. It was quite by accident, therefore, that I became rather serious about a professional career, or at least serious about graduate-level educational preparation for a professional career. My motivation was, I understood, rooted in my rather distinctive personal history. My mother, not a part of the first wave of feminism, had raised me to understand that I *might* have to be self-reliant economically. She, like so very many women in this society, had learned that lesson the hard way, by being left a widow at an early age with five children to support and educate. So my specific family socialization differed in one important respect from the socialization of many of my friends — like myself, white women from middle-strata homes. I had been taught explicitly that I needed to be prepared for contingencies of life that I could not control. Fortunately, with my generation it had become acceptable for a woman to get a college education, but it was not expected that we would use our education professionally. Not surprisingly, given this double message, mine was a generation in which ambivalence about striving and the fear of success were rampant.[3]

Another historical dynamic eventually shaped my professional development. Mine was the "church youth movement generation." My experience in the church — in this case, the United Presbyterian Church — was shaped by the centrality of young adult ministries in post–World War II mainstream Protestantism. Like many of my contemporaries in the halcyon days of the early 1950s, I was a leader in various denominational youth organizations. In these youth organizations, boys were usually elected moderators, as we Presbyterians called our chairpersons, but girls made it to the vice-moderator level and worked very hard at the difficult organizational work of these movements. In my role as perpetual vice-moderator, I was encouraged to believe that I indeed had some leadership ability. My wonderful and distinguished college professor Robert McAfee Brown, whose work and support much influenced me and who surely never thought *not* to encourage me because I was a woman, suggested I study theology at Union Theological Seminary in New York. Because of my serious, if ambivalent, intellectual interests, my aspiration for a theological education, and even, to a degree, my aspiration for a professional career in the church, this suggestion thrilled me. The idea that I should attend seminary also received active support from many liberal male clergy I knew. In this respect I was surely one of the luckier women of my generation. Admittedly, the Presbyterian clergy who encouraged me never imagined any role for me except as a director of Christian education. Until I arrived at Union Seminary I did not even *know* that many women did the regular ministerial theological degree, the Bachelor of Divinity degree, as it was then known.[4] Nor did the possibility of clerical ordination ever enter my consciousness. Since I was headed for campus ministry, I deemed ordination "unnecessary." I hardly made this decision consciously, however, because at that time I could not have tolerated the anxiety of sex role "deviance," not even in aspiration, much less in practice. I now realize that I was drawn to campus ministry not merely because of my own ability, but even more by the graceful and fortuitous circumstance that I actually knew one woman, a serious professional in ministry, who was *not* a local church director of Christian education. The Reverend Elizabeth Heller, a campus minister at the University of Minnesota during my college years, had willy-nilly become my role model. Not surprisingly, I followed the only role model I had known into campus ministry. Fortunately, I was well suited to that work, but, retrospectively, I also came to realize how often women like myself, well socialized to "femininity," followed our projective identifications rather than our own realistic self-assessments. Even today, I believe many women are drawn to church ministry because some professionally employed woman in the church turns out to be the first "nonprivatized" female she has met, the first who has sought fulfillment through work as well as relationship.

In spite of my own vague and inchoate motivation, I consistently received encouragement for my professional interest. After seminary I had several job options and chose to work in campus ministry. The considerable creativity and unconventionality of campus ministry during the late 1950s and early 1960s attracted me, and the openness of many colleagues assured me continuous and much-needed support. Another factor in my survival, however, was undoubtedly my ability to do things the way men did them! I was regularly commended, in indirect ways. Often, I heard, "You *really* are good" — a message tinged with surprise, implying "You are different from what we expected a woman to be." Sometimes, I was told explicitly: "You are really one of the boys." In the fall of 1956 I was examined by the San Francisco Presbytery to become a "Commissioned Church Worker." The Presbyterian Church, USA, was at that very moment debating the question of whether women should be ordained as "Teaching Elders," as we call our clergy. The truth is that I was so out of touch with myself at that point that I neither aspired to be ordained nor even had a clear opinion about the ordination of women. Whether women could be ordained or not was, I imagined, *irrelevant to me!* Still, at my "commissioning examination" one of the clergy, a colleague with whom I have had loving, conflictual relations over subsequent years, rose and exclaimed, "Well, if we have to ordain women, this is the kind we should ordain!"

My own early experience in a professional career in the church was not, then, a story of hostility or an experience of subversion of my self-esteem. But the subtle message communicated by many men was "Because you are like us, that is, *not* like most women, we welcome you as a colleague." During this period, while I was getting positive strokes, many of my women friends working professionally in the church reported quite different experiences and were deeply discouraged. When I was commissioned, just prior to the decision to extend clerical ordination to women, there were at least a dozen Commissioned Church Workers in the Presbytery of San Francisco. When I left the Bay Area six years later, only three of us, myself included, still worked professionally for the church. The shocking thing to me now is that I lived through this experience and *never asked why*. Only later did I join other sisters in asking, "Where Have All the Women Gone?" [5]

I realize now that I lived during these years with an internal psychic split that, given the times, was the cost of the acceptance by male peers that I so much valued. This split expressed itself in a deeply embedded uneasiness that I really must be *different* from other women, tougher, and, therefore, presumably less "feminine." Because I was acceptable to men and could operate in a "male" mode, I felt inadequate as a woman. At the same time, male approval left me feeling superior to other women. A sense of superiority and a deep uneasiness that something was terribly wrong with me as a woman operated in my soul. As a result, my "success" cut me off from other women. I was faintly, though not actively, contemptuous that somehow *they* were not tough enough. I was impatient with their "weakness" and the ease with which *they* became discouraged. Stoical by family background and culture, I was quick to dismiss their "emotionality," much as men often do. But I also felt flawed because I was not "soft" enough; because men were so supportive, I felt uneasy. I was simultaneously a professional success and a "failed" woman. Yet I *was* a woman. In this condition I could not fully own my own power. I felt that my accomplishments were specious, not really mine; feeling weak, I more or less imitated the working styles of those around me, unawares. The result was that though I evidently performed well enough to fool everyone else, I never felt quite "good" about what I did or who I was.

It amazes me that the women's movement "found" me, or reached me at all. I was a perfect candidate for "queen bee" status, as we now call successful women who do not support other women. Yet it was precisely the support of other women that finally healed this split in me and enabled me to come to value myself. This healing also enabled me to continue my struggle to be a strong woman in the church and to have the courage to acknowledge how potent a force sexism really is within it. Please note that both developments — the ability to continue the struggle and the willingness to face the truth about the scope of the struggle and the depth of change needed — resulted from my experience of sisterhood.[6] Because of other women's gifts of support, I can claim that it *is* possible to keep faith in a sexist church. But this same graceful support also helped me to understand that keeping faith involves justice for women and uncompromising challenge to the real injustices of church life, including sexism. My title makes clear that I also believe that the challenging of injustice is not a task for women only; women cannot turn the church around alone, especially where sexism is concerned. Gender roles, like all social roles, are reciprocal, and it is not just for women to struggle alone to eliminate sexism, any more than it is just or right for people of color to carry the struggle against racism alone.

Because many of my male colleagues celebrated my ability as a theological scholar, I was also encouraged in the early 1960s to return to graduate studies. I experienced ambivalence at the prospect of attempting to be a theologian, but once again, if others said that I could, I would try. It was, however, the period when the neo-orthodox synthesis of the 1950s was breaking up. The "death of God" movement was emergent when I returned to graduate school, signaling loss of confidence in the dominant theological options.[7] I became aware rather quickly of a malaise and defensiveness among my theological professors that I had not sensed a decade earlier. While I had to acknowledge that this malaise was in myself as well, it was nevertheless unnerving to find myself experiencing what seemed then a "loss of faith" just as I was beginning doctoral studies in theology. I did not at this point possess any degree of feminist consciousness. I was but partially aware that the neo-orthodox theology I had embraced in my earlier seminary days had ceased to seem plausible to me. This dislocation appeared as a "loss of faith" because I recognized that I could no longer speak confidently of a transcendent God, one who stands as "totally other," "beyond" life, history, and the world. Nor could I maintain my previous confidence in the power of the established churches to directly and positively affect the structures of our society. At one level, I felt that my life's work as a theologian was basically over before it had begun.

Happily, in order to support myself toward the end of my Ph.D. program, I began doing administrative work as an assistant dean of students with special responsibility for women students. It was at this point, sitting in an office at Union Seminary, that I began, really for the first time, to talk deeply with other women about their convictions, experiences, and struggles in theological education and in the church. Typically, through the first year or two of these conversations, I understood myself to be dealing with "their" problems — with whether and to what extent they could survive theological education. The answer that many of them reached through our dialogues (and, I am sad to say, without protest from me) was that they could not survive, that they would be better off leaving the seminary. My old and well-learned attitude that women had to be tough and learn to compromise to "endure" in theological education and professional ministry, though never directly expressed, led me to acquiesce in these younger women's decisions to withdraw.

About this time, the second wave of feminism began to break, exemplified by Betty Friedan's book *The Feminine Mystique*.[8] Her book, expressing a cry of anguish from a woman, like myself well educated, unlike myself a suburban housewife, named the socioeconomic powerlessness of the homemaker, an object of manipulation and caricature by the media. Different as my situation was, the book struck a deep chord in me. Soon, other books and writings began to appear, written by more radical and activist women who had learned the meaning of sexism in the various social justice struggles of the 1960s.[9] As I listened to the voices of these women, I began to put my own history together in a different way. The conversations with women in the seminary began also to resonate and connect with my own story in new ways. At some level these women, mostly young, were describing a vision, a call, a claim to ministry that simply did not fit the existing mode of professional norms for clergy. They were questioning the assumptions of the enterprise of theological education, especially the kinds of questions and approaches that constituted "acceptable" academic work. Their complaints resonated even in my conformist soul, as I heard them insist that to be creative in ministry, their own initiatives and questions had to be taken seriously. I knew that our curriculum made that impossible. Slowly I recognized how much I disvalued women, myself included, and made a connection between my own conformity and my lack of a sense of my power in my work.

It dawned on me, sitting behind my desk in an institution in which I had some influence, some power of agency, some capacity to affect the situation of these women, that *I* had done nothing to actively support their concerns. Furthermore, I saw that every time I confirmed or affirmed a woman's decision to leave seminary, I was cutting myself off from my sisters and weakening the base of support for my own work. I had to acknowledge that those who were teaching *me* what critical consciousness was about and who were giving me the power to own my own strength through their mutual recognition and solidarity were precisely those least valued in the institution I served. Yet I recognized that they were at the same time the most actively caring, the most creative and free of our students in the arts of ministry. For the first time, I saw how much *I* was taken for granted in the seminary and how little I was perceived as a serious academic! I became an activist because of my growing awareness that I could not live productively and well without those sisters and that I needed the enhanced environment of support their presence and creativity offered. I could not, and did not want to, survive in the church if they could not thrive in it as well. It was this burgeoning awareness that turned me around.

As my practice changed, I also gained an intuition that my earlier "loss of faith" was not really a loss of faith at all. It was merely a loss of credulity. It began to dawn on me that I had learned allegiance to a structure of theological authority that was external, not my own. I had, slowly, to learn how deeply unfree and escapist my own, and much of others', so-called Christianity had been. For the first time, I could really ask "What do I really affirm, really deny, theologically?" I was led, finally, to say of women's genuine liberation, "This is *my* fight, this is *my* struggle, *my* life; I am in it, with my sisters, to the end." Once the commitment was clear, the ambivalence overcome, my intellectual perspective began to gain a clarity I had never known before. I felt that for the first time I was asking *my* theological questions, critically appraising all that I had learned in new ways, discovering how other-centered, authority-oriented, and uncreative my own work had been. I discovered that nearly all of my earlier theological judgments had been sustained by the prejudices of my former teachers, with whom I had rarely disagreed because I was so male-dependent. Sadly, I also had to face the truth that my own questions became harder, more probing, and my answers less conventional. The support I received from some previously affirmative male colleagues was much qualified. It had never occurred to me that my cautiousness and restraint, born of ambivalence, had been a source of some of the affirmation I had received from men. I lived to learn that not all of the support I had experienced was due to genuine appreciation of my strength. Being commended for being "one of the boys" had, I understood, also meant being affirmed for playing it safe.

The Feminist Critique of Christianity

Since the early 1970s, when these changes occurred, there has emerged, and I have had a small part in it, a very strong movement of feminist theology within and beyond Christianity.[10] The feminist theological critique of the dominant Christian tradition and of the church, its theology and liturgy, its way of organizing its life cuts so deep that male theologians often try to ignore it or trivialize it or brand it as a mere repetition of ancient errors long discredited as "heresy." [11] I believe quite honestly that this sort of response is defensive nonsense and that the feminist critique is the most important event internal to dominant western Christianity in the last centuries. To my mind, it is an even more important challenge to dominant Christianity than was the intellectual ferment of the Enlightenment, if only because Enlightenment rationalism was so symbiotically tied to the patriarchal religion it challenged. "Reason" replaced "Revelation," but both were hypostatized and portrayed as nonrelational qualities, possessions of subjects, the one of God alone, the other of "man" alone.

Sometimes, of course, Christian feminists themselves do not perceive how deeply our questions cut against the fundamental ethos of western theological scholasticism and philosophic rationalism. Women do not yet take ourselves seriously enough, especially intellectually. Such attitudes are reinforced in us when women in theology are treated as nuisances, superficial thinkers, who merely advance theological ideas long since dismissed by more profound theological "giants." Feminists in theology are often very angry. We have a lot of new, painful awareness to bear and a lot of anger to process and channel. As I have argued already, we have a *right* to this anger.[12] Nevertheless, it takes courage to differentiate and channel such anger clearly. And since even women who are slightly angry terrify those who fear women, our anger is constantly observed, whereas obvious and ongoing rage *at* women goes unperceived and undiagnosed. Resentment that we do not stay in "our place" — that is, play the role of those who mediate good feelings to men — is widespread. Because women are not to deal with ideas or to precipitate or engage conflict, the most articulate feminists are the objects of continuous projection, and they have a very rough time in theological education.

It is helpful through all of this to be aware that from the beginnings of the feminist movement in the United States women have been especially punished for challenging masculinist religion. As I have documented, the earliest feminists recognized that everything on women's agenda of historical liberation depended on a successful challenge of religious teaching and that such a critique was socially dangerous. Unless the presuppositions of patriarchy, pervasive in the major world religions, were exposed, male supremacy could never be ended effectively. What we are doing today in theology, then, is by no means novel. Feminists have always had to learn to face the wrath of those who deemed us "impious" and heretical.

In spite of the rage of dominant theological groups, many of us have learned that in, with, and under these dominant theologies, there is within Christian tradition a marginal, but nevertheless more authentic and empowering message. Women's use of marginal traditions of Christianity is as appropriate as women's use of *all* marginated historical tradition.[13]

The roots of feminism in western Europe and in the United States illustrate this point. The post-Enlightenment political struggles of the rising white European middle class provided one ideological source for feminism. Women were a part of the struggle of this bourgeois revolution, and some of them began to ask why the traditions of the "Rights of Man" did not include women. Mary Wollstonecraft is a classic example of such a woman. Fiery and passionate, she lived at the end of the eighteenth and into the nineteenth century and she became a writer of tracts for the new bourgeois political movement. An early tract was entitled *A Vindication of the Rights of Man*. Then, hearing this message of liberation as relevant to herself, she became aware that "Man" was not recognized as a generic-inclusive term. She penned *A Vindication of the Rights of Woman*[14] as an extension of the message of liberation her male political colleagues did not intend for her to hear. The "secular" root of feminism, Enlightenment political theory, was not intended to be heard by women.

In the previous chapter I have described how the religious root of feminism — Christian social evangelism — reached women in the same way. In the United States religion originally played a positive role in social change. By 1828, when the Second Great Awakening began, currents of political reform merged with religious impulse. The Spirit of God, it was widely believed, was breaking in on this society in a new way, calling it to internal reform. As the "revival" swept the country, women too began to hear these claims and to stand up to pray or speak for the Spirit of God, for social reform, and to testify to God's power to effect change. Out of this revival — the last one that led directly to pressure for social reform — emerged numerous reform movements, serious, organized efforts at social change. The major reform movement focused on the abolition of the institution of slavery. In the emergent abolitionist movement, a few women, including some white women, began to stand up and attack as idolatrous and unthinkable the notion that black people were created by God to be inferior to whites.[15] In rejecting the notion that blacks are "naturally" inferior, these white women began also to hear, *in their own words*, a message that ought also to apply to themselves. For the first time they began to ask "Is woman's nature really proscribed by God as different from and inferior to men?"

Some of us living out of the Christian traditions in which we were raised have made a commitment and taken stands for justice for others. Through this we have heard a story about ourselves and our own possibilities that no one else had been telling us explicitly. It is not so surprising, then, that we have heard in the church a story of liberation that we were not intended to hear. Whenever women or marginalized men stand on their own feet and begin to speak for ourselves, we hear in our own words about change, a hope that must also apply to us. More and more, as women take each other seriously and reinterpret past tradition for ourselves, relating it to *our* possibility, we discover messages of hope in the neglected, suppressed, or marginal traditions of Christianity that we find to be truly liberating.

The Christian story as I have come to understand it out of my experience, informed by feminist consciousness, is not the story told by the dominant tradition as I first learned it in seminary. The way I understand the Christian story is now quite different. My own theology *is* controversial, and by some standards it *is* heretical. Here, the summary of my presuppositions must be oversimplified. Yet coming to understand the Christian story this way — as this vision — is the reason that I am still in the Christian church.

Some Presuppositions Regarding Christian and "Secular" History That Inform a Feminist Theological Stance

I will begin with Jesus, not because one must always begin there but because the Jesus story has been so central to Christian identity. As a feminist, I have come to understand Jesus of Nazareth's life and work very differently than I once did. Jesus was a man born into a remote province of the Roman Empire, in a time when his own and other cultures were suffused with religion. He was a Jew, and a lowly peasant Jew at that. Through a series of circumstances, the details of which are not clear, he left his family and village, thereby flaunting the dominant religious expectation of his people, and began to be an itinerant rabbi or teacher, announcing that something critical was occurring. In the theological language of his time, he called this happening "the inbreaking of the Kingdom of God." [16] What he was about "in word and deed," as we Christians frequently put it, was clarifying and embodying what it meant for people to live out their lives under conditions of the "reign of God." It was, as I have noted, a tremendously "religious" age, with new cults emergent on every hand. In that sense it was very like our own. Jesus called upon the traditions of his people, but he often reversed or reinterpreted them. He did not ask people to be "religious" in the well-recognized ways supported by powerful religious leaders of his time. One way to characterize what he was doing is to say that he proposed a radical, alternative understanding of what it meant to *be* "religious" or "spiritual," challenging many of the most influential and powerful conceptions of religiousness practiced in his culture. We also need to be aware, though, that to characterize Jesus' message as religious is in some respects misleading. Religion was not then the differentiated sphere it has become in our modern western tradition. It is also accurate, and no more anachronistic,[17] to characterize Jesus' teaching primarily as political because he was engaging people in an effort to change their lifestyles, their social relationships, and the ethos of their culture. As a Jew, he drew on several powerful traditions of his people little remembered by his most influential religious contemporaries. He insisted that to be related to God, to participate "in the Kingdom," one needed to *live* a certain way. "The Way" that he recommended and lived out is much disputed and highly controversial. We know that he spoke to those who were ill or psychically or physically maimed, people who saw themselves as invalids, and instructed them to stand up and go on their way. We know that he told some rich people who asked what his teaching meant for them that they would have to turn around, to change their entire way of living, if they were going to "enter the Kingdom of God." There is evidence that he told his closest followers to adopt a radical lifestyle, loving and caring for one another, and that he sent them out to do what he did — calling upon people to live in consonance with the inbreaking "Kingdom of God." His notion of religion was, at the very least, revolutionary, not because it was entirely new or unprecedented but because it was powerfully change-oriented, which is why it is as accurate to describe it in modern parlance as political teaching as it is to call it religious. His early followers, it is reported, called themselves "the people of the Way." It was a way in which fidelity to God was incarnated in new action and new relationships to others.

Living out this conception of "religion" brought Jesus into a great deal of conflict. It was obviously not in the interest of many people to encourage this sort of religion — an active, change-making praxis. The historical record suggests that revolutionaries, that is, intense change-makers, always are met with opposition. Not surprisingly, Jesus actively offended the Roman colonial rulers of Palestine, and eventually he was killed by the authority of the Roman state. He was not executed for any abstract reason, or because he believed that God demanded his self-sacrifice. That is the way the church has often told the Jesus story after the fact, but this way of speaking about Jesus' life and work is a deep distortion of the New Testament story. Jesus was *not* crucified for urging that we sacrifice ourselves for God. He was killed because he insisted on encouraging the acting out of the conditions of God's reign and on getting "the Way" of radical communitarian living under way.

The evidence suggests that such success as the early Christians had in engaging other people in this praxis resulted from people personally responding to these actions and ways of being in the world. This way of relating to each other was different and made a difference to people's sense of well-being. This lifestyle and manner of being together was promising in terms of what it meant to be godly. However, the followers of Jesus were constantly challenged and accused of being dangerous to public order. Christians eventually came to fear the charges being made against them — charges that they were undermining the existing order of power and authority. Fear began to dissipate their energy for change. The early Christians came less and less to talk about staying "on the Way" in terms of God's reign and began, more and more, to substitute beliefs about *Jesus'* extraordinary power, clinging to his memory in the past rather than living toward the future in the pattern of relations they had embraced and affirmed with him. Jesus had, in effect, told them: "Do not point to *me,* do not reverence *me* — live as our profoundest forebears commanded, loving God with a whole heart and loving each other as you love yourselves!"[18] Slowly, being "Christian" ceased to mean living radically under the conditions of God's reign and came to imply believing certain things *about* Jesus and accepting certain propositions *about* God. With this shift from praxis to ideology, those "on the Way" became religious in the way religious people are popularly expected to behave, that is, acting holier than others and finding their distinctiveness in certain beliefs and propositions that assure blessedness. Roman Christians and Jewish Christians retreated to their earlier segregated lifestyles, male and female resumed well-established patterns of traditional gender subjugation. Those who were "masters," owners of slaves, once again grew comfortable about their relationships to slaves. Genuine modeling of "the Way" became rarer and rarer among Jesus' followers. From time to time, some Christians attempted the radical praxis of God's reign, but many Christians, including some Christian teachers or "theologians," grew weary of being viewed as "dangerous" troublemakers and worked instead for social and intellectual acceptance. Eventually, Christianity even became the "official" religion of the Roman Empire. That made it harder and harder to locate any tension between "the Way" of God's reign and the intentions of the Caesars.

The world was changing, though, and within a short time, the imperial power of Rome collapsed. For many centuries there was decentralization and reorganization in areas where Christianity had become the official religion, and, as it spread, Christianity evolved in many different ways. Many forms of Christian "religiousness" were practiced. More and more, however, being "Christian" came to mean living for "another world," not for the reign of God now manifesting itself. Spirituality came to mean living for another world, not for life in the here and now. Late Hellenistic religion had influenced early Christians, encouraging the idea that the "otherworld," an invisible order, above the "merely" physical world of time and space, was the pious Christian's "true home." Much of the time, then, Christian praxis meant concentrating on this *other*, "spiritual" world to find a blessedness and peace clearly denied to most people living out the burdens of this life. Being Christian frequently was presumed to involve keeping oneself "pure" and unsullied by this world, subscribing to a "higher" standard of ascetic denial.

To be sure, there have always been some trends in the Christian movement that challenged this drift toward otherworldliness. It is my conviction that Christian feminism needs to live out of precisely these neglected traditions of life-affirmation. We must reappropriate Christian tradition from a different strata and for different reasons than dominant Christianity has done. We must seek to appropriate the theological struggle and dynamic of those Christian traditions that were world-, nature-, and cosmos-affirming. We need a differing sensibility and principle of interpretation for appropriating the theological past.

How our "hermeneutical principle" differs may be illustrated by an example: Thomas Aquinas is, by all accounts, a major theo-

logical giant in Christian history. Traditionalist theologians celebrate Aquinas because he was presumed to offer an elegant systematic integration of nature and the supernatural. I believe feminists
need to appreciate his accomplishments differently. Feminist criticism to date has focused on his views of women. Like most Christian theologians, Aquinas' formal ideas about women were appalling. We must recognize this without equivocation, but it is also
important for us to acknowledge that Aquinas had a positive feminist significance because he refused to limit the meaning and focus
of Christian theology to a "higher," otherworldly salvation. We can
criticize him but also recognize that from the standpoint of a feminist hermeneutic, he opened the door to fresh theological thinking about our life in time and history. Because of his willingness
to read and respect "dangerous" Greek philosophers, he opened
new theological currents. By affirming that our senses are constitutive of our human intelligence and our proper humanity,
he struck a blow against the accelerating trend of world-denying
spiritualism in Christianity. Aquinas found this world a fascinat-
ing place and wanted Christians to recover the capacity to look
about and see it, touch it, feel it, respect it. He argued that human
reason, human rationality, was not a bad thing, that the created
world is not an evil place. He insisted that supernatural knowledge was no substitute for the use of our intelligence and our
senses, that it is appropriate to enter deeply into the created, natural world. Aquinas initiated a much-needed theological revolution, reintegrating the human capacity for self-directed intelligence into the highly spiritualized theological world of his time,
within the framework of the ongoing church. This sort of reading
of Aquinas — identifying the constructive change he made toward a life-affirming theology — merely illustrates the way we
need to reappropriate past tradition. It should be comforting for
us feminists to remember that it took nearly a century for the
church to accept these changes. Aquinas may be celebrated now
as "*the* theologian" of the Roman Catholic tradition, but we
should not forget that he was an anathematized heretic for nearly
a century.[19]

What I have come to believe, out of my feminist theological
reorientation, is that there are not and can never be any final,
once-for-all adequate theological formulations. The task of theology is "continuous revolution." Aquinas' "new" catholic synthesis, involving the recovery of the role of human intelligence
through the integration into Christianity of other cultural resources, eventually ceased to be adequate as a formulation of
Christian praxis. By making Aquinas "singularly authoritative"
in Roman tradition, long after the historical situation in which

his voice was authentically creative had passed, the papacy weakened the role of the very creative life-affirming values in theology that Aquinas had struggled to articulate. But this is the way all dominant Christianity uses its "theological giants" — as a barrier against creative change.

Protestants also have undermined theological creativity in analogous ways. Luther and Calvin, whom dominant Protestant theologians view as distinctly authoritative, addressed a world where fundamental social and political changes were occurring. A new social and political order was emerging, and both Luther and Calvin understood that theological change was a requirement of their situation. To be sure, both stressed that their theologies represented a recovery of "authentic" Christianity, on the grounds that they were more faithful to scripture than was the reigning Roman theology. This preoccupation with authority makes clear that Luther and Calvin were most decidedly premodern men. Because of their backward-looking preoccupations, neither granted a more positive role to sensuous engagement in life than Aquinas had centuries earlier. Yet each worked to bring about deep and dramatic change in the theological praxis and the sensibilities of Christians in their time. Ironically, many of their heirs celebrated the changes they made, yet they treated their theological insights as final and fixed truths from which further change and dissent are impossible. In Protestant scholasticism, "Reformation" came to be understood as a state of being to be embraced rather than an ongoing challenge of Christian faithfulness.

In light of the proclivity of dominant theologies, I believe feminist sensibility and spirituality must continue to incorporate and appreciate the worldly, secular impulse within theology. This also means appreciating the Enlightenment, which traditionalists dismiss as humanistic. The Enlightenment was a reaction to the endless hostility, fueled by theological arrogance, that characterized the post-Reformation centuries. Many Europeans eventually became weary and wary of the narrow-mindedness of religion. Enlightenment humanism, as I observed before, had a symbiotic relationship to patriarchal Christianity and therefore was not without its own arrogance and presumption. It possessed a certitude about reason that often led to elitist cultural chauvinism. But it also generated new concern for explicit and direct efforts to accomplish political change to enhance human well-being. It encouraged a new concern for human rights — the best part of the modern European outlook. Obviously, feminism as a social movement having a sustained and critical character, no longer merely an episodic and occasional insight of isolated women, became a widespread possibility only after the Enlightenment. Until the adequacy of authoritarian forms of Christianity could be questioned on a broad scale, such a development would have been impossible. We Christian feminists, then, are heirs to the secular Enlightenment tradition as well as to the radical Jewish and Christian traditions. Yet we have to subject all of these traditions to the same searching analysis.[20] In the absence of a world-affirming theological vision, "Enlightenment" secularity can represent a loss of depth and spiritual substance. We feminists cannot embrace just any sort of worldly attitude or religiosity. The key to feminist spirituality is always a consistent praxis of justice.[21]

Even before the Enlightenment, most European Christians had abandoned serious efforts to change society and had entered into activities that ran counter to any previously recognized Christian practice or piety. The rising economic order was embraced, and new patterns of exploitation of others were undertaken. The need for cheap labor to develop the new land "discovered" in America led Europeans to sail to the coasts of Africa to kidnap Africans in large numbers.[22] These victims of European Christian "enterprise" were sold into slavery, and the "peculiar institution" of chattel slavery was born. There was little active dissent from any Christians except the left-wing "sectarians," that is, those who were identified neither with Rome nor with the dominant Reformation leaders. As a result of the slave trade, European whites began to develop an ideology of white supremacy. Like all supremacist ideology, the ideology of white racism gets its formidable power from the need of whites to believe in the rightness of a position of dominance they unjustly achieved, that is, to justify the exploitation of other human beings. Evidently, supremacist doctrine functions to "ease" the consciences of those whose evil acts run counter to their expressed moral and religious ideology.

One of the most striking contradictions that has come to characterize Christianity in the United States, given this history, is the simultaneous strength of otherworldly piety and the theological defense of our social system, including unrestrained economic activity. The "official histories" of this nation invariably stress the deep religious values of our people, but a critical history must acknowledge the extent to which the original European settlers exploited indigenous people, slaves, and poor immigrants in what appears now as a rapacious pattern of so-called national development. The point is important because it makes clear how deeply, to this day, our society is ensconced in a culture of split consciousness. We have a religiosity ostensibly grounded in deep fidelity to an authoritative Christian past on the one hand and a "worldly praxis" devoid of relational-spiritual substance, cynically insensitive to the human consequences of our so-called national development, on the other.

An American "empire" was built from this ambiguous spiritual legacy, and this imperium continues to perceive itself as very "religious" and/or "moral." While many forms of Christianity have flourished in the United States, the mainstream traditions of the Reformation, until quite recently, controlled the style and substance of this imperial religiosity. My early theological education represented a brief renaissance of mainstream Reformation Protestantism, clearly identified with U.S. elites. The "death of God" movement was but a symptom of these groups' cultural displacement. The social justice radicalism of the 1960s was led by black people, whose Christianity was forged out of the distinctive experience of slavery and oppression, by Jews, by social justice-oriented Catholics, by left-wing Protestant "sectarians," and by secular radicals. Together, these groups began to challenge the spiritual hegemony of the U.S. Protestant mainstream. Stirrings from the "third world" indicated further dissent from the dominant Euro-American Christian ethos. Led by some black Christians, a Christian spirituality "from below," voicing the hope of the oppressed, emerged once more, as it always does when political and religious longings coinhere. The civil rights movement and the anti-Vietnam War movement signaled a renewal of a praxis of worldly spirituality. The dominant Christian churches responded ambivalently, uncertain about whether they could or should identify with these "ambiguous" political tides. It was within this ferment that a women's movement emerged, affecting church women, who then demanded fuller direct participation in the church's ministry. In light of this interpretation of the current context of dominant western Christianity, what does feminism portend in the dominant churches? What must we say *to* the church, *about* the church, regarding its ministry and its theology?

Further Implications of Feminism for Christian Ministry and Its Relation to Liberation Theology

Elsewhere I have observed a great irony in the fact that women are now demanding a different approach to Christian ministry in and from the churches, and doing so at just the time in history when the stereotypical image of women and the stereotypical image of the Christian clergyman have become all but identical. Christians perceive the role of their clergy to be especially loving, acquiescent, culturally cautious, and self-sacrificing. They are, in short, to be "feminized." Women in large numbers are now seeking ordination at a point in time when this feminized notion of the "good" professional minister can be used against us, the more so because the sense of "Christian ministry" that feminists in particular embrace is one that rejects a "feminized," spiritualized, and privatistic conception of Christian ministry in favor of enabling Christians to make the connections between faith and embodied — that is, public — action. The feminist theological perspective recognizes our need for ongoing revolution — religious, economic, racial, political, sexual — as well as the need to bring about change holistically. A major source of the complexity of the feminist agenda within Christianity and Christian theology derives from this historical situation. The stereotypical, privatized religiosity in the dominant churches creates a tide strongly resistant to Christian feminist awareness that there can be no separation of spirituality and worldly engagement, that such a split vitiates a foundational praxis that always characterizes authentic spiritual power.

Women of dominant groups have been told in the recent past that we are "especially" fitted for religious vocation, precisely because we are morally "pure." This claim is, of course, nonsense. And quite modern nonsense at that. That women sometimes have been seen as particularly "religious" means only that the church has honored passivity and has called that passivity "spirituality." Yet such affirmation of women's "unique religiousness" works to divert the new feminist Christian movement, and to encourage us not to demand or expect much change. This is why I believe we must insist that women have been the activists, the doers, in human history and, in that capacity, the integrators of those presumed contradictions in the social world that male-dominant spiritualities articulate. This is probably why, until the modern period, Christian male theology has perceived women as *less*, not more, spiritual than men. In any case, feminists are called to be activists in ministry, not especially sanctified peacekeepers.

The feminist conviction that both giving and receiving characterize authentic ministry and are active modes of being in the world means that reciprocity is central to our paradigm of ministry. Our capacity for caring is born out of being cared for, but not in the patriarchal dualist sense that only God's care, in isolation, is genuinely restorative. The style of all authentic ministry is mutual acknowledgment and shared leadership. Solidarity is not a mode of life that can thrive where some are strong and others weak. Strength and vulnerability thrive or die together. This means that, at a time when much theology of ministry calls on the clergy to be *the* servants, *the* sacrificers, we must say instead that the church is called to act collectively, to enhance our common survival and mutual well-being. Just as Jesus' vision never focused on personal sacrifice, abstractly considered, but rather on a praxis consistent with the reign of God, so we are to find ways to be together, a living parable of hope. Such inclusive life affirmation does threaten any power that is not reciprocal power.

The specific Christian feminist theological critique of sexism in Christian tradition needs to be set within this wider horizon. Others in the Christian community also see that dominant Christian theologies do not express adequately a life-affirming perspective. Feminist theology is very much a part of a larger movement of liberation theology in our time, even in spite of the point I have stressed that much "liberation theology" perpetuates male supremacy.[23] One of the joys of my work as a professional woman and theologian over the last fifteen years has been my engagement with those developing a liberation critique from a variety of analyses of oppression. To confront, and be confronted by, liberation theologies emergent in other cultures and structures of oppression I have not experienced directly has greatly deepened my own sense of what an adequate feminist theological agenda involves. The radical analyses of racism and imperialism — cultural and economic — generated by liberation theologies not only have sensitized me to my own racism and cultural chauvinism but have deepened my sense both of women's contribution to all human liberation struggle and to the depth of sexism that victimizes those women who bear the reality of interstructured subjugations.

Far from muting my feminism, these experiences have intensified my probing into the heart of traditionalist Christianity. Male-controlled liberation theology requires the same confrontations that dominant theology demands of feminists. Feminism implies a specific critique of each particular Christian theological culture and tradition. Women within each tradition must develop these critiques, for women are the specific underclass within every group and culture. Insofar as each Christian theological movement, including those on "the underside of history,"[24] appeal to past male-controlled tradition, the way in which male supremacy deforms its message or purported "good news" must be analyzed. Since misogyny has been an active force, profoundly deforming Christianity's own internal structure and ideology for centuries, these distortions run deep in every culture. It is no wonder, then, that the full and honest scope of a feminist critique remains deeply threatening even to liberation theologians.

Over against the resistance of reputed liberation theologians, feminists must appeal to the pivotal thesis of liberation theological method, namely that the good news of God — which is also the experience of the power and presence of God in our midst — is given only as we engage concrete oppression and enter into struggle against it. A feminist faith pilgrimage requires that we all relinquish so-called faith that is merely uncritical identification with male power. Men and women alike require the genuine spiritual rebirth that comes from fighting for the concrete lives and worldly well-being of women. In that engagement, what appears initially as a "loss of faith" will turn out to be a step into genuine nonalienation, that is to say, deeper faith in the power of God-in-relation.[25] Refusal to confront male supremacy keeps hierarchies of all sorts in place.[26]

Important as it is for liberation theologians to come to terms with the critical consciousness of the self-affirming women in their communities, engagement in the liberation theology process has led me to conclude that the deepest resistance to a feminist theological agenda, and the greatest threat to the promise of feminist theology, may well be the *liberal* consciousness of many women and men in the white mainstream of dominant Christianity. The very ideology and ethos that engendered feminism now threatens to compromise it. There is, indeed, a growing tendency for liberal women and men to embrace a pseudo-feminist, immature, and sentimental "pro-woman" rhetoric while refusing to come to terms with the scope of pain and suffering in our world. For liberals a long struggle is needed even to begin to perceive the depth of active evil we face. We have learned, subtly, to construct our lives to evade conflict. Since conflict is intrinsic to life, and therefore to genuine faith, our psychic evasions keep us theologically immature. In a sense, liberalism conditions us to a "happiness fix," to a desperate wish for an antiseptic, "harmonious" world.

White Christian feminists like myself have not escaped this system of socialization. On the contrary, those of us who are white and middle strata are most likely to be raised to be "good girls," encouraged to become addicted to sentimental religion. We are encouraged to become addicted to the "security" of pleasantries from our earliest years.[27] Furthermore, because we are white, and not poor, we do not easily detect the privilege that is ours in a white-supremacist, class-stratified society. Nor do we always recognize that others' suffering is more relentless than our own. Not all white, nonpoor women experience this sort of "feminized" socialization, but many of us have, and the churches have encouraged it. Given this fact, it is, I believe, quite astonishing that so many white feminists, along with a few gay men, have

pressed the critical questions about the full scope of human oppression and Christian theological complicity so relentlessly in
the mainstream churches.

The Specific Feminist Theological Agenda
Within Christianity

The critique we feminists make of Christianity involves a long
agenda for theological change. It requires an extended and profound rethinking of all the language, images, and metaphors central to Christian theology, a re-visioning that will surely not be
exhausted soon. The unrealistic expectations of our opponents
are often aimed at discrediting our work. Those who complain because we have not already or instantly produced liturgies, rituals,
and theological imagery that are exemplary theological alternatives to long-established Christian practice are making an unjust
demand. To expect a decade of feminist work to produce a fully
mature, nonsexist Christian theology that rivals the presumed
grandeur of Elizabethan English, or even the greatest literary
productions created by a huge male theological caste working
over centuries, is silly. Developing a feminist literary tradition,
including a liturgy[28] and a significant corpus of theological reflection, is a task for numerous and culturally diverse women, over
many lifetimes and many generations. And much of our early
work must aim at critical de-construction of existing imagery, the
"digging" necessary to remember the ignored or forgotten work
of our foresisters.

Even so, there are, I believe, three matters of particular urgency on the Christian feminist theological agenda, if we are to
heal the special oppressiveness of masculinist Christian practice
that daily shatters women's lives. Priority must be given not only
to the language of Christian theology but to the images that
Christian theology relies on in describing our God-relation. The
frequent dismissal by male theologians of this matter is itself one
of the great scandals of contemporary Christianity. Christian
male theologians have celebrated God's speaking, as logos, as "the
Word," throughout Christian history. No metaphors for God are
more overworked in Christian theological imagination than the
speech metaphors. The Christian theological community that
claims that God's speaking to us is itself the primary metaphor of
divine disclosure can hardly also insist, with any integrity, that
the issue of sexist theological language and image is a minor
problem. The spiritual schizophrenia expressed here never ceases
to amaze me. Surely one of the reasons that sexism in theological

language can be so readily, if erroneously, dismissed is that many
Christian theologians have lost the capacity to recognize the fundamental, imagistic character of the language in which they confess the faith of the Christian community. If I am right on this
point, then feminist theology, precisely because of women's insistence on the foundational character of image and metaphor,
will contribute to a desperately needed refurbishment of Christian theological imagination.[29]

As I have acknowledged here, it was my early feminist consciousness that made me aware of how glibly some white male
Christian theological colleagues invoked God as "wholly other,"
as "transcendent" to all human time, space, and experience. With
this awareness came a persistent puzzlement at their apparent
inability to notice the complete loss of religious substance and
meaning that followed from this kind of negative, abstract imagery about God. Slowly I began to realize that one of the dynamics
I had previously overlooked was the way in which male gender
primacy masks the effect of the abstractions of these primal God
metaphors used by male theologians. They often operate with a
split consciousness because they employ vague and impersonal
concepts and language about God on the one hand and simultaneously draw on the concrete male imagery of Christian tradition
on the other. Even when these theologians spoke of God as totally
transcendent, they nevertheless did not lose entirely a continuing
analogy between God and their own experience. The positive
analogy between their lives and God was sustained by the male
biblical imagery that their abstract concepts denied. Many men,
I now believe, do not really *experience* the complete spiritual
emptiness of God's "radical transcendence" because their ongoing recital of the stories of scripture and liturgical tradition con-
tinually reiterates images for God that invoke analogies to male
identity and men's experience. This "wholly other" God is, for
them, still Father, Lord, King, all concrete terms of male agency.
He remains, always, whatever else they aver of God, a male image. Men can insist on the complete disconnectedness of God and
"man" yet not have to cope with what it means theologically to
create a total gulf between human experience and God. No wonder male theologians often seem to me not to be hearing what
they are saying!

For many of us women, by contrast, this abstract "otherness"
language, taken together with imagery derived so exclusively
from concrete historical male experience, combines to obliterate
all divine-human connection. Is it any wonder that we protest
and insist that this is not our experience of faith? No positive

analogy for divine-human relationship is present for us. The image and language of "wholly other" and "father" combine to render us totally invisible, empty of any connection to God, and reinforce a double disidentification of ourselves with God. Women are not being ornery or irreverent, then, in protesting male theological practice. Only if we pay attention as much to the sources of our images as to explicit gender references in the structure of language do we see the depth of the problem imposed on a feminist theology.

A second urgent matter for a contemporary Christian feminist theological agenda, touched on in my earlier historical discussion, is the split endemic in dominant Christian tradition, especially the split between spiritualistic mind and body. The sources of this split in dominant theological tradition are many, and I have addressed some of them elsewhere. Here I need only to underscore how much the purported "differences" between male and female, and the social inequality of women, have legitimated and grounded this split. "Male" has been a pervasive symbol for mind, power, intellect, that which is truly "spirit"; female has been symbol for nature, "irrational" feeling, "mere body," earth, the less than fully human. Women *are* body and men (actually, only dominant, power-identified males) *are* mind or reason. In some streams of classic Hellenic and late Hellenistic traditions, women were held to be, literally, deficient in the capacity for reason, and we are still living with that judgment and internalizing it. But even in the more holistic Hebraic tradition, men were most often portrayed as bearing *nepesh*, spirit, more readily able to be the spokespersons for Yahweh's breath and power.

I have already insisted that over the centuries this body/mind split has rendered dominant Christian traditions inept, idealized, incapable of addressing very fundamental issues of life, existence, and intellectuality. Not only has the dualism led to an ascetic, antisexual, antiphysical theology, encouraging dominant Christianity's constant and perpetual spiritualizing of life, but it has conditioned Christian inability to recognize that material well-being and bodily health are fundamental to spiritual blessedness and to authentic "redemption." This split is also clearly implicated in the way in which Christianity, in the modern period, has become not merely complacent toward but actively collusive with capitalist ideology. The inability of Christians to affirm, appreciate, and celebrate pleasure as a gift of God given for our enjoyment is also rooted in this dualism. Christian masochism is the perfect psychological foil to support a workaholic culture that nevertheless finds little or no joy or pleasure in work.

Finally, feminist theology must address the very deep na-
ture/history split in the Christian past, especially in the western
tradition. Since women are held to be "mere" nature, men are
therefore understood as the real historical agents. The sharp dichotomy between history and nature runs through much of our
theology, our ethics, and our reflection, and it conditions our actions and worldviews in ways too numerous to elaborate here.
Those who have analyzed the cultural roots of the ecological crisis
point to the complicity of Christian tradition in encouraging unrestrained "domination" of nature.[30] Even if these charges are
overdrawn, we still have to acknowledge that the "stewardship"
of our avowedly Christian culture in relation to nature has been
appalling. Can anyone really deny that there is no connection between Christianity and a Christian-dominant culture's belief that
it is acceptable to consume resources rapaciously, to plunder and
destroy the land, to control nature in any way we choose? As
Christians, we have learned to think of ourselves as "above" nature, as its superior.

It is not only feminist theology that makes this protest. Feminists press the issue in a foundational way, the more so because
women have been imaged as nature and as bearers of nature,
and we have learned the value of not repudiating this connection. In our identification with nature, we feminists do need to
avoid nature romanticism, which can lead to abdication of historical responsibility by construing human life as merely cyclical
and evolutionist. We do possess the power of historical agency
or creative capacity to affect and change the world. Still, modern Christian theology has overemphasized the nature/history
distinction by interpreting humanity (males) primarily as the
makers of history rather than as subjects of natural/historical
relationship. Technical, not personal-relational, images have been
primary in our conception of nature. What a feminist theological
critique demands, by contrast, is not a complete rejection of human historical agency but a profound recovery of a sense that we
are, ourselves, species-dependent, in nature, culture, and history.
As natural, historical, and cultural creators, we are profoundly
dependent on each other and the rest of the natural/historical/
cultural order. There is in fact a clear dialectic between our responsibility to nature and our capacity to become fresh, creative,
and humane historical-cultural agents. If we do not recover a new
respect for our deep interdependence as natural/historical and
cultural beings, understanding our reciprocity with each other
and nature as a dimension and condition of our freedom, all of
us are doomed.

A Postscript to Feminist Sisters
Who Are Considering Ministry

I conclude this reflection with a special word to those women now in seminary. Obviously, it is my hope that many will choose to take their stand, as I do, in the churches, in some continuity with Christian tradition, attempting to keep faith where sexism is rampant. None of us who do so dare deny that Christianity and the churches have been, and are, profoundly hostile to women. Christian theology, liturgy, and social organization do devalue women. The strongest things that post-Christian feminists like Mary Daly have said about Christianity's sexism are true.[31] What I have argued here is that in order to survive and, even more important, to live well in the church, each of us needs to move more deeply into the feminist critique of Christianity; we cannot run away from it, or flee from it, without losing capacity for truth or denying reality. If we do not opt for the solution Mary Daly proposes — that is, leaving the church because it is so bad for our dignity, health, and well-being — if we do not take that route, we must nevertheless be clear that the reason we do not is that we are called of God to be uncompromising agents of transformation of the church, in the church. The central theological issue is that the Christian church, its pompous self-profession notwithstanding, will not have, and cannot have, a genuine "gospel" either for its community or for anyone else while it teaches that maleness is distinctively holy. Christians will never hear a full gospel in their midst from anyone until we stand our ground as committed feminists, which is to say opponents of all structures of domination, proponents of *all* women's concrete well-being. We must insist that our hard word be heard. Our vocation requires that we accept that God calls us to utter this blunt word, that it is given to the church for its deliverance. Only in this way can we be authentic bearers of "the Way" to/of God.

Simultaneously, though, we need desperately to understand that none of us can work such transformation alone. What I say about this vocation is no appeal for individualistic, promethean prophethood or for some purported promethean power of Sisterhood either.[32] I do urge that we learn, deeply, the meaning of solidarity — solidarity with sisters who struggle and with marginated men who resist. Solidarity is continuous relationship, fidelity to relationship, and mutual accountability. I will never apologize, nor should you, for acknowledging my need for support from sisters and others in our common struggle. Above all, we need never apologize for our dependence on solidarity among women, even if men are threatened by it. We must never apologize for our need for other women's support, in or outside the church. Previously, there has not been genuine sisterhood in the Christian church, except in those attenuated and broken forms appropriate to "femininity," in which women were expected to do "lesser" things together precisely because they were women. For us to seek each other out because we are strong and capable, strong enough to be vulnerable to each other, is right and proper. And this is the only reality that will sustain our ability to keep faith in a sexist church.

We must recognize the cultural backlash against feminism and understand that it is dangerous and unjustified morally. Even when this backlash takes the "liberal" form I have discussed here — that feminism is "superficial," concerning itself with trivial matters instead of the urgent authentic panorama of "real" human problems — we must not be taken in. We must not forget that the material base of this new opposition to feminism is the extended stagflation of an advanced global capitalist economy. Women need to be pushed back into "their place" because our society cannot absorb the kind of pressure for change that we are generating. Both the reactionary and liberal strategies will accelerate. Liberals accommodate to feminism, to the women's movement, in mild and reformist ways but resist any real change. Reactionaries are more direct, crying, "back to the family," back to the "old" values. Ridicule women who speak out! Since women make up 51 percent of the population, reformist accommodation is pursued by finding those women who best "fit in" to the dominant system. A few of us — those who take their cues from the men — are to be rewarded. Tokenism continues, but this does not result in genuine change in the lives of most women. More than ever, women are the major victims in this society, the group most afflicted by the new poverty, the new racism, and the backlash against gender justice. Our solidarity must always span all of these realities. More and more women are unemployed, while others are increasingly marginated in ever more sex-stratified work positions. Homemakers are vulnerable and marginated as never before. Yet all of us, in one way or another, are being "invited" to cease the struggle to communicate across the social lines that divide us.

Those in the churches who imagine that the church will confront other injustice, such as global imperialism, racism, and class oppression, more easily if "noisy" feminist women are silenced are badly mistaken. We must not be intimidated by such illusions. For the mainstream churches to fail to answer the new right, to waver on gender justice and sexual politics, to use lesbians and gay men as scapegoats is to give active aid and comfort to the most powerful forces of reaction in this society. And it is, finally, to perpetuate all the institutions of oppression, not merely those that keep dominant, conformist male supremacy in place. It is the challenge of a feminist theology to make clear why this is so.

A Postscript to Men Who Recognize That Feminism Is Not for Women Only

And, finally, a word to men who have read to this point because you know that feminism is not for women only. Men who have gained awareness of how their personhood and humanity have been deformed by the demands of the masculine role, who will honestly name the cost, in terms of loss of spiritual power, that a misogynist theology exacts, are much needed in the work of ministry today. A feminist commitment requires more than a critique of the male role. It demands strong advocacy *for* women. But gender roles are always reciprocal. *Everyone* is of woman born, so advocacy for women is finally also advocacy for everyone's full humanity.

Increasingly, men are recognizing that feminism has deep theological promise. The issues we are raising regarding the images and language of faith also speak to these men and address the crises of faith through which they are also passing. Several years ago, after I lectured on feminism and christology, no less than four clergymen came up, one by one, to say that mine were the first reflections they had heard from a Christian theologian that had the ring of integrity, that actually spoke to their own very fundamental theological questions about Jesus of Nazareth and what Christians ought to teach about him. One said it had given him courage to face changes he needed to make if he were going to stay in the church. Another said, "As a preacher, I have come to feel like a peddler of 'Christ-ism,' requiring people to recite formulas about Jesus that neither they nor I any longer understand or believe." Feminism is not for women only because we *all* need a recovery of our full, integrated humanity and the power of theological language to engage our genuine struggles.

We also need each other especially to survive and flourish as activists in the dominant churches, where, to a certain extent, white middle-strata people profit from others' oppression. It is easy for us, men and women alike, to lose touch with the genuine scope of social oppression that is the existential condition of most human beings on this globe. Genuine struggle, the capacity to live with conflict and to resist the complacency of the dominant ethos, requires precisely those marks of transcendence born of the acknowledgment of solidarity. Our lives are worth struggling for, but only as a part of this wider struggle. Our lives will come alive, become our own, and prosper spiritually only in *shared resistance* to all that thwarts life's promise. To live through the anger and pain that nonescapist spirituality requires can be a great gift *if* it enables us, together, to resist what threatens this fullness of life. The capacity to know and name one's hurt, to recognize one's vulnerability, to bear suffering in order to work against unnecessary suffering is a blessing. The temptation to permit Christianity to lapse back into an escapist ideology, an accommodation to the power of privilege will be great if we do not learn to hold each other accountable to these realities. The dominant spirituality of our male-controlled religious culture, what Mary Daly coins as "necrophilia — the love of death," [33] *is* genuinely powerful. The solidarity of which we speak in liberation theology is as critical to the lives of feminist men as to women.

Much of my conversation with white males who seek this sort of solidarity has led me to recognize some distinctive problems that men have in experiencing genuine solidarity. Often the feminist analysis is heard by men as a call to deny your own personal power, to abrogate all leadership, or to renounce all personal strength, to embrace passivity. This, of course, is not what is required. More often, what is called for is a more direct and self-aware owning of the power that is already yours, making it more directly accountable to those affected by it. Greater vulnerability to and awareness of your own pain, doubts, and struggles is also important, along with a reduction of unconscious emotional dependence on women. Feminism is a call to genuine strength in women *and* men, a strength born of the power of relationship. Active love and passion for justice sends our roots deep, to discover or recover our connections with all that is. Such shared strength does enable us to keep faith, and we need that strength, for our faith calls us to ongoing, difficult, and challenging work.

THEOLOGICAL REFLECTION
IN THE STRUGGLE
FOR LIBERATION

A Feminist Perspective

The Praxis of Human Liberation

It is no simple matter to characterize the role of theological re-flection in the human struggle for liberation at a genuinely inter-national gathering. For anyone to do liberation theology, it is necessary to develop a critical awareness of how one's specific social location affects one's theological and moral sensibilities. Such analyses do not easily "translate" across international boun-daries or across cultural or racial lines. I want to begin, however, with one of the matters we have in common. All of us are stu-dents, faculty, or "senior friends" [1] of the university, persons who live out our lives in academic institutions or are closely identi-fied with the intellectual life and the enterprise of higher educa-tion. Whatever our differences of culture, ethnicity, or politics, most of us are positively identified with academic life and its values. Throughout much of the world today, universities have replaced religious institutions as the conveyors of social values and prestige. They play a central role in molding cultural and so-cial elites. Institutions of higher learning have become primary purveyors of status. Education is now perceived as the source of those qualities of "wholeness" and "dignity" that ground self-worth. In the modern world, under western hegemony, a full life is deemed to require intellectual mastery, and one's competence is assessed chiefly by academic certification. The expectation that competence comes with certification is presumptuous at best. Nonetheless, the social prestige of intellectual elites is, increas-ingly, a global phenomenon. Do we possess a critical awareness

---

* This essay is an expansion and revision of two papers delivered originally to international gatherings. I have retained the framework I used in addressing an academic-based international audience of political progressives who were also skeptical of feminism.

235

that our institutional identification gives us class prerogative, even privilege, within our own societies and cultures? Developing this critical consciousness is basic to our own liberation theological process. Resisting the elitism of university life, with others who also seek to make intellectual life answerable to the well-being of subjugated people, has to be one of our theological priorities.

For each of us, critical consciousness is forged, whether early or late, by acknowledging the social contradictions that shape not only our collective existence but our personal lives as well. The distance between our elite status and our ideological commitment to just and democratic community represents only one contradiction. Awareness of contradictions is never the result of isolated intellectual striving. It comes from a process of concrete engagement, an entering into struggle against oppressive conditions that also involves being drawn into collective effort to overcome these conditions. Such consciousness takes hold only in concrete engagement; it is through the struggle that we acquire more profound awareness of the range of social oppression and its interconnectedness.

Each of us must learn to extend a critical analysis of the contradictions affecting our lives in an ever-widening circle, until it inclusively incorporates those whose situations differ from our own. This involves naming structures that create the social privilege we possess as well as understanding how we have been victims. Recognizing both realities — privilege and oppression — is necessary. For me, an obvious case in point is my need to develop awareness of the social contradictions involved in being a liberation theologian *and* a citizen of the United States. A painful process of learning had to occur before I grasped what it meant that my country occupies the center of a still-expanding global capitalist system of production that creates social relations of exploitation here and in every other nation. I have had to face the painful truth that this political-economic system pressures vast numbers of people across the globe to relinquish valued social, cultural, and economic patterns. It is a system that integrates whole societies into a mode of production generating new patterns of human exploitation and reinforcing and worsening ancient forms of racism and sexism and the already inequitable distribution of social resources. As a United States citizen, and middle-strata by birth, I have been socialized to a "bourgeois" consciousness that masks these realities.[2] How did I eventually come to accept the bitter truth about my own nation's current role in our world?

Or, equally to the point, how have I been able to acknowledge that, as a white person, I am the recipient of incredible privilege in a nation in which racism remains the most powerful barrier to the upward mobility of which my homeland boasts? How have I learned to acknowledge my own need to confront honestly what it means to be white in a country and a world where the madness of white racism seems to be reaching its most massive fruition? For four centuries this racism has festered like cancer, reducing many whites to twisted paranoid perceptions they cannot even recognize.

A liberation theological perspective presumes that any transcendence of received and conferred identity that I or anyone else comes to possess is not gained from generalized knowledge of social theory learned on an academic pilgrimage. Nor is it the fruit of hearing some universally proclaimed Christian mandate — even one that calls us to identify with the oppressed. A liberation theological perspective rejects any account of science, philosophy, or theology that presumes either that its truths are grounded in abstract knowledge or that there are clear and universal rational or revelational formulas that assure scientific, philosophical, or theological veracity. Such undialectical universalism merely perpetuates the patronizing benevolence always characteristic of those whose social location enables them to assume they have intellectual riches to give to the poor.

The crucial point here, so central to an adequate understanding of liberation theology, is that critical consciousness and, therefore, genuine social and spiritual transcendence, do not and cannot emerge apart from our refusing complicity in destructive social forces and resisting those structures that perpetuate life-denying conditions. For me, a white, middle-strata American, this has meant beginning at the most obvious point where I have been a victim of subjugation — as a woman who has lived under that most ancient contradiction of male gender supremacy. Women's subjugation to men was my concrete entry point into struggle. My active engagement in this struggle has enabled me to gain sensitivity to the wider dynamics of human oppression. A slowly won commitment never to be complicit in my own or my sisters' oppression, if I can avoid it, and to develop a praxis aimed to overcome sexist subjugation and oppression has grounded my further comprehension of what doing theology in service of, and as an aspect of, a praxis of human liberation means.

The Critical Role of Feminism in the Work of Liberation Theology

It is necessary, especially in an international Christian context, to emphasize the seriousness of feminism as a source of critical consciousness in western society. The strong tendency of all male-stream thought[3] and of those institutions dominated by masculinist perceptions (which definitely include international academically focused organizations of presumed "progressive" Christian persuasion) is to trivialize the liberation of women or to fail utterly to grasp the depth of world historical change needed to dislodge male supremacy. This complacency must be challenged. Typically, it takes the form of a charge that feminism is a "white, middle-class women's affair." Given the historical origins of feminism in its literary expressions, as well as the sort of feminism on which the media currently focus, there is some truth to this charge. But it is also true that women have been engaged in every human venture and active in every human struggle for liberation.

In my own nation's history, working-class women and black and other women of color have participated deeply in their communities' struggles. Bourgeois historians and media reporters have never identified these engagements as "feminism," but every woman who refuses to "stay in women's place" is a resister of sexism. The ideological shortcomings of any given feminist theory, determined by the social location of its adherents, is irrelevant to the wider need for a feminist perspective within any theory of human liberation. Because women's subjugation is a cross-cultural historical reality, no liberation theory is adequate that denies an explicit feminist sensibility. The objective conditions for a theoretically developed critique of male supremacy have emerged among women only when some forms of material oppression have been overcome. Nevertheless, male supremacy remains a life-denying structure from which all women need release, and the ideological weaknesses of white feminism must be corrected without evading the truth of its critique of male supremacy. No liberation perspective ever emerges full-blown, with ideological purity, free of the distortions of the social conditions that give rise to it. Feminism can and will grow.

Still, no white feminist dares deny the failure of white feminism, and of early Euro-American feminism as a movement, to name and integrate racism and class privilege at the level of practice and theory.[4] Conversely, anyone committed to human liberation needs to remember and respect the struggle of Euro-American feminism. In the United States, the tensions between white feminists and black people, female and male, that emerged after the emancipation of slaves resulted from the way the dominant white male system played black male suffrage off against female suffrage.[5] It was because white women accommodated these white male strategies and failed to engage racism as a structure of oppression that white feminism took a racist turn. Just as white feminists must name and overcome white racism in our history, incorporating the legacy of black women's and men's struggle into our remembered past of liberation struggle, so all who strive for human liberation must come to appreciate the significance of white Euro-American feminists' organized resistance to sexism. As it is, very few presumed radicals take seriously or understand — much less respect and celebrate — the historical struggles that have made both antiracism and resistance to male supremacy profound collective forces in our world. Few except feminists — and there *are* feminists in every liberation movement — are aware that women's well-being has been and will continue to be the fruit of collective struggle. Nor do the failures of Euro-American feminism discredit its demand for women's liberation, any more than the failures of antiracist or socialist movements discredit the moral validity of racial justice and genuine economic democracy.

A mature liberation perspective, then, recognizes that the objective, structural realities of racism, classism, and male supremacy are tenacious and that each operates globally and interacts dynamically. Those who trivialize these contradictions, thereby downplaying the pervasive destructive effects of cultural and sociopolitical white supremacy, misogyny, or class privilege, demonstrate that their own concern for genuine human liberation is a pseudo-commitment, a disguised effort to preserve European cultural hegemony, rule by light-skinned people, or male control.

Feminism, especially, is in its early stages as a world historical force. Across the globe, left-wing males have accommodated slowly, if at all, to a feminist critique of the ideology of male supremacy, though there are some cultural variations in males' responses. While some liberal feminists have used this truth to evade a critical analysis of class and political-economic oppression or even racism, some radical men have failed to grasp the inevitably reactionary character of all efforts to keep women "in our place." We have far to go before each and every liberation movement and liberation theological process reaches the point where the perspectives and experience of women are given central voice and integrated power in strategies of change. Until this occurs, there is a critical role for feminism as a distinctive ideology in the ongoing work of liberation theology.

A concrete praxis of justice does require some prioritizing of strategic goals in the liberation struggle. But strategies against oppression are much the poorer if they are not informed by a deepening consciousness of the interstructuring of oppression that operates in society. To be sure, all contradictions are now exacerbated by the political economy of capitalism. However, we will never see a socialist political economy with a fully human face until each of the sociocultural contradictions generated by past exploitative human social relations is acknowledged and resisted. We need not appeal to some future utopian state of affairs to justify our need for inclusive strategies of change. Rather, we can observe that where social revolutions have been carried through without multidimensional sensitivity to sociohistorical contradictions — that is, without sensitivity to religious, racial, and ethnic hatred and oppression and without acknowledgment of sexual politics — it is often hard to distinguish the faces of the liberators from those of previous oppressors. An adequate theology of liberation requires a holistic theoretical and analytical perspective. Nothing less deserves respect as a serious theory of human liberation. Feminist theology, in particular, insists on this so adamantly because relationality is central to its theory of reality. Everything in life *is* related to everything else.[6] A theology of liberation must be capable of an analysis that clarifies how oppression is interstructured. And such reflection must, as an absolute criterion, avoid what Michelle Russell calls "taking our own particular form of victimization, isolated from a collective context, and making that our morality."[7]

Specific Feminist Theological Challenge to Liberation Theology

The insight emergent from liberation theology — that our ability to grasp the broader, multifaceted, global reality of oppression hinges on our pursuing an interested engagement in the struggle for our own dignity and well-being — correlates with a basic feminist insight, one that traditional Christians resist. However, feminist insistence that personal struggle for fulfillment is neither aberrant nor selfish flies in the face of much Christian theological interpretation. Too many Christians, even of the progressive sort, still believe, in accord with male-stream Christian teaching, that an irresolvable theological and moral tension exists between self-assertive or self-interested acts (that is, those involved in the struggle for our/my liberation) and "loving" and "good" Christian acts. Nevertheless, we feminists maintain that radical Christian theology should be predicated on the assumption that there is no ontological split between self/other; there is no monolithic polarity of self-interested action versus other-regardingness. All people — each of us-in-relation-to-all — have a mandate, rooted in God, to the sort of self-assertion that grounds and confirms our dignity *in relationship.* Self-assertion *is* basic to our moral well-being. The human struggle for liberation is precisely the struggle to create the material, spatial, and temporal conditions for all to enjoy centered, self-determined social existence.

Feminist theological reflection has developed a further, and complex, critique of the Christian tradition's masculinist idolatry. The analysis of sexual politics voiced by feminism involves a thoroughgoing demystification of the all but universal structures of male supremacy. In so doing, it goes beyond the critical stance toward dominant Christianity that the most progressive male-generated liberation theology has developed. Progressive masculinist Christians tend to acknowledge that dominant Christian theology is class-bound, even perhaps subtly racist. Nevertheless, the deep Christian complicity in oppression is rarely applied to the contradiction of male supremacy, male social privilege, and compulsory heterosexism as a social institution.

Liberationist Christians must come to terms with the fact that the subjugation of women to men antedates both the early Israelite tradition and Jesus' own praxis of human liberation. This means that resistance to or witness against the oppression of women is, at best, very muted in scripture. Such egalitarianism as existed in the early Christian community by virtue of its communitarian radicalism was forgotten soon afterward by developing patristic Christianity. This historical reality defies those who would too simplistically identify scripture and tradition with full human liberation.[8] Nor can liberation theology evade the fact that Christianity, as it passed through numerous cultures, nearly always absorbed the worst negative valuations of women and social forms of subjugating women within those cultures. It is important to insist that any testimony to a Christian gospel that fails to explicitly acknowledge this bitter truth is not liberative for the majority of human beings, namely women. Nothing can be said to be "good news" for women, including those who are also victims of the racist and classist dynamics of oppression, if a vicious Christian complicity in the historical oppression of women is muted or denied.

A central contention of a feminist theological analysis is that the suppression of women and women's status as property of men are dialectically related to the mystification of women's "nature." Whenever it is claimed that women are "opposite" or "complementary" to men in their human nature, whether or not the implication is that women are therefore best suited to reproductive and domestic functions, such mystification is at work. Feminist analysis has revealed that the separation of mind and body lies at the core of western Christian spirituality. Women's blessedness, in our dominant Christian theology, accrues only through the fruit of our wombs, that is, it is derived from our biological or "natural" condition. Men's blessedness, by contrast, is the product of free historical agency — at worst as dominion and control of the world and at best, as stewardship of all life. Women, then, are seen as nature, men as history.

Karl Marx interpreted religion's propensity to this sort of dualistic idealization and spiritualizing of reality. He insisted that alienated religion is the fruit of exploitation, which under capitalism takes the form of a split between the person and her sensuous labor. Turning wage labor into a commodity, according to Marx, leads to the alienation of human beings from their own productive capacity.[9] Spiritualizing life contributes to the loss of meaning in concrete activity. A feminist analysis offers a further and complementary explanation for why alienated religion is so marked by a spirituality of otherworldliness, mortification of the body, and withdrawal from the solidarity of real flesh and blood community. The persistence and pervasiveness of world-denying spirituality is not explained adequately as simply a result of human alienation from sensuous productive activity or work. Alienated religion is also related to even more direct body alienation. Bodily control of humans by each other, exemplified in slavery or through males' sexual access to women, is an exploitation even more terrible than subjugation to wage labor. The master's control of the slave's body and the husband's or state's control of a woman's sexuality and reproductive power are fearful forms of exploitation that the flight from the body and from sensuality in dominant religion abets. The mind/body and intellect/will dichotomies that infect dominant theologies are bred more by racism and misogyny — the hatred of nonwhiteness and femaleness — than Marx's analysis recognizes.

A feminist critique also helps explain why such dominant theologies, even when they speak of identification with the oppressed, still imply chiefly an intellectual identification, not cohabitation, embodied commitment, or a deeply shared engagement. Both western Christian theology and western Marxism (not, of course, authentic "people's Marxism"[10] but bourgeois, academic Marxism) tend to exemplify this sort of idealist body/mind split. Whenever theory is granted absolute priority over the broader wisdom of lived-world sensuous experience, such body-denying idealism is present. There is a tendency in academic theory, Christian and/or radical, to eclipse the daily realities of cultural imperialism, racism, male gender supremacy, and compulsory heterosexism by subsuming all human suffering under one analytic category: class oppression. To resist a more complex appreciation of structural oppression on grounds that it diverts real class struggle epitomizes the disembodied abstractionism against which a liberation theological hermeneutic must protest. Radicals who respond this way exemplify the difficulty dominant males have sensing the concrete character of real oppression or human liberation. Lack of a concrete, embodied sense of how theoretical analysis relates to action leads theorists to imagine that the power to control a situation properly rests with those who have the "purest" conceptual definition of that situation. By contrast, a genuine liberation perspective is accountable to a praxis that gives priority to the concrete well-being of people, and so its starting point also must be concrete.

Learning How to Learn: From Conscientization to Social Analysis

Consciousness-raising, or "conscientization" — what I have called the entry point of a liberation theological process — happens when collective storytelling, a process of naming with others our shared situation, gets under way. Conscientization involves recognition that what we have experienced, in isolation and silence, as private pain is in fact a public, structural dynamic. *My* life is now perceived in a new way in light of *your* stories. Together we slowly re-vision our reality so that what appeared, originally, to be an individual or personalized "problem" or even a human "failing," is exposed as a basic systemic pattern of injustice. The reality of oppression, exploitation, or subjugation becomes clear as we "learn together" to grasp the common meaning of our lives.[11] Until each participant in the process of reflection has been empowered to break silence and name her or his own story, the pedagogy of liberation is violated. As Sheila Rowbotham has observed, silence among the oppressed always signifies the absence of hope. If the oppressed are silent while theologians or other intellectuals speak, no empowerment occurs. Muteness is always the enemy of authentic change:

> When the conception of change is beyond the limits of the possible, there are no words to articulate discontent, so it is sometimes held not to exist.
> This mistaken belief arises because we can only grasp silence in the moment in which it is breaking. . . .
> This is particularly important for women, because we come from such a long silence. We must structure

our own connections. The revolutionary must listen
carefully to the language of silence.[12]

There can be no question that liberation struggles require deep
and genuine intellectual resources, but the inability of intellectuals to participate with authentic mutuality can destroy a liberation process. We often reproduce social relations of oppression
unawares in our very efforts to "share" our expertise.

Intellectuals like ourselves need to learn how to learn[13] from
those whom we often are only too eager to "lead." The test of the
seriousness of our commitment is whether we welcome having
those who were previously silent wrest our theory from us, alter-
ing and transforming it through their unique appropriation. If we
are not eager for this to occur, our expressed hope for revolutionary change is just one more presumptuous act of bad faith. "Solidarity with the oppressed" is a slogan sometimes bandied about
by academic theologians. Genuine solidarity involves not mere
subjective identification with oppressed people but concrete an-
swerability to them. Solidarity *is* accountability, and accountability means being vulnerable, capable of being changed by the oppressed, welcoming their capacity to critique and alter our reality.

A further implication of our theological method is that a genuine process of liberation theological reflection will confront and
conflict with the dominant theology and culture. If conflict does
not occur, a theological process is bogus, controlled "from above."
We intellectuals are clever at conceptualizing reality precisely to
control situations and to avoid confrontation and conflict. Direct
conflict and confrontation, so abhorrent to elites, is controlled by
withholding opinions or evading or refusing hard questions. Furthermore, we who are Christian intellectuals have also often
learned to structure our praxis so as to give the appearance of
active concern without running love's risks of vulnerability. We
are, by virtue of a hollow, patriarchal Christianity, masters at
avoiding conflict and, therefore, mutuality. Reducing love to subjective attitude rather than equating it with active engagement
enables us to remain above the struggle.

A further strategy of intellectuals fearful of conflict is to de-
flect the seriousness of disagreement by appealing to the desirability of pluralism. Celebrating pluralism to mitigate the importance of issues at stake in conflict is a common strategy among
liberals who do not wish to change. Demands for justice are rejected not as reactionaries reject them — as dangerous schemes —
but as purported threats to authentic human diversity. Pluralism
is celebrated as *the* major intellectual virtue; but the tepid atmo-
sphere among liberal, "enlightened" intellectuals betrays their

presumption that nothing important is reflected in intellectual disagreement. Thus, appeals to pluralism also often mask a deep anti-intellectualism within liberalism itself; tolerance of difference enables intellectuals to avoid defending their own positions, which are vulnerable to public scrutiny, or conceals their refusal to face their own investment in the status quo. A liberation theological process is, by comparison, tough-minded and direct. Life and death issues *are* at stake in the way we perceive, analyze, and envision the world and therefore in what we say of God and human hope. The critical intellectual task of theology is the serious one of reappropriating all our social relations, including our relations to God, so that shared action toward genuine human and cosmic fulfillment occurs.

The Emancipation of Theology and Liberation Social Ethics

By contrast to dominant theologies, then, liberation theologies are intrinsically historical, physical, time-bound. There is no "core" of life or reality to be "essentialized." "Reality" [14] is concrete, a material, interactive cosmic-world-historical process. Our agency or action is set within ongoing temporal-historical processes and webs of interrelations. From this perspective, an analysis is theological if, and only if, it unveils or envisions our lives as a concrete part of the interconnected web of all our social relations, including our relations to God.

Older, established Christian theologies envisioned theology as an abstract, universal, intellectual perspective. By contrast, the horizon to which an adequate liberation perspective aspires, given twentieth-century reality, is not only globally inclusive but respectful of our cosmic environment. Precisely because we live in a world historical situation in which one geopolitical economy controls all people and our interactions with the rest of nature, global perspective is today *the* appropriately universal perspective of a Christian theology. An inclusive social theory is required to ground our theological analytic work because the new global system controls the life and death prospects of all of us. The dynamics of this system impinge on all human life in the poorest and the richest nations, in villages and in urban centers everywhere. The uprooted and impoverished peasant in the "third world" and the homeless, hungry, unemployed urban worker in advanced capitalist nations are both victims of global patterns of exploitation. Since the global capitalist mode of production pervades and controls all our social relations, we can no longer afford to analyze any of the patterns of exploitation shaping our own community's reality in discrete isolation.

Even though, as I have already insisted, racism, sexism, and its corollary, compulsory heterosexism, predate the rise of capitalist political economy, a global analysis of political economy is basic to a full account of how these ancient contradictions are now structurally maintained and reinforced. Racism is entrenched in and accelerates through a capitalist mode of production. New patterns of white racist exploitation of blacks and other people of color replace the racist patterns and institutions of capitalism's earlier phases. Chattel slavery as an institution of total labor exploitation has given way to apartheid and ghettoization. Late monopoly capitalism has also transformed gender inequality in subtle and complex ways, reinforcing some ancient patterns of male supremacy, undermining others, while deepening the workload and socioeconomic vulnerability of the vast majority of women on this planet. All of the ancient contradictions of human social relations are now filtered through the reality of class conflict, that is, antagonistic social relations patterned by the exploitative relations of economic production and capital formation. It is a truism of radical analysis that these lines of class conflict — patterned social powerlessness and structural economic dependency — have reproduced themselves at the global level such that most nations are now class-bound, unable to break the cycle of economic exploitation. So-called economic underdevelopment is, after all, only the pattern of dependency that results when weaker nations are penetrated and organized to serve the interests of those who control capital at the center of the global system. Clarifying these sociohistorical connections makes it possible for us to forge a properly universal perspective that genuinely reveals how our common humanity in relation to God is being undermined. By exposing the dynamics that keep people in bondage and that prevent right relationship among human communities and persons, we are doing properly theological work. Part of the "epistemological privilege" of the struggling poor is that they do not credit God with sanctifying widespread human bondage and oppression.

Social analysis, then, is the phase of the liberation theological process that enables us to make these connections. It is an intellectual challenge of the highest order to enable an imaginative process that exposes the connections between people's suffering and the history of political-economic exploitation.[15] Middle-strata people in our societies must not be disregarded in the liberation theological process of conscientization and social analysis. The passivity of the nonpoor in the wake of these changes appears formidable, though we should not, as many do, mistake this passivity as simple political reaction. The patterns of structural oppression that I have just enumerated impinge on middle sectors of affluent societies in increasingly destructive ways. Many middle-strata people are experiencing a new sense of powerlessness and loss of political and economic control over their own lives. Conscientization is critical here as well as among the poor. Liberation theology must go on wherever structural oppression genuinely disempowers human life.

Recently I heard a distinguished educator, a feminist who has done remarkable work resisting the militarization of my own nation, protest the idea that most people in the United States have become self-preoccupied, that they are not interested in great public issues of justice and peace.[16] Our perception that such people are unaffected and unconcerned, she argued, is a misapprehension based on our failure to grasp human problems concretely enough. To mobilize people in the struggle for justice, she stressed, it is necessary to begin where they live. She reported that she asked her students to walk the streets of the town or city where they grew up and to identify the global connections of every business, government facility or office, organization, church, or religious organization that they encountered. She then required them to draw lines across the globe from their local communities, via each organization and institution, to the many places on this planet to which they were related, so that they would begin to grasp the concrete meaning and scope of these connections. As I listened to this woman, a great teacher, I reflected on the widespread ineptitude of so much formal education in empowering people really to grasp what is going on. In the liberal, bourgeois sectors of affluent societies, the problem of social myopia is acute. Cultural blindness is reinforced daily by an ideology that submerges real, lived-world existing social relations under myths of "progress" and "individuality." If critical consciousness is to develop more widely among people "in the middle," we need to find ways to help them connect their "personal pains" to the wider dynamics of a social system that exploits countless others far more ruthlessly.

In the affluent nations the dream of "upward mobility" mystifies many working people's reality. Amid affluence, proletarian status and poverty are stigmas of a sort that those from less wealthy societies find difficult to comprehend. In my country, working-class status is frequently experienced, *ipso facto*, as personal failure. Class in the United States is experienced by the worker as a wound to self-respect, and he or she often adamantly hides the suffering it causes from others.[17] The lack of a sense of dignity is then often channeled into resentment against those who are even more deprived in the pecking order of social privilege. The result is an exacerbation of racism and sexism.

A further implication of this methodology that places social analysis at the starting point is that "social ethics," traditionally conceived as subservient and deducible from theological tradition, here becomes prolegomenon to more specific doctrinal utterance. The circle of socioethical analysis is an intrinsic part of the theological hermeneutic circle[18] because liberation theologians insist that theological sensibility depends on and is formulated in the fuller social praxis of which it is a dimension. "Praxis" is here understood as the total complex of action, including all the reflection embedded in that action. Liberation theologians insist that only a praxis aimed at emancipation can yield a "truthful" theological interpretation and vision. "Emancipatory practice" is precisely an ongoing struggle against structures of oppression and toward realization of the conditions for alternative social relations that enable nonexploitative relations to occur.

Christian theological interpretation of a situation escapes being "ideological," in the Marxian sense of that term — that is, a perspective that masks such oppression — only if it expresses emancipatory criteria. These criteria must include unveiling the dynamics operating structurally within society and within Christianity itself that hold human beings in bondage. Christians must also resist direct or indirect complicity in sanctifying historical evil within our churches or in society as "necessary" or "inevitable." Any social analysis is dialectically related to the explicitly ethical question What are we, as Christians engaged in this particular situation, to do? What form must our struggle for liberation take?

Much socioethical analysis carried out within liberation theology has been criticized for failure to incorporate many dimensions of traditional ethical analysis needed to develop an optimal social ethic. These charges are dubious because when a liberation ethic is developed, it cannot always be shared in published form. The strategic reflection of oppressed and marginated groups cannot always be safely made public without betrayal of the struggle for change. Nor does the socioethical analysis of one liberation struggle readily translate from one cultural context to another. The particularity, as well as the political precariousness of liberation praxis, gives the properly socioethical work of liberation theology a different cast from the genre of abstract, formalistic ethics characteristic of dominant Christian groups. Such analysis will not be developed at international conferences, though we may hope for the day when international conferences will aim at an inclusive sharing of these more concrete analyses as an expression of truly ecumenical Christian work.

The Stages of Human Liberation

To clarify the full implications of a liberation social ethics methodology, a summary of its stages may be useful.[19] Identifying these stages does not imply that they must or will emerge in linear sequence. The stages are analytically, not sequentially, discrete dimensions of liberation social ethic work.

The entry point of conscientization, already discussed, is both the theological and ethical starting point. Clarification of the group's concrete historical experience of oppression or subjugation, carried out communally, begins the work of ethics/theology. This collective "naming" process fosters the ability to reflect on one's shared situation as structurally conditioned and also enables people to enter into the basic stance that precipitates ethical reflection itself: the power or capacity to be "the subjects of our lives."

The second phase of the method is more theoretical and involves explicit *historical socioethical analysis* aiming to connect our historical narratives of specific, experienced oppression to the broader historical framework. The methods of liberation theology and ethics must always be historical, which means that our social theory must be historical as well. Genuine historical perspective enables several forms of empowerment. It aids recovery of social memory and awareness of the struggles of our forebears. It aims to represent the past to us in a specific way — as the result of collective human agency. To be sure, human agency is here understood not in some simple, individualistic, or voluntarist sense. Emancipatory historiography enables us to see that the past has a human face, that human actions, patterned over time, are the source of social structures and institutional practices that have come to function as real, objective constraints on the lives of our forebears and on us. This means that though we recognize the objectivity of historical structures, we cannot interpret the present as a realm of sheer chance or "natural necessity"; what has been done can be undone.[20] Furthermore, where there is and has been oppression, there is also, always, a history of survival and resistance to oppression that needs to be recalled and celebrated for the marks of dignity, courage, and potential it bears. The relevance of historical data must be judged by the need to understand how past collective action, as privilege and resistance to privilege, has led to our present situation. There must also be an effort to clarify how the structural interaction among varying dynamics of oppression have differently affected the lives and perceptions of our own group and others. For example, how do the burdens of men and women within our group vary, and what has conditioned these differences in the past? How do the historical dynamics of sexism, racism, and classism prevent solidarity from developing within our community? Here, as I have insisted, the critical interpretations of the most marginated must be accepted as "correcting" the subjective blind spots in our own experience. "Objectivity" here means openness to others' history and to the critical claims that history bears and also the ability to learn from others' historical experience.

We need to remember that those who exercise privilege and control in the present also control "official" history. "Official" history suppresses the stories of resistance and dissent against the status quo and presents the past either as the triumph of the deserving or as inevitable.[21] Critical history breaks open the past, in its full complexity, and re-presents that past as bearing a story of human struggle against domination. Even failed resistance bears powerful evidence of human dignity and courage that informs our contemporary vocations. Our remembered forebears and colleagues in struggle energize our lives as we live through the pressures and risks that real resistance to oppression always involves. There are also lessons to be learned from those who have struggled for a future of hope and possibility. Assuredly, these lessons are never simple, nor do they solve our own dilemmas of choice or reduce the need for well-developed moral sensibility or strategic intelligence in the present. Past history is not a treasure trove of moral formulas or solutions to problems. Often it is from past mistakes that we need most urgently to learn. But there is some truth in the aphorism that those who know nothing of the past are doomed to repeat it.

A further aspect of this sociohistorical ethical method is *careful examination of the roots and ongoing dynamics of oppression or subjugation.* The roots of oppression are important, not because they lead us to understand the past for "its sake" (whatever that might mean) but because, as I emphasized earlier, the past continues to live on, embedded in present social relations. While it is epistemologically futile to seek single causes of oppression, it is morally significant to illuminate the way that oppression has formed the identities of both the powerful and the exploited. Without such analysis, it will never be clear to us, much less to those who have internalized oppression, why it is absurd to believe that the poor are poor due to lack of virtue, or women weak because of their "natures," or black people "unintelligent" because of genetic endowment. Failure to see the powerful force of social structure on groups and persons renders us manipulable by myths elaborated to sustain social domination.

Because a sociohistorical method does not lead automatically to our finding "good strategies" or "right actions" for the present, several other stages of a liberation socioethical analysis need to be systematically pursued if we are to arrive at a well-considered sense of what we are to do. These stages must include *clarification of our solidarities and loyalties*. Every socioethical stance is pervasively influenced by the loyalties to groups and institutions that its strategic historical project aims to serve. Since a liberation social ethic makes solidarity with the marginated and oppressed people a presumption of its method, solidarity must also be an explicit methodological criterion of a liberation ethical analysis. Continued accountability is the measure of the integrity of our ethic. Historically, much social change, whether realized from liberal or radical intent, has lost its transformative dynamic because those charged with responsibility for change have subtly betrayed their expressed accountability. There is some truth to the aphorism that "absolute power corrupts absolutely," [22] and there is no place in a liberation process for absolute, that is, unaccountable, power. The development of specific mechanisms and organizational patterns that ensure accountability is the real test of any liberation social ethic.

Even if structures of accountability are attended to, *explicit attention needs to be paid to clarifying a movement's options for action*. Movements for social change have long recognized the importance of calculating the consequences of alternative strategies of action, but liberation ethics must recognize the importance of both the realistic and the utopian/imaginative functions of consequentialist thinking. Assessing possible consequences of action requires great realism and cautious projection of scenarios for that action, just as conservatives have always contended. The danger of realism in ethics is not related, as idealists sometimes assume, to the hard-headedness of realists. Rather, the limitations of realism invariably rest in one of two perversions of the professed "hard-headedness." On the one hand, so-called realists may imbibe a subtle identification with the powerful as leaders enjoy their own newly acquired power. On the other hand, "realism" often degenerates into myopic short-term thinking; that which "works" in the most immediate sense commends itself, without reference to longer-term effects. Realism always must be constrained not by abstract idealism but by continuing, long-term loyalty and accountability to those whom change is intended to serve. The absence of genuine accountability ensures that realism will degenerate into the crassest type of political pragmatism, which always functions to protect established privilege. An absence of realism, though, threatens a movement for change, because naiveté and lack of hard assessment of possible consequences of strategic options inevitably rebounds to the disadvantage of those already weak and dispossessed.

What few realists who identify with established power ever recognize is that realism, in assessing consequences, also requires imagination. The best strategic reflection not only enables us to anticipate undesirable consequences of proposed change but, more important, enables us to avoid some of the negative consequences of the strategies that are proposed. A serious politics of liberation must be an artful politics, one that generates conditions for cooperation. When strategic analysis becomes crassly utilitarian, it is often because cynicism has dampened the humane and imaginative powers of those chosen to spearhead social change. Failure of imagination leads to degenerate forms of realism.

Another critical stage of social ethics within a liberation theological process is required to ensure the integrity of its specifically moral dimension. We have an explicit responsibility *to examine continuously strategic options in light of the moral norms espoused in and intrinsic to the liberation process itself.* Some social radicals, for understandable reasons, are skeptical about the role of specifically normative moral analysis in human liberation. The formalism of much bourgeois moral theory seems to imply that moral norms may be arrived at by rational analysis abstracted from emancipatory commitment and struggle. As a result, normative ethics has sometimes been suspect among those who seek change. Furthermore, the central moral norms of much formalistic ethics, including liberal theories of justice, have been inadequate, and this has deepened many activists' distrust of moral theory. By insisting that justice is merely a procedural, not a substantive, matter or by commending the occasional relevance of a vague principle of benevolence that, at best, functions to mitigate individual self-interest, liberal moral philosophers have provided a tepid set of norms that apply only in selected aspects of our life, chiefly those governed by face-to-face relations. These norms are also embraced in an ahistorical, abstract way that obscures the pervasiveness of real historical evil. The moral person that most moral philosophy conjures is one moderately concerned for living conscientiously within social convention but also a person who eschews a "passion for justice" [23] as unseemly and excessive moral partisanship.

A liberation ethics, grounded in a communitarian conception

of human nature, requires a deep transformation of our moral norms. Implicit in the experience of liberation struggle is, as I have already observed, a radically relational understanding of justice as rightly ordered relationships of mutuality within the total web of our social relations. The givenness of reciprocal, interdependent social relations must be presupposed in liberation moral theory. All of our norms must be reciprocal, stressing mutuality both of responsibility and of control. Genuine equality in this model must mean equal dignity-in-relation and in-power. Obligations and virtues must be shaped and articulated from values that serve dignity and respect in our social relations.

In spite of the limits of conventional bourgeois moral theory, the elaboration and defense of liberation moral norms must be made explicit. To be sure, our attitudes toward all moral norms, like our attitudes toward social theory and theological tradition, must be critical. Nevertheless, no motive for justice is ever strong enough to sustain an automatic or spontaneous realization of the visions of justice that liberation movements initially generate. Norms are essential criteria of self-evaluation. We must treat norms for what they are: human constructs that state our presumptions about what constitutes the general direction acts should take to qualify as "moral." Since norms are conceptual formulations of envisioned values, they may be expressed as principles of action. In life, situations have a tendency to overwhelm principle; all human action is complex and is "contestable in principle." [24] Nevertheless, the very abstractness of principles enables them to function as ongoing tests of our consistency, helping us assess our fidelity to the vision of justice we profess. We need not imagine that norms are ahistorical or are themselves exempt from criticism. Serious attention to principles of justice, however, ensures that we do not presume the automatic integrity of our own actions, as if nothing was to be learned from the moral dialectic that subjects our actions to public principles and criteria.

Most current discussion of moral theory presumes that good moral reasons for action are those classified either as "deontological" — focused by duties or obligations legislated by past moral and religious tradition or social convention — or "utilitarian" — shaped by the concrete consequences that actions actually have. A frequently voiced charge against liberation ethics these days is that its moral theory is either a form of situation ethics, which is to say that it eschews norms altogether, or that it is crassly "utilitarian." [25] The charge often is made that the central principle of classical utilitarianism — that social actions are justified if they accomplish the greatest good for the greatest number of persons — is also the basic moral principle of liberation ethics. This accusation rests on a misconception. The defects of classic utilitarianism are many, and I will not elaborate them here. The theory rested on two assumptions obviously at variance with liberation ethics: that the "subjective" happiness of individuals can be quantified to provide an adequate measure for assessing social welfare and that value balancing applies to whatever subjective goals human agents happen to hold as good. At the very least, over against classic utilitarianism, a liberation ethics presumes that there are basic human needs that constitute minimum social well-being and that these are foundational to any definition of human welfare.

The structure of a liberation ethics is neither strictly deontological nor utilitarian. Deontological approaches give so much weight to the presumptions of past moral experience that their adherents do not critically reflect on what those principles meant in their original context or consider whom their invocation served. Deontologists tend to romanticize the past, failing to understand that only those moral principles that protect existing privilege gain "uncontestable" status in social convention.[26] Unqualified deontology is always status quo-oriented. Utilitarianism, properly formulated, is preferable from a liberation perspective because its logic is not overwhelmingly constrained by past, dominant conceptions of moral obligation. However, utilitarian theory frequently does not envisage goals or values in a temporal frame adequate to incorporate the visions of change needed to bring about genuine justice. All ethics that engages political reality requires some utilitarian component, but a wider teleological sense, what Dorothy Emmet has called "a sense of human vocation," is also required.[27]

The principles of communitarian-egalitarian justice that we espouse do not possess either the self-evidence of rational moral intuition that some traditional deontologists claim for their principles or the self-evident authority of "divine revelation" that other deontologists invoke. Liberation norms express a visionary and communitarian sensibility born of the fragmentary human experience of solidarity and grounded in the struggle against oppression. This struggle generates respect for the concrete, embodied needs that all human beings have — for dignity, food, shelter, health, bodily integrity, nonalienating labor, and cultural creativity. Such respect is learned, and it *is* learned, by *refusing subjugation* that denies the conditions of dignity. No principle can replace concrete engagement as *the* formative element in any morality worth the name. We do not make a fetish of principles or overgeneralize their universality by ignoring conditions that justify their exceptions,[28] as those identified uncritically with dominant moral theory seem frequently to do. But like them, we take seriously the need to test our actions by the principles of well-being we profess.

Many object to this category of basic foundational human need on which a liberation social ethic rests. The claim is made that human "need" is too subjective a ground for a social ethic. Yet it is, in fact, utilitarianism that is arbitrarily subjective. A liberation ethic cannot justify the neglect of basic human needs for some simply because many others are willing to ignore them. The simplistic, monistic balancing principle of classic utilitarianism is ruled out precisely because, for us, the minimum conditions of human welfare are manifest. Perhaps individuals have a moral right to neglect the basic conditions for their own well-being, but in a liberation ethics no one has a moral right to override basic conditions for others' well-being in order to have "liberty" inconsistent with others' basic welfare.

The much-reiterated liberal objection to this sort of teleologically grounded understanding of "basic need" is also subjectivistic. It is said that one cannot define justice substantively without also imposing a definition of value or good on people that thereby limits their subjective freedom to direct their lives. Because a liberation ethic incorporates a substantive notion of social good, our ethic is said to impede the free working of human choice, reducing options and threatening human liberty. Against such objections, we need to insist that a conception of "basic human need" is not arbitrary. There may be some room for disagreement as to which human needs are genuinely foundational and which elective, but the human needs identified above — for dignity, food, shelter, and so on — are hardly elective from the standpoint of human survival and well-being. From a liberation ethics standpoint, no one has a right to luxury or even to less essential "enhancement needs" [29] if those needs are satisfied at the price of others' basic dignity or physical survival. Certainly "liberty" that is sustained by dehumanizing structures of exploitation is not morally defensible.

Because liberation ethics assesses moral norms within a broader sociohistorical analytic frame, we are clear, as many contemporary moral philosophers are not, that identifying norms is only one dimension of moral reasoning. The perennial moral dilemmas that beset all human socioethical action are not resolved by narrow normative analysis. Identifying normative principles and weighing means in terms of their consistency with one's moral ends are elements in a liberation ethical process, not the whole of it.

Many accusations about the moral adequacy of liberation theology and ethics, however, have little to do with our implicit or explicit methodology. Much criticism of our social ethics takes the form of specious argument that rips liberation theology out of its historical context. For example, Euro-American white male academics often condemn liberation theological ethics because it "endorses" armed revolution and violence that established dominant theological ethics is presumed to eschew. It is time to expose the hypocrisy of this criticism directly. To be sure, few liberation theologians, with some conspicuous exceptions,[30] embrace pacifism, either in its philosophical absolute or Christian confessional forms.[31] However, we rarely pause to ask how many neo-orthodox or liberal, white Euro-American male theological ethicists and moral theologians actively embrace either of these forms of pacifism themselves! The implication that liberation theologians give any more frequent normative endorsement to the use of violence than most just-war proponents is preposterous. If we were to compare most western white male Christian ethicists' views on the use of U.S. military force with liberation theologians' specific views regarding justification for force in social revolution, we would quickly recognize that the reputed insensitivity of liberation theologians to violence is a chimera, the result of *ad hominem* argument. It is an ideological ploy aimed to discredit liberation theology. The fully justified contention of liberation theologians that violence is already pervasive in their existing social systems and that such violence is inflicted chiefly on the dispossessed and powerless is largely discounted by the critics of liberation theologies. The latter insist that the existing order of things is largely benign or, at worst, in need of marginal improvement — an astonishing claim in the world we know. Furthermore, many of them are quite prepared for their nations to use military might in opposition to presumed "threats" to the "civilization" or "pax Americana."

The basic disagreement here has nothing to do with matters of principle. It is an argument about the moral quality of existing social systems. It is a dispute about facts, not an argument about moral norms at all. Failure to assess the gravity of existing moral evil allows those identified with established power to posture great moral purity about the relation of means and ends and about the application of principles. Those who believe change is urgent because ongoing evil is great are made to appear unprincipled. It is easier to charge others with insensitivity to means/ends dilemmas than to answer their accusation about refusal to countenance change in the face of great evil because of self-interest. Nor is there any need to remind oppressed people of the terrible cost of violence or to point out to them that violence breeds violence. These are realities they know from the arbitrary brutality in which their daily existence is immersed. The moral question that faces our world is whether or when the use of violence to end violence is justified. Dominant ethicists, who so often romanticize just-war traditions, forget that this was precisely the question the just-war tradition attempted to address. Liberation theologians are facing the same dilemma. The moral presumption in favor of nonviolence must not be confused with the actual existence of nonviolence in our world. To discuss moral principles of non-violence as if nonviolence existed is a fallacy of moral reasoning that renders a discussion untruthful from the outset. The all but unending caricature of liberation theology on this point can no longer be tolerated, given that the present global system is maintained by continuous, brutal, and unrelenting violence, in the face of which many of liberation theologies' major critics are all but silent.

An adequate Christian liberation socioethical analysis must incorporate one further phase, to which I alluded when I described the internal critique of Christianity generated by feminism. *Our critical socioethical work is not complete until the hermeneutic of liberation is brought to bear on the internal history of Christianity itself.* We cannot complete our work without scrutinizing our appropriation of scripture/tradition. Failure to do so means that Christians cannot enter into the struggle for human liberation in genuine good faith. Among other things, we must recognize that Christian spirituality, too, must be transformed if it is to become a genuine, engaged worldly spirituality. To subject ourselves and our churches to critique is to keep faith with them by challenging them to return to the path of liberating praxis. Theological fidelity never means merely obeisance to what the churches currently claim as theological "truth." Rather, it means candidly and judiciously facing our own community's complicity in those roots and structures of oppression our social analysis lays bare. Authentic spiritual maturity requires a conception of theological truthfulness as an ongoing process.

The various movements of liberation theology have, each in their own way, contributed to such an internal critical task. Latin American theological reflection has clarified both Roman Catholic and Protestant church complicity in economic exploitation, in European imperialism, and in the suppression of native American culture in Latin America.[32] Black liberation theologians in the United States have identified latent and overt legitimations of racism and white supremacy in our dominant traditions.[33] African and Asian Christians' liberation theologies have exposed dominant Christian complicity in racism and in the cultural imperialism that has suppressed the humanly important, age-old cultural traditions of their peoples.[34] And I have already stressed the role of feminist theologies, now joined by gay liberation theology, in exposing Christian complicity in sexism and misogyny and its fetishistic support of compulsory heterosexism. Not to acknowledge Christian complicity in domination to ourselves, to our communities, and to others is to vitiate a Christian liberation vision at the outset. If we don't use Christian candor, those who have been our victims will sense our lack of integrity even if we hide it from ourselves. Any notion that God's self-disclosure gives Christians superior wisdom and status that separates us from our common humanity is a virulent Christian spiritual contamination that we must confront continuously.

The striking difference between the way liberation theologies and dominant theologies understand the scope of theological work, including the intrinsic relation of social ethics and theology, can be traced to resistance to this historical sociocritical method. Euro-American, white male dominant theologians usually embrace either a general, abstract, "essentialist" method that they call "foundational theology," or they presume proper theological work to involve attending to scripture and tradition in isolation from the sociohistorical nexus and fuller human setting in which these sources are embedded. Both options avoid accepting the particularity of their way of seeing the world. Dominant theologians fail utterly to understand why a concrete critical analysis of oppression has to be intrinsic to theological method — precisely because just such historical-social particularity is the basis of all our knowledge of the world.

We would be wealthy if we had a dime for each time white Euro-American male theologians described liberation theology either as "mere" sociology or as "political" or ideological," as though their own work could not also be so characterized. Since each Christian theological perspective, without exception, contains already implicit, if not explicit, assumptions about all our social relations, such accusations are vacuous. Those whose privilege is served by an abstracted or spiritualized theology maintain their ideological bias by insisting that theological language is a discrete discourse on divine-human relationships. What they mean is that our theological relations run between "the self" (read "individual," "inner reality") and "God." Their imaginations detach God, self, and/or religion from the social relations in which we live, and they insist that we should conceive reality this way as well. So theology becomes an effort to clarify the "essence" of things — the nature of Man (sic), the nature of God as "He is in Himself" (sic) — either by bracketing history to "reach" ontological structure or by treating scripture/tradition as a spiritualized language and message not identifiable with anything in human culture. Theology, it is claimed, illumines the "core" of biblical faith or its ontological "essence." Social relations are something "added on" to this core or essential structure. From this perspective, theological work focuses either on an effort to locate the enduring, unchanging nature of things in the flux of finitude or on the effort to keep pristine "tradition" intact. In this model, "real" theology begins not with our life situation in relation to each other and God but with the divine/human relation abstracted from all (other) social relations.

Beginning with a critical analysis of our social relations is, we liberationists contend, the only way to a nondualistic theology, a theology that does not subordinate our relations to God and each other to those destructive dualisms endemic in Christian theology: nature/supernature; material body/spirit; time/eternity; finitude/infinity; existence/essence; reason/revelation; world/church; or nature/history. Accepting the all-inclusive character of our relationality means that theological utterance too is relational. We never speak of God in isolation from other relations.

What in dominant theology is the exclusive focus of theological work becomes in liberation theology a responsive moment within a larger theological process — the reengagement with scripture/tradition in light of critical awareness of our existing situation. Confession, usually considered the proper starting point of dominant theological utterance, here occurs as a response to our situation, a call not to accept existing bondage as either divine intention or the last word about our lives or God's creation. While the focus of such confession is on dialogue with Christian tradition, including scripture, the intent of this dialogue differs from traditional theology. The intent is not merely to reassert tradition but to ask: Does our tradition express a word genuinely liberating for this historically specific community of persons? Because various communities experience the dominant Christian traditions differently, given the cultural particularities of oppression and subjugation, we cannot expect liberation theologies to produce a simple, homogeneous reenvisagement of what Christians should confess. There are real tensions among liberation theologies. Nevertheless, they agree that only through an emancipatory praxis and an inclusive theological process can the meaning of Christian faith be articulated with integrity.

Annunciation and Celebration: The Reconstructive Phase of Liberation Theology

The reconstructive phase of liberation theology is possible only when the critique of society and tradition has been addressed self-consciously. The formation of liberating spirituality occurs as we together remember, name, and celebrate the presence and power that sustains our struggle. We need liberating spirituality (call it "authentic religion," if you will) because we require not only a relationally just, nonexploitative society that respects our needs but also an ongoing rebirth of vision, imagination, and hope for human and cosmic inclusivity. We need human cultures and societies that manifest and sustain aesthetic sensibility, diversity, beauty, and moral passion. We need a spiritual reorientation that encourages love, reverence, and appreciation for all that is creative in nature and in human life and culture.

We will not witness such spiritual transformation if we perpetuate hostility to religion as such, nor will we awaken it if we develop a mindless amnesia about the pluriform, humanly beautiful manifestations of spirituality that have existed throughout history. A *critical* appreciation of religion is not an irreligious spirit. Antireligion is not helpful because it fosters reaction and increases the strength of that sort of disembodied religion identified with dominant power that always bears the marks of alienation: rigidity, lack of creativity, compulsive repetition. Like everything else concrete and embodied, religion can never be successfully suppressed or eradicated.[35] It can only be transformed. Religious persons and institutions, like political persons and institutions, are *de*formed by participation in oppression. They are transformed by incorporating a genuinely moral resistance to oppression. Since religion does not just wither away, no one can eschew an affirmative, critical theological task anymore than they can reject moral responsibility. A worldly spirituality, one born of affirmation and love of the real, tangible cosmos and of our shared humanity within the created world, is possible, but only if it is based on the presupposition that love of neighbor and love of God are coterminous. Any invocation of the love of God to perpetuate injustice, any uncritical respect for the givenness and "authority" of existing social relations of domination, perpetuates alienated religion. Since there is no possibility of separating these social relations, attempting to do so impoverishes our spirituality. A spirituality motivated by caring and respect for our relation to God, to each other, and to the cosmos depends on our participation in emancipatory history. To love God is to love that concrete power that, through us and the cosmos (always reciprocally), transforms nature, history, society, and human personal life toward community, toward relations of mutual respect. God is personal because God is richly related to all that is, and so we must be. The unequivocal no we must utter is not, as in neo-orthodox Christianity, the no to human power as opposed to God's power but the no to those forms of human power that distort all of our social relations, including our relations with God. It is possible to say no to this sort of human disorder and at the same time offer a full-hearted yes to human good and to a God-and-neighbor-centered respect for all things.

To sustain resistance to evil, the constructive phase of a liberation theological process needs to include both *annunciation* and *celebration*. What we creatively reappropriate and re-present as liberating or God-bearing in our past tradition needs to be rehearsed and annunciated[36] to keep hope alive.

Annunciation feeds hope, but so does celebration. Wherever there is genuine resistance to evil and solidarity in struggle, there is also the human experience of joy. Dominant theologies enjoin us to a spirituality in which "worship" implies a singular, total devotion toward God, even a detachment from each other, an act of subservience to the only One truly worthy of adoration. By contrast, a liberating theology discourages attitudes of subservience, commending instead a spirit of conviviality and mutual vulnerability. Those who have a strong investment in the status quo know little of deep joy *or* deep pain. Not to know either is to lack the resources for celebration. To be tied to the present order is to be filled with anxiety that we may lose what we already have: power, wealth, prestige, control, or even vicarious identification with those things. By contrast, where people really engage deeply and humanly on behalf of their own and their sisters' and brothers' needs, rituals of shared empowerment emerge that authentically express and support the longing for justice that is nurtured or reborn in us, together. Such ritual or liturgy, we can be sure, is not endlessly preoccupied with whether it is "orthodox" or "traditional." Traditions live only through their fresh, creative reappropriation by people immersed in life.

That the dominant theological language and images of western theology have lost their capacity to elicit spontaneous, dynamic, imaginative power is, I believe, clear enough. What is less clear, even to Christian radicals at times, is the degree of innovation in theological language, image, and ritual necessary to draw forth the latent power of hope and celebration among those who resist evil. Dominant Christianity's language and rituals, like its appeals to "scripture" and "tradition," reveal an immense conventionality and repetitiveness. In contrast, the spontaneity and imagination of the Christian body of oppressed people attest the capacity of communities to birth the Spirit together.

The suppression of spiritual spontaneity is not the central theological problematic of dominant Christian theology, however. The deepest shortcoming of such theology is in what it teaches us about our action. Much Christian theology and liturgy cultivates masochism. Not only are self-denial and sacrifice demanded of Christians (and, more especially, as I observed earlier, of women) but its interpretations of Jesus' work — that is, its christology — imply a masochistic reading of our relation to Jesus and his relation to God. Some christological formulas even suggest that God "the Father" is to be understood as a sadist who demands a masochistic sacrifice from "the Son." Here human redemption is, in essence, conceived as a sadomasochistic transaction between God and "Man."

As I have already observed, such christology fundamentally misrepresents the earlier New Testament tradition about Jesus. His fidelity consisted of an unqualified praxis of annunciation of God's "kingdom" or, better, "commonwealth," present but still to come, a praxis that he would not renounce. In Dorothee Sölle's phrase, "Jesus may be understood as our representative, as one who stands in for us toward the time when we may stand ourselves." [37] But Jesus is not, as dominant christology has insisted, the possessor of a unique relation to God. We may, with Sölle, honor him as an irreplaceable forerunner in the process of redemption, but not as our replacement in that work. Juan Luis Segundo has insisted that putting theology in the context of the struggle for human liberation is necessary for the liberation of theology.[38] Feminists such as Carter Heyward have gone further, insisting that unless we return full humanity to our brother Jesus, making Jesus' word and work reciprocal with our own, his God-bearing cannot be, in any sense, good news for us.[39]

Many of us feminist Christians have patterned our understanding of what it means to be Christian on the image of that neglected closest follower of Jesus, Mary Magdalene. The synoptic gospels suggest that she was the last to leave the cross and the first to sit at the tomb. She is reported to have told the male disciples that Jesus had risen from the dead, but they did not believe her. Many of us feminists believe that liberation theology would do well to envisage Mary Magdalene not merely as a female disciple but as a prototype of all those followers of Jesus who speak and are not heard, those whose testimonies and visions have been denied and discounted by Christianity itself.[40]

It is the unacknowledged friends of Jesus, the Mary Magdalenes among us, who know most deeply the meaning of the Christian theological and moral virtues and can identify what hope, faith, and love mean in our time. From the voices of those long silenced, we can conclude that today Christian hope at least means this: that we are given the power to sustain the struggle, to resist oppression, even when the empirical horizon for human hope is dim and remote, as it surely is now. To have faith means that moving on, in struggle, we trust our communal power of relation to sustain us, that we can learn what we need to know. Christian love — both God's love for us and ours for God and each other — means this: that we discover and experience, in the power of praxis and solidarity, a new wellspring of caring that fuels our passion, so that nothing can destroy or break our shared capacity to pursue actively a justice long denied. God's grace to us, here and now, takes the form of an infinite, unquenchable longing for justice that will not be defeated even by death. We cannot say much more of God or of God's grace to us than this, because we do not yet see the face of God clearly. José Porfirio Miranda has reminded us, rightly, that God's countenance becomes visible only when justice rolls down like water and mercy like an ever-flowing stream.[41] That time is not yet at hand. And where the passion for justice is quenched, God is no longer known. In struggle, we catch intimations of the face of God and a foretaste of a commonwealth where the genuine joy in life can be shared. Our celebration goes on in that anticipation.

It is in this sense that liberation theology is utopic. As liberation Christians, we live not out of acquiescence to authority but out of vision, out of utopia (literally, "no place"), out of an experience of deep anticipation born of our shared commitment to justice. To live out of such a vision when the face of history appears to support the victory of evil is to experience the power of God as genuine transcendence. Celebration and annunciation, then, is the phase of our theological process that enables reengagement in resistance and feeds our souls to continue the everspiraling circle of our theological praxis, returning us to our daily engagement, grounding our power of praxis. Through it all, we discover the concrete reality of divine and human transcendence present in radically human engagement in the quest for justice. We Christians should be the first to understand that genuine experiences of transcendence are rare in the world in which we live. They are not secured by theological formulas that endlessly reiterate the importance of transcendence, either God's or our own. The genuine experience of transcendence arises in the ecstatic power emergent between those who have connected with each other, intimately engaged with God, in emancipatory praxis. Passion for justice, shared and embodied, is the form God takes among us in our time.[42]

Notes

Index

Notes

Introduction

1. Beverly Wildung Harrison, *Our Right to Choose: Toward a New Ethic of Abortion* (Boston: Beacon Press, 1983).

2. Mary Daly's *Gyn/Ecology* (Boston: Beacon Press, 1978) exemplifies this position. Harrison engages Daly's theoretical perspectives in several essays in this collection.

3. Aside from the straightforward stance that biological determinants are morally relevant, there is a more complicated view that gender relations have been and still are primarily determined by childrearing practices. Since universally women have been primary care providers for infants and children and since women tend to relate to daughters differently than to sons, some personality and social relations have been "determined" in this way. This theory may have some bearing on Carol Gilligan's theoretical perspective, *In a Different Voice* (Cambridge: Harvard University Press, 1982). A question to bring to this more cultural perspective is whether its coherence would depend in some measure on a view that biologically based gender differences in men and women result in qualitatively different moral perceptions.

4. For instance, see Starhawk, *The Spiral Dance* (San Francisco: Harper and Row, 1979), and *Dreaming the Dark* (Boston: Beacon Press, 1982).

5. This framework for analyzing justice is from Ch. Perelman, *The Idea of Justice* (London: Routledge and Kegan Paul, 1963). Perelman notes that these conceptions of justice are not consistent among themselves, and one needs to make a case for elevating one aspect of justice over any of the others. All aspects agree, however, that justice is a principle of action in which beings of the same category must be treated in the same way. They disagree about what is the ethically relevant category.

6. Harrison makes the point that "to each her due" is not a satisfactory notion of justice when rank or status is the dominant aspect of justice. See "The Dream of a Common Language," *Annual of the Society of Christian Ethics* (1983), p. 15. Also see Margaret Farley, R.S.M., "New Patterns of Relationship: Beginnings of a Moral Revolution," in *Woman: New Dimensions*, ed. Walter J. Burghardt, S.J. (New York: Paulist Press, 1976), p. 53. Farley indicates, "Given the interpretations of women's 'nature' as inferior, there was no question of violating the principle of giving 'to each her due' when women were placed in subordinate positions or denied rights which were accorded to men."

7. Carol Gilligan, *In a Different Voice* (Cambridge: Harvard University Press, 1982).

8. Margaret Farley, R.S.M., "Sources of Sexual Inequality in the History of Christian Thought," *Journal of Religion* 56 (April 1976), p. 165. Farley notes, "And whether woman was thought consciously to be a threatening force in the dialectic of history, or a temptress of men throughout all history, or a symbol of what men feared within themselves, she appears throughout the centuries in Christian writings as a special agent of evil. It is almost unnecessary to cite in this regard the texts of Justin Martyr, Irenaeus, Tertullian, of Origen, Augustine, Jerome, of Thomas Aquinas and Bonaventure, of Luther, John Knox and the Puritans."

9. Ronald M. Green, *Religious Reason* (New York: Oxford University Press, 1978), p. 26. Green explains, "Morality may be thought of as one of two basic ways of ordering social disputes. One way relies upon force and is the antithesis of reason. The other way relies on principles to which all could agree."

10. Harrison makes the point that "too many Christians, even of the progressive sort, still believe, in accord with male-stream Christian teaching, that an irresolvable theological and moral tension exists between self-assertive or self-interested acts (that is, those involved in the struggle for our/my liberation) and 'loving' and 'good' Christian acts. Nevertheless, we feminists maintain that radical Christian theology should be predicated on the assumption that there is no ontological split between self/other; there is no monolithic polarity of self-interested action versus other-regardingness." See "Theological Reflection in the Struggle for Liberation" in this collection. Also see Preston N. Williams, "Impartiality, Racism, and Sexism," *Annual of the Society of Christian Ethics* (1983), pp. 147–159.

11. Harrison, in "Theological Reflection in the Struggle for Liberation" in this book, argues that objectivity "means openness to others' history and to the critical claims that history bears and also the ability to learn from others' historical experience." With regard to universalism, she claims, "The horizon to which an adequate liberation perspective aspires, given twentieth-century reality, is not only globally inclusive but respectful of our cosmic environment. Precisely because we live in a world historical situation in which one geopolitical economy controls all people and our interactions with the rest of nature, global perspective is today the appropriately universal perspective of a Christian theology."

12. See Ruth Smith, "Feminism and the Moral Subject," in *Women's Consciousness, Women's Conscience*, ed. Barbara Hilkert Andolsen, Christine E. Gudorf, and Mary D. Pellauer (New York: Seabury Press, 1985). Also see Eleanor Humes Haney, "What Is Feminist Ethics: A Proposal for Continuing Discussion," *Journal of Religious Ethics* 8, no. 1 (Spring 1980), p. 120.

13. For a fuller discussion of this double standard, see Anne Wilson Schaef, *Women's Reality: An Emerging Female System in the White Male Society* (Minneapolis: Winston Press, 1981), pp. 78ff.

14. Harrison, "Misogyny and Homophobia: The Unexplored Connections" in this book.

15. See Harrison, "Theology and Morality of Procreative Choice" in this book.

16. Harrison examines the basis of theological arguments against procreative choice and comes to this conclusion. *Our Right to Choose: Toward a New Ethic of Abortion.*

17. Carol Gilligan, *In a Different Voice*, gives close attention to precisely this issue. While Harrison and Gilligan may disagree about the place of justice in feminist moral theory, they converge in their commitment to affirming the worth of women's well-being in moral reflection. Eleanor Haney in "What Is Feminist Ethics?" proposes nurture and friendship as feminist values but says, "The feminist task is to wrench these rules and principles from their destructive context" (p. 122).

18. Barbara Hilkert Andolsen gives careful attention to this question in "Agape in Feminists Ethics," *Journal of Religious Ethics* 9, no. 1 (Spring 1981), pp. 69–83.

19. Marjorie R. Maguire, "Personhood, Covenant, and Abortion," *Annual of the Society of Christian Ethics* (1983), p. 120.

20. I am using the formulation of Margaret Farley, R.S.M., "An Ethic for Same-Sex Relations," in *A Challenge to Love*, ed. R. Nugent (New York: Crossroad Publishing, 1983), p. 94.

21. Farley, "An Ethic for Same-Sex Relations," p. 98, and Harrison, "Theology and Morality of Procreative Choice" in this book.

22. Harrison, "The Power of Anger in the Work of Love" in this book. Also see Farley, "Sources of Sexual Inequality," p. 175.

23. Harrison, "The Equal Rights Amendment: A Moral Analysis" in this book.

24. Katie Geneva Cannon in "Moral Wisdom in the Black Women's Literary Tradition," *Annual of the Society of Christian Ethics* (1984), pp. 171–192, makes the point that this perspective is characteristic of white women, but not of black women. Black women were never under the illusion that the moral tradition ever included them. See "Resources for a Constructive Ethic in the Life and Work of Zora Neal Hurston," *The Journal of Feminist Studies in Religion* I, no. 1, 1985, pp. 37–54.

The Power of Anger in the Work of Love

1. Mary Daly, *Gyn/Ecology: The Metaethics of Radical Feminism* (Boston: Beacon Press, 1978), pp. 30ff. Mary Daly's work rightly has shaped most discussion and debate among women in theological and religious studies. Few, if any, male scholars seem to appreciate the importance of Daly's critique of Christian theology as exemplary patriarchy, perhaps because it is easier to ignore her claims than to offer a serious rejoinder. I have chosen to take public issue with Daly here not to give aid and comfort to those who think her work "too angry" and "too man-hating" but because, with the publication of *Gyn/Ecology*, Daly enters directly into "metaethics," or a discussion of the foundations of particular moral claims. It will not do, as Rebecca Porper did in *Union Seminary Quarterly Review* 35, nos. 1 and 2 (Fall, Winter 1979–1980), pp. 126–128, simply to treat the book as "beyond academic categories." Many of Daly's complaints about "methodolatry" in academia are on target, but she is also developing a substantive conceptual position herself, so her own method (consisting of operative assumptions and appeals for justification) deserves scrutiny. Daly is concerned about anti-intellectualism among women. It would be an exemplification of such anti-intellectualism not to hold her accountable for the factual and moral claims she makes or for her explicit or implicit methodological moves.

2. Daly, *Gyn/Ecology*, pp. 27–31.

3. My differences with Daly are numerous and beyond full classification here. Methodologically, I believe Daly has not repudiated adequately the extreme abstract rationalism of her Roman Catholic philosophical background, nor has she completed the shift from static ontic categories to the process categories she often celebrates. Carter Heyward is correct in claiming that Daly remains philosophically a subjective idealist. Carter Heyward, "Speaking and Sparking; Building and Burning," *Christianity and Crisis* 39, no. 5 (2 April 1979), p. 69. I assume a connection between subjective idealism and the body/mind dualism of the western tradition. The test of one's philosophical epistemology always becomes clear at the level of action. Idealism produces a critique of concepts, but it does not produce a historically concrete critique of institutions (that is, collective practice) or an alternative strategy for action. Even when Daly is correct about the depth of misogyny, her historical analysis of it lacks concreteness, nuance, and accuracy, and the book does not open the way to a strategy of change for a real, material world. It is not surprising that many begin to connect Daly's position with the ancient Gnostic movements, which in their developed form became dualistic.

4. As noted above, the quality of Daly's historical scholarship leaves much to be desired, especially in light of the growing amount of competent feminist research available on some of the historical periods about which she writes. Daly seems unwilling to draw on the work of distinguished women colleagues whose training is in historical scholarship and who are better able

to do historical analysis. The record of women's oppression is powerful enough, when carefully reconstructed, to ground Daly's claims without recourse to casual and noncontextual historical judgments. Daly often rips historical materials out of their cultural context, as for example in condemning the practice of "African genital mutilation" without noting that male subincision rites are part of the same cultural practice, or in condemning *both sides* of the sometimes contradictory treatment women in the United States receive at the hands of gynecologists. The result of this has been that many of Daly's critics have dismissed her substantive claims because of easily disputable historical overgeneralization.

5. Daly, *Gyn/Ecology*, pp. 413ff. As this manuscript was going to press, Mary Daly's *Pure Lust* (Boston: Beacon Press, 1984) appeared. A perusal suggests that Daly has shifted her position somewhat from some of the views criticized here. This analysis was, of course, focused on Daly's work through *Gyn/Ecology*.

6. I am assuming here that a "feminist moral theology" arises from the in-depth experience of women's struggle for life and from the consciousness that emerges through that struggle to live and to maintain a culture that expresses our lives. Such experience produces a critique of dominant, male-articulated Christian and secular theological, philosophical, and moral assumptions. I want to stress that for me *biological gender does not ground this point of view; women's historical* struggle for life grounds it. I agree with Mary Daly that a feminist perspective — in this case a feminist moral theology — cannot assume the adequacy of any male notions of "reason" or "revelation." However, since I am philosophically a dialectical materialist, I believe that critique of tradition equals transformation of tradition. The goal of a feminist moral theology, then, as Daly suggests, is to expose the death-dealing assumptions in the male-articulated tradition. However, contrary to Daly, I insist that women's culture has also been alive and concretely implicated in the real historical past of existing religious communities. The goal is to break the male monopoly on past and present interpretation so as to thereby displace patriarchal (that is, idolatrous) tradition with a humanly inclusive one.

7. I want to stress the similarity of hermeneutical assumptions made by feminists and by other liberation theologians even though many male-articulated liberation theologies often relish misogynist and masculinist idolatrous assumptions. See, for example, Juan Luis Segundo, *The Liberation of Theology* (Maryknoll, N.Y.: Orbis Press, 1976), pp. 37–38, n. 55. Segundo would reserve the term "Christian" for the male element in revelation. From the standpoint of the method of feminist theology, it is well to remember that women are not a minority. This means that the liberation theologies of all communities and groups must be transformed by the experience of women in those groups. If the world survives at all, all theologies will be forced to the feminist assumption since women are the underclass within every historical group. However, this also means, as noted here, that the liberation of women is "the longest revolution."

8. Roman Catholic theologian Matthew Fox has particularly stressed this theme of sensuality and spirituality. Happily, he notes the connection between feminist theology and the recovery of a spirituality of sensuality. Matthew Fox, *On Becoming a Musical Mystical Bear* (New York: Paulist Press, 1972), pp. ix–xxvi. He pursues this theme in other books, including *A Spirituality Named Compassion* (Minneapolis: Winston Press, 1979).

9. Sojourner Truth's speech was recorded in *History of the Women's Suffrage Movement*, vol. 1, reprinted in *The Feminist Papers*, ed. Alice Rossi (New York: Bantam, 1973), pp. 426–429.

10. Mary Daly, *Beyond God the Father* (Boston: Beacon Press, 1973), pp. 35, passim.

11. Susanne Langer, *Mind: An Essay On Human Feeling*, vol. 1 (Baltimore: Johns Hopkins University Press, 1967). Langer traces in minute detail the

evolution of organic structure from invariant process to motivated act as the major transition point between mind and the rest of nature.

12. See "Sexism and the Language of Christian Ethics" in this book.

13. The best available study of the values and virtues intrinsic to a feminist ethic, which also stresses this nurturance theme, is Eleanor Humes Haney, "What Is Feminist Ethics: A Proposal for Continuing Discussion," *Journal of Religious Ethics* 8, no. 1 (Spring 1980), pp. 115–124.

14. Nelle Morton, "The Rising of Women's Consciousness in a Male Language Structure," *Andover Newton Quarterly* 12, no. 4 (March 1972), pp. 177–190.

15. The phraseology is from the Boston Women's Health Collective, *Our Bodies, Ourselves* (New York: Simon and Schuster, 1973). This work has been one of the most powerful influences in transforming women's self-understanding during the past decade.

16. An important work that elaborates this theme is James B. Nelson, *Embodiment: An Approach to Sexuality and Christian Theology* (Minneapolis: Augsburg Press, 1979).

17. See especially Rosemary Ruether, *New Woman: New Earth* (New York: Seabury Press, 1975).

18. See especially Tom F. Driver, *Patterns of Grace: Human Experience As Word of God* (New York: Harper and Row, 1977). Recognition of the problem is also receiving attention in the works of theologians such as Charles Davis and Harvey Cox and, as noted above, Matthew Fox.

19. Happily, a few recent works by male colleagues in Christian ethics stress the importance of body and feeling in moral epistemology in a way consonant with my thesis here. See *Embodiment*, James B. Nelson and Daniel Maguire, *The Moral Choice* (New York: Doubleday, 1978).

20. See Haney, "What Is Feminist Ethics," and Anne Kent Rush, *Getting Clear: Body Work for Women* (New York: Random House, 1972).

21. Martin Buber, *I and Thou*, trans. Walter Kaufmann (New York: Scribner's, 1970), pp. 67f.

22. See, for example, Barry Commoner, *The Closing Circle* (New York: Knopf, 1971).

23. Carter Heyward, *The Redemption of God: A Theology of Mutual Relation* (Washington, D.C.: University Press of America, 1982).

24. John R. Wikse, *About Possession: The Self as Private Property* (University Park, Pa.: The Pennsylvania University Press, 1977).

25. Wikse, *About Possession*, pp. 44–45.

26. Wikse, *About Possession*, pp. 12–13.

27. A major source for the deprecation of mutuality in Protestant Christian ethics was Anders Nygren's study *Agape and Eros* (Philadelphia: Westminster Press, 1953). Among those who followed Nygren was Reinhold Niebuhr. See Gene Outka, *Agape: An Ethical Analysis* (New Haven: Yale University Press, 1972), pp. 7–92. An early critique of Nygren never adequately appropriated was Daniel Day Williams, *The Spirit and Forms of Love* (New York: Harper and Row, 1968). Roman Catholic writers have usually included a more positive role for mutuality in ethics than have Protestants, but the critique of sacrifice proposed here is relevant to Roman Catholic writers.

28. For an excellent critique of orthodox christologies, see Heyward, *The Redemption of God*, and Dorothee Sölle, *Christ the Representative* (Philadelphia: Fortress Press, 1967) and *Political Theology* (Philadelphia: Fortress Press, 1974).

29. Adrienne Rich, *Lies, Secrets and Silence* (New York: Norton, 1979).

30. Jules Girardi, "Class Struggle and the Excluded Ones," trans. and distributed by New York Circus, from *Amor Cristiano y Lucha de Classes* (Sigueme, Spain, 1975).

31. Thomas Aquinas argued, following Aristotle, that male and female "natures" differed because biological structure differed. This two natures idea runs deep in Christian theology. Daly has, of course, reversed the traditional argument, making women alone expressive of full rationality. She continues the traditional dualism, however.

32. Within a liberation theology method, "thinking" or "reflection" is, of course, a moment *within* praxis. We "do" theology, which includes our naming, interpretation, and analysis of our world, in the process of acting to change it in a life-giving direction.

Sexism and the Language of Christian Ethics

1. My understanding of the role of moral reasoning in ethics is elaborated in greater detail in Beverly Wildung Harrison, *Our Right to Choose: Toward a New Ethic of Abortion* (Boston: Beacon Press, 1983), pp. 12–27, 187–200, and passim.

2. How one defines "the moral point of view" depends on what "moral theory" one accepts. For a summary of some current assumptions about moral theory, see James Childress and Thomas L. Beauchamp, *Principles of Biomedical Ethics* (London: Oxford University Press, 1983), especially chapters 1 and 2. A less reductionist approach to moral theory is found in Dorothy Emmet, *The Moral Prism* (New York: St. Martin's Press, 1979). See also Kai Nelson, "The History of Ethics" in *The Encyclopedia of Philosophy*, vol. 3, ed. Paul Edwards (New York: Free Press, 1973), pp. 81–117.

3. Full examination of this point is outside the scope of this essay. To put the matter briefly, however, I agree that Divine Command discourse is not per se adequate as a moral claim. My convictions about God warrant my moral judgments and valuations indirectly. I do not have the right to dismiss others' moral arguments because they do not concur with my sense of what God commands, nor do I have the right to reject questions about the bearing of Divine Commands on human well-being that nonbelievers may press upon me. See Paul Helm, ed., *Divine Commands and Morality* (New York: Oxford University Press, 1981).

4. Habermas's suggestion that social theorists should focus on the systematic distortion that institutional power imposes on communication has been influential in my work. I find Habermas's recent work flawed by idealist assumptions and psychologisms, however. Compare Jürgen Habermas, *Toward a Rational Society: Student Protest, Science, and Politics* (Boston: Beacon Press, 1971) and his *Theory of Communicative Action: Reason and the Rationalization of Society*, vol. 1 (Boston: Beacon Press, 1984).

5. My notion of power-in-relation is dependent on the work of Carter Heyward, *The Redemption of God: A Theology of Mutual Relation* (Washington, D.C.: University Press of America, 1982), especially chapter 1. See also Carter Heyward, *Our Passion for Justice: Images of Power, Sexuality, and Liberation* (New York: Pilgrim Press, 1984).

6. Barrie Thorne and Nancy Henley, eds., *Sex Difference in Language, Speech, and Nonverbal Communication* (Rowley, Mass.: Newbury House, 1975). The study of sexism in language has begun to demonstrate that in linguistic history is buried a heavy burden of misogyny.

7. In technical ethical terms moral obligation is a claim on our action that expresses the conditions (in some moral philosophy, though not in Christian ethics, the minimal conditions) for human well-being. Some moral theories define obligation more narrowly, as the general characteristic of the universalizability of acts, that is, that actions are morally obligatory if all people in similar circumstances should do them.

8. Numerous citations throughout this book document this claim. Of special importance is Peggy Reeves Sanday, *Female Power and Male Dominance: On the Origins of Sexual Inequality* (Cambridge: Cambridge University Press, 1981).

9. See in this connection Rosemary Ruether, *New Woman/New Earth: Sexist Ideologies and Human Liberation* (New York: Seabury Press, 1978), and The Cornwall Collective, eds., *Your Daughters Shall Prophesy: Feminist Alternatives in Theological Education* (New York: Pilgrim Press, 1980).

10. A useful discussion of Piaget's work on ego development and its relation to moral development is found in Walter Conn, *Conscience: Development and Self-Transcendence* (Birmingham, Ala.: Religious Education, 1981).

11. Harrison, *Our Right to Choose.*

12. Karl Barth, *The Church Dogmatics,* vol. III/2 (Edinburgh: T. and T. Clark, 1970), pp. 274–285, 632f. I do not mean to suggest that Barth's theological framework provides the same justifications as mine for why we should interpret human evil this way.

13. Winthrop Jordan, *White Over Black: American Attitudes Toward the Negro* (Chapel Hill: University of North Carolina Press, 1968).

14. Roland Sampson, *The Psychology of Power* (New York: Vintage, 1968). See also, D. V. Hiller and Robin Sheets, eds., "Women and Men: The Consequences of Power," Office of Women's Studies, University of Cincinnati, 1977.

15. See especially Dorothy Dinnerstein, *The Mermaid and the Minotaur: Sexual Arrangements and Human Malaise* (New York: Harper and Row, 1976); Nancy Chodorow, *The Reproduction of Mothering* (Berkeley: University of California Press, 1978); and Adrienne C. Rich, *Of Woman Born: Motherhood as Experience and Institution* (New York: Norton, 1976).

16. In spite of his critical attitude toward the church's attitude toward women, Reinhold Niebuhr's usual tendency is to romanticize interpersonal family relations. See *The Nature and Destiny of Man,* vol. 1 (New York: Scribner's, 1941–1943), pp. 282f.

17. An editorial Niebuhr wrote in 1949 exemplifies the complex blend of his views on women. In it, he strongly endorses the moral superiority of secular society over church because of the latter's treatment of women but presumes women's interests to be innately related to motherhood. Reprinted in Reinhold Niebuhr, *Essays in Applied Christianity,* D. B. Robertson, ed. (New York: Mendian Books, 1959), pp. 93–95.

18. For a characterization of how theological liberalism has supported women's oppression, see Ann Douglas, *The Feminization of American Culture* (New York: Knopf, 1977).

19. Before revising this essay I read Nancy Jay's suggestive "Gender and Dichotomy," *Feminist Studies* 7, no. 1 (Spring 1981), pp. 39–56. Jay's work, focusing on a sociology of religion relevant to women, has provided a deeper awareness of how religious systems, as such, develop as part of the legitimation system of male supremacy. Her essay suggests that logic itself is shaped by the patriarchal system such that a dualism-creating logic of exclusion develops — if *A,* then not *B.* This supports my thesis.

20. Mary Daly's solution to this problem has been to create a new language to describe women's reality. See *Gyn/Ecology: The Metaethics of Radical Feminism* (Boston: Beacon Press, 1978).

21. This is, I realize, a hotly contested issue among feminists. In my view, too little attention is paid to the most rigorous scientific research on this issue. See below, notes 24 to 26. See also John M. Broughton, "Women's Rationality and Men's Virtues," and Deborah Nails, "Social-Scientific Sexism: Gilligan's Mismeasure of Man," both in *Social Research: Women and Morality* 50, no. 3 (Autumn 1983), pp. 595–642 and 643–664, respectively.

22. Mary Daly, *Beyond God the Father* (Boston: Beacon Press, 1973). Her *Gyn/Ecology* is also relevant here, as is *Pure Lust* (Boston: Beacon Press, 1984).

23. Penelope Washbourn, ed., *The Seasons of Women* (New York: Harper and Row, 1982). This section originally appeared in Beverly Harrison, "Feminism and Process Thought," *Signs* 7, no. 3 (Spring 1982), pp. 704–710.

24. Joseph Pleck, *The Myth of Masculinity* (Cambridge: MIT Press, 1981).

25. Robert Green, *Sexual Identity Conflict in Children and Adults* (New York: Basic Books, 1974). See also John Money and Patricia Tucker, *Sexual Signatures* (Boston: Little, Brown, 1975).

26. John Money and Anke A. Earhardt, *Man and Woman: Boy and Girl* (Baltimore: Johns Hopkins University Press, 1973).

27. Eleanor Maccoby and Carolyn Jacklin, *The Psychology of Sex Differences* (Stanford: Stanford University Press, 1974).

28. See "The Effect of Industrialization on the Role of Women in Society" in this book.

29. See also Beverly Wildung Harrison, "The New Consciousness of Women: A Socio-Political Resource," *Cross Currents* 24, no. 4 (Winter 1975), pp. 445–462.

30. For example, see Mary Daly, *Beyond God the Father*, chapter 5.

31. An important treatment of this problem appears in Jean Baker Miller, *Toward a New Psychology of Women* (Boston: Beacon Press, 1979).

32. Gordon Rattray Taylor, *Rethink: A Paraprimitive Solution* (London: Secker and Warburg, 1972), pp. 27–47.

33. Taylor, *Rethink*.

34. Carter Heyward, *Our Passion for Justice*, pp. 243–247. The argument that such images are necessary to protect "divine transcendence" is brilliantly refuted in this work.

35. My indebtedness to Dorothee Sölle in this whole section should be obvious to all who know her work. See especially *Beyond Mere Obedience* (Minneapolis: Augsburg Press, 1970; Philadelphia: Fortress Press, 1980).

36. Karl Barth, *The Epistle to the Romans* (London: Oxford University Press, 1933).

37. Dietrich Bonhoeffer, *Ethics* (New York: Macmillan, 1965). There was little such awareness in his fragmentary work on ethics.

38. Bonhoeffer, *Ethics*, pp. 248ff., 286–287, and Dietrich Bonhoeffer, *Letters and Papers from Prison* (New York: Macmillan, 1967).

39. See *The Humanity of God* (Richmond: John Knox Press, 1960). See also *Church Dogmatics*, 3:2 (Edinburgh: T. and T. Clark, 1960), pp. 26–54.

40. Barth, *Church Dogmatics*, 3:4 (Edinburgh: T. and T. Clark, 1961), pp. 116–240.

41. Barth, *Church Dogmatics*, 3:4, pp. 169f.; Clifford Green, "Liberation Theology? Karl Barth on Women and Men," *Union Theological Seminary Quarterly Review* 29, nos. 3 and 4 (Spring, Summer 1974), pp. 221–231.

42. Karl Barth, *Church Dogmatics*, 3:4, pp. 161f. Barth's criticism of Simone de Beauvoir's *The Second Sex* clarifies his hostility to women's equality. See also *Church Dogmatics*, 2:1 (Edinburgh: T. and T. Clark, 1958), pp. 288–329, especially p. 303.

43. Rudolf Bultmann, *History and Eschatology: The Presence of Eternity* (New York: Harper Torchbooks, 1962). A brilliant appreciation and critique of Bultmann on this particular point is found in Dorothee Sölle, *Political Theology* (Philadelphia: Fortress Press, 1974).

44. Frederick Dennison Maurice, *The Conscience: Lectures on Casuistry* (London: Macmillan, 1868).

45. F. D. Maurice, *The Life of F. D. Maurice* (London: Macmillan, 1884).

46. This is similar to the point H. Richard Niebuhr stressed in *The Responsible Self* (New York: Harper and Row, 1963).
47. Dorothee Sölle, *Christ the Representative* (Philadelphia: Fortress Press, 1967).
48. This insight about faith being expressed in action is well developed in H. Richard Niebuhr. See Beverly Wildung Harrison, *H. Richard Niebuhr: Towards a Christian Moral Philosophy* (Ann Arbor, Mich.: Xerox University Microfilms, 1974), pp. 170–203.

The Effect of Industrialization on the Role of Women in Society

1. Probably the first feminist to observe this was Alice Clark in a work first published in 1919: *Working Life of Women in the Seventeenth Century* (London: Frank Cass and Company, 1919), reprinted by Biblio Distribution Center of Totowa, N.J., 1968. See Valentina Borreman, "Technique and Women's Toil," *Cross Currents* (Winter 1982–1983), pp. 420f.
2. Philippe Aries, *Centuries of Childhood* (New York: Vintage, 1960). For an excellent feminist treatment of women's changing lives, see Rosalind Pollack Petchesky, *Abortion and Woman's Choice* (New York: Longmans, 1983), part I. See also Jean Louis Flandrin, *Families in Former Times* (Cambridge: Cambridge University Press, 1979).
3. Margaret Mead, "The American Woman Today," in *The World Book Year Book*, 1969, pp. 78–95; Peggy Reeves Sanday, *Female Power and Male Dominance: On the Origins of Sexual Inequality* (Cambridge: Cambridge University Press, 1981); Evelyn S. Kessler, *Women: An Anthropologist's View* (New York: Holt, Rinehart, and Winston, 1976); Rayna Reiter, ed., *Towards an Anthropology of Women* (New York: Monthly Review Press, 1975); Michelle Zimbalist Rosaldo and Louise Lamphere, eds., *Woman Culture and Society* (Stanford: Stanford University Press, 1974).
4. Judith R. Walkowitz, "Male Vice and Female Virtue: Feminism and the Politics of Prostitution in Nineteenth-Century Britain," in *Class, Race, and Sex: The Dynamics of Control*, eds. Amy Swerdlow and Hanna Lessinger (Boston: G. K. Hall, 1983). See also Florynce Kennedy, *Color Me Flo* (Englewood Cliffs, N.J.: Prentice-Hall, 1976).
5. Thorstein Veblen, *The Theory of the Leisure Class* (New York: Penguin, 1979). Gerder Lerner, "The Lady and the Mill Girl: Changes in the Status of Women," *Midcontinental American Studies* 10 (Spring 1969), pp. 5–15.
6. Rosalyn Baxandall, Linda Gordon, Susan Reverly, *America's Working Women: A Documentary History 1600 to the Present* (New York: Vintage–Random House, 1976), especially pp. 85–131; Kathleen McCort, *Working Class Women and Grass-Roots Politics* (Bloomington: Indiana University Press, 1977). See also, Alice Clark, *Working Life of Women in the 17th Century*.
7. Lillian Breslow Rubin, *Worlds of Pain: Life in the Working Class Family* (New York: Basic Books, 1976). Also see Kathy Kahn, *Hillbilly Women* (New York: Avon, 1974).
8. Harriet Martineau, *Society in America*, vols. 1–3 (London: Sanders and Otley, 1837).
9. Elizabeth Cady Stanton, et al., eds., *The History of Woman Suffrage*, vol. 1 (New York: Fowler and Weels, 1881), p. 80.
10. Eugene D. Genovese, *Roll, Jordan, Roll: The World the Slaves Made* (New York: Pantheon, 1972), pp. 81f., passim.
11. Betty Friedan, *The Feminine Mystique* (New York: Norton, 1963).

12. Hilda Scott, *Does Socialism Liberate Women?* (Boston: Beacon Press, 1979); Alena Heitlinger, *Women and State Socialism* (Montreal: McGill–Queen's University Press, 1979), p. 94, and *Feminism and Socialism* (New York: Pathfinder, 1972); Marilyn J. Boxer and Jean H. Quatert, *Socialist Women: European Socialist Feminism in the 19th and Early 20th Century* (New York: Elsevier North-Holland, 1978); Mari Jo Buhle, *Women and America's Socialism: 1870–1920* (Urbana: University of Illinois Press, 1983).

13. All women experience the pressure of the split between home and workplace in a formative way, but this does not mean that women are all equally disadvantaged by it. Political-economic (class) oppression and racism further oppress most women. Nothing in my analysis should be read as positing a uniform theory of "women's experience." Compare Michelle Russell, "Women, Work and Politics in the United States," in *Theology in the Americas*, ed. Sergio Torres and John Eagleson (Maryknoll, N.Y.: Orbis Press, 1976), pp. 341–350.

The Role of Social Theory in Religious Social Ethics

1. John C. Bennett, *The Radical Imperative* (Philadelphia: Westminster Press, 1976), pp. 124, 142–164.

2. The historical context of the emergence of radical social thought makes clear that "socialism," for all its ideological and theoretical variations, involved the conviction that socializing economic relations is conditional to sustaining genuine democracy. Historically, not all socialists analyzed the specific sources of capitalism's evils the same way, but all agreed that further *political* democracy was not possible without institutionalizing *economic* democracy in some new ways. The analysis of religious socialists who were idealists and of socialists who were materialists differed because of their variant theories of knowledge. Christian socialists have been represented in both genres. See, for example, Paul Tillich, *The Socialist Decision*, trans. Franklin Sherman (New York: Harper and Row, 1977), and John Lewis, *Marxism and the Open Mind* (Trenton, N.J.: Rutgers University Press, 1959); also see James Weinstein, *The Decline of Socialism in America, 1912–1925* (New York: Vintage, 1967).

   Prior to the last decade, several of the best discussions of Christianity and radical social thought with which I am familiar appeared in John Lewis, Karl Polanyi, and Donald Kitchen, *Christianity and the Social Revolutions* (New York: Scribner's, 1936). In light of my critique of Reinhold Niebuhr in this essay, it should be noted that that volume contained one of Niebuhr's early assessments of communism as religion, "Christian Politics and Communism as Religion."

3. The student in question, Eugene Jones, has since completed an excellent comparative study of the assumptions about value, the conceptions of agency, and respective views of economic distribution in neo-Marxian and neoclassical theory. I am indebted to his work at several points as well as to studies by other former students cited elsewhere in this chapter. "The Justice Imaginable: The Conceptions of Action and the Possibilities of Justice Delimited in Neo-classical and Marxian Value and Distribution Theories" (unpublished diss., Union Theological Seminary, New York, pending).

4. Ralph Potter, "The Logic of Moral Argument," in *Toward a Discipline of Social Ethics: Essays in Honor of Walter Muelder*, ed. Paul Deats, Jr. (Boston: Boston University Press, 1972), pp. 117f. For several spirited rejoinders, see the methodological essays contained in *The Journal of Religious Ethics* 5, no. 1 (Spring 1977), especially Joseph C. Hough, Jr., "Christian Ethics as Advocacy," pp. 115–113, and Glen H. Stassen, "A Social Theory Model for Religious Social Ethics," pp. 9–37. Here I use the hybrid term "social theory/social science" to refer to all those disciplines encompassing the hu-

man sciences and to indicate the range of self-understandings about the nature of social science present within each field. On the Marxian views of science, see Stanley Aronowitz, "Science and Ideology," Current Perspectives in Social Theory (1980), pp. 75–101. Also see G. A. Cohen, Karl Marx's Theory of History: A Defence (Princeton: Princeton University Press, 1978), pp. 326–344.

5. James Gustafson popularized this term for characterizing unfruitful methodological debates in "Contextualism: A Misplaced Debate," in New Theology No. 3, ed. Dean G. Peerman and Martin Marty (New York: Macmillan, 1966), pp. 69–102.

6. Here I am following Roger Shinn's characterization of ideology, in Forced Options: Social Decisions for the Twenty First Century, in Religious Perspectives, vol. 27, ed. Ruth Nanda Anshen (San Francisco: Harper and Row, 1982). For a characterization of the thesis that ideology is a cultural system, see Clifford Geertz, "Ideology as a Cultural System," in Ideology and Discontent, ed. David Apter (Glencoe, Ill.: Free Press, 1964), pp. 47–76. An excellent collection of essays by radical social theorists on ideology and social science is Robin Blackburn, ed., Ideology in Social Science: Readings in Critical Social Theory (New York: Vintage, 1973). Also see Gerard Fourez, Liberation Ethics (Philadelphia: Temple University Press, 1982), particularly part 1. Fourez's treatment of ideology in ethics is excellent. His account of the nature of ethical debate vis-à-vis cultural relativity is too subjectivist and individualistic, however.

7. Some radical political economists, whose work I commend here, have helped illumine the importance of ideology by paralleling differing ideological social-theoretical accounts of social issues. Compare David Gordon, ed., Problems in Political Economy: An Urban Perspective (Lexington, Mass.: D. C. Heath, 1977); David Mermelstein, ed., Economics: Mainstream Readings and Radical Critique (New York: Random House, 1976); and E. K. Hunt and Howard Sherman, Economics: An Introduction to Traditional and Radical Views 4th ed. (New York: Harper and Row, 1981).

8. The continuing regard for Niebuhr is reflected in James Gustafson, "Christian Ethics," in Religion: Humanities Scholarship in America Series, ed. Paul Ramsey (Englewood Cliffs, N.J.: Prentice-Hall, 1965); Donald Meyer, The Protestant Search for Political Realism 1919–1941 (Berkeley and Los Angeles: University of California Press, 1960); Paul Merkley, Reinhold Niebuhr: A Political Account (Montreal: McGill–Queens University Press, 1975); and Nathan Scott, ed., The Legacy of Reinhold Niebuhr (Chicago: University of Chicago Press, 1974).

9. Useful criticisms of Niebuhr on this point may be found in several essays and in the discussion section of Harold R. Landon, ed., Reinhold Niebuhr: A Prophetic Voice in Our Time (Greenwich, Conn.: Seabury Press, 1962); in John C. Bennett, "Realism and Hope After Niebuhr," Worldview 15 (May 1972), pp. 4–14; Ronald H. Stone, Realism and Hope (Washington, D.C.: University Press of America, 1977); and Stanley Hoffman, Contemporary Theory in International Relations (Westport, Conn.: Greenwood Press, 1977).

10. During the Depression, Niebuhr stressed the centrality of economic power to political control. During this period, his formulations often sounded as though he believed economic power had primacy in determining sociopolitical dynamics. Compare Reinhold Niebuhr, Moral Man and Immoral Society (New York: Scribner's, 1932), Reflections on the End of an Era (New York: Scribner's, 1934), and Christianity and Power Politics (New York: Scribner's, 1934). Careful reading of these texts reveals a shifting conviction within the same work about the relation of economic and political power, however.

11. See, for example, these books by Reinhold Niebuhr: The Irony of American History (New York: Scribner's 1952) and Christian Realism and Political

Problems (New York: Scribner's, 1953). The most revealing of Niebuhr's book-length publications, in terms of the hold of philosophical idealism on his perspective, is *The Self and the Dramas of History* (New York: Scribner's, 1955). Note in particular his postulating self-divine relations and self-eternal relations apart from society and community.

12. Reinhold Niebuhr, *The Structure of Nations and Empires* (New York: Scribner's, 1959) and *Man's Nature and His Communities: Essays on the Dynamics and Enigmas of Man's Personal and Social Existence* (New York: Scribner's, 1965).

13. For example, Michael Novak, "On Needing Niebuhr Again," *Commentary* 15 (September 1972), pp. 52–62. Robert Benne, *The Ethic of Democratic Capitalism: A Moral Reassessment* (Philadelphia: Fortress Press, 1981). The strong tide of neoconservative Christian ethics has accelerated with the well-funded support of the American Enterprise Institute for Public Policy Research. A rather more subtle "defense" of Niebuhr at the expense of the Latin American liberation theology movement (which, however, is not entirely clear), is Dennis McCann, *Christian Realism and Liberation Theology: Practical Theologies in Conflict* (Maryknoll, N.Y.: Orbis Press, 1981). An equally unfortunate regurgitation of Niebuhr's evaluation of Marx has been popularized by Denis Goulet, "Secular History and Teleology," *World Justice* (September 1966), pp. 5–18.

14. It is important to remember that Niebuhr denied that Christian theology or ethics could give direct legitimation to any particular political or economic system. Some neoconservatives, such as Novak and Benne, formally follow Niebuhr's method in giving capitalism only indirect or penultimate "baptism." However, Niebuhr would not approve their passionate partisanship for the penultimate superiority of capitalism. Even in his mature years, Niebuhr might well have preferred that the United States approximate Britain or Sweden in its social welfare standards. He also tended to assume that the New Deal was more successful in eradicating poverty than it actually was.

15. Niebuhr, in fact, all but equated Marxism and communism. For a collation of his writings on this topic, see Harry R. Davis and Robert C. Good, eds., *Reinhold Niebuhr on Politics* (New York: Scribner's, 1960), particularly pp. 3–11, 26–36, 180–192, 213–225, 261–268, and 298–320. Niebuhr also misunderstood Marx's analysis of "the means of production." He identified Marxism as a critique of *private property* not of *private ownership and control of the means of production, The Irony of American History*, pp. 95, 117, and *passim, Children of Light and the Children of Darkness* (London: Nisbett and Company, 1945), pp. 28, 65, 79, and *passim*. A popular, typically appreciative summary of Niebuhr's views on Marxism is contained in June Bingham, *Courage to Change: An Introduction to the Life and Thought of Reinhold Niebuhr* (New York: Scribner's, 1961). To appreciate the distance between Niebuhr's earliest intellectual assumptions and Marx's, see Louis Tietje, "Was Reinhold Niebuhr Ever a Marxist? An Investigation into the Assumptions of His Early Interpretation and Critique of Marxism" (Unpublished doctoral diss., Union Theological Seminary, New York, 1984).

16. Something of this tone suffuses McCann, *Christian Realism and Liberation Theology*. When I presented the original version of this paper, several questioners were incredulous that I would affirm the merits of neo-Marxian theory and specifically asked me how a Christian could do so, citing Reinhold Niebuhr as "authority" for their views on the "idolatry" of Marxism.

17. Louis Tietje, "Was Reinhold Niebuhr Ever a Marxist?" is an indispensable work for assessing Niebuhr's treatment of Marx.

18. See Ronald H. Stone, *Reinhold Niebuhr: Prophet to Politicians* (Washington, D.C.: University Press of America, 1981). I consider this the best work on Niebuhr's thought, but Stone fails to analyze seriously the relation between Marx and Niebuhr and presumes that Niebuhr's early views were heavily indebted to Marx. See also Merkley, *Reinhold Niebuhr*, pp. 82f.

19. Karl Marx, A Contribution to the Critique of Political Economy, Frederick Engels, ed., Samuel Moore and Edward Aveling, trans. (New York: Modern Library, 1936), introduction and passim. Karl Marx, Grundrisse, David McLellan, ed. and trans. (New York: Harper Torchbooks, 1972), pp. 16–58. Compare with Cohen, Karl Marx's Theory of History, pp. 326f., and Alfred Schmidt, The Concept of Nature in Marx (London: New Left Books, 1971), pp. 95–126.

20. See especially Reinhold Niebuhr, The Nature and Destiny of Man: A Christian Interpretation (New York: Scribner's, 1949), and Faith and History: A Comparison of Christian and Modern Views of History (New York: Scribner's, 1946), passim.

21. See, for example, The Self and the Dramas of History, pp. 114f., 133–140.

22. See, for example, H. Richard Niebuhr, The Social Sources of Denominationalism (New York: Holt, 1929); also Kingdom of God in America (Chicago: Willet, Clark, 1937). I interpret the importance of Niebuhr's work in "H. Richard Niebuhr: Towards a Christian Moral Philosophy" (unpublished doctoral thesis, Union Theological Seminary, New York, 1974).

23. Ernst Troeltsch, The Social Teaching of the Christian Church, 2 vols., trans. Olive Wyon, introduction by H. Richard Niebuhr (New York: Harper Torchbooks, 1960). H. Richard Niebuhr did his doctoral thesis on Troeltsch. For differing views of Troeltsch and Weber's relationship, see Henry Stuart Hughes, Consciousness and Society (New York: Knopf, 1958), and Carlo Antonio, From History to Sociology (Detroit: Wayne State University Press, 1957), pp. 59–70.

24. For example, James Gustafson, Treasure in Earthen Vessels: The Church as a Human Community (New York: Harper, 1961); Kenneth W. Underwood, Protestant and Catholic, Religions and Social Interaction in an Industrial Community (Boston: Beacon Press, 1957).

25. Nothing in this essay critiquing nonradical social theory is meant to deny the importance of culture in social theory or to deny the insensibility of many Marxists, with obvious exceptions such as Gramsci and Mao, to cultural factors. Compare David McLellan, Marxism After Marx (Boston: Houghton Mifflin, 1979). However, many of the neo-Marxist social theorists I cite here are deeply aware of the dangers of analytic reductionism and accept the accountability of social theory to concrete communities of suffering people. See Michael Albert, What Is to Be Undone: A Modern Revolutionary Discussion of Classical Left Ideologies (Boston: Porter Sargent, 1974), and Michael Albert and Robin Hahnel, Un-Orthodox Marxism (Boston: South End Press, 1978).

26. See H. H. Gerth and C. Wright Mills, eds., From Max Weber: Essays in Sociology (New York: Oxford University Press, 1958); Max Weber, The Protestant Ethic and the Spirit of Capitalism (New York: Scribner's, 1952) and The Theory of Social and Economic Organization (New York: Free Press, 1947).

27. This criterion of historicity needs more amplification than I can give it here. It is not merely the history of ideas, but of cultural and social institutions that is relevant.

28. See above, n. 12.

29. The phrase is from W. B. Yeats, "The Second Coming." See Marvin M. Ellison, The Center Cannot Hold: The Search for a Global Economy of Justice (Washington, D.C.: University Press of America, 1983). Ellison's work is invaluable for clarifying the ideological dimensions of the debate on economic development in social theory, ecclesiastical discussion, and theological ethics.

30. For example, Max Stackhouse, who strongly utilizes Weber in his social ethics, joined several neoconservative theological ethicists on the Editorial

Board of a militantly anti-Marxian, antiliberationist journal that purports to focus on economic ethics, *This World*.

31. Alvin W. Gouldner, "Anti-Minotaur: The Myth of Value-Free Sociology," *Social Problems* IX (Winter, 1962), pp. 99–213, and *The Coming Crisis of Sociology* (New York: Avon, 1971); see also Leon Bramson, *The Political Context of Sociology* (Princeton: Princeton University Press, 1961).

32. This is the force of Carlo Antonio's critique, *From History to Sociology*, not only of Weber but of the entire German historical school. Compare Guenther Roth, "Political Critiques of Max Weber" in Dennis H. Wrong, ed., *Max Weber* (Englewood Cliffs, N.J.: Prentice-Hall, 1970), pp. 195–210.

33. Antonio, *From History to Sociology*. See Harrison, "H. Richard Niebuhr," pp. 296f.

34. This is obvious particularly in his later methodological essays. Compare Max Weber, *The Theory of Social and Economic Organization* (New York: Free Press, 1947), and *The Methodology of the Social Sciences* (New York: Free Press, 1969), especially pp. 182ff. A nonradical social scientist who acknowledges the tendency in Weber's work for the promised role of the historical subject to disappear is Milton M. Gordon, *Human Nature, Class, and Ethnicity* (Oxford: Oxford University Press, 1978). On Weber's subtle capitalist bias, compare Cohen, *Karl Marx's Theory of History*, p. 320.

35. See Ellison, *The Center Cannot Hold*. See also John O'Connor, *The Fiscal Crises of the State* (New York: St. Martin's Press, 1973); John Blair, *Economic Concentration: Structure, Behavior, and Public Policy* (New York: Harcourt Brace Jovanovich, 1972); Samir Amin, *Unequal Development: An Essay on the Social Formations of Peripheral Capitalism* (New York: Monthly Review Press, 1976); Andre Gunder Frank, *Capitalism and Underdevelopment in Latin America*, 2nd. ed. (New York: Monthly Review Press, 1969); Paul Baran, *The Political Economy of Growth* (New York: Monthly Review Press, 1957). It should be noted that there is among these neo-Marxists a deep theoretical division about the basic mechanisms that precipitate economic crisis. Important issues are at stake here. See Robert Brenner, "The Origins of Capitalistic Development: A Critique of Neo-Smithian Marxism," *New Left Review* (July–August 1977), pp. 25–92, and Erik Olin Wright, "Alternative Perspectives in Marxist Theory of Accumulation and Crisis," in Jesse Schwartz, ed., *The Subtle Anatomy of Capitalism* (Santa Monica: Goodyear Publishing Co., 1977). See also Thomas Weisskopf, "Alternative Theories of Economic Crisis," in *U.S. Capitalism in Crisis, The Union of Radical Political Economist Perspectives* (New York: Union of Radical Political Economists, 1978).

36. A standard interpretation of Marshall's role here is contained in Phyllis Deane, *The Evolution of Economic Ideas* (Cambridge: Cambridge University Press, 1979), pp. 93–124. See also Alfred Marshall, *Principles of Economics*, 2 vols., 9th ed. (London: Macmillan, 1961). Marshall was John Maynard Keynes's teacher. See J. M. Keynes, *Essays in Biography*, vol. 10, *Collected Writings of John Maynard Keynes* (Cambridge: Cambridge University Press, 1972). On the relationship of Keynes and Marx, a critical work is Paul Mattick, *Marx and Keynes: The Limits of Mixed Economy* (Boston: Porter Sargent, 1969).

37. Tom L. Beauchamp and Norman E. Bowie, *Ethical Theory and Business* (Englewood Cliffs, N.J.: Prentice-Hall, 1979).

38. See, for example, Charles Powers, John G. Simon, and Jon Gunnemann, *The Ethical Investor: Universities and Corporate Responsibility* (New Haven: Yale University Press, 1972); Charles Powers, *People/Profits: The Ethics of Investment* (New York: Council on Religion and International Affairs, 1972) and *Social Responsibility and Investments* (Nashville, Tenn.: Abingdon Press, 1971).

39. A good philosophical analysis of the conceptions of rationality implicit in these theories is found in Martin I. Hollis and Edward J. Nell, *Rational Eco-*

Notes / 281

nomic Man (Cambridge: Cambridge University Press, 1975). See also the important comparative study by Jones, *The Justice Imaginable* and also Nancy C. M. Hartsock, *Money, Sex, and Power: Toward a Feminist Historical Materialism* (New York: Longman, 1983), pp. 19–54.

40. While to designate something as an "exogenous" factor does not technically commit a neoclassical economist to the judgment that it is irrelevant to social policy deliberation, it does enable the neoclassical economist to offer a professional normative judgment on what is optimal economic behavior that may contradict her or his own moral sense. Compare, for example, Lester Thurow, *The Zero-Sum Society: Distribution and the Possibilities for Economic Change* (New York: Basic Books, 1980), which contains sensitive reflections on the social effects of current economic policy with the advice he offers investors when he appears on the Public Broadcasting Service "Wall Street Journal."

41. Churches have taken a lead in this work. The Interfaith Center on Corporate Responsibility maintains a program on church shareholder and investor activity with corporations on social and financial issues. "Corporate Responsibility" is their newsletter published ten times a year. Rm. 566, 475 Riverside Drive, the National Council of Churches, N.Y., N.Y., 10115; (212–870–2623).

42. See, for example, Philip J. Wogaman, *The Great Economic Debate: An Ethical Analysis* (Philadelphia: Westminster Press, 1977). Wogaman includes "conservationism" as a fifth "type," but the moral evaluation is actually focused on the ideological spectrum I am concerned with in this essay.

43. Neoclassical economists utilize two ideologies—conservative (laissez-faire) or liberal (social welfare). The conservatives sometimes assume that the "free market" describes an earlier historical state of affairs, but their philosophy of social science may, at the same time, presume that theoretical models of the market need not describe the real world because neoclassical theory is a "pure" science. Such inconsistencies are rife in the field of economics.

44. See Blair, *Economic Concentration,* and Paul Baran and Paul Sweezy, *Monopoly Capital: An Essay on American Economy and Social Order* (New York: Monthly Review Press, 1966).

45. Milton Friedman, *Capitalism and Freedom* (Chicago: University of Chicago Press, 1981). While Friedman is the most consistent ideologist of the right, one notices that his advice to Chile's Fascist regime did *not* include recommendations for reducing state control of the economy or military spending. The limited state is desirable in the United States, less so in the third world.

46. It cannot be emphasized too much, given prevailing misperceptions about Marx's views, that for him *the* task of social science is to demystify appearances and to identify the actual character of concrete social relations. To argue, as many theologians, including Niebuhr, have done, that Marx's aim is to develop a scientific theory of socialism is erroneous. It is even worse to interpret Marx as providing a scientific "blueprint" for revolution. I also agree with G. A. Cohen's assessment that Marx anticipated that social science would not be necessary if capitalism is transcended. See Cohen, *Karl Marx's Theory of History,* pp. 326–344. Much responsibility for the widespread misinterpretation of Marx's theory of science falls on Karl Popper for the false claims made in *The Open Society and Its Enemies,* vol. 2 (Princeton: Princeton University Press, 1966). A recent theological interpretation of Marx that reflects an accurate reading on this point and recognizes Popper's misleading influence is Nicholas Lash, *A Matter of Hope: A Theologian's Reflections on the Thought of Karl Marx* (South Bend, Ind.: University of Notre Dame Press, 1982), pp. 210–230. Lash even suggests that Marx gave too little attention to the question of the future. I agree.

47. Charles Lindblom, *Politics or Markets* (New York: Basic Books, 1977).

48. Again, a caveat is in order regarding the social theory used to explicate the *meaning* of class conflict. As a radical, I presume that the term "class"

means a group that shares objective conditions of social privilege or social exploitation. In conservative or liberal social theory "class" means "social strata." Many "misplaced debates" in Christian ethics follow from confusing these two vastly different notions of class. See James Stolzman and Herbert Gamberg, "Marxist Class Analysis Versus Stratification Analysis as General Approaches to Social Inequality," *Berkeley Journal of Sociology* 18 (1973–1974), pp. 105–125. See also Bertell Ollman, "Marx's Use of 'Class,' " *American Journal of Sociology* 73 (March 1968), and Pat Walker, *Between Labor and Capital* (Boston: South End Press, 1979).

49. In this regard, Hunt and Sherman, *Economics: An Introduction to Traditional and Radical Views,* and Deane, *Evolution of Economic Ideas,* are helpful. See also Maurice Dobb, *Theories of Value and Distribution Since Adam Smith* (Cambridge: Cambridge University Press, 1973).

50. In fact, "competence" in graduate-level education in economics requires that both theories be mastered. However, the politics of graduate faculties of economics is, evidently, as ideologically determined as are theological faculties. See Leo Lifschultz, "Could Karl Marx Teach Economics in America?" *Ramparts* 12, no. 9 (April 1974), pp. 27–59.

51. See Eugene Jones, "Bibliography: The Reality of Social Class as Theological and Ethical Problem" (unpublished, 1980). Jones's bibliography highlights radical literature, though it also includes other perspectives.

52. These debates among political economists can be traced in publications of the Union of Radical Economists and in the following journals: *Monthly Review, New Left Review, Radical America, Review of Radical Political Economics, Insurgent Sociologist,* and *Socialist Revolution* (now called *Socialist Review).* See also McLellan, *Marxism After Marx.*

53. I concur with Stanley Aronowitz, "Science and Ideology," regarding the negative effects of Habermas's and Althusser's work on the Marxian theory of science. McLellan contends, and I believe he is right, that the structuralists and Frankfurt School reflect a lack of confidence in the working class and a loss of interest in politics. *Marxism After Marx,* p. 333. Marxism, no less than Christianity, requires praxis as its presupposition.

54. See below, p. 227f. and 261f. I am here presuming the sort of feminist theological perspective commonly designated as "feminist liberation theology." See Beverly Wildung Harrison, *Our Right to Choose: Toward a New Ethic of Abortion* (Boston: Beacon Press, 1983), pp. 91–118. This mode of theological work is related to a broader movement of feminist theory known as "socialist-feminist theory." See Carol Robb, "Frameworks in Feminist Ethics," *Journal of Religious Ethics* 9 (Spring 1981), pp. 48–68. See also Hartsock, *Money, Sex, and Power.*

55. The so-called Christian-Marxist dialogue has too often been characterized by an overabstract focus and Christian idealist imperialism. See, for example, Paul Lehmann, Jürgen Moltmann, and Charles C. West in *Openings for Marxist-Christian Dialogue,* ed. Thomas W. Ogletree (Nashville, Tenn.: Abingdon Press, 1969). Ogletree's introductory essay is useful.

In a feminist liberation perspective, praxis as resistance to concrete suffering is the norm for collaboration, not conceptual agreement. Solidarity and common accountability in resisting concrete human suffering are more important than intellectual agreement. In sum, *social theoretical* formulations are to be judged by how well they clarify the sources of oppression of poor black women. *Theological* formulations are to be judged by how profoundly they give voice to the sources of hope such women experience.

56. McCann, *Christian Realism and Liberation Theology.* See also Charles C. West, *Communism and the Theologians* (New York: Macmillan, 1958), and Jon Gunnemann, *The Moral Meaning of Revolution* (New Haven: Yale University Press, 1979).

57. Here I am arguing that a neo-Marxian, anticapitalist social theory is an irreducible dimension of the social theory we need. Nevertheless, as most

of the theorists I have cited recognize, a neo-Marxian analysis must also incorporate both an antiracist and feminist analysis. The contradiction not only of production but of reproduction must be identified. See Rosalind Pollack Petchesky, *Abortion and Woman's Choice: The State, Sexuality, and Reproductive Freedom* (New York: Longman, 1984); Manning Marable, *How Capitalism Underdeveloped Black America: Problems in Race, Political Economy and Society* (Boston: South End Press, 1983); Cornel West, *Prophesy Deliverance: An Afro-American Revolutionary Christianity* (Philadelphia: Westminster Press, 1982).

58. The point here is not that it is wrong to be concerned about the maldistribution of wealth, but rather that such maldistribution is a symptom of unjust social relations. Welfare liberalism, which addresses only the redistribution of wealth, not its control and ownership, does not affect exploitative social relations directly.

59. The presumption that religious ethicists are accountable to the concrete experience of people underlies my entire concern here. Methodologically, my assumption is that the morality suffuses everyday life. See John Sabini and Maury Silver, *Moralities of Everyday Life* (Oxford: Oxford University Press, 1982).

60. For an interesting account of the inability of neoclassical economic theory even to *incorporate* women's reality, see Nancy Barrett, "How the Study of Women Has Restructured the Discipline of Economics," in Elizabeth Longland and Walter Gove, eds., *A Feminist Perspective in the Academy: The Difference It Makes* (Chicago: University of Chicago Press, 1983), pp. 101–109.

61. Among members of the Union of Radical Economists, this commitment is explicit. Also journals such as *Dollars and Sense*, produced by a collective of economists, aim to make critical economic information widely available. It is also worth noting that many radical political economists collaborate in their research, a rarity in academia. See *Dollars and Sense*, published monthly, Somerville, Massachusetts, Economics Affairs Bureau, Inc.

62. I am presuming that Marx's views may be described appropriately as a philosophical anthropology. I would not go so far as Carol Gould has done in describing Marx's position as "a social ontology" because Marx does not follow the methodology of philosophical ontology. He does develop an identifiable conception of human nature. Gould's presentation of Marx is accurate even if her general label is misleading. See Carol C. Gould, *Marx's Social Ontology: Individuality and Community in Marx's Theory of Social Reality* (Cambridge, Mass.: MIT Press, 1978).

63. Michael Parenti, *Democracy for the Few* (New York: St. Martin's Press, 1980). See also Bertram Gross, *Friendly Fascism: The New Face of Power in America* (Boston: South End Press, 1980).

64. There is also important moral theoretical work to be done in this connection so that we may develop a fully feminist-socialist theological conception of justice. See Allen W. Wood, "The Marxian Critique of Justice" and "Marx on Right and Justice: A Reply to Husami," in *Marx, Justice, and History: A Philosophy and Public Affairs Reader*, ed. Marshall Cohen, Thomas Nagel, and Thomas Scanlon (Princeton: Princeton University Press, 1980), pp. 3–41, 106–134.

Sexuality and Social Policy

1. I have complained of a related confusion elsewhere. See the discussion in particular of Christopher Lasch's work, 293, n. 7 below.

2. See above, pp. 274, ns. 24–27, and below, pp. 284, n. 4, 293, n. 5. For a telling critique of empiricist social science, see Liam Hudson, *The Cult of the Fact* (New York: Harper and Row, 1972).

284 / Notes

3. "Unexceptional action guides" are, in contemporary moral philosophic par-

3. "Unexceptional action guides" are, in contemporary moral philosophic parlance, rules or principles that do not admit of conditions or exceptions.
Most moral philosophers and Christian ethicists believe that we should treat
rules and principles as if they create a presumption for or against acts such
that we need to marshall serious reasons if they are not to be honored.
Nevertheless, Christian sexual ethics continues to be discussed as if unexceptional rules exist. See below, p. 302, n. 28. See also Gerard Fourez,
Liberation Ethics (Philadelphia: Temple University Press, 1982), particularly
parts 1 and 2. I share Fourez's assumption that such rigid rules reflect taboo
structures and that these are maintained often by the ideology of dominant
groups to serve their interests. See also John Lewis, Marxism and the Open
Mind (Trenton, N.J.: Rutgers University Press, 1957), pp. 211f.

4. References valuable in discussing sex roles are found throughout the notes
of this book, especially those for essays 1, 3, and 7. See also Peter Gabriel
Filene, Him/Her Self: Sex Roles in Modern America (New York: Harcourt
Brace Jovanovich, 1974). Also Helen S. Astin, Allison Parelman, and Anne
Fischer, Sex Roles: A Research Bibliography (Washington, D.C.: Center for
Human Services, 1975).

5. Robin Ruth Linden, Darlene R. Pagano, Diana E. H. Russell, and Susan
Leigh Star, eds., Against Sadomasochism: A Radical Feminist Analysis (East
Palo Alto, Calif.: Frog in the Well, 1982); also Pamela Kearon and Barbara
Mehrhof, "Rape: An Act of Terror," in Radical Feminism, eds. A. Koedt,
E. Levine and A. Rapone (New York: Quadrangle, 1973); Maria Roy, ed.,
Battered Women: A Psychosociological Study of Domestic Violence (New
York: Van Nostrand Reinhold, 1977), and Carol Vance, ed., Pleasure and
Danger: Exploring Female Sexuality (Boston: Routledge and Kegan Paul,
1985).

6. Bonnie Mass, Population Target (Toronto: Toronto Women's Press and Latin
American Working Group, n.d.). Dr. Helen Rodriguez, "The Social Politics
of Technology," Women's Rights Law Reporter 7, no. 5 (1983). Also see
Beverly Wildung Harrison, Our Right to Choose: Toward a New Ethic of
Abortion (Boston: Beacon Press, 1983), p. 272, n. 20; p. 273, n. 29.

7. Andrea Dworkin, Woman Hating (New York: Dutton, 1974), pp. 22–24.

8. Mary Breasted, Oh—Sex Education (New York: New American Library,
1971).

9. This analysis of the need for change in both dimensions of women's lives
is the hallmark of socialist-feminist theory. Important works of this genre
of theory are cited throughout this work. Others of critical importance for
understanding feminist socialist theory are Rosalind Pollack Petchesky,
Abortion and Woman's Choice: The State, Sexuality, and Reproductive
Freedom (New York: Longman, 1984); Zillah R. Eisenstein, ed., Capitalist
Patriarchy and the Case for Socialist Feminism (New York: Monthly Review
Press, 1979); Batya Weinbaum, The Curious Courtship of Women's Liberation and Socialism (Boston: South End Press, 1978), and Nannerl O. Keo-
hane, Michelle Z. Rosaldo, Barbara Gelpi, eds., Feminist Theory: A Critique
of Ideology (Chicago: University of Chicago Press, 1982).

10. This thesis is dramatically documented in Hilda Scott, Does Socialism Liberate Women? (Boston: Beacon Press, 1974).

11. Louise Kapp Howe, Pink Collar Workers: Inside the World of Women's
Work (New York: Putnam, 1977).

12. See above, n. 9, and below, p. 285, ns. 15–17, 290, n. 7, and 292, n. 6.

13. Rosalind Pollack Petchesky, "Reproduction and Class Divisions Among
Women," in Amy Swerdlow and Hanna Lessinger, eds., Class, Race, and Sex:
The Dynamics of Control (Boston: G. K. Hall, 1983), pp. 221–241.

14. "Women in Today's Economic Crisis," in U.S. Capitalism in Crisis (New
York: Union of Radical Political Economists, 1978), pp. 69–77; Barbara
Ehrenreich and Deirdre English, "The Manufacture of Housework," Social-
ist Revolution 5, no. 4 (October–December 1975). Oli Hawrylyshyn, The

Economic Value of Household Services: An International Comparison of Empirical Estimates (New York: Praeger, 1976).

15. United States Department of Labor, Bureau of Labor Statistics, *The Social and Economic Status of the Black Population in the United States: An Historic Overview, 1790–1978.* See also p. 284, nn. 12–14 and p. 292, n. 6.

16. Cherrie Moraga and Gloria Anzaldua, eds., *This Bridge Called My Back: Writings by Radical Women of Color* (New York: Kitchen Table Press, 1981); Cherrie Moraga, *Loving in the War Years* (Boston: South End Press, 1983); Elizabeth Higginbotham, "Laid Bare by the System: Work and Survival for Black and Hispanic Women," and Angela Jorge, "Issues of Race and Class in Women's Studies: A Puerto Rican Woman's Thoughts," in Swerdlow and Lessinger, eds., *Class, Race, and Sex.* Also see Miranda Davies, ed., *Third World, Second Sex: Women's Struggles and National Liberation, Third World Women Speak Out* (London: Zed, 1983).

17. Michelle Russell, "Women, Work and Politics in the United States," in *Theology in the Americas,* eds. Sergio Torres and John Eagleson (Maryknoll, N.Y.: Orbis Press, 1976), p. 350.

18. Leo Kanowitz, *Women and the Law: An Unfinished Revolution* (Albuquerque: University of New Mexico Press, 1974), and Shana Alexander, ed., *A State by State Guide to Women's Legal Rights* (New York: Wollstonecraft, 1975).

19. There has been a tremendous upsurge in incidents of vandalism, arson, and assaults directed at abortion clinics and their personnel. In August 1982, the operator of an abortion clinic and his wife were kidnapped by a radical antiabortion group protesting government failure to denounce abortion. The couple were released unharmed. Nathaniel Sheppard, Jr., "Abortion Doctor and Wife Are Freed," *New York Times,* 21 August 1982, p. A7. See also Andrew Merton, *Enemies of Choice: The Right-to-Life Movement and Its Threat to Abortion* (Boston: Beacon Press, 1981). Antiabortion tactics are monitored by the Religious Coalition for Abortion Rights in its newsletter *Options.* See also Roz Kramer, "The Great Abortion Battle of 1981," *Village Voice* 21, no. 1, 1981, pp. 1, 14–15, and Lisa Cronin Wohl, "Anti-abortion Violence on the Rise: How Far Will It Go?" *Ms.* (October 1984), pp. 135–140.

20. The National Conference of Catholic Bishops has made curtailment of federal funding for contraceptive research a major priority. See Kenneth A. Briggs, "Catholics Beginning an Expanded Drive Against Abortions," *New York Times,* Vol. 126, No. 43670 1977, pp. 13, 20. Boyce Rensberger, "Lag in Research on Birth Control Found Despite Increasing Need," *New York Times,* 17 November 1976. This report on the Ford Foundation's study on contraception research projected that to maintain the 1976 levels of research, which cost less than $150 million, by 1980 half a billion dollars would be required worldwide. Expenditures have increased little since then.

21. Bernard Barber, *Research on Human Subjects* (New York: Russell Sage Foundation, 1973), p. 108. See also Joy Katz, *Experimentation with Human Beings* (New York: Russell Sage Foundation, 1972); Ellen Frankfort, *Vaginal Politics* (New York: Quadrangle, 1972); Toni Cade, "The Pill: Genocide or Liberation," in *The Black Woman,* ed. Toni Cade (New York: New American Library, 1970), pp. 162–169.

22. Herbert Aptheker, "Sterilization, Experimentation and Imperialism," *Political Affairs* 53, no. 1 (January 1974). Also see *Health Policy Advisory Center Bulletin,* no. 62 (New York, January–February 1975), 4, Cherrie Moraga, *Loving in the War Years* (Boston: South End Press, 1983), pp. 98–144; and Angela Y. Davis, *Women, Race and Class* (New York: Random House, 1981). Also see Petchesky, "Reproduction and Class Divisions Among Women," and Lourdes Beneria and Gita Sen, "Women's Role in Economic Development: Practical and Theoretical Implications of Class and Gender Inequalities," in Swerdlow and Lessinger, *Class, Race, and Sex.*

23. The phrase is from William Ryan, *Blaming the Victim* (New York: Vintage, 1971).

24. See n. 5 above. Marie Fortune clarifies these dynamics in a wider discussion of sexual abuse, *Sexual Violence: The Unmentionable Sin, An Ethical and Pastoral Perspective* (New York: Pilgrim Press, 1983).

25. In a new study, Diana Russell reports that 19 percent of the women she interviewed acknowledged experiences of marital rape. See *Rape in Marriage* (New York: Macmillan, 1982).

26. Marilyn Frye, "Some Reflections on Separatism and Power," *Sinister Wisdom* 6 (Summer 1975), 30–39. On the impact on women of recovering bodily self-direction, see Audre Lourde, *Uses of the Erotic: The Erotic as Power* (Trumansburg, N.Y.: Crossing Press, 1978).

27. See n. 5 above and n. 29 below.

28. See n. 4, p. 275, and p. 284, n. 5. Compare Susan Brownmiller, "Speaking Out on Prostitution," in *Radical Feminism: An Anthology*, eds. Anne Koedt, Ellen Levine, and Anita Rapone (New York: Quadrangle, 1973), and Kate Millet, "Prostitution: A Quartet for Female Voices," in *Women in Sexist Society*, eds. Vivian Gornick and Barbara Moran (New York: Basic Books, 1971).

29. Compare Ellen Willis, "The Challenge of Profamily Politics: A Feminist Defense of Sexual Freedom," in Swerdlow and Lessinger, *Class, Race, and Sex*, pp. 325–338; Deirdre English, Amber Hollibaugh, and Gayle Rubin, "Talking Sex," *Socialist Review* (1981), pp. 43–62; and Robin Morgan, *Going Too Far: A Personal Chronicle of a Feminist* (New York: Vintage, 1978), pp. 163–169. See also Laura Lederer, *Take Back the Night: Women on Pornography* (New York: Morrow, 1980), and Robin Morgan, *The Anatomy of Freedom: Feminism, Physics and Global Politics* (New York: Doubleday, 1984).

30. Joseph Pleck and Jack Sawyer, *Men and Masculinity* (Englewood Cliffs, N.J.: Prentice-Hall, 1974), and Letty Cottin Pogrebin, *Growing Up Free: Raising Your Child in the 80's* (New York: Bantam, 1981).

31. Merle Longwood, "Divorce as an Occasion for Moral Reconstruction," in *Annual of the Society of Christian Ethics, 1984* (Waterloo, Ontario: Council on the Study of Religion, 1984), pp. 229–248.

Theology and Morality of Procreative Choice

1. I use the traditional Roman Catholic term intentionally because my ethical method has greater affinity with the Roman Catholic model.

2. The Christian natural law tradition developed because many Christians understood that the power of moral reason inhered in human beings qua human beings, not merely in the understanding that comes from being Christian. Those who follow natural law methods address moral issues from the consideration of what options appear rationally compelling, given present reflection rather than from theological claims alone. My own moral theological method is congenial to certain of these natural law assumptions. Roman Catholic natural law teaching, however, has become internally incoherent by its insistence that in some matters of morality the teaching authority of the hierarchy must be taken as the proper definition of what is rational. This replacement of reasoned reflection by ecclesiastical authority seems to me to offend against what we must mean by moral reasoning on best understanding. I would argue that a moral theology cannot forfeit final judgment or even penultimate judgment on moral matters to anything except fully deliberated communal consensus. On the abortion issue, this of course would mean women would be consulted in a degree that reflects their numbers in the Catholic church. No a priori claims to authoritative moral reason are ever possible, and if those affected are not consulted, the teaching cannot claim rationality.

3. For a critique of these positions, see Paul D. Simmons, "A Theological Response to Fundamentalism on the Abortion Issue," in *Abortion: The Moral*

Issues, ed. Edward Batchelor, Jr. (New York: Pilgrim Press, 1982), pp. 175–187.

4. Most biblical scholars agree that either the early Christians expected an imminent end to history and therefore had only an "interim ethic," or that Jesus' teaching, in its radical support for "the outcasts" of his society, did not aim to justify existing social institutions. See, for example, Luke 4 and 12; Mark 7, 9, 13, and 14; Matthew 25. See also Elisabeth Schüssler Fiorenza, "You Are Not to be Called Father," *Cross Currents* (Fall 1979), pp. 301–323. See also her *Bread Not Stone: The Challenge of Feminist Biblical Interpretation* (Boston: Beacon Press, 1985).

5. Few Roman Catholic theologians seem to appreciate how much the recent enthusiastic endorsement of traditional family values implicates Catholicism in Protestant Reformational spirituality. Rosemary Ruether is an exception; she has stressed this point in her writings.

6. Helmut Thielicke, *The Ethics of Sex* (New York: Harper and Row, 1964), pp. 199–247. Compare pp. 210 and 226ff. Barth's position on abortion is a bit more complicated than I can elaborate here, which is why one will find him quoted on both sides of the debate. Barth's method allows him to argue that any given radical human act could turn out to be "the will of God" in a given context or setting. We may at any time be given "permission" by God's radical freedom to do what was not before permissible. My point here is that Barth exposits this possible exception in such a traditional prohibitory context that I do not believe it appropriate to cite him on the pro-choice side of the debate. In my opinion, no woman could ever accept the convoluted way in which Barth's biblical exegesis opens the door (a slight crack) to woman's full humanity. His reasoning on these questions simply demonstrates what deep difficulty the Christian tradition's exegetical tradition is in with respect to the full humanity and moral agency of women. See Karl Barth, "The Protection of Life," in *Church Dogmatics*, part 3, vol. 4 (Edinburgh: T. and T. Clark, 1961), pp. 415–22.

7. Compare Beverly Wildung Harrison, "When Fruitfulness and Blessedness Diverge," *Religion and Life* (1972), vol. 41, no. 4, pp. 480–496. My views on the seriousness of misogyny as a historical force have deepened since I wrote this essay.

8. Marie Augusta Neal, "Sociology and Sexuality: A Feminist Perspective," *Christianity and Crisis* 39, no. 8 (14 May 1979), pp. 118–122.

9. For a feminist theology of relationship, see Carter Heyward, *Toward the Redemption of God: A Theology of Mutual Relation* (Washington, D.C.: University Press of America, 1982).

10. Neal, "Sociology and Sexuality." This article is of critical importance in discussions of the theology and morality of abortion.

11. Susan Teft Nicholson, *Abortion and the Roman Catholic Church*, JRE Studies in Religious Ethics II (Knoxville: Religious Ethics Inc., University of Tennessee, 1978). This carefully crafted study assumes that there has been a clear "antikilling" ethic separable from any antisexual ethic in Christian abortion teaching. This is an assumption that my historical research does not sustain.

12. Jean Meyer, "Toward a Non-Malthusian Population Policy," in *The American Population Debate*, ed. Daniel Callahan (Garden City, N.Y.: Doubleday, 1971).

13. See James C. Mohr, *Abortion in America* (New York: Oxford University Press, 1978), and James Nelson, "Abortion: Protestant Perspectives," in *Encyclopedia of Bioethics*, vol. 1, ed. Warren T. Reich (New York: Free Press, 1978), pp. 13–17.

14. H. Richard Niebuhr often warned his theological compatriots about abstracting acts from the life project in which they are embedded, but this warning is much neglected in the writings of Christian moralists. See "The Christian Church in the World Crises," *Christianity and Society* 6 (1941).

15. John T. Noonan, Jr., *A Private Choice: Abortion in America in the Seventies* (New York: Free Press, 1979). Noonan denies that the history of abortion is related to the history of male oppression of women.

16. We know now that the birth control pill does not always work by preventing fertilization of the ovum by the sperm. Frequently, the pill causes the wall of the uterus to expel the newly fertilized ovum. From a biological point of view, there is no point in the procreative process that can be taken as a clear dividing line on which to pin neat moral distinctions.

17. The most conspicuous example of corporate involvement in contraceptive failure was the famous Dalkan Shield scandal. Note also that the manufacturer of the Dalkan Shield dumped its dangerous and ineffective product on family planning programs of third world (overexploited) countries.

18. Catholic moral theology opens up several ways for faithful Catholics to challenge the teaching office of the church on moral questions. However, I remain unsatisfied that these qualifications of inerrancy in moral matters stand up in situations of moral controversy. If freedom of conscience does not function *de jure*, should it be claimed as existent in principle?

19. I elaborate this point in greater detail in "The Power of Anger in the Work of Love" in this book.

20. For example, Paul Ramsey gave unqualified support to U.S. military involvement in Southeast Asia in light of just-war considerations but finds abortion to be an unexceptional moral wrong.

21. See Richard A. McCormick, S.J., "Rules for Abortion Debate," in Batchelor, *Abortion: The Moral Issues*, pp. 27–37.

22. One of the reasons why abortion-on-demand rhetoric — even when it is politically effective in the immediate moment — has had a backlash effect is that it seems to many to imply a lack of reciprocity between women's needs and society's needs. While I would not deny, in principle, a possible conflict of interest between women's well-being and the community's needs for reproduction, there is little or no historical evidence that suggests women are less responsible to the well-being of the community than are men. We need not fall into a liberal, individualistic trap in arguing the central importance of procreative choice to issues of women's well-being in society. The right in question is body-right, or freedom from coercion in childbearing. It is careless to say that the right in question is the right to an abortion. Morally, the right is bodily self-determination, a fundamental condition of personhood and a foundational moral right. See Beverly Wildung Harrison, *Our Right to Choose: Toward a New Ethic of Abortion* (Boston: Beacon Press, 1983).

23. A theory is crassly utilitarian only if it fails to grant equal moral worth to all persons in the calculation of social consequences — as, for example, when some people's financial well-being is weighted more than someone else's basic physical existence. I do not mean to criticize any type of utilitarian moral theory that weighs the actual consequences of actions. In fact, I believe no moral theory is adequate if it does not have a strong utilitarian component.

24. For a perceptive discussion of this danger by a distinguished Catholic priest, read George C. Higgins, "The Prolife Movement and the New Right," *America*, 13 Sept. 1980, pp. 107–110.

25. Philip J. Murnion, ed., *Catholics and Nuclear War: A Commentary on the Challenge of the U.S. Catholic Bishops' Pastoral Letter on War and Peace* (New York: Crossroads, 1983), p. 326.

26. I believe the single most valid concern raised by opponents of abortion is that the frequent practice of abortion, over time, may contribute to a cultural ethos of insensitivity to the value of human life, not because fetuses are being "murdered" but because surgical termination of pregnancy may further "technologize" our sensibilities about procreation. I trust that all

of the foregoing makes clear my adamant objection to allowing this insight to justify yet more violence against women. However, I do believe we should be very clear that we stand ready to support — emphatically — any social policies that would lessen the need for abortion *without* jeopardizing women's right to control our own procreative power.

Misogyny and Homophobia: The Unexplored Connections

1. Dorothea Krook, *Three Traditions of Moral Thought* (Cambridge: Cambridge University Press, 1959), pp. 333–347.
2. Krook, *Three Traditions of Moral Thought*, p. 342.
3. James B. Nelson, *Embodiment: An Approach to Sexuality and Christian Theology* (Minneapolis: Augsburg Press, 1979). See also his *Between Two Gardens: Reflections on Sexuality and Religious Experience* (New York: Pilgrim Press, 1983).
4. Rosemary Radford Ruether, *New Woman: New Earth* (New York: Seabury Press, 1975); Linda Gordon, *Woman's Body, Woman's Right: A Social History of Birth Control in America* (New York: Penguin, 1974); also "Women: Sex and Sexuality," *Signs* 5, no. 4 (Summer 1980), reprinted as Catherine R. Stimpson and Ethel Specter Person, eds., *Women: Sex and Sexuality* (Chicago: University of Chicago Press, 1980).
5. The theme of enforced heterosexuality as a social institution has been widely discussed by feminist theorists. However, heterosexism has been subtly internalized in feminist theory also. Now it is being recognized that heterosexism, historically, was a necessary extension of the system of sexist control aimed at assuring women's compliance to heterosexuality as "natural," because women's emotional bonding is otherwise likely to be with other women, as men's usually is with other men. See the excellent elaboration of this thesis in Adrienne Rich, "Compulsory Heterosexuality and Lesbian Existence," *Signs* 5, no. 4 (Summer 1980), pp. 631ff. See also Ann Ferguson, Jaquelyn N. Zita, and Kathryn Pyne Addelson, "On 'Compulsory Heterosexuality and Lesbian Existence': Defining the Issues," *Signs* 7, no. 1 (Autumn 1981), pp. 158–199. See also Lillian Faderman, *Surpassing the Love of Men: Romantic Friendship and Love Between Women from the Renaissance to the Present* (New York: Morrow, 1981).
6. John Boswell, *Christianity, Social Tolerance, and Homosexuality: Gay People in Western Europe from the Beginning of the Christian Era to the Fourteenth Century* (Chicago: University of Chicago Press, 1980). Boswell notes that etymologically *homophobia* means "fear of sameness," not "fear of homosexuality." He therefore declines to use the term, though he admits the force of the phenomenon to which it refers. While I am an admirer of Boswell's work, I find this to be a linguistic affectation. It is a mistake to assume that meaning can be discovered in etymology apart from usage.
7. See John J. McNeill, *The Church and the Homosexual* (Kansas City, Mo.: Sheed, Andrews, and McMeel, 1976), and Letha Scanzoni and Virginia Mollenkott, *Is the Homosexual My Neighbor? Another Christian View* (San Francisco: Harper and Row, 1978). Useful cross-cultural data on homosexuality may be found in Clellan S. Ford and Frank A. Beach, *Patterns of Sexual Behavior* (New York: Harpers, 1951).
8. Boswell, *Christianity, Social Tolerance, and Homosexuality*, pp. 50ff.
9. Boswell, *Christianity, Social Tolerance, and Homosexuality*, pp. 50ff.
10. Elaine Pagels, *The Gnostic Gospels* (New York: Random House, 1979). Elisabeth Schüssler Fiorenza, "Word, Spirit and Power: Women in Early Christian Communities," in *Women of Spirit: Female Leadership in Jewish and Christian Traditions*, ed. Rosemary Ruether and Eleanor McLaughlin (New York: Simon and Schuster, 1979); also see Fiorenza's *In Memory of Her: A*

Feminist Theological Reconstruction of Christian Origins (New York: Cross-roads, 1983). On the relationship of hierarchy and sex negativity, see Samuel Lauechli, Power and Sexuality: The Emergence of Canon Law at the Synod of Elvira (Philadelphia: Temple University Press, 1972).

11. Marie August Neal, "Sociology and Sexuality: A Feminist Perspective," Christianity and Crisis 39, no. 8 (14 May 1979), pp. 118–122.

12. I place these terms in quotes because I do not believe that they designate objective psychological qualities. Psychological perspectives that presume the meaningfulness of these terms invariably result in a subtle perpetuation of sexism. An adequate theory of psychosexual identity can deal with the differences and similarities in men's and women's psychological/historical experience without resort to either term. Studies that document the dubiousness of both notions in psychological research are James Harrison, A Critical Evaluation of the Psychological Concepts of Masculinity and Femininity (Unpublished doctoral diss., New York University, February 1975), and Joseph Pleck, The Myth of Masculinity (Cambridge: MIT Press, 1981).

13. This thesis that we learn equality or lack of it through early sex role socialization is only now being recognized. See Jean Baker Miller, Toward A New Psychology of Women (Boston: Beacon Press, 1976), and Roland Sampson, The Psychology of Power (New York: Vintage, 1968). These discussions and numerous others in the feminist literature only begin to open up this crucial issue of how we learn, or fail to learn, equality.

14. On this theme of spirituality and sensuality, see the writings of Matthew Fox, On Becoming a Musical Mystical Bear (New York: Paulist Press, 1979) and A Spirituality Named Compassion (Minneapolis: Winston Press, 1977). Also see Tom F. Driver, Patterns of Grace: Human Experience as Word of God (New York: Harper and Row, 1977).

The Older Person's Worth in the Eyes of Society

1. H. Richard Niebuhr, The Meaning of Revelation (New York: Macmillan, 1970), p. 48. Cf. also pp. 8–12, 42f.

2. H. Richard Niebuhr, "Ernst Troeltsch, Philosophy of Religion: A Dissertation Presented to the Faculty of the Graduate School of Yale University" (unpublished manuscript, 1924), p. 77.

3. The understanding that knowledge is socially constructed has given rise to a sociology of knowledge perspective in sociology that has been summarized and elaborated in Peter Berger and Thomas Luckmann, The Social Construction of Reality: A Treatise on the Sociology of Knowledge (Garden City, N.Y.: Doubleday–Anchor, 1967). This work is useful as a sketch of mainstream academic assumptions about the social construction of knowledge, but it fails to take seriously the reality of power and dominant group privilege in the noetic construction process.

4. Jer. 31:29.

5. For purposes of this analysis, "power" is the ability to act on and effectually shape the world around us, particularly through collective action and institutional policy. To have power means to have access to physical resources and wealth, to knowledge, and to the loci of social decision-making and to be able to impact institutional and social policy.

6. Jonathan Cobb and Richard Sennett, The Hidden Injuries of Class (New York: Random House, 1972), and Lillian Breslow Rubin, Worlds of Pain: Life in the Working Class Family (New York: Basic Books, 1976).

7. For a description of the inequities in our society, see Eugene Toland et al., "World Justice and Peace: A Challenge to American Christians," Church Research and Information Project (Maryknoll, New York). See also Frances Fox Piven and Richard A. Cloward, Regulating the Poor: The Functions of

Public Welfare (New York: Pantheon, 1971) and *The New Class War* (New York: Pantheon, 1982); Barry Bluestone and William and Mary Stevenson, *Low Wages and the Working Poor* (Ann Arbor: University of Michigan Press, 1973); William A. Domhoff, *Who Rules America?* (Englewood Cliffs, N.J.: Prentice-Hall, 1968) and *The Higher Circles: The Governing Class in America* (New York: Vintage, 1970); and Stanley Aronowitz, *Food, Shelter, and the American Dream* (New York: Continuum, 1974).

8. William Ryan, *Blaming the Victim* (New York: Vintage, 1971).

9. Michael Lewis, *The Culture of Inequality* (Amherst: University of Massachusetts Press, 1978), especially part 1, pp. 3–88, and Stanley Aronowitz, *False Consciousness: The Shaping of the American Working Class* (New York: McGraw-Hill, 1973).

10. Here I am not assuming the characterization of capitalism's distinctiveness offered by capitalist neoclassical economic theory. Rather, I take the distinctive characteristics of a capitalist system to be those identified by Karl Marx. That is, what is distinctive about capitalism is neither unrestricted markets nor the existence of private property per se. Rather, its distinctive feature is the private control of the *means of production* — resources, machines, and other people's labor. Karl Marx, *Capital*, vol. 1 (New York: International Publications, 1967), pp. 579–712.

11. There are, of course, exceptions. Remnants of "the household economy" still function, but most persons' lives are shaped by the separation of economic and cultural activity. Compare Scott Burns, *The Household Economy: Its Shape, Future, and Origin* (Boston: Beacon Press, 1975); Cobb and Sennett, *Hidden Injuries of Class;* and Studs Terkel, *Working* (New York: Pantheon, 1974).

12. Terkel, *Working.* See Rosalyn Baxandall, Linda Gordon, and Susan Reverly, *America's Working Women: A Documentary History, 1600 to the Present* (New York: Random House–Vintage, 1976).

13. Eli Zaretsky, *Capitalism, the Family and Personal Life* (New York: Harper and Row, 1976).

14. Seymour Melman, *Our Depleted Society* (New York: Holt, Rinehart, and Winston, 1965). The most vigorous Christian ethical challenge to this "efficiency" thesis was formulated by Harry Ward. See, for example, *The Profit Motive: Is It Indispensable to Industry?* (New York: New York League for Industrial Development, 1924), especially pp. 18–24, 28–31.

15. Among books that describe this reality well are Seymour Melman, *Pentagon Capitalism* (New York: McGraw-Hill, 1970); Richard J. Barnet, *The Roots of War* (Baltimore: Penguin, 1973); and John Blair, *The Control of Oil* (New York: Random House, 1978).

16. For a spirited rejoinder to this sort of thinking that clarifies the "family as fetish" mentality of dominant groups and the hostility to actual families and children, see Letty Cottin Pogrebin, *Family Politics: Love and Power in an Intimate Frontier* (New York: McGraw-Hill, 1983).

17. The most socially devastating stigmatization falls on the young who are nonwhite, a shocking index of our racism. Though we tolerate unemployment levels of over 20 percent among white youth, we accept a disastrous unemployment rate of over 50 percent among black young people. Furthermore, rates of female unemployment are higher than rates for males in all groups. What this means is that over half of the black children born into this society will never have access even to the lower thresholds of wage labor. Lack of such access is a loss of access to the minimal threshold of survival power in a society such as ours. To put the matter in capitalist (money) terms, the social side effects of such disempowerment are incalculably costly to everyone's social well-being. On the interrelationship of racism and class, see Oliver C. Cox, *Caste, Class and Race* (New York: Monthly Review Press, 1972). See also, William K. Tabb, *The Political Economy of the Black Ghetto* (New York: Norton, 1970).

18. A general work that reliably treats this topic is Douglas Kimmel, *Adulthood and Aging: An Interdisciplinary Developmental View*. (New York: Wiley, 1980). A resource on women and aging is *Age Is Becoming: An Annotated Bibliography on Women and Aging*. (Oakland: Task Force on Older Women, 1976).

19. H. Richard Niebuhr et al., *The Church Against the World* (New York: Willet, Clark, 1935), pp. 1–13, 123–156.

20. Useful discussions of aging and sexuality are contained in The United Church of Christ, *Human Sexuality: A Preliminary Study*. (New York: Pilgrim Press, 1977); Alex Comfort, *A Good Age* (New York: Crown Publishers, 1976); Douglas Kimmel, "Adult Development and Aging: A Gay Perspective," *Journal of Social Issues* 34, no. 3 (1978), pp. 113–130.

21. In fact, typical "nuclear family households" now constitute slightly more than one-third of all the living units in the United States. And in nearly half of these nuclear family units, the mother works outside the home. All these statistics are worth studying. James B. Nelson, *Embodiment: An Approach to Sexuality and Christian Theology* (Minneapolis: Augsburg Press, 1979), notes that nuclear families account for 37 percent of living units, single adults without children 19 percent, single parents with children 12 percent, remarried couples with children 11 percent, childless couples with no children at home 11 percent, experimental family forms 6 percent, three-generation households 4 percent. See also, Letty Cottin Pogrebin, *Family Politics*, pp. ix–x, 1–19.

The Equal Rights Amendment: A Moral Analysis

1. Leo Kanowitz, *Women and the Law: An Unfinished Revolution* (Albuquerque: University of New Mexico Press, 1974); Barbara A. Brown, Ann E. Freedman, Harriet Katz, and Alice M. Price, *Women's Rights and the Law: The Impact of ERA on State Laws* (New York: Praeger, 1977); Barbara Allen Babcock, Ann E. Freedman, Eleanor Holmes Norton, Susan C. Ross, *Sexual Discrimination and the Law* (Boston: Little, Brown, 1975, supplement 1978).

2. California Commission on the Status of Women, *Impact ERA: Limitations and Possibilities* (Millbrae, Calif.: Les Femmes Publishers, 1976).

3. For discussion of this theory, see Barbara A. Brown, Thomas Emerson, Gail Falk, and Ann E. Freedman, "The Equal Rights Amendment: A Constitutional Basis for Equal Rights for Women," 80, *Yale Law Journal* 871 (1971), reprinted in Babcock et al., *Sexual Discrimination and the Law*.

4. H. L. A. Hart, "Are There Any Natural Rights?" and Richard Wasserstrom, "Rights, Human Rights, and Racial Discrimination," in *Rights*, ed. David Lyons (Belmont, Calif.: Wadsworth, 1979), pp. 14–25, 46–57. On the importance of feminist notions of equality, see Louise Marcil-Lacoste, "The Trivialization of the Notion of Equality," *Discovering Reality*, ed. Sandra Harding and Merill B. Hintikka (Dordrecht, Holland: Reidel Publishing Company, 1983), pp. 121–137.

5. In this book I cite the most important literature that challenges so-called scientific justifications of gender difference. See, for example, Ann Oakley, *Sex, Gender and Society* (New York: Harper and Row, 1972); Martin Duberman, *Gender and Sex in Society* (New York: Praeger, 1975); and Clarice Stasz Stoll, *Sexism: Scientific Debates* (Reading, Mass.: Addison-Wesley, 1973). A generally reliable overview of the gender differences that actually have been confirmed empirically is Eleanor Maccoby and Carolyn Jacklin, *The Psychology of Sex Differences* (Stanford: Stanford University Press, 1974). Even some of the limited number of differences they confirm have been challenged by later researchers.

6. Karen Stallard, Barbara Ehrenreich, and Holly Sklar, *Poverty in the American Dream* (Boston: South End Press, 1983). Alice Amsden, ed., *The Economics of Women and Work* (New York: St. Martin's Press, 1980). The term

"feminization of poverty" was recently coined to designate alarming global trends. Interpreters believe that over 80 percent of the desperately poor are women and their dependent children. Others predict that by 1990, ninety percent of those so classified will be from this group. See also Ann H. Stromberg and Shirley Harkness, eds., *Women Working: Theories and Facts in Perspective* (Palo Alto, Calif.: Mayfield Publishing, 1978).

7. It may startle some readers that I lump together crass ideologists such as George Gilder and Michael Novak with the widely revered Freudian psychiatrist Bruno Bettelheim and the "moderate" historian Christopher Lasch. Feminists, however, cannot let subtle antiwomen ideology go unnamed anymore than blatant misogyny. What these men all have in common is their intellectual effort aimed to provide a rationale that discredits sex role change. All are also nostalgic about the family. Bettelheim uses a wooden Freudianism to justify his views, Lasch a historical cynicism. Bruno Bettelheim, *The Uses of Enchantment* (New York: Random House–Vintage, 1977), pp. 11, 83, 111f., 320, n. 83, and *Surviving and Other Essays* (New York: Random House-Vintage, 1980), pp. 221–238, 370–386; Christopher Lasch, *The Culture of Narcissism: American Life in an Age of Diminishing Expectations* (New York: Warner Books, 1979) and *Haven in A Heartless World* (New York: Basic Books, 1979). For an analysis of Lasch's assumptions about women, see Berenice M. Fisher, "The Wise Old Men and the New Women: Christopher Lasch Besieged," *History of Education Quarterly* 19, no. 1 (1978), pp. 125–141. Michael Novak, *Democracy and Mediating Structures: A Theological Inquiry* (Washington, D.C.: American Enterprise, 1981), *The Spirit of Democratic Capitalism* (New York: Simon and Schuster, 1982), *The Denigration of Capitalism* (Washington, D.C.: American Enterprise, 1979), *Towards a Theology of the Corporation* (Washington, D.C.: American Enterprise, 1981); George Gilder, *Visible Man* (New York: Basic Books, 1978) and *Wealth and Poverty* (New York: Bantam, 1982).

8. Michael Lewis, *Culture of Inequality* (Amherst: University of Massachusetts Press, 1979).

The Politics of Energy Policy

1. The term is taken from the well-known book that aims to help women develop a holistic view of health and sexuality. The Boston Women's Health Collective, *Our Bodies, Ourselves* (New York: Simon and Schuster, 1972). The analogies between our alienation from nature and our alienation from the body have been widely recognized by feminists and, increasingly, integrated into discussions of ecojustice.

2. An important source for understanding what I mean by "the ecological perspective" is Barry Commoner's *The Closing Circle* (New York: Knopf, 1971).

3. The centrality of relationship in feminist theory and its implications for theology and ecology are nowhere better developed than in the work of Carter Heyward. See above, nn. 23, 28, and 5, pp. 271, 272. Outstanding discussions of the task of feminist theory in relation to ecology/nature are found in Ynesta King, "Feminism and the Revolt," and Joan L. Griscom, "On Healing the Nature/History Split in Feminist Thought," *Heresies: A Feminist Publication on Art and Politics*, 4, no. 1 (1981), pp. 12–16, 4–9.

4. Pamela McAllister, ed., *Reweaving the Web of Life: Feminism and Nonviolence* (New York: New Society Publishers, 1982); Starhawk, *The Spiral Dance: A Rebirth of the Ancient Religion of the Great Goddess* (San Francisco: Harper and Row, 1979) and *Dreaming the Dark: Magic, Sex, and Politics* (Boston: Beacon Press, 1982); Charlene Spretnak, ed., *The Politics of Women's Spirituality* (New York: Anchor, 1982); Elizabeth Dodson Gray, *Green Paradise Lost* (Wellesley, Mass.: Roundtable Press, 1982).

5. Carole Pateman, *Participation and Democratic Theory* (Cambridge: Cambridge University Press, 1970).

6. See, for example, Aldo Leopold, "The Conservation Ethic," in *The Ecological Conscience*, ed. Robert Disch (Englewood Cliffs, N.J.: Prentice-Hall, 1970).

7. The term is borrowed from Richard Bond, "Salvationists, Utilitarians, and Environmental Justice" (Mimeographed essay presented to the Group for Interdisciplinary Educational Research, Ramapo College Colloquium, Mahwah, N.J., 1975).

8. The phrase is standard in contemporary discussion of moral philosophy. Compare John Rawls, *A Theory of Justice* (Cambridge: Harvard University Press, 1971), pp. 3ff. When moral philosophers like Rawls make this point, they generally mean to *restrict* the norm of justice to the specific arena of institutional relations. The biblical norm of justice does not lend itself to such restriction. For a critique of the liberal theory of justice, see Michael J. Sandel, *Liberalism and the Limits of Justice* (Cambridge: Cambridge University Press, 1982). My own views on this norm are further elaborated in "The Dream of a Common Language: Toward a Normative Theory of Justice in Christian Ethics," Society of Christian Ethics, *Annual of the Society of Christian Ethics, 1983* (Waterloo, Ontario: Council on the Study of Religion, 1983), pp. 1–25. Obviously, I have borrowed this title from Adrienne Rich.

9. An important theological analysis of this view of justice is found in Gustavo Gutierrez, *A Theology of Liberation* (Maryknoll, N.Y.: Orbis Press, 1973), especially part 4. See also Gutierrez, *The Power of the Poor in History* (Maryknoll, N.Y.: Orbis Press, 1983).

10. Cf. Matt. 25:30–46; Mark 1:21–28, 10:35–45; and parallels. For an excellent discussion of the contemporary significance of such texts, see Dorothee Sölle, *Political Theology* (Philadelphia: Fortress Press, 1974), chapters 3–8.

11. For clarification of various metaphors of justice, see Eugene Outka, *Agape* (New Haven: Yale University Press), pp. 75–92.

12. *Exploring Energy Choices: A Preliminary Report* (New York: Energy Policy Project of the Ford Foundation, 1974), pp. 23–28.

13. Robert Engler, *The Brotherhood of Oil* (New York: New American Library, 1977), chapter 4.

14. Dramatically different ways of assessing government costs of nuclear power development can be seen by comparing Richard Munson, ed., *Countdown to a Nuclear Moratorium* (Washington, D.C.: Environmental Action Foundation, 1976), and John Francis and Paul Albrecht, eds., *Facing Up to Nuclear Power* (Philadelphia: Westminster Press, 1976).

15. Engler, *Brotherhood of Oil*, and John Blair, *The Control of Oil* (New York: Random House, 1978), pp. 371–400.

16. Blair, *The Control of Oil*, chapters 4, 7, 8; Engler, *Brotherhood of Oil*, pp. 139–198.

17. Alexander Cockburn and James Ridgeway, "Carter's Powerless Energy Policy," *New York Review of Books*, 24 May 1977, pp. 31–36.

18. Robert Leckachman, "Carter's Energy Plan: Grade It C for Effort," *Christianity and Crisis* 37, no. 8 (16 May 1977), pp. 98–99.

19. For a summary of the complex compromise initially adopted on natural gas pricing, see *The New York Times*, 10 Nov. 1978, pp. D1, D14. Needless to say, this compromise has been totally undermined by Reagan administration policy.

20. Those interested in studying the corporate positions can obtain a booklet containing major advertisements run by the Mobil Oil Corporation during the debate: P.O. Box NP, Mobil, 150 East 42nd Street, New York, NY 10017.

21. *New York Times*, 17 April 1977, p. E7, no. 6.

22. *New York Times*, 17 April 1977, p. E7, no. 8.

23. *New York Times*, 17 April 1977, p. E7, no. 6.

24. This way of distinguishing "need" and luxuries is informed by Denis Goulet, *The Cruel Choice: A New Concept in the Theory of Development* (New York: Atheneum, 1973), pp. 240f. Those who argue that "need" is too subjective to be used in ethics should ponder Agnes Heller, *The Theory of Need in Marx* (London: Allison and Busby, 1978).

25. Campaign for Human Development, United States Catholic Conference, *Poverty in American Democracy* (Washington, D.C., 1974). This study is a refutation of the argument that it is the poor who benefit chiefly from government expenditures. See also Eugene Toland et al., *World Justice and Peace: A Challenge to American Christians* (Maryknoll, New York: Church Research and Information Project, 1976).

26. Michael Harrington, *The Other America* (New York: Macmillan, 1970). U.S. poverty data is updated in Michael Harrington, *The New American Poverty* (New York: Holt, Rinehart and Winston, 1984), pp. 77f. and 207–229.

27. E. J. Kahn, "Who, What, Where, How Much, How Many," *New Yorker*, 15 Oct. 1973. United States Commission on Civil Rights, *Civil Rights Digest* (Spring 1974), pp. 20f. Elizabeth Higginbotham, "Laid Bare by the System: Work and Survival for Black and Hispanic Women," in *Class, Race, and Sex: The Dynamics of Control*, ed. Amy Swerdlow and Hanna Lessinger (Boston: G. K. Hall, 1983), pp. 200–215. See also Eugene Jones, "Getting to the Roots" (Unpublished manuscript, Union Theological Seminary, New York, 1984). Using data provided by the U.S. government, Jones recalculated poverty levels, replacing the government's thirty-year-old food cost index with an index adjusted to account for inflation rates. He discovered that rather than the over 34 million poor reported by the government, that there are between 63 and 69 million persons in the United States who should be so classified. Harrington's estimates in the work cited in note 26 are somewhat lower.

28. For specification regarding the role played by these groups in advanced industrial society, see Barbara and John Ehrenreich, "The Professional-Managerial Class," *Radical America* 11, no. 2 (March-April 1977), pp. 7–31, and "The New Left and the Professional-Managerial Class," *Radical America* 11, no. 3 (May–June 1977), pp. 7–22. Debate as to whether it is appropriate to designate this group as a class has been vigorous. In spite of this controversy, the Ehrenreichs' thesis regarding the distinctive role of this group in the contemporary economy is important. These essays and a debate about them are in Pat Walker, ed., *Between Labor and Capital* (Boston: South End Press, 1979).

29. Leonard Silk, "Economic Scene: Energy Prices and Inflation," *New York Times*, 7 Nov. 1978, p. 68.

30. Production increases and reduced consumption due to economic slowdowns temporarily stabilized and slightly reduced gasoline prices, but these adjustments do not fully reflect the market price reduction.

31. Bob Swierczek and David Tyler, "Energy and the Poor," *Christianity and Crisis* 38, no. 15 (16 Oct. 1978), pp. 242–246.

32. Cockburn and Ridgeway, "Carter's Powerless Energy Policy."

33. Richard Grossman and Gail Daneker, "Jobs and Energy" (Washington, D.C.: Environmentalists for Full Employment, Spring 1977).

34. Richard Grossman, "Energy and Employment," *Christianity and Crisis* 28, no. 15 (16 Oct. 1978), p. 247f.

35. For specification of some U.S. aid policies related to energy that can help the poor, see Swierczek and Tyler, "Energy and the Poor."

36. See Douglas Still, "Ways to Influence Energy Systems," in *Energy Ethics* ed. Dieter T. Hessel (New York: Friendship Press, 1979), pp. 72–96.

The Early Feminists and the Clergy

1. As quoted in R. Pierce Beaver, *All Loves Excelling: American Protestant Women in World Mission* (Grand Rapids, Mich.: Eerdmans, 1968), p. 105. Beaver does not identify the source of the quotation. His account of the activities of women in the mission enterprise makes clear the extent of change with respect to women's activity in the churches in the nineteenth century.

2. "Discontent" was, by the conventions of the time, a woman's major spiritual failing, perhaps analogous to being "neurotic" today. Women were always being charged with it, and they turned the charge to good account for the purposes of their movement. Compare Lucy Stone, "Disappointment Is the Lot of Woman," in *Feminism: The Essential Historical Writings*, ed. Miriam Schneir (New York: Vintage, 1972), pp. 106–109.

3. In fact, the reactions to such events were often more violent in the 1870s than they had been earlier. Elizabeth Cady Stanton, Susan B. Anthony, and Matilda Joclyn Gage, *The History of Woman Suffrage*, vol. 1 (New York: Fowler and Weels, 1881), pp. 481ff., 531ff., passim.

4. "Pastoral Letter: The General Association of Massachusetts (Orthodox) to the Churches Under Their Care," 1837, in *The Feminist Papers*, ed. Alice Rossi (New York: Bantam, 1974), pp. 305ff.

5. The deepest expression of these tensions can be traced in debates about the post–Civil War settlement and enfranchising slaves. A major schism among women's rights advocates (male and female) arose over the Fourteenth Amendment. The version adopted guaranteed "males" the right to vote, thereby introducing the term "male" into the Constitution. Some abolitionists agreed to this compromise, but feminists wished to avoid any wording that did not enfranchise black men and white and black women. Before this amendment, feminists had expected that women would be enfranchised by a judicial decision that would set aside the unwritten tradition that the "rights of man" referred only to males. After adoption of the Fourteenth Amendment, only a brutal constitutional amendment process could secure suffrage for women. See Eleanor Flexner, *Century of Struggle* (New York: Atheneum, 1971), pp. 142–163.

6. See below, page 198f. and p. 297, n. 26.

7. See Stanton et al., *History of Woman Suffrage*. So appreciative were these "radical" feminists of support from the clergy that they marked a sermon sympathetic to women's rights preached in Syracuse, N.Y., in 1845 as worthy of a full paragraph in their documentary history of events that led to the suffrage movement (p. 40).

8. See Beverly Harrison, "Sexism and the Contemporary Church," in *Sexist Religion and Women in the Church*, ed. Alice Hageman (New York: Association Press, 1974), especially pp. 205f.

9. Rossi, *Feminist Papers*, p. 413.

10. See below, pp. 199f. and 227f.

11. The Seneca Falls Declaration is recorded in Stanton et al., *History of Woman Suffrage*, pp. 70–75, and in Rossi, *Feminist Papers*, pp. 415–421.

12. Stanton et al., *History of Woman Suffrage*, p. 75.

13. Weld, however, did not withdraw support. He remained a stout feminist. Many who had signed the Seneca Falls Declaration did withdraw their names. Stanton et al., *History of Woman Suffrage*, p. 78.

14. Stanton et al., *History of Woman Suffrage*, cf. pp. 76 and 124. At one early convention, men were not permitted to speak. The women recorded: "Never did men so suffer," having to sit and listen. However, this is the only early occasion recorded when that procedure was adopted (p. 110).

15. The same dynamic exists today between secular and religious feminists. The strength of feminism in the churches is little appreciated by academic

feminists because the force of social movements as a generating source of feminism is recognized insufficiently.

16. Rossi, *Feminist Papers*, p. 246.

17. The point Rossi misses is that class consciousness among the feminists is related to the extent to which they had been touched by New England, especially Bostonian, intellectualism. Hence, the more religiously "sophisticated" feminists were more likely to manifest a certain attitude of noblesse oblige, and (alas!) racism in later years (Stanton and Anthony) than those who were evangelicals. Their "sexual prudery" also needs to be understood in context. Many feminists found sex distasteful because they, like many women of the time, experienced sexual relations as the "price" they had to pay males for "protecting" them. Marriage was no choice for nineteenth-century women.

18. Angelina Grimké, "An Appeal to the Christian Woman of the South," *The Anti-Slavery Examiner*, vol. 1 (Sept. 1836). Compare Rossi, *Feminist Papers*, pp. 282–322.

19. Stanton et al., *History of Woman Suffrage*, pp. 78f.

20. Stanton et al., *History of Woman Suffrage*. On one occasion the presence of and request to speak by ex-slave Sojourner Truth nearly caused a riot. Frances Gage insisted that she be given the floor, whereupon she silenced the crowd by delivering her famous "Ain't I a Woman" speech, which Gage recorded for posterity. Schneir, *Feminism*, pp. 93–95. The later dynamics of racism in the women's rights movement betrayed its early egalitarian heritage. Compare Angela Davis, *Women, Race and Class* (New York: Random House, 1981); Bell Hooks, *Ain't I a Woman: Black Women and Feminism* (Boston: South End Press, 1981); Barbara Andolsen, "Racism in the 19th and 20th Century American Feminist Movements: An Ethical Appraisal (Unpublished thesis, Vanderbilt University, Nashville, Tenn., 1981); Betina Aptheker, *Woman's Legacy: Essays on Race, Sex and Class in American History* (Amherst: University of Massachusetts Press, 1982).

21. Alexis de Tocqueville, among others, and Harriett Martineau in Rossi, *Feminist Papers*, pp. 125ff.

22. Frances Murray and Martineau came to the United States to see for themselves the effects of the "new world" freedom on women. John Stuart Mill also cited the American experience of women as evidence on the point.

23. Rossi, *Feminist Papers*, pp. 254f.

24. Beaver, *All Loves Excelling*, p. 43.

25. Stanton et al., *History of Woman Suffrage*, p. 80.

26. Stanton's theism was extremely sophisticated philosophically. In later life she granted no special authority to scripture but thought that, sexism aside, the Bible could hold its own with the wisdom of the ages. See her Introduction and various exegetical contributions to *The Woman's Bible* (New York: European Publishing Company, 1895). The theological sophistication of the early feminists is especially noteworthy in view of the fact that the first generation had had no formal schooling of any sort. An important analysis is Mary Pellauer in "The Religious Social Thought of Three United States Woman Suffrage Leaders: Towards a Tradition of Feminist Theology" (Unpublished diss., University of Chicago Divinity School, Chicago, 1980).

27. Pellauer, "Religious Social Thought."

28. "Full moral person" meant in the nineteenth century what "being fully human" means today. For the "radical" feminists, moral personhood meant both intellect and sensibility. They did not accept the conventional split between intellect and feeling.

29. See Stanton et al., *History of Woman Suffrage*, pp. 76, 143f., passim, and Schneir, *Feminism*, pp. 99f.

30. While they infrequently attended women's rights meetings, letters from them were often read. Stanton et al., *History of Woman Suffrage*, p. 353, passim.

31. Stanton et al., *History of Woman Suffrage*, p. 133.

32. Stanton et al., *History of Woman Suffrage*, p. 75. It is to their credit that they record this fact and confess that they nearly left the meeting "in disgust" at the prospect of a woman presiding officer.

33. As happened at a temperance meeting at the 1853 World's Fair when Antoinette Brown arrived to participate. Stanton et al., *History of Woman Suffrage*, pp. 507f. The women had learned, from their abolitionist days, that prayer frequently "softened the mob" (p. 285).

34. Harrison, "Sexism and the Contemporary Church." For an excellent discussion of the use of theology as a buffer against social change, see Dorothee Sölle, *Political Theology* (Philadelphia: Fortress Press, 1973).

35. H. Richard Niebuhr bears some responsibility for misstating the "faith" and "culture" issue by adopting an ambiguous definition of culture (borrowed from Bronislaw Malinowski) in his book *Christ and Culture* (New York: Harper, 1951), p. 32. Malinowski's definition is ambiguous because he defined culture as both the total process of human activity and as an *artificial*, secondary environment. The latter definition buys in on the older notion of "culture" as "high culture" or *conscious* activity. Anthropologists no longer admit that definition. "Culture" is now used as a field-encompassing concept.

36. This was a point made often by H. Richard Niebuhr. See "The Christian Church and the World Crisis," *Christianity and Society* 6 (1941), pp. 11–17.

37. Somewhat erroneously. See H. R. Trevor-Roper, "The Great Witch Craze of the Sixteenth and Seventeenth Centuries and Other Essays" (New York: Harper Torchbooks, 1967). The too-easy confidence that Protestant Christianity raised the status of women is beautifully illustrated in Beaver's generally admirable work. He blithely records the adamant opposition of Hindu upper-class fathers to the education of their daughters. To understand how similar they were to American fathers of the nineteenth century, he should read the autobiographical accounts of the feminists. Nor did male churchmen contribute much to the changing attitude of U.S. fathers in this regard. Beaver, *All Loves Excelling*, p. 69.

38. New York State had passed the first law giving women property rights in 1848. It took twelve years of work to get the change. Stanton led the fight and had ventured testimony on the subject to a New York Assembly committee. New York set a good precedent. Later the new western states followed suit in their constitutions.

39. It is one of the many virtues of Beaver's study that he so clearly and candidly documents the contention that it was the power of women to raise money that generated real pressure for change in the nineteenth-century churches.

Keeping Faith in a Sexist Church

1. I discuss the reasons for this in "Sexism and the Contemporary Church: When Evasion Becomes Complicity," in *Sexist Religion and Women in the Church: No More Silence!*, ed. Alice L. Hageman (New York: Association Press, 1974), pp. 195–216.

2. Harrison, "Sexism and the Contemporary Church." Some scholars question the thesis that there was so marked a setback to the feminist movement. See Alice Rossi, ed., *The Feminist Papers* (New York: Bantam, 1973), pp. 279f., and Dale Spender, *There's Always Been a Women's Movement this Century* (London: Pandora Press, 1983). I agree with Rayna Rapp and Ellen

Ross, "The Twenties' Backlash: Compulsory Heterosexuality, the Consumer Family, and the Waning of Feminism," in *Class, Race, and Sex: The Dynamics of Control,* ed. Amy Swerdlow and Hanna Lessinger (Boston: G. K. Hall, 1983), pp. 93–107.

3. Matina S. Horner, "Toward an Understanding of Achievement-Related Conflicts in Women," *Journal of Social Issues* 28 (1972), pp. 157–175. Horner's research precipitated wide discussion of the way in which women's socialization creates ambivalence toward success. Since then, some subsequent research has suggested that younger women have made progress in overcomin this sort of ambivalence. My generation did not find it easy to do so.

4. This professional theological degree is now standardized as the Master of Divinity (M.Div.) degree.

5. Marian Derby, "Where Have All the Women Gone?" (Mimeographed papers, World Division of the United Methodist Board of Missions, New York, undated).

6. Early in the second wave of feminism, I shared the exuberance of others regarding sisterhood. See Robin Morgan, ed., *Sisterhood Is Powerful: An Anthology of Writings from the Women's Liberation Movement* (New York: Vintage, 1970), and Mary Daly, *Beyond God the Father: Toward a Philosophy of Women's Liberation* (Boston: Beacon Press, 1973). For me, the existential support of other women has been real and substantive, but I now am more sensitive to the depth of divisions among women as well. See Nancy Richardson, ed., for the Cornwall Collective, *Our Daughters Shall Prophesy* (New York: Pilgrim Press, 1980); the Mudflower Collective, *God's Fierce Whimsey: The Role of Feminism in Theological Education* (New York: Pilgrim Press, 1985); and Carter Heyward, "An Unfinished Symphony of Liberation: The Radicalization of Christian Feminism Among White U.S. Women," *Journal of Feminist Studies in Religion* 1, no. 1 (1985), pp. 99–118.

7. Thomas J. J. Altizer, *The Gospel of Christian Atheism* (Philadelphia: Westminster Press, 1966), and Thomas J. J. Altizer and William Hamilton, *Radical Theology and the Death of God* (Indianapolis: Bobbs-Merrill, 1966).

8. Betty Friedan, *The Feminine Mystique* (New York: Norton, 1963).

9. Robin Morgan, *Sisterhood Is Powerful,* passim.

10. Mary Buckley and Janet Kalven, *Womanspirit Bonding* (New York: Pilgrim Press, 1984). See, for example, Susanna Heschel, ed., *On Being a Jewish Feminist* (New York: Schocken, 1983); Elizabeth Koltun, ed., *The Jewish Woman: New Perspectives* (New York: Schocken, 1976); Judith Plaskow, "God and Feminism," *Menorah* 3, no. 2 (1982), pp. 1–5; Mary Daly, *Gyn/Ecology: The Metaethics of Radical Feminism* (Boston: Beacon Press, 1978); Starhawk, *The Spiral Dance: A Rebirth of the Ancient Religion of the Great Goddess* (San Francisco: Harper and Row, 1979); Carol P. Christ, *Diving Deep and Surfacing: Women Writers on Spiritual Quest* (Boston: Beacon Press, 1980); Carol P. Christ and Judith Plaskow, eds., *WomanSpirit Rising: A Feminist Reader in Religion* (San Francisco: Harper and Row, 1979); Naomi Goldenberg, *Changing of the Gods: Feminism and the End of Traditional Religions* (Boston: Beacon Press, 1979). For a compendium of writings on feminist spirituality, see Charlene Spretnak, ed., *The Politics of Women's Spirituality* (New York: Doubleday-Anchor, 1982).

11. Peter Berger, *Pyramids of Sacrifice: Political Ethics and Social Change* (New York: Basic Books, 1976).

12. See "The Power of Anger in the Work of Love" in this book.

13. Elisabeth Schüssler Fiorenza, *In Memory of Her: A Feminist Theological Reconstruction of Christian Origins* (New York: Crossroads, 1983); Elizabeth Fox Genovese, "Placing Women's History in History," *New Left Review* 133 (May–June 1982), pp. 5–29.

14. Mary Wollstonecraft, *A Vindication of the Rights of Woman* (New York: Norton, 1967).

15. See, for example, Alice Rossi, *Feminist Papers*, pp. 258f., 282–322. See also "Lucretia Mott" in Miriam Schneir, ed., *Feminism: The Essential Historical Writings* (New York: Vintage, 1972), pp. 100f.

16. While I have used the most literal English translation of the New Testament phraseology here, I prefer the Puritan terminology "Commonwealth of God" as more appropriate.

17. The charge is frequently made that a political reading of the Christian New Testament is anachronistic. In fact, it is just as anachronistic to refer to the Jesus movement and the early Christian community as religious. Cult and piety were not differentiated from the organization of the social order or politics until much later, after the culture of the Mediterranean basin was Romanized and Europeanized. See Donald R. Kelley, *The Beginning of Ideology, Consciousness and Society in the French Reformation* (Cambridge: Cambridge University Press, 1981), for an analysis of the differentiation of the political sphere in society.

18. See, for example, Matt. 12:38–42, 46–50; 19:16–30; 20:25–28; 22:34–40; 23:1–13 and parallels in Luke and Mark.

19. Joseph Pieper, *The Silence of St. Thomas*, trans. John Murray, S.J., and Daniel O'Connor (Chicago: Regnery, 1957).

20. Both Dorothee Sölle and Carter Heyward have explored the strengths and weaknesses of Enlightenment liberalism: Dorothee Sölle, *Suffering* (Philadelphia: Fortress, 1975) and *The Truth Is Concrete* (London: Burns & Oates, 1967); Carter Heyward, *Our Passion for Justice: Images of Power, Sexuality, and Liberation* (New York: Pilgrim Press, 1984).

21. My conviction regarding the irreplaceability of justice as a fundamental moral norm derives from my belief that no other moral norm, including "caring," adequately incorporates the structural-relational dimensions of life that justice illumines. On this point, my position is evidently in disagreement with Carol Gilligan's. There are hints of this sharp contrast between justice and caring in her published work, *In a Different Voice: Psychological Theory and Women's Development* (Cambridge: Harvard University Press, 1982), pp. 59, 100f., and especially p. 174. More recently in public presentations, she has explicitly denied the relevance of justice to women's morality.

22. Robert William Fogel and Stanley L. Engerman, *Time On The Cross* (Boston: Little, Brown, 1974).

23. See "Theological Reflection in the Struggle for Liberation" in this book.

24. Gustavo Gutierrez, *The Power of the Poor in History: Selected Writings*, trans. Robert R. Barr (Maryknoll, N.Y.: Orbis Press, 1983).

25. Carter Heyward, *The Redemption of God: A Theology of Mutual Relation* (Washington, D.C.: University Press of America, 1982), p. 2 and passim. Also see her " 'In the Beginning Is the Relation': Toward a Christian Ethic of Sexuality," *Integrity Forum* 7, no. 2 (Lent 1981), pp. 1–6.

26. Cherrie Moraga, *Loving in the War Years* (Boston: South End Press, 1983).

27. Barbara Welter, *Dimity Convictions: The American Woman in the Nineteenth Century* (Athens, Ohio: Ohio University Press, 1976). See also Nancy Boyd-Franklin, "Black Family Life-Styles: A Lesson in Survival," pp. 189–199, Bonnie Thornton Dill, " 'On the Hem of Life': Race, Class, and the Prospects for Sisterhood," pp. 173–188, and Cheryl Townsend Gilkes, "From Slavery to Social Welfare: Racism and the Control of Black Women," pp. 288–300, in Swerdlow and Lessinger, *Class, Race and Sex*. Katie G. Cannon, "Moral Wisdom in the Black Women's Literary Tradition," *The Annual of the Society of Christian Ethics, 1984* (Waterloo, Ontario, 1984), pp. 171–192. It has been suggested that "the good girl" syndrome characteristic of middle-strata white women may be the result of a largely unconscious fear of violence. Given the denial tendencies characteristic of white culture and the pervasiveness of violence, this may be true.

28. I do not mean to imply that feminists have lacked creativity in changing liturgy. See Linda Clark, Marian Ronan, and Eleanor Walker, *Image-Breaking, Image-Building: A Handbook for Creative Worship with Women of Christian Tradition* (New York: Pilgrim Press, 1981).

29. The feminist theologian who has sensitized many of us to this point most dramatically is Nelle Morton. See *The Journey Is Home* (Boston: Beacon Press, 1985).

30. Lynn White Jr., "The Historical Roots of Our Ecological Crisis," in David and Eileen Spring (eds.), *Ecology and Religion in History* (New York: Harper & Row, 1964), p. 25.

31. Mary Daly, *Beyond God the Father* and *Gyn/Ecology*.

32. Daly's sense of the power of sisterhood is promethean. See *Beyond God the Father*, chapter 5.

33. Daly's definition of *necrophilia* is found in *Gyn/Ecology*, p. 59.

Theological Reflection in the Struggle for Liberation

1. The term "senior friends" is used widely in Student Christian Movement circles to refer to those faculty or church-related persons concerned for higher education who relate to, but are not directly members of, such movements. The original audience for this section of the essay was the World Student Christian Movement General Assembly in Colombo, Sri Lanka, January 1977.

2. See above, p. 299, n. 6, and p. 300, n. 27.

3. The phrase is Mary O'Brien's in *The Politics of Reproduction* (London: Routledge and Kegan Paul, 1981), pp. 5ff.

4. See above, p. 300, n. 27, and p. 297, n. 20. See also Michelle Russell, "Black-Eyed Blues Connection," in *All the Women Are White, All the Blacks Are Men, but Some of Us Are Brave*, ed. Gloria Hull et al. (Old Westbury, Conn.: Feminist Press, 1981), pp. 196–207.

5. The machinations of U.S. senators were aimed at dividing white feminists and black people. See "The Feminists and the Clergy" in this book. See also Barbara Smith, "Racism and Women's Studies," in Hull, *All the Women Are White*, pp. 48–51.

6. On the theology of relationship, see Alice Walker, *The Color Purple* (New York: Harcourt Brace Jovanovich, 1982). "Everything is related to everything else" is the official slogan of a feminist ecology group. See Joan L. Griscom, "On Healing the Nature/History Split in Feminist Thought," *Heresies: A Feminist Publication on Art and Politics* 4, no. 1 (1981).

7. Michelle Russell, "Women, Work and Politics in the United States," in *Theology in the Americas*, ed. Sergio Torres and John Eagleson (Maryknoll, N.Y.: Orbis Press, 1976), p. 350.

8. Elisabeth Schüssler Fiorenza, *In Memory of Her: A Feminist Theological Reconstruction of Christian Origins* (New York: Crossroads, 1983), and *Bread Not Stone: The Challenge of Feminist Biblical Interpretation* (Boston: Beacon Press, 1985). Phyllis Trible, *Texts of Terror* (Philadelphia: Fortress Press, 1984).

9. Karl Marx, *The Grundrisse*, ed. and trans. David McLellan (New York: Harper and Row, 1971), pp. 59–76, 117–147.

10. I have heard this phrase used among Latin American liberation theologians to refer to the nondogmatic and fully critical awareness of the destructiveness of capitalism. The term is contrasted with the nonexistential interest of academics in Marxism. See above, p. 279, n. 25. Compare pp. 75–76 above.

11. The phrase has been popularized by Paolo Freire, *Pedagogy of the Oppressed*, trans. Myrna Bergman Ramos (New York: Herder and Herder, 1970) and *Education For Critical Consciousness* (New York: Seabury Press, 1973).

12. Sheila Rowbotham, *Woman's Consciousness, Man's World* (Harmondsworth, England: Penguin, 1973), pp. 29–30.

13. Juan Luis Segundo, *The Liberation of Theology*, trans. John Drury (Maryknoll, N.Y.: Orbis Press, 1976), pp. 178–182. I do not, of course, accept Segundo's astonishing equation of divinity and maleness, pp. 37–38, n. 55.

14. How one defines *reality* is critical to how one grounds ethical reasoning. See Anthony Battaglia, *Toward a Reformulation of Natural Law* (New York: Seabury Press, 1981), and Sandra Harding and Merill B. Hintikka, eds., *Discovering Reality* (Dordrecht, Holland: Reidel Publishing Company, 1983).

15. Miriam Wolf Wasserman and Linda Hutchinson, *Teaching Human Dignity: Social Change Lessons for Every Teacher* (Minneapolis: Education Exploration Center, 1978).

16. The feminist in question is Elise Boulding, whose work in peace education is superlative. See *The Underside of History: A View of Women Through Time* (Boulder, Colo.: Westview Press, 1976).

17. See above, p. 281, n. 46, pp. 290, 291 and nn. 6, 7, 10.

18. For a discussion of the hermeneutic circle, see Juan Luis Segundo, *Liberation of Theology*, pp. 1–73. For a criticism of Segundo's position, see Elisabeth Schüssler Fiorenza, "Toward a Feminist Biblical Hermeneutics: Biblical Interpretation and Liberation Theology," ed. B. Mahan and Dale Richesin in *The Challenge of Liberation Theology* (Maryknoll, N.Y.: Orbis Press, 1981), pp. 91–112.

19. The stages I use here were first suggested to me by Carol S. Robb, in a paper she presented to the Consultation on Social Ethics in Feminist Perspective and later published as "Frameworks in Feminist Ethics," *Journal of Religious Ethics 9* (Spring 1981), pp. 48–68.

20. Michael Albert, *What Is to Be Undone: A Modern Revolutionary Discussion of Classical Left Ideologies* (Boston: Porter Sargent, 1975).

21. See Simone Weil, *The Need for Roots* (London: Routledge and Kegan Paul, 1952), p. 225.

22. The aphorism is Lord Acton's, used in a letter to Bishop Mandell Creighton, April 5, 1887.

23. See Carter Heyward, *Our Passion for Justice: Images of Power, Sexuality, and Liberation* (New York: Pilgrim Press, 1984).

24. This is an important point in understanding the nature of ethics. A "moral dilemma" is, by definition, one that is contestable. Otherwise ethical reasoning would not be needed. See Dorothy Emmet, *The Moral Prism* (New York: St. Martin's Press, 1979), especially pp. 1–17.

25. Beverly Wildung Harrison, *Our Right to Choose: Toward a New Ethic of Abortion* (Boston: Beacon Press, 1983), pp. 14ff. Suggestive defenses of utilitarian theory are contained in Tom L. Beauchamp's discussion of suicide in *Matters of Life and Death: New Introductory Essays in Moral Philosophy*, ed. Tom Regan (New York: Random House, 1980), pp. 67–108.

26. See above, pp. 129f. and 302, n. 3.

27. Dorothy Emmet, *The Moral Prism*, treats this theme well. Pp. 5–17, 144–158.

28. I subscribe to the thesis that universalization has a key role in moral reasoning, both as a rational criterion for testing action guides themselves — what sort of society would it be if everyone did the proscribed or prescribed action? — and also as a test of acts — that is, I should do what I would want anyone to do in the same or analogous circumstances. I believe, however, that some Christian ethicists assume inflated and unjustified theories of universalization, for example, that there is a hierarchy of obvious and unexceptional moral principles or that a Christian ethic must be committed

to an abstract, ideal formula of the good, whose meaning is unspecific and unrelated to context. Persons who construe a Christian ethic in this way seem, almost invariably, to accuse those with a different moral theory of being "unprincipled." These criticisms of liberation ethics predictably involve claims alluded to here — that liberation theologians are "crassly utilitarian," that we embrace violence, as if violence were a moral norm. Such criticisms seem to me to derive from ahistorical and asocial abstractness in the use of moral theory. There is ambiguity in moral theory as to what is meant by the "overridingness" of moral principles.

29. See above, p. 295, n. 4.

30. An obvious exception among liberation theologians is Dom Helder Camara, *The Spiral of Violence,* trans. Della Couling (London: Sheed and Ward, 1971).

31. Compare, for example, G. H. C. MacGregor, *The New Testament Basis of Pacifism* (New York: Fellowship Publications, 1960), and A. J. Muste (New York: 1951). *Essays of A. J. Muste,* ed. Nat Hentoff (Indianapolis: Bobbs-Merrill, 1967).

32. See especially Gustavo Gutierrez, *A Theology of Liberation* (Maryknoll, N.Y.: Orbis Press, 1973), and Enrique Dussel, *History and the Theology of Liberation,* trans. John Drury (Maryknoll, N.Y.: Orbis Press, 1976).

33. See, for example, James Cone, *A Black Theology of Liberation* (Philadelphia: Lippincott, 1970); *For My People* (Maryknoll: Orbis Books, 1974); Cornel West, Caridad Guidote, and Margaret Coakley, eds., *Is Liberation Theology for North America? The Response of First World Churches* (New York: Theology in Americas, 1978).

34. Gerald H. Anderson, ed., *Asian Voices in Christian Theology* (Maryknoll, N.Y.: Orbis Press, 1976).

35. My assumption regarding the perennial character of expressions of human religiousness is related to the irreducible character of ritual and the need for creativity in human life. See Harrison, *Our Right to Choose,* chapter 4.

36. Gustavo Gutierrez, *Theology of Liberation,* pp. 265–272.

37. Dorothee Sölle, *Christ the Representative: An Essay in Theology After the "Death of God"* (Philadelphia: Fortress Press, 1967).

38. Juan Luis Segundo, *Liberation of Theology.*

39. Carter Heyward, *The Redemption of God: A Theology of Mutual Relation* (Washington, D.C.: University Press of America, 1982).

40. Elisabeth Schüssler Fiorenza, *In Memory of Her.*

41. José Porfirio Miranda, *Marx and the Bible: A Critique of the Philosophy of Oppression,* trans. John Eagleson (Maryknoll, N.Y.: Orbis Press, 1974).

42. Carter Heyward, *Our Passion for Justice.*

Index

Abortion, 115–117, 288, 289n26; abortion on demand rhetoric, 288n22; critical historical review of, 119–126; federal funds for, 97; legal, 84, 88, 92, 93, 97, 125; and moral theory, xv, 126–131; social policy dimensions of debate on, 131–134; in theological context, 117–119
Academic life, 235–236
Action, clarifying movement's options for, 251–252
Activity, as mode of love, 8–12
Adams, James Luther, 63
Agape, defined, 28
Ageism, 152; mythologies obscuring sources of, 155–157; overriding cultural values and shaping, 157–161. *See also* Older persons
Alienation, in religion, 242–243; from body and nature, 293n1
Alimony, 104
American Academy of Religion, 54–55
Andolsen, Barbara, 268n10,n18, 297n20
Anger: denied, 15; relation of our acts of love to, 14–15
Annunciation, celebration and, 259, 261–263
Anti-body dualism, xvii, 75, 136, 138, 229
Antiradical legacy: disciplinary impact of, 67–74; of social theories used in Christian ethics, 58–63
Antisexual bias, Christianity's, 139–144
Anti-Vietnam War movement, 223
Aquinas, Thomas, 219–221, 272n31
Aries, Philippe, 45
Aronowitz, Stanley, 282n53, 291n9
Asexuality, 139, 164

Barmen Declaration (1934), 36
Barth, Karl, 26, 35, 37, 38, 118, 272n12, 274n38–42, 287n6
Beaver, R. Pierce, 193–194
Be-ing: and do-ing, 10–11; God as, 10
Bennett, John C., 54, 73, 276n1
Bettelheim, Bruno, 173
Biblicism, 116, 121
Birth control, *see* Contraception

Black, Liberation Theology, 202, 257
Black vs. white women, stereotypes of, 50–51; Black women, 51, 89, 95, 98, 238–243, 269n24, 276n13, 282n55, 285n16,n17,n21,n22, 286n26, 295n27, 297n20; Black vs. white women, 296n5, 300n27
Bodily integrity, right to, xvi, 129–131
Body, Christianity's neglect of, 129, 135–136. *See also* "Our bodies, ourselves"
Body/mind dualism, xvii, 12–13, 149, 229, 241–242, 269n3
Body-right, 129–130
Body-space, 129–130, 149, 150
Bonding, male, 141–142, 143
Bonhoeffer, Dietrich, 36–37, 274n37,n38
Boswell, John, 139, 289n6,n8,n9
Bourgeois gentlewoman, rise of, 46–48
Browders, Sandra, 19
Brown, Antoinette, 200, 201, 202
Brown, Robert McAfee, 208
Buber, Martin, 15
Bultmann, Rudolf, 38
Business ethics, 68–69

Calvin, John, 221
Cannon, Katie Geneva, 268n24
Capitalism, 55, 68–78 *passim*, 246
Carter, Jimmy, 178–180, 184, 186, 189
Celebration, annunciation and, 259, 261–263
Celibacy, 139; clerical, 120, 142
Center for Family Planning Services, 99
Chauvinism, 28, 120, 141, 221
Child-centered families, effect of, on women's role, 44–46
Child custody laws, 104, 204
Children, well-being of, 162–163
Christian-marxist dialogue, 282n55
Christianity: and Thomas Aquinas, 219–221; contradictions characterizing, 222–223; early, 216–219; feminist critique of, 214–216, 257; liberation theology and, 257–259; specific feminist theological agenda within, 227–230

305

308 / Index

Beverly Wildung Harrison is Professor of
Christian Social Ethics at Union Theolog-
ical Seminary in New York and author of
*Our Right to Choose: Toward a New Ethic
of Abortion.* Carol S. Robb is Assistant
Professor of Christian Social Ethics at San
Francisco Theological Seminary in San
Anselmo, CA.